Recent Financial Crises

Analysis, Challenges and Implications

Edited by

Lawrence R. Klein

Benjamin Franklin Professor of Economics Emeritus, University of Pennsylvania, USA and 1980 Nobel Laureate in Economic Sciences

Tayyeb Shabbir

Associate Professor of Finance, California State University, Dominguez Hills and Adjunct Associate Professor of Finance, Wharton School, University of Pennsylvania, USA

Edward Elgar

Cheltenham, UK • Northampton, MA, USA

Published by
Edward Elgar Publishing Limited
Glensanda House
Montpellier Parade
Cheltenham
Glos GL50 1UA
UK

Edward Elgar Publishing, Inc.
William Pratt House
9 Dewey Court
Northampton
Massachusetts 01060
USA

A catalogue record for this book
is available from the British Library

ISBN-13: 978 1 84376 642 1
ISBN-10: 1 84376 642 6

Printed and bound in Great Britain by MPG Books Ltd, Bodmin, Cornwall

Contents

List of contributors vii
List of abbreviations ix

Introduction 1
Lawrence R. Klein and Tayyeb Shabbir

PART I ANALYSIS OF CURRENCY CRISES

1 Asia before and after the financial crisis of 1997–98: a retrospective essay 23
Lawrence R. Klein and Tayyeb Shabbir

2 Indicators and analysis of vulnerability to currency crisis: Thailand 69
Pranee Tinakorn

PART II CURES AND REFORMS

3 The next financial crisis 121
Barry Eichengreen

4 Capital controls, financial crises and cures: simulations with an econometric model for Malaysia 134
Lawrence R. Klein, Roberto S. Mariano and Süleyman Özmucur

5 The case of the missing market: the bond market and why it matters for financial development 148
Richard J. Herring and Nathporn Chatusripitak

PART III ANALYTICAL ISSUES PERTAINING TO THE RECENT CRISES

6 Investment, growth and productivity during the East Asian Financial Crisis 197
F. Gerard Adams and Tayyeb Shabbir

7 What really happened to Thai wage rates during the East Asian Financial Crisis? 221
Jere R. Behrman, Anil B. Deolalikar and Pranee Tinakorn

8 Exchange rate or wage changes in international adjustment? Japan and China versus the United States 240
Ronald I. McKinnon

9 Adjustment to China's CPI-based inflation rate to account for 'true' cost of living, 1993–2004 260
Lawrence R. Klein, Huiqing Gao and Liping Tao

10 Estimating China's core inflation rate 296
Deming Wu

Index 329

Contributors

F. Gerard Adams, McDonald Professor of Economics at Northeastern University and Professor of Economics, Emeritus, University of Pennsylvania, USA

Jere R. Behrman, William R. Kenan, Jr Professor of Economics, University of Pennsylvania, USA

Nathporn Chatusripitak, PhD candidate at the Wharton School, University of Pennsylvania, USA

Anil B. Deolalikar, Professor of Economics and Director of the Public Policy Initiative at University of California, Riverside, USA

Barry Eichengreen, George C. Pardee and Helen N. Pardee Professor of Economics and Political Science, University of California, Berkeley, USA

Huiqing Gao, Division Chief, Department of Economic Forecasting, State Information Center, China

Richard J. Herring, Jacob Safra Professor of International Banking, Wharton School, University of Pennsylvania, USA

Lawrence R. Klein, Benjamin Franklin Professor of Economics Emeritus, University of Pennsylvania, USA

Roberto S. Mariano, Dean, School of Economics and Social Studies, Singapore Management University, Singapore

Ronald I. McKinnon, William D. Eberle Professor of International Economics, Stanford University, USA

Süleyman Özmucur, Research Specialist in Economics, University of Pennsylvania, USA

Tayyeb Shabbir, Associate Professor of Finance, California State University, Dominguez Hills and Adjunct Associate Professor of Finance, Wharton School, University of Pennsylvania, USA

Liping Tao, Senior Economist, Department of Economic Forecasting, State Information Center, China

Pranee Tinakorn, Dean and Professor of Economics, Thammasat University, and Research Consultant at the Thailand Development Research Institute (TDRI), Bangkok, Thailand

Deming Wu, Senior Financial Economist, Risk Analysis Division, The Office of the Comptroller of the Currency, Washington, DC, USA

Abbreviations

APEC	Asia-Pacific Economic Cooperation
ARIC	Asia Regional Information Center
ASEAN	Association of Southeast Asian Nations
BDC	Thai Bond Dealing Center
BERI	Business Environmental Risk Intelliegence
BIS	Bank for International Settlements
BOT	Bank of Thailand
CA	current account
CAC	collective action clause
CPI	consumer price index
CQM	Current Quarter Model
DVP	delivery versus payment
EMEAP	Executives' Meeting of the East Asia-Pacific Central Banks
EMS	European Monetary System
ERM	exchange rate mechanism
FDI	foreign direct investment
GDP	gross domestic product
ICR	International Country Risk
ICRG	International Country Risk Guide
IIF	Institute of International Finance
IMF	International Monetary Fund
IMFC	International Monetary and Financial Committee
LES	linear expenditure system
LIBOR	London Interbank Offered Rate
M1	The smallest of several measures of the stock of money in an economy, consisting primarily of currency held by the public and demand deposits
M2	A measure of the stock of money in an economy that includes, in addition to everything in M1, savings deposits and other relatively liquid assets such as small certificates of deposit and money market mutual funds
MAE	mean absolute error
MAEMAPE	mean absolute percentage error
MLR	minimum lending rate

NESDB	National Economic and Social Development Board
NPL	non-performing loan
OECD	Organisation for Economic Co-operation and Development
PBC	People's Bank of China
PPP	purchasing power parity
QPS	quadratic probability score
REER	real effective exchange rate
RMSE	root mean square error
ROSC	Review of the Observance of Standards and Codes
RPI	retail price index
SAFE	State Administration for Foreign Exchange
SDDS	Special Data Dissemination Standard
SDR	Special Drawing Right
SEC	Securities and Exchange Commission
SET	Stock Exchange of Thailand
SIMEX	Singapore International Monetary Exchange
SVAR	structural vector autoregression
TDRI	Thailand Development Research Intsitute
TFP	total factor productivity
TRIS	Thai Rating and Information Services Company Limited
TSD	Thailand Securities Depositary Corporation
VECM	vector error correction model
WPI	wholesale price index

Introduction

Lawrence R. Klein and Tayyeb Shabbir

1 ABOUT THIS BOOK

This volume has been assembled to focus on specific analytical as well as policy-related issues pertaining to recent financial crises, most notably the Asian Financial Crisis of 1997–98 and the ripple effects that translated into uncomfortably close calls in Russia, Brazil and, somewhat later, full-blown crises in Turkey and Argentina. Of course, much has been said and written about the various aspects of these recent crises. However, motivated by the belief that the issues raised by and surrounding these recent crises (in fact, financial crises in general) are of ongoing importance, and despite a perspective gained by scholarly analyses of these crises, there are important lessons to be learned and analytical issues that can be explored even further.

It may be noted that the papers included in this volume have been specifically prepared for it and thus have the distinction of being original and not reprints, affording an analysis that the respective authors are sharing for the first time.

Thematically, we have divided the chapters into three parts. Besides providing an introduction, Part I addresses the issues of predictability of currency crises; Part II consists of chapters that focus on a set of reforms or 'cures' for preventing and/or ameliorating the after-effects of a crisis and, finally, Part III consists of a set of econometric studies that address several issues of analytical interest pertaining to labor market behavior, investment and productivity, exchange rate adjustments and estimation of China's core inflation rate, as well as the 'true' cost of living index for China over the twenty-year period that spans the Asian Financial Crisis.

A brief guided tour of the contents of the specific chapters is given in section 3, while in section 2 below we note the important questions raised by the recent financial or currency crises.

2 QUESTIONS OF IMPORTANCE RAISED BY THE RECENT FINANCIAL CRISES

The last decade or so has been marked by a significant number of major financial crises including the Mexican ('Tequila') Crisis (1994–95), the Asian Financial Crisis (1997–98), the Russian Bond Market Default (1998), the Turkish Banking Crisis (2000) and the Currency Crisis that followed (2001) and the Argentinean Financial Crisis (2002). While most of the affected countries, to a lesser or a greater degree, have apparently recovered from the immediate negative consequences of these crises, the outcome could have been much worse in terms of the time to recover and sustainability of crisis-free development. In any event, there exist the relatively longer-run effects of these recent crises, which are still in the process of unwinding. These secular after-effects are relevant, both for practical as well as analytical or academic reasons. In practical terms, several of the affected countries are still grappling with the secular aftermath of these crises. In addition to the adoption of country-specific economic and financial sector reforms, these countries are still facing social sector issues, such as income distributional effects and setbacks to trends towards poverty alleviation that so strongly characterized the 1980s and the early 1990s. On the other hand, in analytical terms or broad-based academic terms, we still need to make sure that that the appropriate lessons from these crises have been learned, and more importantly are being instituted, regarding the workings and reform of the global financial system. While much scholarly work focused both on the analytical and policy-oriented issues has already been undertaken, we believe that there are still very important issues that need to be addressed regarding the nature of these crises. The following is a selective list of some of these important issues that are of special interest to us.

2.1 Nature and Dynamics of the Crises

How much have we learned about the nature and the dynamics of these crises? In particular, are these crises predictable to any appreciable or practical extent – say, enough to be able to allow us to develop an early warning system? What are the factors that make economies vulnerable to financial crises? (Chapter 1 by Klein and Shabbir as well as Chapter 2 by Tinakorn.) Again, can the policy-makers recommend policies that will soften the impact of, if not eliminate such crises? (Chapter 3 by Eichengreen.)

2.2 Lessons Learned

What kinds of specific lessons have we learned, if any, from these episodes? What kinds of economic, fiscal, monetary and perhaps even political reforms will be necessary in order to ameliorate the vulnerability of a country to a financial crisis? In this respect, it is heartening to note that considerable progress has already been made in instituting certain reforms of the global financial system that have evidently been inspired by the recent financial crises. Prodded by the IMF and the Bank for International Settlements (BIS), increasingly countries now report the value of non-performing loans (NPLs) as a way of monitoring the commercial banking sector. In addition, there has been a consistent trend towards emphasizing the importance of maintaining transparency and prudent risk management by private financial institutions (such as the hedge funds) as well as the central banks of the respective countries. The latter are now routinely expected to furnish prompt and regular reports regarding the amount as well as the disposition of the international reserves they manage. The occurrences of these recent financial crises have taught us the importance of continuing to strengthen these trends.

Since the affected countries have mostly recovered, at least economically, from the recent crises, there is a real danger that, for practical purposes, a significant complacency may set in. Obviously, we must guard against this possibility – revisiting the question of the lessons learned and how best to implement them to minimize recurrence and/or to mitigate the severity of future crises. The description of one very important way to do just that can be found in Chapter 3 by Eichengreen.

2.3 'Cures' for the Crises

The next set of issues is often presented under the rubric of 'cures' for financial crises – actually they are the generally recommended reforms apparently motivated by the experience of financial crises. We will discuss three such broad categories of the so-called 'cures': appropriate exchange rate policy, capital market reforms and private business governance.

2.3.1 Appropriate exchange rate policy

Regarding the question of the appropriate exchange rate policy, to many, the appropriate policy is simply to have no deliberate policy at all! 'Let the market take care of the issue completely', they declare. While it is true that, in retrospect, the 1997–98 Asian Crisis marked a watershed 'event' that has convinced many of the desirability of a completely flexible exchange rate, many subtleties still need attention and the question of the appropriate choice of an exchange rate system is not an open and shut case, as it is sometimes made out to be. There are questions regarding the desirability and/or feasibility of a single world or wide-area currency, or in general, the extent and the mechanism for managing exchange rates in the context of the new global financial architecture. Increasingly, private capital flows have come to dominate trade flows and have thus lent a historically high level of volatility in price behavior in this important market. The capital mix has changed – there is, for example, more foreign direct investment (FDI) and less capital flow on official account.

Again, there are important unresolved issues concerning how best to deal with chronic current account imbalances (surpluses as well as deficits), management of international reserves by the central banks, possibilities of currency contagion, current account-induced flows and debt flows. A particularly vexing question is the appropriate policy response to a trade surplus in the case of a large, fast-growing creditor country such as China. It turns out that an often-recommended solution – appreciation of the yuan relative to the US dollar – may do little to rectify the problem if the underlying cause of the hugely favorable trade surplus for China is to be found in international wage differentials estimated to be in the range of 20 or 30:1 in favor of China, even though the differential has been narrowing lately (Chapter 8 by McKinnon).

2.3.2 Capital market reforms

Besides currency reforms, capital market reforms are also critical for the emerging economies. In this regard, there are two dominant issues and we will refer to them as (a) optimal degree of liberalization and (b) relative completeness of the scope of capital market instruments or institutions.

Capital market liberalization is desirable because it increases efficiency through better allocation of resources. However, such efficiency gains may come at a price since liberalization, inter alia, makes the economy more vulnerable to contagion and a host of other external shocks. Obviously, these two opposing effects need to be balanced, leading naturally to the notion of the 'optimal capital market liberalization'. There is a related question of what is the 'safe' rate at which transition should take place? Such a determination of optimality would depend, in part, on having on hand analyzes of the various policies that can be used to mitigate the downside of capital market liberalization. One such policy, to contain the potential vulnerability due to openness on account of capital market liberalization, can be the adoption of capital controls. However, such policy needs to be designed precisely and thoughtfully, with assessment of relevant side-effects. There are relatively few studies that undertake such an assessment. However, Klein, Mariano and Özmucur (Chapter 4) introduce an econometric case study of Malaysia, which assesses the effects of capital controls, to help manage the financial crisis of 1997–98 in that country and finds that the capital controls there had many positive and desired effects in terms of economic stabilization.

Regarding the other issue that we have termed 'relative completeness of the scope of capital market', it has been noted that the emerging economies lack well-functioning bond markets, even when they have fairly well developed equity markets. This is as if one leg is missing, and it makes the country less resilient in the face of a potential financial crisis. However, the study of bond markets in emerging economies is starting to receive increasingly greater attention. There is a burgeoning interest in the study of questions such as the role of a viable bond market in improving the efficacy of financial intermediation in these countries as well as how a robust bond market may be a useful buffer to prevent or soften a future crisis. (Chapter 5 by Herring and Chatusripitak is a case study of the Thai bond market in relation to the 1997–98 Asian Financial Crisis; a related, yet independently arrived at, analysis of the importance of a bond market may be found in Chapter 3 by Eichengreen.)

2.3.3 Private business governance

Finally, regarding the third aspect of the capital market reforms, we want to note that corporate governance is an important issue in this respect. Indeed, it is one of the host of other emerging issues that pertain (albeit indirectly at times) to the possibility of future financial crises in emerging economies. The question of corporate governance, in part, encompasses concerns about the role of minority shareholders, full disclosure and transparency, prudent risk management and the role of the board of directors as independent overseers. It also takes up behavioral issues such as conflict of interest and use of inside information (Chapter 3 by Eichengreen).

2.4 Secular Aftermath of the Asian Financial Crisis 1997–98

While the various economic indicators have shown sustainable and solid improvement in the majority of the affected countries, their respective social indicators are definitely still lagging relative to the pre-crisis trends. The financial crisis in Asia left a deep mark in terms of social upheaval in these countries, many of which were unprepared for such an eventuality. We need to evaluate the income distributional impact in the medium- to the long-run sense as well as to assess the state of the present and future adequacy of the social safety nets in emerging economies that may be especially prone to financial crises (Chapter 1 by Klein and Shabbir). One particularly important question pertains to the behavior of the real wage rate in the affected countries pre- versus post-Asian Crisis. (Chapter 7 presents a case study of Thailand regarding real wage rate behavior pre- versus post-Asian Crisis.)

2.5 Focus on New Developments in the Asian Region

We feel that in any discussion of the recent financial crises, in addition to reflecting on the past, we ought to be forward-looking as well. In this spirit, we want to note the emerging developments in East Asia/or Greater Asia as a region. Our primary interest in this region lies in particularly focusing on countries that were directly affected by the Asian Crisis of 1997–98, such as South Korea and Thailand, as well as China and Japan, which were only indirectly involved in one or the other aspect of the above crisis because they are important actors in the region. Finally, we also want to indulge in a prospective look at India as an emergent regional economic powerhouse and thus see how the future may look in the wake of post-crisis Asia, where China and India have emerged as the relatively fastest-growing dynamic and open economies (at least in the aspects of trade flows), which may be the dominant part of the 'New Asian Miracle' going forward and thus may stand to gain the most from any valuable lessons that the recent financial crises can teach us. We will, thus, divide the relevant region into three groups: East Asian directly affected countries China and Japan and India (South Asia).

2.5.1 East Asian directly affected countries

An important question is, how will the experience of the last crisis transform the affected countries? It seems that each of the affected countries has been responding in unique fashion when it comes to the speed of recovery, depth of the commitment to reforms and adoption of longer-run reforms to prevent or mitigate the effect of the 'next crisis'. There are some initial hints that these countries may no longer represent a monolithic group that seemingly followed a nearly uniform mantra for growth. Also, these countries, albeit in varying degrees, each maintained a peg of their respective currency to the US dollar. Instead, it seems that many of these countries will be following fairly differentiated paths from now on. These idiosyncrasies in the chosen development strategies are important both from a policy perspective as well as their theoretical perceptions of growth and development. Is a new paradigm of growth emerging that may lessen the future possibility of financial contagion?

2.5.2 China and Japan

China's case is important from many points of view. China of course, has been growing tremendously fast since reform in 1978. It is poised to be a dominant part of future economic prosperity of the region – a 'New Asian Miracle', if you will. Its openness in terms of trade flows makes it vulnerable to crises. However, it has a longstanding policy of minimal variations in the exchange rate in the face of persistent current account surpluses. This is just the opposite of what Thailand faced on the eve of the crisis in 1997–98, and decidedly is a relatively better situation to be in than Thailand was when it faced shortages of international reserves rather than having to worry about disposal of surplus. However, an imbalance is an imbalance, all the same. Thus, China is also at the center of the debate about the appropriate exchange rate and the capital controls policies to adopt. These are issues that have been an intimate part of the financial crisis experience. China is also an obviously important player through its trade and direct investment links to the region. Thus focusing on China is only natural.

However, we know that some people have expressed a degree of skepticism about the veracity of China's growth statistics. This is an aspect of the Chinese economy that is of interest to us. Besides addressing the question of China's 'true' growth rate, we are also interested in exploring what role China may have played – a stabilizing or a destabilizing one – during the 1997–98 Asian Crisis.

Of course, China is a major regional power and thus very strategic. However, the debate about China's exchange rate posture has captured wide attention. Its policy of nearly fixed parity of yuan per dollar and capital controls in the face of burgeoning current account surpluses has exposed the currency to potentially destabilizing speculative and political pressure because vested interests feel effects of large competition from many countries. While these pressures are of a different nature in comparison with those that Thailand had to face in the weeks and months preceding the bhat devaluation of 2 July 1997, still, in a fundamental sense, both kinds of such pressures represent essentially two sides of the same coin if the fundamental goal is to avoid exchange rate instability. The major question, of course, is whether we have learned enough from the previous crises so that we can more confidently determine the optimal degree of openness of a country's capital and exchange rate markets.

The other important regional power, Japan, is currently showing some signs of a nascent recovery from a long slump. However, the question still remains whether Japan has recovered enough to lend a strong helping hand in the event of the next crisis erupting.

2.5.3 India (South Asia)

There are historic changes afoot in South Asia as well. India, in particular, has started to emerge as an Asian 'giant', side by side with China. Both these countries have enjoyed strong growth in the real sector (GDP) although they reached high growth in unique fashion – China's has been a case of growth led now by exports of manufactured goods, while India's growth has been fueled by growth of service sector activity (especially in the information technology [IT], financial and health sectors). While each of these countries have exhibited impressive rates of GDP growth in recent years, there are significant financial sector issues such as stock and bond market reform, greater transparency and better corporate governance that still need attention. It is clear that going forward, financial sector and capital market reforms will be necessary for the continued success of these countries while keeping in mind some of the important ways – political and structural – in which these countries differ from each other. However, the important point is that, as the new players on the growth playing field so to speak, these countries' reliance on open trade and foreign direct investment flows makes them vulnerable to financial crises. It is worth watching to see whether lessons from the recent crises were learned well. During the crisis period, neighbors and other competitors blamed China for stealing their export markets. Now they enjoy China's import appetite. As for India, advanced countries blame 'white collar' unemployment problems on India's burgeoning service sector, but should be benefiting from reduced operating costs in the near future.

3 SALIENT POINTS OF THE CONTRIBUTIONS TO THE VOLUME

The following is a brief guided tour of the contents and the themes explored in the various chapters in this volume.

Chapter 1: 'Asia Before and After the Financial Crisis of 1997–98: A Retrospective Essay' by Lawrence R. Klein and Tayyeb Shabbir

Since financial crises can be costly both in economic, as well as, societal terms, it is only natural to inquire whether such crises are predictable. Besides providing a brief introduction, this chapter reviews the various approaches to prediction of currency crises. In this respect, the authors conclude that while econometric predictive models can be very useful in identifying various indicators of 'vulnerability', such exercises are not a cure-all. Therefore, exploring the various aspects of the aftermath of a financial crisis is also quite important. In this regard, the authors focus on the income distributional consequences of the Asian Financial Crisis of 1997–98 as well as its impact on the poverty alleviation trends in the affected countries.

Chapter 2: 'Indicators and Analysis of Vulnerability to Currency Crisis: Thailand' by Pranee Tinakorn

This chapter by Professor Tinakorn is a case study of Thailand, a country that has the dubious distinction of being the first country in Asia whose currency succumbed to speculative pressures on 2 July 1997, setting off well-known ripple effects, which impacted not only some of the neighbors, but also Russia and Brazil. This series of currency crises (and, in many instances, follow-up banking crises) prompted anew many efforts to 'predict' currency crises so as to pre-empt them or, more realistically, decrease the vulnerability to such harmful episodes. In this spirit, Tinakorn's study is an important attempt to identify an early warning system.

Tinakorn uses time-series monthly data from January 1992 to December 2000 for Thailand to estimate a probit model as well as a 'signals' model à la Kaminsky et al.[1] (1998) to analyze the indicators of a currency crisis in Thailand. Tinakorn defines a currency crisis as when 'there is an accumulated three month depreciation in exchange rate of 15 percent or more; or there is an accumulated three-month depletion in net international reserves, of 15 percent or more'. It is important to consider net international reserves, which are gross reserves adjusted for swap obligations of the Bank of Thailand (BOT) – a decidedly better measure than just the equating of currency crises to (realized) currency depreciation, since the monetary authority may successfully ward off speculative attacks by depleting international reserves. (This is an interesting point since anyone focusing only on gross reserves would have missed the fact that swap obligations had skyrocketed for BOT in 1996–97 during this [ex post] 'window of vulnerability' for the country.)

This study's main finding is that, in the case of Thailand, there are several early warning indicators of a currency crisis that are worth watching. The following seven are supported simultaneously by the 'signals' analysis as well as the estimated probit model for the country: export growth, ratio of current account to GDP, real exchange rate misalignment, growth of M2/international reserves, ratio of fiscal balance to GDP, real GDP growth rate and change in stock prices. Further, the signals analysis identifies the following four indicators in addition to the above seven: terms-of-trade growth, ratio of short-term external debt to international reserves, growth of domestic credit/GDP and inflation rate.

Thus, in hindsight, an awareness of the above set of early warning indicators by the policy-makers in Thailand would have been helpful in either handling the management of the international reserves better and/or it might have enabled them to negotiate a less contractionary package with the IMF, thus possibly ameliorating some of the extreme effects of an unanticipated devaluation and the contraction of the economic activity that necessarily followed. However, there is an important issue of transparency. A former IMF official has indicated in a lecture at the University of Pennsylvania that Thailand's international reserve accounts were in trouble prior to the crisis outbreak, but the international institution would not have made that known to the public on its own authority in advance, for an obvious fear of panic in the financial markets.

Chapter 3: 'The Next Financial Crisis' by Barry Eichengreen

In this chapter, Barry Eichengreen contends that, as of spring 2005, the 'next' financial crisis for emerging economies may already be brewing but it may or may not materialize since, as a result of some of the lessons learned from the East Asia Crisis of 1997–98, we have a more stable global financial system as well as improved country-specific financial sectors rendering emerging economies less vulnerable to any impending crisis. However, lest we feel tempted to rest on our laurels, the author lists an agenda for future reforms, in addition to providing an excellent assessment of the reforms that have already been put in place.

Eichengreen maintains that, as of spring 2005, the following factors constitute a 'potentially fatal cocktail' that may foretell a crisis in emerging economies:

1. Rising US interest rates as a result of the FED's (Federal Reserve's) reversal of its easy monetary policy it had adopted as of spring 2001. In the past, US domestic interest rate increases have been harbingers of financial problems in emerging markets.
2. The ever-increasing US 'twin deficits' – the current account deficit as well as the dudget deficit.
3. The international oil price increases, which may lead to a significant slowdown in China's growth momentum, which will mean a negative ripple effect throughout the emerging economies since China has lately emerged as a significant engine of regional as well as global economic growth.

While the above factors may appear to be clouding the horizon for the emerging economies, Eichengreen stresses that 'no ill effects are evident yet' perhaps due to the reforms instituted since the last crisis in 1997–98. He singles out ten reforms already instituted as noteworthy, namely, lengthening the maturity structure of emerging economies' debt, their smaller current account deficits, larger foreign reserve stockpiles, relatively greater flexibility of the exchange rate mechanisms, greater fiscal 'responsibility' as well as reduced leverage in international financial systems, greater multilateral surveillance of the financial systems, greater financial sector transparency, incorporation of collective action clauses in sovereign debt instruments, and, finally, comparatively greater transparency of the IMF itself.

Besides noting the already instituted reforms that have been motivated by the lessons learned from the recent financial crises, Eichengreen also stresses that we need to continue on this path. He stresses five such future reform targets in emerging economies: continuity of earlier reforms, improved credit and bond markets, enhanced exchange rate flexibility, feasibility to borrow in own currency on the world capital markets and continued governance reforms at the Bretton Woods Institutions.

One unique feature of Eichengreen's chapter is that while assessing the reforms put in place in the last few years, he also sheds light on the 'costs' of such reforms – a hitherto neglected area of research and analysis. In this regard, if one were to add a 'sixth' item to the above agenda for future reforms, it could be the goal of maximizing the 'net [of costs] benefits' of these reforms that are inspired by a desire to learn from the past crises.

Chapter 4: 'Capital Controls, Financial Crises and Cures: Simulations with an Econometric Model for Malaysia' by Lawrence R. Klein, Roberto S. Mariano and Süleyman Özmucur

Liberalization of capital account is generally favored as a desirable policy as it can lead to greater availability of capital and increased efficiency. These 'pro-growth' effects, however, may be tempered by the fact that liberalization of capital account can render a country more vulnerable to financial crises due to an enhanced exposure to external shocks.

In the face of a financial crisis when the domestic policy-makers often experience the feeling of a loss of control of their economy, an imposition of capital controls (at least temporarily) is often advocated as a solution. Such controls, it is argued, can help to bring under control the possibility of panic-driven flight of capital and uncontrolled depletion of international reserves in the wake of a crisis. However, such controls are generally disfavored by those who hold the relatively orthodox view that considers any interference whatsoever with the 'market mechanism' as counterproductive.

On the eve of the 1997–98 crisis, Malaysia imposed capital controls to manage the financial crisis. This chapter by Klein–Mariano–Özmucur is a description of use of a simultaneous equation macroeconometric model – a method to study the possible impact of capital controls while taking account of the various feedback effects. Such a model is estimated for Malaysia. The model is a fairly detailed one with 438 equations and 607 variables. Such detail allows the authors to supplement a traditional macroeconomic model by incorporating a very thorough specification of the external sector; in particular, the authors specify capital account, foreign direct investment as well as portfolio investment, as endogenous to the model.

The major conclusion of this chapter is that capital controls in Malaysia had a number of desirable effects on important macroeconomic indicators such as the real GDP growth rate (the net effect was an increase of 0.07 percent over the post-crisis period, 1998–2001). The GDP deflator (whose rate of change, of course, measures inflation rate) would also have been higher in the absence of capital controls. Thus, generally speaking, in the case of Malaysia, the capital controls helped the policy-makers manage the crisis better and the economy enjoyed many positive stabilization benefits with minimal negative effect on foreign direct investment inflows. It is, however, important to recognize that the success of capital controls seems to be contingent on the particular 'context' in which they are imposed, quality of policy intervention and the initial conditions in the economy.

Chapter 5: 'The Case of the Missing Market: The Bond Market and Why It Matters for Financial Development' by Richard J. Herring and Nathporn Chatusripitak

Over the last decade, there has been an increased interest in analyzing the role of financial institutions and financial markets in economic growth and development. However, the main focus has been on equity markets, and bond markets have been almost entirely overlooked. This chapter by Herring–Chatusripitak, concentrating particularly on Asian economies, tries to redress this situation by seeking to explain how the absence of a well-functioning bond market may adversely affect other markets, savers, investors and banks, and, in particular, how it may render the economy more vulnerable to a financial crisis. It concludes with an analysis of recent financial development in Thailand to illustrate both the problems associated with the absence of bond markets and the proposed solutions.

The authors assert that absence of well-functioning bond markets can make an otherwise vibrant economy more vulnerable to a financial crisis (as was the case in East Asia during the mid-1990s). One major implication of the absence of a bond market is that the economy lacks a market-determined term structure of interest rates that accurately reflects the opportunity cost of funds. This deficiency can make firms under- or over-invest relative to the societal efficient allocation on whether the firm's internal rate of discount is too high or too low (the latter was the case in the early to mid-1990s in East Asia). Also, lack of 'true' term structure will impede accurate pricing of equity in the stock market as well as pricing of credit risk. Again, in the absence of a well-functioning bond market, hedging in the derivatives (including foreign exchange) market will be relatively more expensive, if it is possible at all. As a result, market participants may end up assuming more financial risk than they would choose if there were efficient derivatives markets, just as the Asian Financial Crisis in 1997 showed that many market participants had accepted excessive exposure to foreign exchange risk. The greater risk obviously increases the vulnerability to a financial crisis.

Perhaps the most worrisome implication of an underdeveloped bond market is that, in such economies, the banking sector is more vulnerable to inefficiencies, liquidity shocks and falling prey to 'moral hazards' of the kind often referred to as 'crony capitalism'. Lack of competition from the bond market makes banks 'too big', leads them to prefer short-term credit, which in turn, leads to biases in firms' investment policies in favor of short-term assets and away from longer gestation ventures. Also, lack of opportunity for the banks to rely on the bond market to spread their own portfolio risk makes these highly leveraged institutions more vulnerable to a liquidity shock with obvious and often immediate repercussions for the rest of the economy.

In Thailand, prior to the 1997 Financial Crisis, the bond market was severely underdeveloped. As a result, Thai firms tended to over-invest, the efficiency of investment was declining and the economy was heavily reliant on bank lending. Consequently, when the banks suffered heavy losses, new lending ceased and firms had to halt investment projects, resulting in prolonged and painful economic contraction. Since then, the Thai government has begun to implement a number of reforms to stimulate development of both primary and secondary bond markets. These include developing a yield curve for government bonds, efforts to promote risk management and market liquidity, centralizing the clearing and settlement of bonds, upgrading accounting and disclosure standards, and active participation in regional initiatives to strengthen Asian bond markets. These changes have markedly improved the liquidity of the government bond market, and the Thai bond market is more than four times larger, relative to GDP, than before the crisis. The Thai example shows that bond markets do matter for financial development, and that an expanded role for the bond market may be used to rebuild financial systems after the crisis.

Chapter 6: 'Investment, Growth and Productivity during the East Asian Financial Crisis' by F. Gerard Adams and Tayyeb Shabbir

In this chapter, Adams–Shabbir examine the impact of the 1997 East Asian Financial Crisis on real GDP growth and total factor productivity (TFP) of the East Asian countries during and after the crisis. Rather than taking the more typical approach to analyzing the crisis and its impact in terms of such factors as financial flows, exchange rate misalignment and contagion, the authors approach the crisis from a production input/factor productivity perspective.

In the first place, the authors look at the financial crisis and its impact on the growth record of East Asian countries, by comparing a number of growth characteristics pre- and post-crisis. The impact was uneven with apparently minimal effect on China yet with serious recessionary effect on the economies of Thailand, South Korea and Indonesia. In general, real GDP growth rates fell sharply in 1997–98 due to the crisis, and although the post-crisis period shows renewed growth, it is at substantially lower growth rates than in the pre-crisis period. Also, post-crisis relative to pre-crisis, there was a downward trend in labor productivity growth. In addition, compared with the exceptionally high values for the investment/GDP ratio, there was a sharp drop in this investment share, and post-crisis recovery was of a relatively smaller magnitude. In fact, the downward swing in investment was not matched by a similar swing in domestic saving, hence foreign inflows turned to outflows. Finally, though exports recovered in the post-crisis period, and somewhat offset the lower investment share, the export growth for this period was also lower than its pre-crisis rate.

The authors then seek to disentangle growth of output into that attributable to increased inputs and the residual factor, or total factor productivity. This residual represents the difference between the growth of total output and the weighted sum of labor and capital input and includes all elements not taken into account in the computation of growth inputs, including technological change, economies of scale, the composition of output, the role of exports and the cyclical position of the economy. The authors define unexplained TFP as the change in TFP less the business cycle effect less the industrial/export effect. Statistics show that total labor and capital input growth remain lower post-crisis than pre-crisis.

They next undertake a statistical analysis of the factors associated with the growth of TFP. To measure the effect of the 1997 Financial Crisis on TFP, during which there were severe declines in production, they perform regressions linking TFP to a series of dummy variables covering the 1998–2001 periods. They find that declines in production, particularly in 1997 and 1998, have clear impacts on TFP, that the loss in productivity growth associated with this period was not made up in later years, and that the coefficient of a time-trend variable was significantly negative. They also perform regressions linking TFP to other variables such as increasing exports, share of investment, and industrialization, and find that change in industrial output and change in exports make significant contributions to TFP change. Other measured factors, including foreign direct investment, did not show up with statistical significance. Unexplained TFP growth is relatively small. Thus the ultimate equation explaining TFP growth indicates that productivity growth in East Asia varies considerably with cycles in business activity and depends greatly on the expansion of industrial production and exports.

Chapter 7: 'What Really Happened to Thai Wage Rates during the East Asian Financial Crisis?' by Jere R. Behrman, Anil B. Deolalikar and Pranee Tinakorn

In their chapter, Behrman, Deolalikar and Tinakorn (BDT) explore what happened to real wage rates during the Asian Financial Crisis of the late 1990s. The most important earning asset of most members of developing countries is their labor, therefore what happens to real wage rates is important because of (a) the implications for the purchasing power of workers' income and the design of effective anti-poverty and social safety net policies, (b) the impact on time allocations of workers, and (c) the implications for the extent to which labor market adjustments occur through price rather than quantity effects.

Conventional wisdom and most of the claims in previous literature indicate that real wage rates fell considerably in Thailand due to the crisis. This chapter uses as its benchmark a World Bank (2000) study of the behavior of the aggregate Thai wage rates as a result of the crisis. This World Bank study estimates that the Thai real wage rate fell by 4.6 percent during the crisis. The methodology used was to subtract the percentage change in the number of employed workers between the pre- and post-crisis period from the percentage change in the aggregated real wage earnings between the pre- and post-crisis period. However, BDT argue that the methodology used in the World Bank and other studies is subject to at least four possibly important limitations that may make a considerable difference in understanding what really happened to real wage rates and what the implications are for policy. The chapter then examines these four limitations in detail.

First, the World Bank assumes that the number of wage recipients is a fixed share of total employment. But the composition of employment shifted from wage to non-wage workers, and this *by itself* creates a bias of 2.5 percentage points in World Bank estimates (implying 'true' change of −4.6% + 2.5% = −2.1%). Second, it assumes that hours worked are constant, but, in fact, hours worked did change, which, again *by itself*, creates a bias of 5.5 percentage points (implying a 'true' change of −4.6% + 5.5% = 0.9%). Third, the World Bank weights wage recipients proportionately to their hours worked to obtain the mean wage rates across wage recipients; whereas BDT feel that it is more appropriate to weight individuals equally and estimate that this aspect of the World Bank methodology by itself causes a bias of 1.4 percentage points (implying a 'true' change of −4.6% −1.4% = −6.0%). If *all of these first three biases were corrected*, the World Bank estimate would change to an *increase* of 2 percent in Thai real wage rates during the crisis.

However, more importantly, BDT contend a fourth issue related to the above World Bank methodology. This issue concerns the World Bank study's assumption that no change took place in the composition of wage recipients between the pre- and post-crisis periods. Instead the BDT study looks at data for all workers and for subcategories defined by the three observed characteristics of gender, age and schooling and finds that as a result of the crisis, wage employment shifted relatively from females to males, from younger to older workers, and from lower-schooled to higher-schooled individuals – all shifts from lower to higher real wage categories. The failure to account for these important compositional changes in World Bank estimates means that the estimated overall average real wage rate change is biased *upwards*. The authors' best estimate of how much real hourly wage rates declined due to the crisis is 7.8 percent (due to the methodology used by BDT, their estimate is free from the first three biases that the World Bank study had to contend with).

The major conclusion of the study was that the methodology used by the World Bank presents a misleading picture of what happened to Thai real wage rates during the Asian Financial Crisis. Although the biases in the World Bank study are partially offsetting, the severity of the impact of the crisis on declines in the real wage rate is underestimated by 3.2 percentage points or about 40 percent (comparing a World Bank estimate of a 4.6 percent decline with this study's preferred estimate of a 7.8 percent decline). This study notes that even the decline of 7.8 percent is probably an underestimate of the true decline because of the probable compositional changes that occur because of unobserved characteristics such as ability and motivation. The authors feel that the best solution would be for longitudinal labor force data to be collected as a matter of routine so that comparisons could be made for the wage rates for the same individuals over time. If these longitudinal surveys are not available, then a second-best solution is to follow the methods in this chapter, in particular controlling for compositional changes with respect to observed characteristics such as gender, age and schooling.

Besides the above question of computing the 'true' magnitude of the decline in the Thai real wage during the 1997 crisis, the BDT study also examined the claim that the poorer and more vulnerable suffered most in the crisis and found some, but limited, support for that claim. Regression estimates showed that youths fared worse than prime-age adults, but that some other groups typically characterized as more vulnerable fared relatively well: those with primary or less schooling, females and older adults.

Chapter 8: 'Exchange Rate or Wage Changes in International Adjustment? Japan and China versus the United States' by Ronald I. McKinnon

In this chapter, McKinnon puts forth an analysis that concludes that, under the world dollar standard, a discrete appreciation by a dollar creditor country of the United States, such as China or Japan, has no predictable effect on its trade surplus. Currency appreciation by the creditor country will slow its economic growth and eventually cause deflation but cannot compensate for a saving–investment imbalance in the United States. Under a fixed exchange rate, however, differential adjustment in the rate of growth of money wages will more accurately reflect international differences in productivity growth. International competitiveness will be better balanced between high-growth and low-growth economies, as between Japan and the US from 1950 to 1971 and China and the US from 1994 to 2005, when the peripheral country's dollar exchange rate is fixed so that its wage growth better reflects its higher productivity growth. Also discussed is the qualified case for China moving toward greater flexibility in the form of a very narrow band for the yuan/dollar exchange rate, as a way of decentralizing foreign exchange transacting.

One important implication of the McKinnon hypothesis as articulated in this chapter is that even if we made some desirable changes in the yuan/dollar exchange rate, the hope of narrowing the China–US trade surplus may not materialize since the more important determinant of the Chinese advantage is its relatively lower wage rate. According to available data, anecdotal evidence indicates that it may be as high as 20 to 30:1 in China's favor compared with about 5 to 10:1 in India's favor when we compare India versus China. However, it is interesting to note that China's relative advantage in wage competitiveness may already be narrowing and the dynamic implications of this trend towards the exchange rate and trade policy vis-à-vis China should be very instructive and important to watch.

Chapter 9: 'Adjustment to China's CPI-based Inflation Rate to Account for the "True" Cost of Living, 1993–2004' by Lawrence R. Klein, Huiqing Gao and Liping Tao

In this chapter, the authors Klein, Gao and Tao (KGT), in a pioneering study, adjust China's Consumer price index (CPI) to account for the 'true' cost of living for 1993–2004, a period that covers the Asian Financial Crisis period 1997–98.

Chinese economic growth since 1978 has certainly been spectacular in magnitude, and, as a result, many scholars have drawn the conclusions that the numerical size of Chinese economic growth is overstated. However, that is not the opinion of the authors of this chapter. In order to examine China's growth rate, they have focused on its rate of price level change as measured by a consumer price index – the inflation rate that can be used to convert nominal GDP to real GDP. They argue that the magnitude of inflation has been overstated, because it does not take into account quality change or lifestyle change. Hence, they estimate an adjustment to China's CPI by estimating the 'true' economic cost of living index, using the linear expenditure system (LES). The true 'cost' of living in China can indicate how much the inflation might be lowered, and the real growth rate correspondingly increased, for the economy as a whole.

The LES equation can be written as:

$$(p_{it}q_{it} - p_{it}\gamma_i) = \beta_i\left(r_t - \sum_{j=1}^{n} p_{jt}\gamma_j\right); \sum_{i=1}^{n}\beta_i = 1$$

expenditure on the *i*-th category	minimum subsistence expenditure on the *i*-th category	total income	total minimum subsistence expenditure on all categories	βi = marginal propensity to consume out of supernumerary income.

This equation is expressed in current value prices (nominal). Goods and services are grouped into eight classes: food; clothing; household facilities; medicine and medical services; transportation, post and communication services; educational, cultural and recreation services; residential; and miscellaneous commodities and services. Each of these aggregate groups can be treated as a non-inferior good. Engel curves separately relate expenditure on each group to total income, and the part of the Engel curves that the authors of this chapter use for parameter estimation is in a linear range. They use cross-section data from family budgets (for both urban and rural populations) to estimate the parameters γ_i, which represent necessary or minimum levels of consumption for each grouping of goods and services, and they use time-series aggregates to estimate the parameters β_i, which represent marginal propensities to consume.

Using these parameter estimates, they evaluate the 'true' cost of living index. They find a lower inflation rate across both urban and rural populations on the basis of 'true' cost of living, compared with standard CPI calculations, which translates into higher growth rates for real consumption. If nominal consumption rates were adjusted using this lower inflation rate, KGT estimate a higher real consumption growth of 9.32 percent on a per capita basis and 9.57 percent on a household basis (versus 7.65 percent and 6.65 percent, respectively without such an adjustment). Because the authors see persistent overestimates of the price deflator for consumption, they conclude that one or two percentage points should be added to the growth rate. Although they determine this for consumption, they argue that close to the same order of magnitude should be considered for GDP as well.

In addition, the authors offer another approach to adjusting the official published price indexes, which takes into account a variety of indicators of life quality or lifestyle in a wider sense. Using ten such indicators, they compute an index as a ten-element weighted average, which grows from 100 in 1980 to 115.47 in 2002. This indicates an estimated growth rate of $r =$ 0.65596 percent, nearly double that for the United States in the period 1980–2000. Thus they conclude that the adjustment to China's growth rate could be as high as 1 percent or more.

The adjustment of the US inflation rate for quality of life and other changes has been broadly accepted, so it seems reasonable to adjust China's price indexes for the same reasons. In fact, lifestyle changes in China have been much greater than for the United States.

Chapter 10: 'Estimating China's Core Inflation Rate' by Deming Wu

The premise of this chapter by Deming Wu is to ascertain the 'core' inflation rate for China in the same manner as is routinely adopted for other advanced economies such as the United States. This constitutes a very sound and extremely interesting methodological exercise with important policy implications as well. The empirical estimates obtained as a result of this effort are a very important statistic that allows us to characterize properly the stabilization policy in China. This is an important element both domestically as well as in the context of the debate pertaining to China's perceived role in the Asian Crisis of 1997–98 when, at times, it was criticized for being too 'deflationary'. One of the main findings of the chapter is that China's core inflation rate – an idea familiar to the US macro-empiricists – was positive unlike the observed official overall inflation rate, which was negative. This implies that, judged by the same standards as adopted, say, in the US for determining the inherent or underlying true inflation rate by looking at the 'core' inflation rate, China pursued a rather expansionary monetary policy during 1997 and 1998. Thus, if anything, China was a stabilizing influence in East Asia during the crisis period. It is evident that this chapter makes very important contributions methodologically as well from a policy perspective in the context of the debate on the Asian Financial Crisis of 1997–98.

NOTE

1. Kaminsky et al. (1998).

REFERENCES

Kaminsky, G.L., S. Lizondo and C.M. Reinhart (1998), 'Leading Indicators of Currency Crisis', *IMF Staff Papers*, **45** (1), March.
World Bank (2000), *The: Workers and the Crisis*, Bangkok: Social Monitor 4.

PART I

Analysis of Currency Crises

1. Asia before and after the financial crisis of 1997–98: a retrospective essay

Lawrence R. Klein and Tayyeb Shabbir

1 INTRODUCTION

It is common knowledge that the Asian Financial Crisis refers to the onset and the aftermath of the currency crashes with attendant sharp declines in output growth and plummeting stock markets in many of the previously fast-growing countries in East Asia during 1997–98. Amongst the countries were particularly hit hard were Thailand, Republic of Korea, Indonesia, Malaysia and the Philippines (often dubbed the 'Affected Five'). For this group of countries, the average decline in the 1997 real GDP growth was about 10 percent from the trend value in 1996, the currency devaluations ranged from 30 percent to 80 percent and stock markets declined by as much as 70 percent, which was the case in Indonesia.

Occurring on the heels of past economic achievements of historic proportions, these severe economic shocks were particularly painful as expectations of an ever-increasing living standard had to be sharply and suddenly pared down in these countries. After all, during the three decades preceding the crisis, these East Asia countries had enjoyed a period of remarkable economic growth as well as social sector achievements. The decades leading up to the crisis had witnessed an average real GDP annual growth rate of more than 7 percent, a decline in poverty from an incidence of six in ten to two in ten, income per capita increases of up to ten-fold in Korea and four-fold in Indonesia, Malaysia and Thailand, nearly 100 percent primary school enrollment, remarkable reductions in infant mortality and increases in life expectancy. Unfortunately, the Asian Crisis of 1997–98 had suddenly but surely put all of these past achievements in serious jeopardy. It was rightly feared that the Asian Crisis will be costly both in economic and societal terms. However, the majority of the analyses of the costs of this crisis have focused on its economic or financial aspects while the disruptive social or societal impact of this episode has been relatively ignored; in fact, one of the three major goals of the present study is to contribute towards rectifying the understanding of this imbalance. The other two goals are to present a retrospective overview of the nature and efficacy of the econometric predictive models of currency crisis as well as the identification of the pre- versus post-crisis pattern of macroeconomic indicators of 'vulnerability' for the 'Affected Five' countries in order to note the appropriate lessons that may be learned.

Three major goals of this chapter are to:

1. Review the different theories that motivate the specification of econometric predictive models of currency crises. Given the relatively high cost of these financial crises, being able to assess their relative predictability can be a very worthwhile exercise.
2. Identify the macroeconomic indicators that mark the 'vulnerability' of a particular economy to a financial crisis. This can be very useful in order to learn the appropriate lessons from the historical patterns and thus, hopefully, allow the policy-makers to devise appropriate policies to minimize the chances of a crisis even when precise predictions may not be forthcoming.
3. Focus on the impact of the 1997–98 Asian Crisis on the social sectors and poverty reduction efforts of the 'Affected Five' countries, in order to provide an illustration of the negative societal impact that such financial crises often inflict in addition to the customary analysis of economic loss.

The chapter is arranged in the following manner. Section 2 presents an overview of the currency crisis theories and econometric predictive models that have been inspired by them; section 3 presents a discussion based on the pre- versus post-crisis patterns of certain macroeconomic indicators in the case of the East Asian countries affected by the 1997–98 crisis; section 4 examines the statistical relationship between financial crisis, poverty alleviation and income distribution, again, using East Asia as the basis of this case study and, finally, section 5 contains concluding comments.

2 CURRENCY CRISIS THEORIES[1]

The theoretical literature on currency crises can be categorized into three 'generations', each delineated by the underlying mechanism that brings about the crisis. The first generation focuses on 'fundamentals', and emphasizes the role of unsustainable government policies that are incompatible with a pegged exchange rate, and which eventually lead to its collapse. The canonical model here was presented in Krugman (1979), based on a government that is financing persistent budget deficits through monetization. This simplest of models suggests that in the period leading up to a speculative attack, one should notice a gradual decline in reserves. It also suggests that budget deficits and excessive growth in domestic credit may be potential early warning indicators for speculative attacks. Extensions of the basic model look at other factors that may force the government to abandon the peg. For example, expansionary policy may lead directly to a worsening of the current account through a rise in import demand; the same result may occur indirectly through a rise in the price of non-tradables and the subsequent overvaluation of the real exchange rate.

Thus, the behavior of external sector variables such as the trade balance, the current account deficit and the real exchange rate may provide some warning regarding the vulnerability of a country to a speculative attack. Further, other potentially useful indicators in this respect are possible measures of the 'quality of existing debt', say, the proportion of non-performing loans of the banking system.

Second-generation models were motivated by episodes such as the exchange rate mechanism (ERM) crisis in 1992–93, where some of the countries did not seem to possess the characteristics described in first-generation models. This led researchers such as Obstfeld (1994) to enrich existing theories of currency crises. The key element in second-generation models is recognition that there are both benefits *and* costs to maintaining a peg, and that market participants' beliefs over whether a peg will not hold or can affect a government's cost of defending it. The circularity inherent in second-generation models – that government policy is affected by expectations, and expectations are affected by government policy – leads to the possibility of multiple equilibria and self-fulfilling crises. These second-generation models suggest that anything that affects a government's decision whether to maintain a peg or not – because of unemployment, inflation, the amount and composition of debt, financial sector stability and so on – might contain information on the likelihood of a crisis occurring. Also, evidently, the inflexibility of the ERM system prevented potentially helpful policy actions. This crisis brought to the forefront the potential for conflict between a member country's goals and the restrictions of the system. On the other hand, we saw later in 1997–98, Hong Kong, with its very strict parity with US dollar, let interest rates go extremely high, but they had big reserves when attacked by the speculative hedge funds and could withstand these shocks.

The third generation of currency crisis models focuses on the issue of contagion, or why the occurrence of a crisis in one country seems to affect the likelihood of a crisis occurring in other countries. Masson (1998) suggests three possible reasons why crises seem to come in clusters. First, there may actually be common external shocks (for example, fluctuations in world interest rates) that affect all the countries involved. Second, there may be spillover effects from one country to another due to trade competitiveness effects or portfolio rebalancing effects. Lastly, speculative attacks might spread from country to country merely on the basis of market sentiment or herding behavior. This class of models suggests that early warning systems should include external variables such as LIBOR (London Interbank Offered Rate) dynamics or the economic growth rate of trading partners that indicates a critical trouble in a trading partner economy or in 'similar countries' that should be taken into account.

2.1 Early Warning Systems

Recent efforts such as those of Demirgüç-Kunt and Detragiache (1998); Eichengreen and Rose (1998); Kaminsky and Reinhart (1998, 1999); Kaminsky et al. (1998); Kumar et al. (2003); and Pérez (2005) towards devising an early warning system for an impending financial crisis have taken two related forms.

The first approach estimates a probit or logit model of the occurrence of a crisis with lagged values of early warning indicators as explanatory variables. This approach requires the construction of a crisis dummy variable that serves as the endogenous variable in the probit or logit regression. Classification of each sample time-point as being in crisis or not depends on whether or not a specific index of vulnerability or speculative pressure exceeds a chosen threshold. For currency crises, the index of vulnerability is often based on a weighted average of the following three variables:

- percentage changes in nominal exchange rates;
- percentage change in gross international reserves;
- difference in local and key foreign short-term interest rates.

Other possible determinants of relevance include current account balance, inflation rate and domestic fiscal balance. Explanatory variables typically come from the real, financial, external and fiscal sectors of the economy, but, in one way or another, often involve international economic relations.

The second method uses a signaling or leading-indicator approach to get a more direct measure of the importance of each potential explanatory variable. Apart from constructing a crisis dummy variable, the approach also constructs binary variables from each explanatory variable – thus imputing a value of 1 (a 'signal') or 0 (no signal) for each explanatory variable at each point in time in the sample – based on whether each variable exceeds a chosen threshold or not. These signals are classified according to their ability to call a crisis: a signal is a 'good signal' if a crisis does occur within a specified period (usually 24 months), and is a 'false signal' otherwise. Thresholds are chosen so as to strike a balance between the risk of having many false signals and the risk of missing many crises. More precisely, a signal-to-noise ratio is computed for each explanatory variable over the sample period – as a quantitative assessment of the value of the variable as a crisis indicator. This is done by classifying each observation of the binary signaling variable into one of the following four categories:

	Crisis occurs within 24 months	No crisis occurs within 24 months
Signal	A	B
No signal	C	D

Thresholds are then chosen to maximize the signal-to-noise ratio [A/(A+C)]/[B/(B+D)]. Based on this metric, Kaminsky et al. (1998) find that the best early warning indicators for currency crises include exports, deviations of the real exchange rate from trend, M2/reserves, output and equity prices.

Whether this approach or a probit/logit approach is used, to cover a wider sample for purposes of estimating incidence probabilities for a crisis, many studies have been typically made of a panel of countries – and usually with some homogeneity assumptions about crisis behavior across countries.

2.1.1 Drawbacks in the above approaches

Despite the current popularity of these approaches,[2] they have some drawbacks, which include the following (see Abiad, 2002 and Mariano et al., 2002 for a more detailed discussion):

- There may be an inadequate treatment of serial correlations inherent in the dynamics of a crisis. Neither the probit/logit approach nor the signaling approach give us information on dynamics, showing how long crisis periods tend to last – nor do they give information about what variables affect the likelihood of the end of a crisis period.
- Artificial serial correlations may even be introduced inadvertently through the explicit manner in which the crisis dummy variable is constructed. Many previous studies focus primarily on predicting the onset of a crisis, that is, the first period when speculative attacks occur. To achieve this in their binary crisis variable, they make use of so-called 'exclusion windows', which remove any crisis signals that

closely follow previous crisis signals. This procedure can introduce artificial serial correlations; see Abiad (2002).

- Classification errors may result when constructing the crisis dummy variable (either as a false signal of a crisis, or a missed reading of a crisis). Because the threshold used to delineate crisis periods from tranquil periods is arbitrarily chosen, misclassification of crisis episodes can occur. If the threshold is too high, for example, some periods of vulnerability may not be detected.
- There needs to be a better framework for significance testing of the influence of explanatory or indicator variables (in the signaling approach). The signaling approach could be improved if it were based on an explicit stochastic model. As with many indicator models, it needs formal testing in order to assess its performance vis-à-vis other approaches.
- There may be possible inconsistencies in the estimation of crisis incidence probabilities because of heterogeneity across countries. It is possible that the variables that are important in determining crisis likelihoods for one country are unimportant for another country. And even if the same variables affected crisis likelihoods for all countries, the degree of likelihood of a crisis occurring may differ from one country to the next.

2.2 Markov-switching Approach[3]

Recently, a newer approach to the early warning methodology tries to address these drawbacks. This approach constructs for each individual country a Markov-switching, autoregressive model that allows intercepts, lag coefficients and error variances to switch stochastically over time according to the value taken by a latent Markov chain, describing the vulnerability of the country's currency to speculative attacks (Mariano et al., 2003). In a related work, Martinez-Peria (1999), applies a Markov-switching model to speculative attacks, but the primary purpose in that paper is to evaluate the ability of the model to date crisis periods and to see whether market expectations affect crisis probabilities. Here the focus is on the use of the model as an early warning system. The Mariano et al. (2003) model is a predictive model of a currency crisis and consists of two parts.

First, a Markov chain model of the unobservable financial vulnerability of the country, say S_t. It argues that what we observe are indicators of this latent attribute of the country. It assumes two states:

- normal ($S_t = 0$);
- vulnerable ($S_t = 1$).

This model further assumes that the Markov chain is of order 1, with transition probabilities that are time-varying through dependence on observable indicator variables. In Mariano et al. (2002, 2003) there are reports of results that are based on the following indicator variables:

- deviations of real effective exchange rate from trend (*REERDEV*);
- month-to-month percentage changes in the ratio of M2 to international reserves (*M2RATIO*);
- month-to-month percentage changes in real domestic credit (*DCR*).

Second, a Markov regime-switching time-series model of percentage changes in nominal exchange rates. This model differs from standard cases in the sense that it includes the unobservable state variable S_t as an additional endogenous variable. With the inclusion of S_t, we introduce the notion that the exchange rate dynamics behave in a different fashion, depending on whether financial conditions are normal ($S_t = 0$) or vulnerable to currency pressures ($S_t = 1$). The Mariano et al. (2002, 2003) model reflects this by allowing the parameters in the relevant time-series model to change in value over time, as financial conditions become normal or vulnerable.

2.2.1 Markov-switching model in some detail

Let S_t be a two-state Markov chain of order 1 with transition probabilities p_t and q_t, so that at any given time t, S_t can take on two values, 0 or 1, according to the following probability law:

$$\Pr(S_t = 0 | S_{t-1} = 0) = p_t \quad \text{and} \quad \Pr(S_t = 1 | S_{t-1} = 1) = q_t.$$

Further, let

y_t = month-to-month percentage changes in nominal exchange rates,
$\mathbf{x_t}$ = the vector of exogenous variables at time t to be used to explain y_t,
$\mathbf{z_t}$ = the vector of exogenous variables at time t to be used as indicators of currency vulnerability, which may overlap with $\mathbf{x_t}$.

We assume also that the transition probabilities vary over time according to values of indicator variables in the following manner:

$$p_t = \mathbf{F}(\mathbf{z}_t'\gamma) \quad \text{and} \quad q_t = \mathbf{F}(\mathbf{z}_t'\delta),$$

where $\mathbf{F}(\cdot)$ is the standard unit Gaussian cumulative distribution function.

The second part of the model consists of a univariate linear model for y_t:

$$y_t = \alpha s_t + x_t' \beta s_t + \sigma s_t \varepsilon_t.$$

In this model, the model parameters (α, β, σ) are subscripted by S_t – indicating that their true (unknown) values are shifting between two sets of possible parameter values: (α_0, β_0, σ_0) and (α_1, β_1, σ_1) depending on whether financial conditions are normal or vulnerable.

The estimation procedure we use is direct maximization of the likelihood, where the likelihood function is calculated by using an iterative process, described in detail in Hamilton (1994). Collect all the parameters of the model into a single vector $\theta = (\alpha_0, \beta_0, \sigma_0, \alpha_1, \beta_1, \sigma_1, \gamma', \delta')$. Using information available up to time t, Ω_t, we can calculate for each time t (using the iteration below) the value of $\Pr(s_t = j|\Omega_t; \theta)$, the conditional probability that the t-th observation was generated by regime j, for $j = 1, 2, \ldots N$, where N is the number of states (in this chapter, $N=2$). We will stack these conditional probabilities into an $(N \times 1)$ vector $\hat{\boldsymbol{\xi}}_{t|t}$.

Using the same iteration, we can also form forecasts regarding the conditional probability of being in regime j at time $t+1$, given information up to time t: $\Pr(s_{t+1} = j|\Omega_t; \theta)$, for $j = 1, 2, \ldots N$. Collect these forecast probabilities in an $(N \times 1)$ vector $\hat{\boldsymbol{\xi}}_{t+1|t}$. Lastly, let η_t denote the $(N \times 1)$ vector whose j-th element is the density of y_t conditional on s_t.

The optimal inference and forecast for each date t can then be found by iterating on the following equations:

$$\hat{\boldsymbol{\xi}}_{t|t} = \frac{(\hat{\xi}_{t|t-1} \circ \eta_t)}{\mathbf{1}'(\hat{\xi}_{t|t-1} \circ \eta_t)}$$

$$\hat{\boldsymbol{\xi}}_{t+1|t} = \mathbf{P}_{t+1} \cdot \hat{\xi}_{t|t}$$

where $\mathbf{P}_t$ is the $(N \times N)$ transition probability matrix going from period $t-1$ to period t (for the two-state model in this chapter; $\mathbf{P}_t$ is the 2×2 matrix $[p_t\ 1 - p_t;\ 1 - q_t\ q_t]$), and $\circ$ denotes element-by-element multiplication. Given an assumed value for the parameters, θ, and an assumed starting value for $\hat{\boldsymbol{\xi}}_{1|0}$ (the unconditional probability of s_t at $t=1$), we can then iterate on the above equations to obtain values of $\hat{\boldsymbol{\xi}}_{t|t}$ and $\hat{\boldsymbol{\xi}}_{t+1|t}$ for $t = 1, 2, \ldots T$. The log likelihood function $L(\theta)$ can be computed from these as

$$L(\theta) = \sum_{t=1}^{T} \log f(y_t|X_t, Y_{t-1}; \theta)$$

where

$$f(y_t|X_t, Y_{t-1}; \theta) = \mathbf{1}'(\hat{\xi}_{t|t} \circ \eta_t).$$

One can then evaluate this at different values of θ to find the maximum likelihood estimate.

2.2.2 Empirical results for Markov-switching models of currency crises

The Markov-switching predictive models of currency crises of the type outlined above have recently been estimated for Argentina (Alvarez-Plata and Schrooten, 2003), Turkey (Mariano et al., 2004) as well as countries in Southeast Asia[4] (Brunetti et al., 2003 and Mariano et al., 2003).

In the case of the Argentinean crisis of 2002, Alvarez-Plata and Schrooten (2003) estimate a two-regime Markov-switching model with constant (exogenous) transition probabilities. They find evidence of regime switch prior to the crisis; however, they merely *assume* the cause of this shift to be changes in 'expectations of private investors'. This ignores the (testable) alternative possibility of structural determinants of transition probabilities. On the other hand, Mariano et al. (2004) for Turkey, and Mariano et al. (2003) for Southeast Asian countries, estimate a Markov-switching model with constant as well as time-varying transition probabilities.

For the Southeast Asian countries of Indonesia, Malaysia, the Philippines and Thailand, Mariano et al. (2003) report that the transition probabilities are affected by the real effective exchange rate, money supply relative to international reserves and real domestic credit. However, the estimated model does not perform uniformly well across the sample countries. Whereas for some currency depreciation episodes like those in 1981, 1984 and 1997 for Thailand and in 1997 for Malaysia, the model provides strong early warning signals, but for other episodes, such as in 1997 for Indonesia and the Philippines, the model manages at best to generate only weak warning signals. Incidentally, a related study, Brunetti et al. (2003), extended the Mariano et al. (2003) model to account for conditional heteroskedasticity of the exchange rate depreciations – the volatility is hypothesized not only to switch between two regimes but to follow a GARCH process within each regime. The preliminary results reported in Brunetti et al. (2003) claim improved forecast performance. Further, this study also notes that stock market returns are an additional determinant that may affect transition probabilities in addition to those reported in Mariano et al. (2003).

The formal econometric predictive models like the Markov-switching model discussed above are very useful tools. While their formal structure is an extremely desirable feature, due to technical limitations, they can also restrict the scope of the discussion necessary to get a broad sense of the possible determinants of the vulnerabilities of economies to a currency crisis. Thus, in the following section, we present an analysis based on certain observable important indicators of vulnerability of an economy to a currency or a financial crisis in general.[5]

3 VULNERABILITIES OF THE 'AFFECTED FIVE'

3.1 Competing Hypotheses as Explanations of the Crisis[6]

The literature that has been inspired by the East Asian Crisis of 1997–98 proffers two competing hypotheses as the possible causes of currency crisis – the 'contagion' hypothesis versus the 'vulnerability' hypothesis.[7]

According to the 'contagion' view, the capital flight in Thailand induced by expectations of an impending devaluation of the bhat relative to the US dollar (to which it was pegged), had negative informational 'spillover' effects that doomed some of the neighbors by casting doubt in the minds of the investors about otherwise 'healthy' economies.

The 'vulnerability' hypothesis, on the other hand, maintains that some economies were inherently vulnerable to a crisis because of relatively long-term deterioration in economic fundamentals. This predisposed them to crisis when faced with shocks that may lead to expectation of exchange rate devaluation.

The above set of rival explanations can be distinguished such that the 'contagion' factor is analogous to a 'trigger' and 'vulnerability' means susceptibility to a country crisis on fundamental grounds.

Of course, in their respective extreme forms, the contagion and vulnerability hypothesis afford significantly different interpretations as well as policy implications, whereas the vulnerability hypothesis implies that the relative susceptibility of an economy can be ascertained with the aid of observable indicators. Also, high levels of vulnerability make a crisis inevitable and any random event could actually provoke it. On the other hand, extreme versions of the contagion hypothesis deny or certainly minimize the significance of observable indicators of vulnerability. Most of the literature dealing with the East Asian Crisis of 1997–98 has taken an intermediate stance.

After all, the pure contagion explanation has had to contend with the question that if Thailand spread the virus, how did Thailand become affected in the first place? Evidently, it is hard to escape having to rely on an explanation that is based on deteriorating fundamentals in Thailand before 1997. Again contagion theory fails to explain why some countries such as Singapore, Taiwan and China proved to be resilient to the spreading 'virus'.

We feel that the intermediate position is the most tenable one and thus examining the determinants of vulnerability in terms of critical real as well as financial sector indicators is a very useful exercise. In the analysis that follows, we examine the pre- as well as post-crisis pattern of certain critical macroeconomic fundamentals to provide an assessment of the dynamics of the economies of the 'Affected Five' before and after the 'breakpoint' marked by the 1997–98 crisis.[8]

3.2 Examining the Pre-crisis and Post-crisis Patterns of 'Fundamentals'

As evident from the data trends in current account deficit, export growth rate, government budget fiscal balance and other pertinent macroeconomic variables such as the real exchange rate overvaluation, the 'Affected Five' countries (Thailand, Republic of Korea, Indonesia, Malaysia and the Philippines) were vulnerable before the outbreak of the currency crisis of the baht on 2 July 1997. The problem is particularly telling if one looks at the increase in the current account deficit and the slowdown in the export growth rate. This, accompanied by the fragility of the financial sector, in particular, the upsurge in the proportion of non-performing loans, contributed greatly to the currency and, more broadly, the financial crisis that followed. Tables 1.1–1.5 (and the corresponding Figures 1.1–1.5) below present the pertinent data for the pre- as well as post-crisis period (1993–2004) and additional comments for each of the 'Affected Five' countries separately.[9] On the other hand, Figure 1.6 through Figure 1.11 present the comparative data for all of the 'Affected Five' countries for several important indicators considered one at a time.

As can be seen from Table 1.1 and Figure 1.1, before 1997, Thailand's CA (current account) balance (as a percentage of GDP) had deteriorated sharply from –5.41 percent in 1994 to –7.89 percent in 1996, while its export growth had declined precipitously from an average growth of 20.11 percent during 1993–95 to a decline of –1.91 percent in 1996, and the fiscal balance (as a percentage of GDP) dropped significantly from 3.01 percent in 1995 to 0.94 percent in 1996. These indicators clearly pointed to Thailand's serious vulnerability to a crisis, which, of course, unfolded on 2 July 1997.

In the years following the onset of the crisis in 1997, while Thailand had started showing definite signs of turnaround in its external sector indicators as early as 1998 (the CA deficit had turned positive by then), this recovery was not across the board – in fact, the GDP growth rate registered a steep decline in 1998. Indeed, it was not until 1999, that a firmer and more broad-based recovery milestone was reached when, in addition to a sustained CA surplus, the GDP growth rate turned significantly positive, and both the growth rates of exports as well as imports were positive. Thus, for all

Table 1.1 Macro indicators: Thailand

Year	1993	1994	1995	1996	1997	1998	1999	2000	2001	2002	2003	2004
CA (% of GDP)	−4.90	−5.41	−7.88	−7.89	−1.97	12.66	10.17	7.61	5.41	6.06	5.57	4.39
Export Growth* (%)	13.36	22.15	24.82	−1.91	3.76	−6.78	7.42	19.52	−6.92	5.71	18.18	21.56
Import Growth* (%)	12.35	18.44	31.85	0.62	−13.37	−33.75	16.94	31.34	−2.82	4.45	17.35	26.04
Fiscal Balance (% of GDP)	1.89	2.69	3.01	0.94	−1.50	−2.79	−3.33	−2.23	−2.40	−1.41	0.40	0.13
Real GDP Growth (%)		8.99	9.24	5.90	−1.37	−10.51	4.45	4.76	2.14	5.41	7.03	6.17
REER (1996 = 100)	90.78	92.28	91.54	100.00	93.71	82.39	85.61	79.56	78.11	82.16	80.49	79.12
Inflation Rate (%)	3.31	5.08	5.79	5.83	5.60	8.08	0.30	1.55	1.66	0.60	1.81	2.77

Notes:
Def.: REER = real effective exchange rate index (1996 = 100).
* Based on [{Index(t)/Index ($t-1$)} − 1] × 100 where Index value for 1996 = 100.

Source: http://aric.adb.org.

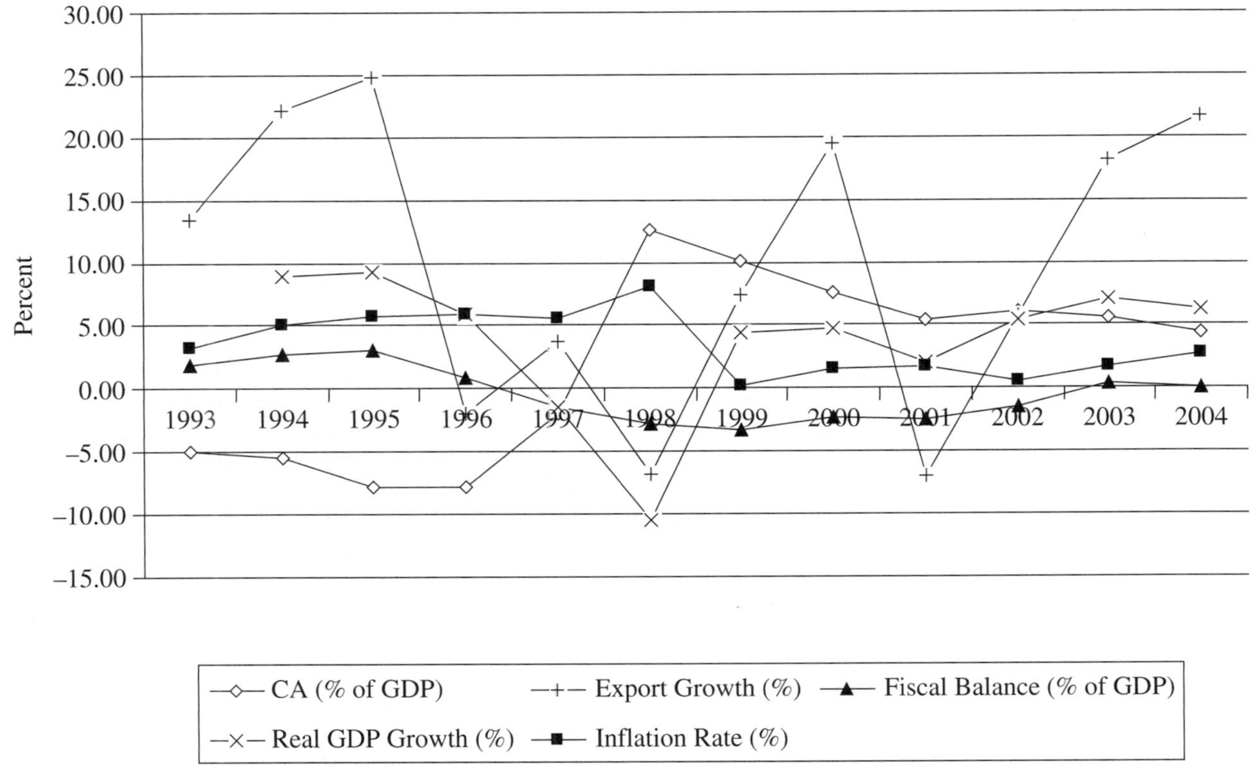

Figure 1.1 Macro indicators: Thailand

practical purposes, 1999 is the year that marks the onset of the post-crisis recovery for Thailand even though fiscal balance took a little longer to recover and started to improve only in 2000.

The Republic of Korea (Table 1.2 and Figure 1.2), in a scenario similar to Thailand's, exhibited plenty of pre-crisis signs of vulnerability – its CA (as a percentage of GDP) turned to a deep deficit in 1996 (–4.41 percent) from a slight surplus of 0.29 percent in 1993, while its export growth slowed down significantly from an average of 18.10 percent p. a. during 1993–95 to a relative trickle in 1996 (3.72 percent) and its real GDP growth that averaged 8.59 percent p. a. for 1994–95, registered at only 6.75 percent in 1996.

While the crisis meant a sharp decline for Korea's real GDP growth rate (–6.69 percent in 1998), as a whole, it was relatively the least hampered by the crisis amongst the group of 'Affected Five' countries. In 1999, Korea's real GDP growth rate recovered vigorously (10.89 percent), its fiscal deficit started declining as well, and, in fact, turned to a surplus by 2000, which has proven sustainable since. Again, following a decline of 2.83 percent in 1998, the export growth rate resumed a positive trend with the exception of a drop in 2001 on account of the recession in the US, a major importer of Korean manufactured goods (average export growth of 17.35 percent p. a. during 1999–2004, excluding 2001, which compares favorably with the average of 18.10 percent p. a. for the pre-crisis 'miracle' years of 1993–95. The country's current account balance also turned positive starting in 1998 though this happened primarily because of a relatively much steeper drop in its trend import growth, which had dropped to –35.50 percent in 1998; import growth did in fact turn positive by the following year and still the CA balance stayed positive.

In general, ex post, the trajectory of Korea's macroeconomic recovery from the crisis was a 'V-shaped' rather than a 'U-shaped' one – that is, quick and sharp rather than dull and drawn out. (See Figure 1.6 in this chapter for comparative changes in real GDP growth rate for the 'Affected Five' countries.)

In addition, in the aftermath of the crisis, Korea has had relatively the most to show for its efforts to clean up its financial sector both in terms of the reform of the corporate ownership structure and decreased frequency of the non-performing loans as a proportion of the total debt of the banking system (though no statistics have been noted in the tables in this regard).

Table 1.3 and the corresponding Figure 1.3 look at the case of Indonesia whose economy, like that of Thailand and Korea, exhibited pre-crisis increase in external sector imbalance (CA deficit increased from –1.45 percent of GDP to –3.41 percent of GDP). However, unlike the Thai or

Table 1.2 Macro indicators: Republic of Korea

Year	1993	1994	1995	1996	1997	1998	1999	2000	2001	2002	2003	2004
CA (% of GDP)	0.29	−0.96	−1.73	−4.41	−1.70	12.58	6.02	2.65	1.93	1.27	1.96	4.05
Export Growth* (%)	7.31	16.75	30.25	3.72	4.97	−2.83	8.59	19.89	−12.67	8.00	19.29	30.97
Import Growth* (%)	2.48	22.13	32.02	11.26	−3.81	−35.50	28.38	34.01	−12.08	7.82	17.55	25.52
Fiscal Balance (% of GDP)			0.33	0.26	−1.54	−4.22	−2.71	1.25	1.32	3.80	1.12	0.72
Real GDP Growth (%)	5.49	8.25	8.92	6.75	5.01	−6.69	10.89	9.33	3.10	6.35	3.10	4.64
REER (1996 = 100)	91.93	94.13	95.67	100.00	95.98	79.50	86.89	90.03	87.56	93.71	95.52	97.13
Inflation Rate (%)	4.79	6.27	4.45	4.92	4.44	7.52	0.81	2.26	4.31	2.77	3.51	3.59

Notes:
Def.: REER = real effective exchange rate index (1996 = 100).
* Based on [{Index(t)/Index ($t-1$)} − 1]×100 where Index value for 1996 = 100.

Source: http://aric.adb.org.

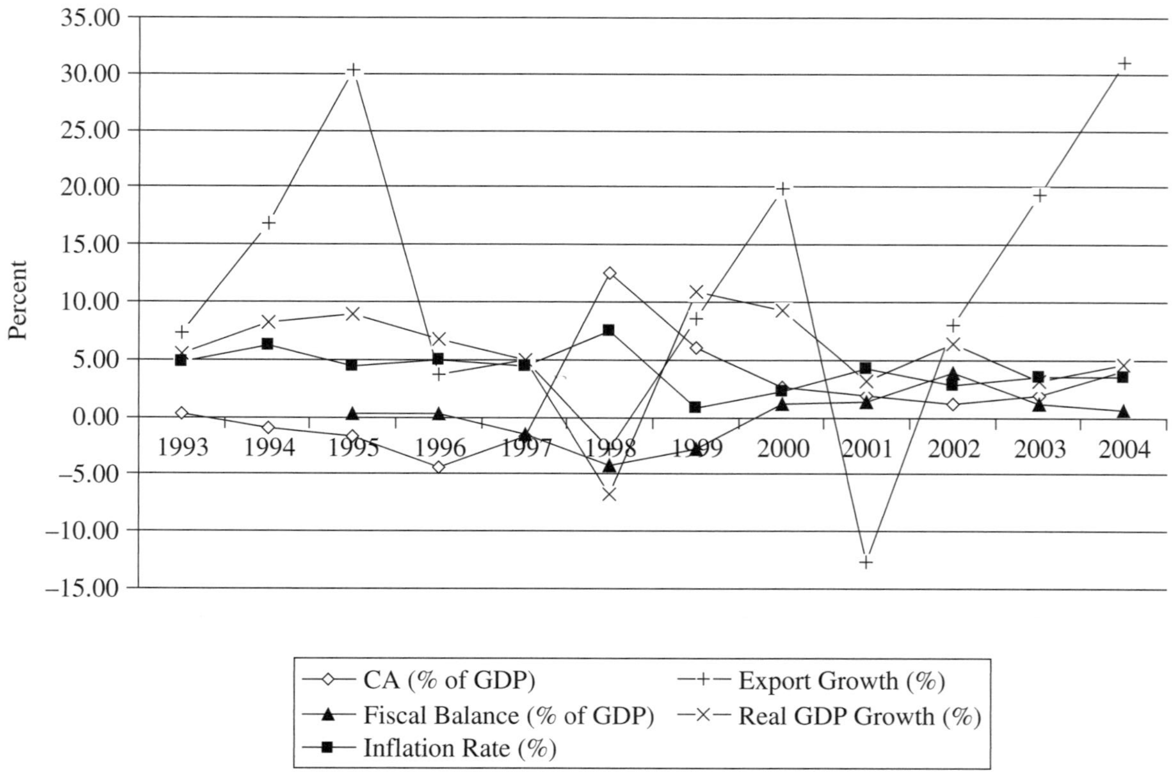

Figure 1.2 *Macro indicators: Republic of Korea*

Table 1.3 Macro indicators: Indonesia

Year	1993	1994	1995	1996	1997	1998	1999	2000	2001	2002	2003	2004
CA (% of GDP)	−1.45	−1.67	−3.34	−3.41	−2.22	4.27	4.11	5.3	4.87	4.3	3.40	1.21
Export Growth* (%)	7.88	9.31	13.39	9.68	7.28	−8.6	−0.37	27.66	−9.34	1.49	6.82	17.24
Import Growth* (%)	3.71	12.95	27.03	5.66	−2.91	−34.41	−11.2	38.06	−7.62	1.06	4.03	42.93
Fiscal Balance (% of GDP)	0.61	0.94	2.22	1.16	−0.67	−2.95	−1.15	−1.19	−3.77	−1.76	−1.65	−1.24
Real GDP Growth (%)		7.54	8.22	7.82	4.7	−13.13	0.79	4.92	3.44	3.66	4.88	5.13
REER (1996 = 100)	93.02	93.63	91.26	100.00	95.46	48.07	68.06	64.19	63.44	77.92	83.39	78.48
Inflation Rate (%)	9.69	8.52	9.43	7.97	6.14	56.15	19.96	3.93	11.54	11.84	6.75	6.08

Notes:
Def.: REER = real effective exchange rate index (1996 = 100).
* Based on [{Index(t)/Index ($t-1$)} − 1]×100 where Index value for 1996 = 100.

Source: http://aric.adb.org.

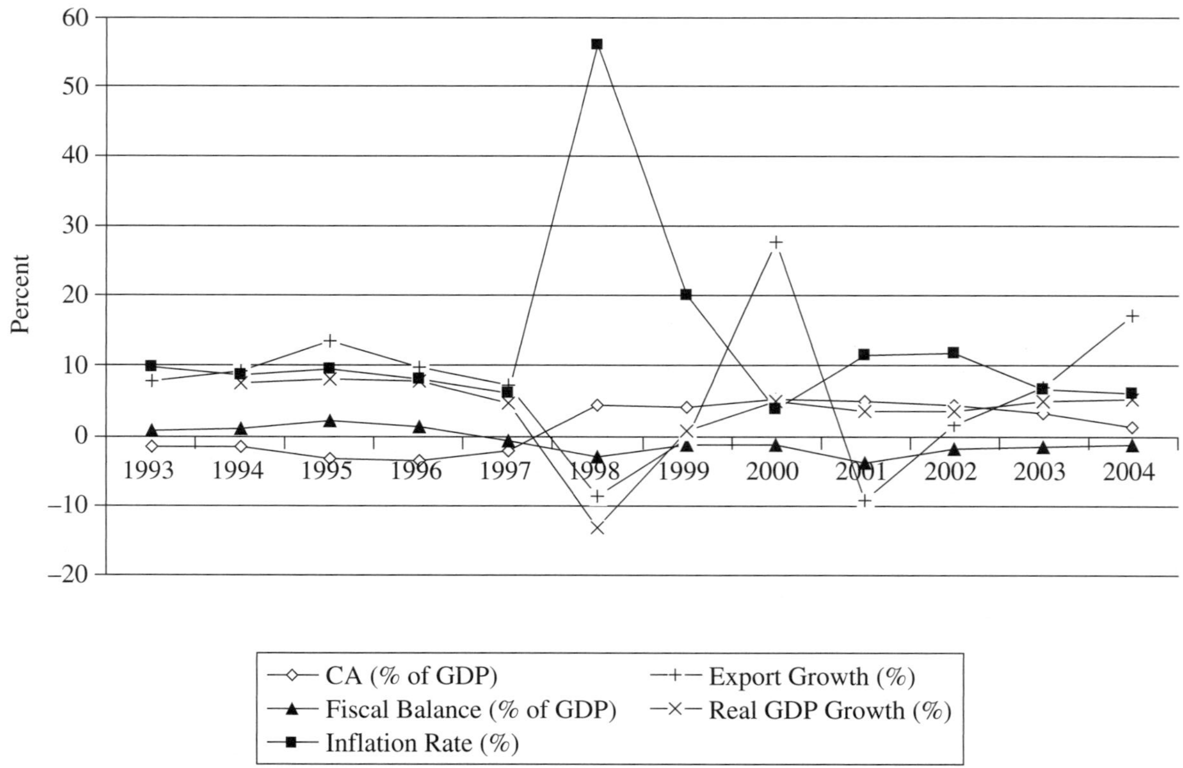

Figure 1.3 Macro indicators: Indonesia

Korean cases, Indonesia showed a far less pronounced drop in export growth, partly perhaps because Indonesia has 'less to lose'. However, while not being in the vanguard of the 'New Asian Miracle', Indonesia had started to show real promise when the Asian Crisis struck in 1997. Thus Indonesia was affected significantly as evidenced from the fact that it suffered a negative real GDP growth rate of 13.13 percent for 1997 as compared with an average growth rate of 7–8 percent p. a. for the early to mid-1990s period.

After the crisis, Indonesia recovered to essentially a relatively low trajectory of GDP growth rate in the 3–4 percent p. a. range. Notice that unlike others in the group of 'Five Affected' countries, import growth in Indonesia was negative as far into the future as the year 2001 and its post-crisis fiscal deficit continues to persist through to 2004, the end of our sample period. Also, Indonesia's post-crisis economic recovery was accompanied by relatively higher inflation rates as compared with the other countries in the same cohort. Indonesia was also a victim of relatively greater amount of political and social turmoil in the aftermath of the Asian Financial Crisis.

Table 1.4 and the corresponding Figure 1.4 present the facts for the Malaysian case. In terms of the possible indicators of vulnerability, Malaysia's export growth dropped to a relatively anemic 5.93 percent in 1996 from an average of 20.10 percent p. a. during the 1993–95 period. Its import growth slowed down considerably as well, essentially stagnating in 1996 compared with an average growth rate of 25.46 percent p. a. during 1993–95. Regarding the country's CA balance, a somewhat classic indicator of crisis vulnerability, Malaysia's case indicated an overall trend of relatively worsening CA deficits that increased during 1994 and 1995 compared with 1993. (However, the year 1996 showed a substantial CA deficit reduction compared with the preceding year.)

After the 1997–98 crisis, Malaysia's GDP growth rate was fairly quick to recover – the country experienced a negative GDP growth rate in only one year, 1997, and recovered smartly the following year. Thus, Malaysia resembles Korea in this respect. However, what has been unique about Malaysia's policy reaction to the Asian Crisis was its institution of capital controls – a policy that was at odds with the standard IMF prescription for other countries in East Asia in similar straits at the time. The Malaysian capital control program was looked at with a fair amount of skepticism when it was put in place. After all, Malaysia did not enjoy the huge foreign exchange reserves that China and Hong Kong possessed, to back up their retention of fixed dollar pegs. However, in the end, the steady and sustained Malaysian macroeconomic recovery won over several of the skeptics. Thus, in the aftermath of the Asian Crisis, Malaysian GDP recovered fairly

Table 1.4 Macro indicators: Malaysia

Year	1993	1994	1995	1996	1997	1998	1999	2000	2001	2002	2003	2004
CA (% of GDP)	−4.47	−6.05	−9.78	−4.8	−5.18	13.53	15.92	9.14	8.27	7.82	12.82	12.57
Export Growth* (%)	15.72	24.74	25.85	5.93	0.41	−6.75	15.34	16.08	−10.45	5.92	11.60	20.52
Import Growth* (%)	14.32	30.55	31.52	0.1	0.68	−26.14	12.08	25.35	−10.03	7.98	4.84	25.92
Fiscal Balance (% of GDP)	0.21	2.26	0.84	0.72	2.35	−1.77	−3.15	−5.75	−5.51	−5.62	−5.30	−4.32
Real GDP Growth (%)	9.9	9.21	9.83	10.00	7.32	−7.36	6.14	8.55	0.32	4.12	5.42	7.14
REER (1996 = 100)	93.42	92.53	93.93	100.00	99.08	81.53	82.33	80.94	87.28	89.49	84.79	78.48
Inflation Rate (%)	3.56	4.94	4.06	3.49	2.67	5.27	2.74	1.52	1.41	1.83	1.09	1.42

Notes:
Def.: REER = real effective exchange rate index (1996 = 100).
* Based on [{Index(t)/Index ($t-1$)} − 1] × 100 where Index value for 1996 = 100.

Source: http://aric.adb.org.

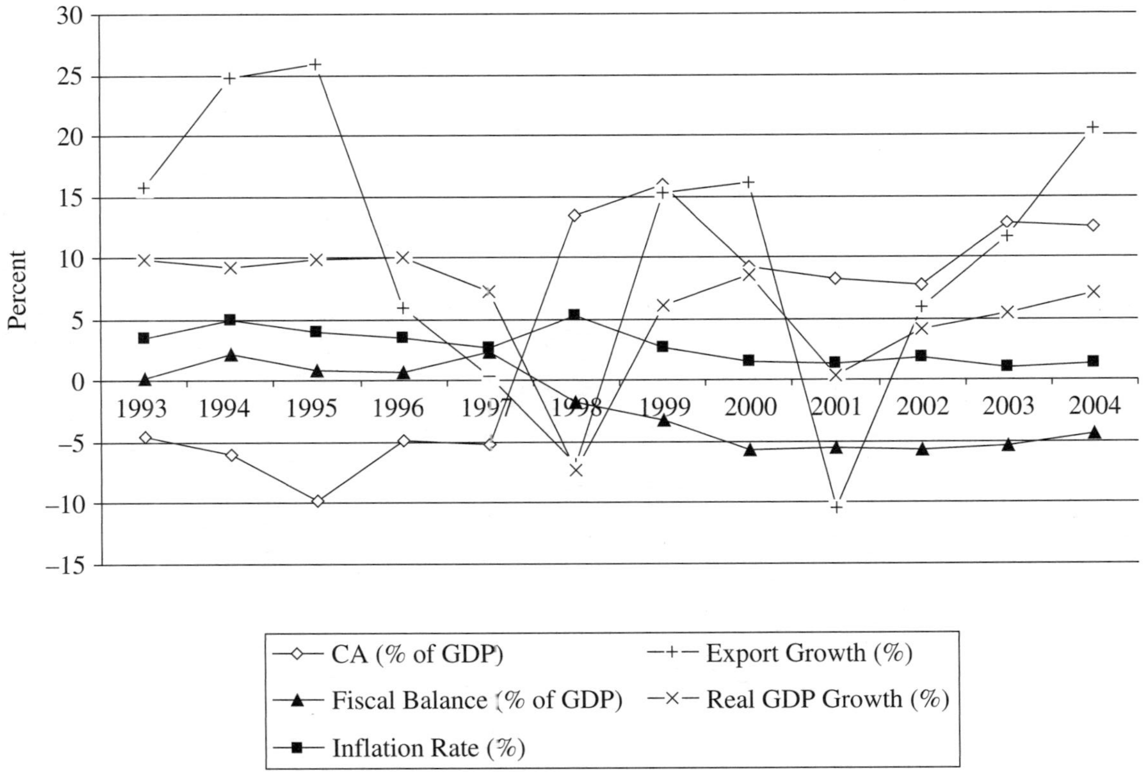

Figure 1.4 Macro indicators: Malaysia

quickly while maintaining a low and stable inflation rate, though fiscal balances were continuing to worsen well into the 1990s and even early in the new decade.[10]

Finally, referring to Table 1.5 and the corresponding Figure 1.5, we turn to a discussion about the Philippines – a country that had just started to show promise when the Asian Crisis hit in 1997. In fact, relative to its ASEAN (Association of Southeast Asian Nations) partners, the Philippines were relatively more vulnerable – its GDP growth rate had averaged only about half of what Korea had been able to achieve in the years leading up to the Asian Crisis; further, for the period, early to mid-1990s, the Philippines suffered from a current account deficit in the range of 4–5 percent of GDP. The country also had its share of political instabilities and crises and, collectively, these pre-crisis vulnerabilities made the recovery period somewhat anemic. Here it is important to note that the 'Marcos Regime', which lasted for almost two decades from 1965–85, had been replaced by a relatively democratic institution only for about ten years when the Asian Crisis occurred. Thus, the Philippines were somewhat 'late bloomers' whose ascent to a sustained higher economic stage was significantly interrupted by the crisis in 1997. Still the country appears to have made a sustained, albeit modest-sized, recovery from the crisis. However, the future prospects of the country would depend on continued political stability that the country has enjoyed of late, getting the increasing fiscal deficit under control and continuing to make progress in terms of the financial sector and governance-related reforms.

Incidentally, many of the above observations regarding the pre- versus post-crisis relative performance of the 'Affected Five' countries can also be visualized in an alternative format as presented in the following set of Figures 1.6–1.11. Here each figure displays information about a given economic indicator across countries rather than across economic indicators for one country at a time as above. In particular, note that Republic of Korea's GDP growth rate was relatively the fastest to recover after the crisis (Figure 1.6) and, relatively speaking, Indonesia had to suffer from the highest rate of inflation in the aftermath of the crisis (Figure 1.11).

3.3 Did We See the Asian Financial Crisis of 1997 Coming?

The above heading poses a particularly interesting question of obvious importance. There may not have been a siren song of pre-crises warning, but several researchers made important observations that noted the development of some unusual patterns that presaged the crises.

Table 1.5 Macro indicators: The Philippines

Year	1993	1994	1995	1996	1997	1998	1999	2000	2001	2002	2003	2004
CA (% of GDP)	−5.54	−4.56	−4.49	−4.77	−5.27	2.36	9.18	8.36	1.84	5.39	1.76	2.37
Export Growth* (%)	15.78	18.53	29.36	17.78	22.8	16.93	18.78	8.69	−15.57	9.51	2.91	9.52
Import Growth* (%)	21.2	21.23	24.38	22.22	10.81	−17.46	3.59	12.26	−4.15	7.17	3.14	8.82
Fiscal Balance (% of GDP)	−1.48	1.07	0.59	0.29	0.06	−1.88	−3.75	−4.06	−4.0	−5.24	−4.66	−3.86
Real GDP Growth (%)	2.12	4.39	4.68	5.85	5.19	−0.58	3.4	5.97	2.96	4.43	4.62	6.03
REER (1996 = 100)	81.67	87.55	90.58	100.00	100.6	85.14	91.29	82.47	79.9	82.01	75.47	71.48
Inflation Rate (%)	6.88	8.36	8.03	9.01	5.97	9.7	6.68	4.31	6.12	3.1	3.48	5.98

Notes:
Def.: REER = real effective exchange rate index (1996 = 100).
* Based on [{Index(t)/Index ($t-1$)} − 1] × 100 where Index value for 1996 = 100.

Source: http://aric.adb.org.

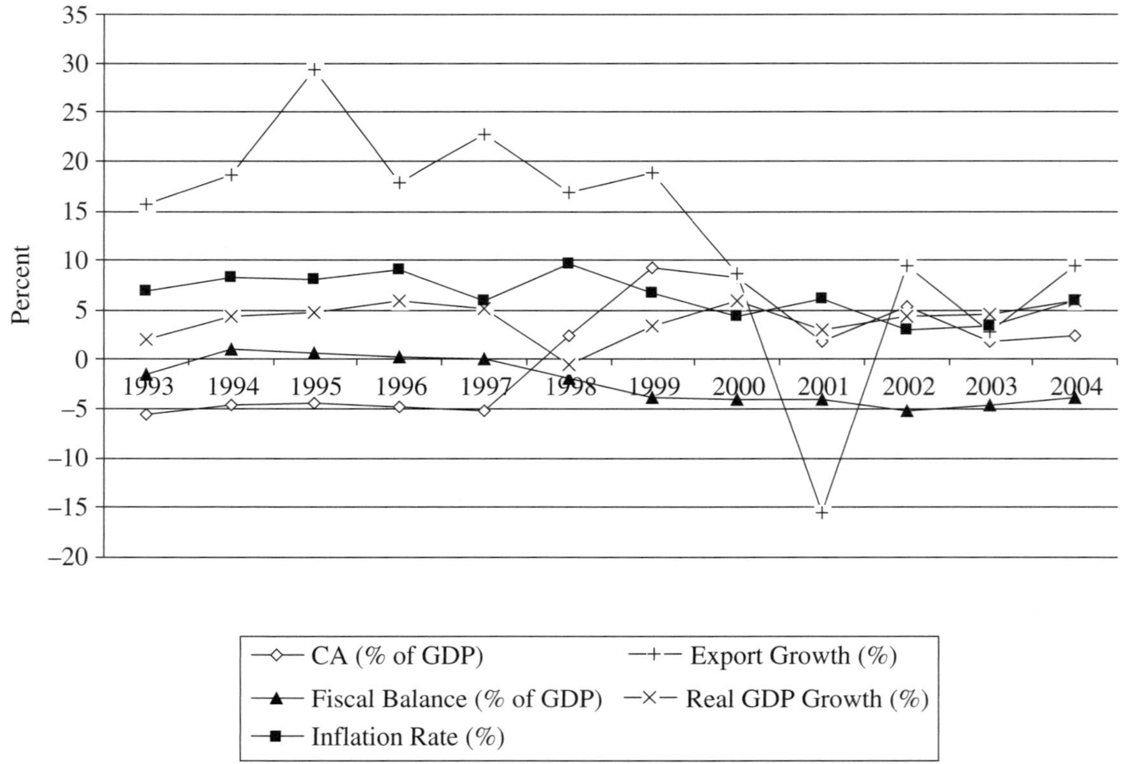

Figure 1.5 Macro indicators: The Philippines

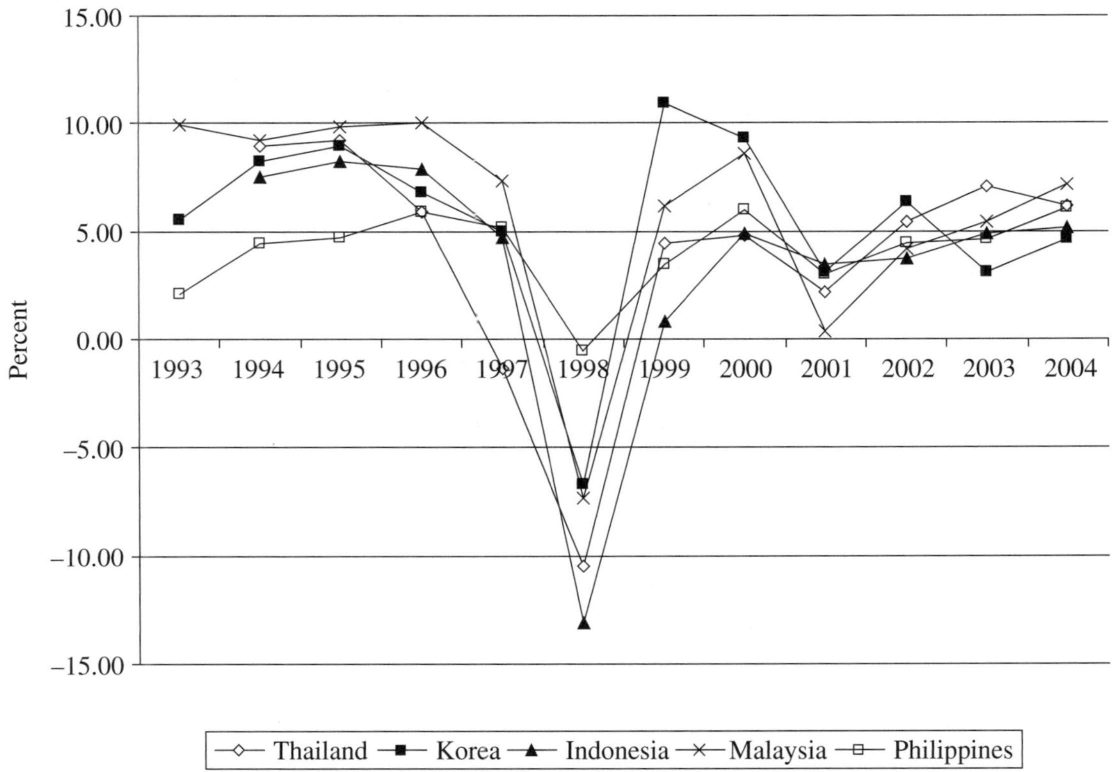

Figure 1.6 Relative real GDP growth rates (%) for the Asian 'Affected Five'

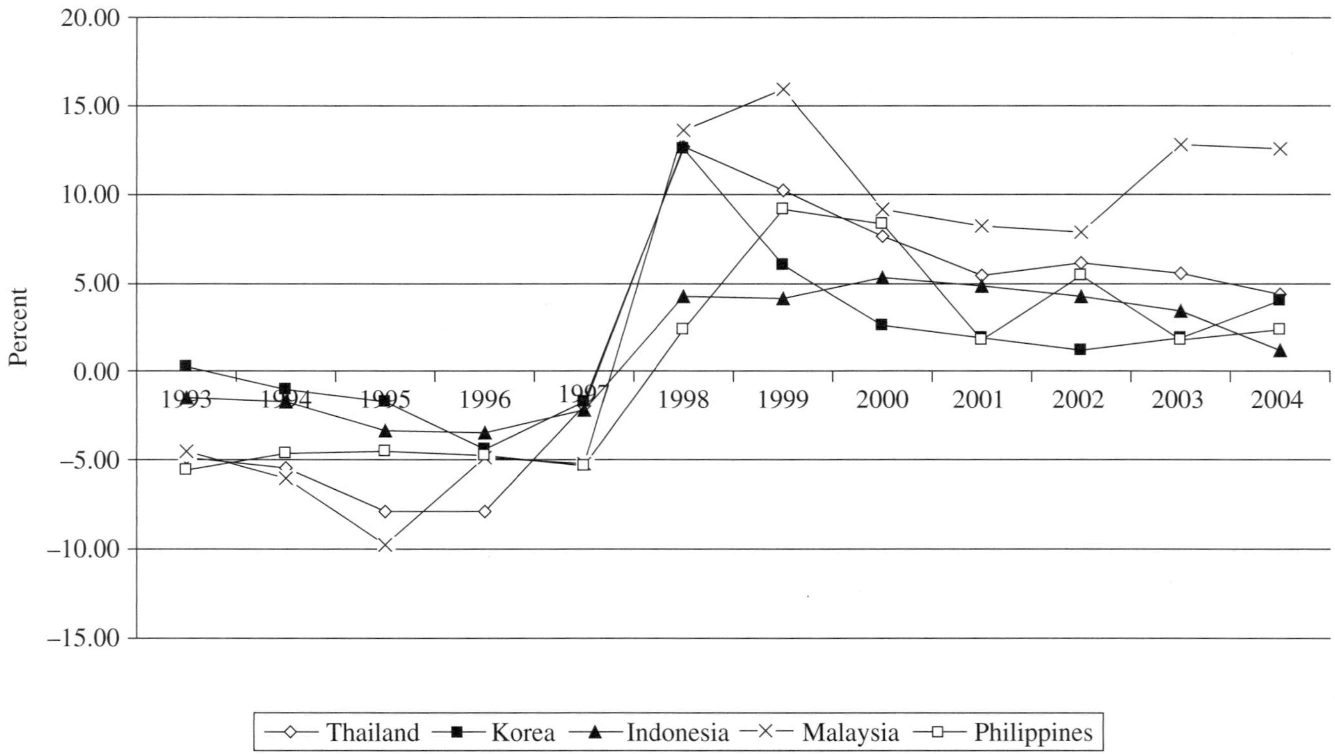

Figure 1.7 Relative current account (as % GDP)

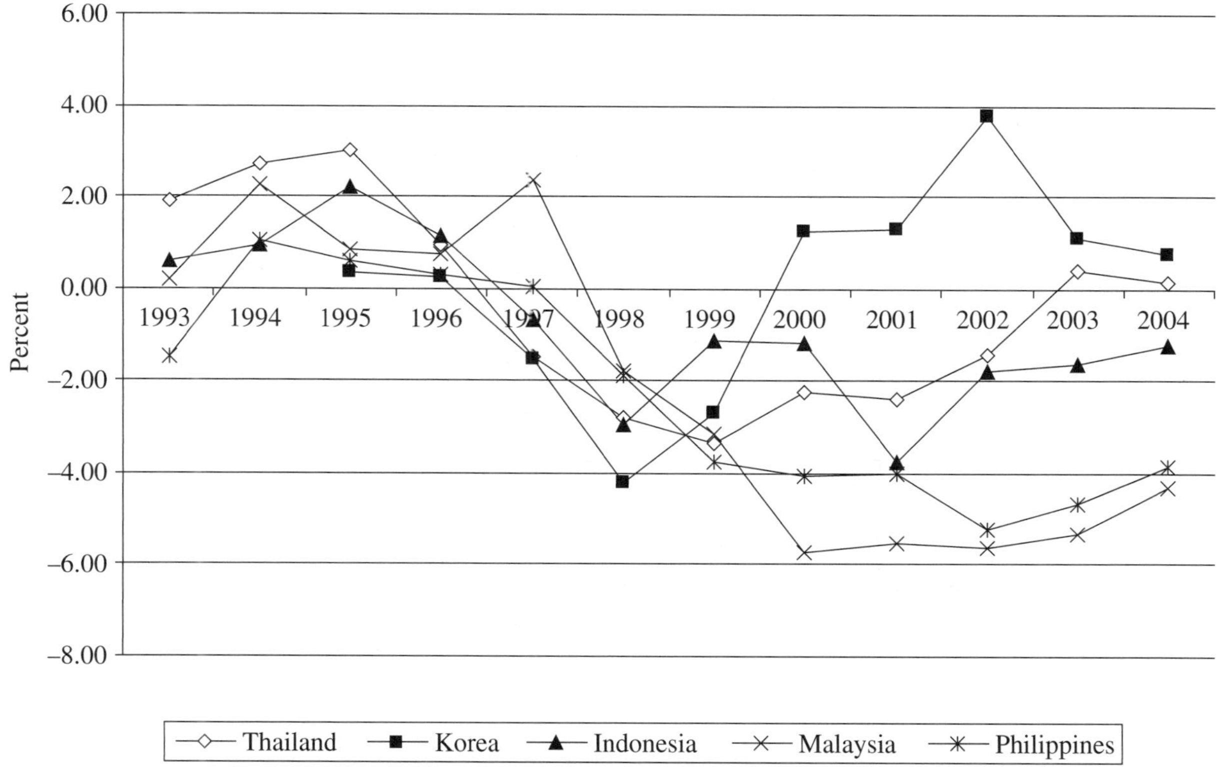

Figure 1.8 Relative fiscal balance (as a % GDP)

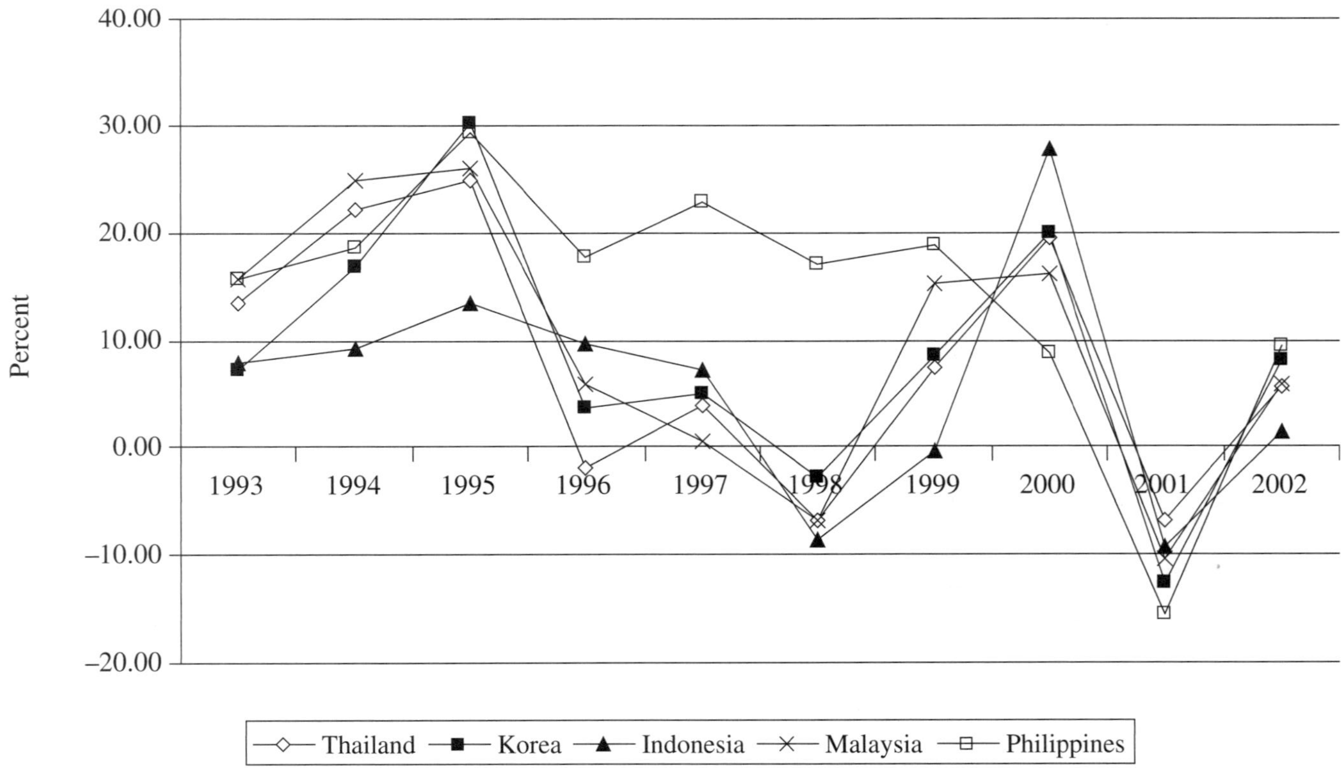

Figure 1.9 Relative export growth rates (%)

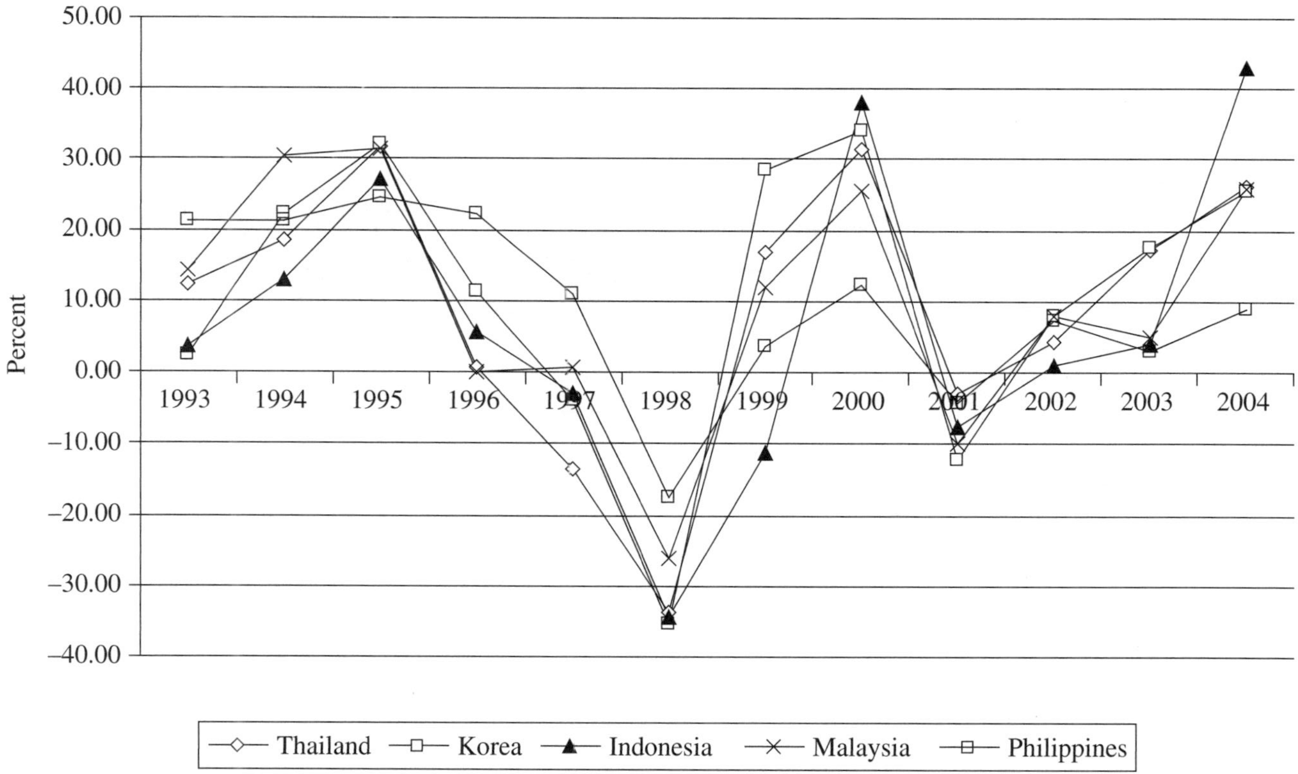

Figure 1.10 Relative import growth rate (%)

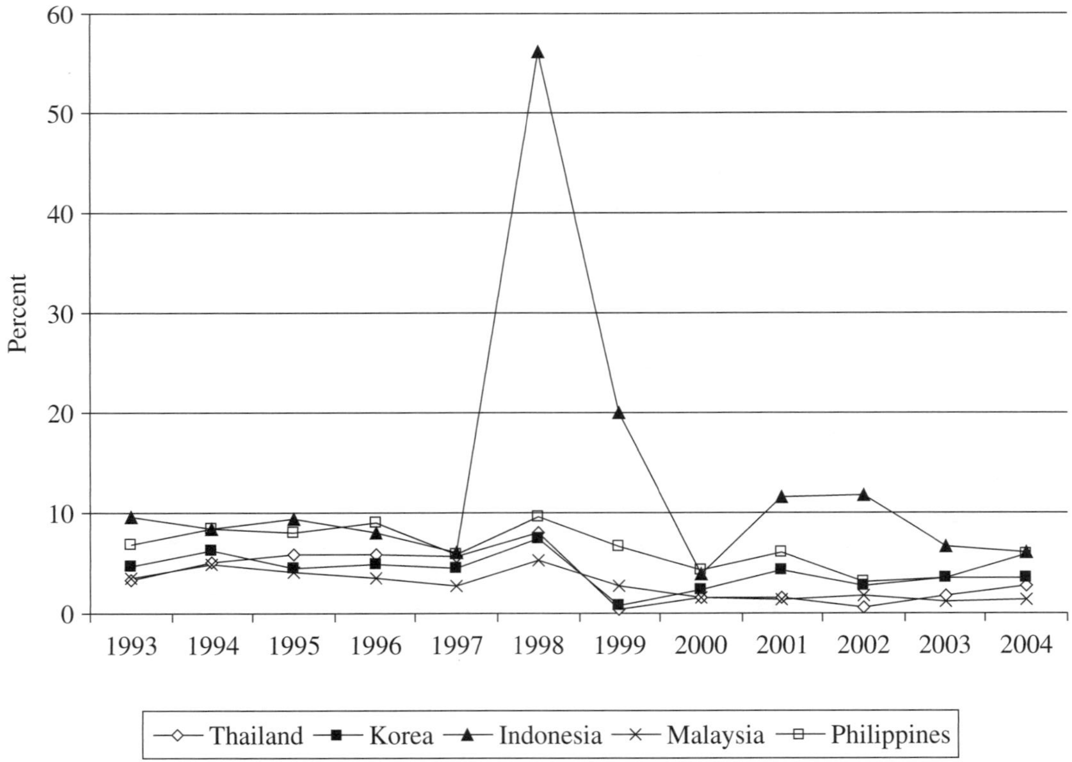

Figure 1.11 *Relative inflation rates (%)*

For one, Krugman (1994) asserted that since the high GDP growth rate of the Asian 'tigers' was fueled primarily by 'Soviet-style' accumulations of machinery, infrastructure, and other factor inputs rather than 'efficiency' gains, these growth rates will 'slow down'. Also, there were many other discussions, albeit often of a generic nature, about the possibility of the appearance of the 'Mexican Crisis' of December 1994 and early 1995 in other countries. A somewhat specific case of such analysis is Lau (1995) who noted, in an ex ante sense, that Thailand and Indonesia were the most likely venues for a Mexican-type financial crisis to occur.

On the other hand, Inada et al. (2000) is a retrospective simulation exercise that concludes that one factor at the heart of the difficulty in East Asia was the fact that many of these countries had, to a significant extent, pegged their currencies to the US dollar, which grew relatively very strong, and many of these countries, such as Thailand, did not act early enough (as China did in 1994) to devalue their currencies, which would have averted or significantly ameliorated the impact of the currency crises. Of course, the Chinese exchange rate action was not in response to a pending crisis, but was a move to unify their exchange rate policies in January 1994 and hold the renminbi-dollar rate at constant par from that time forward. However, the other East Asian countries failed to react to that move by China and thus lost export trade share accordingly.[11] It is interesting to note that in this new century, China's growth has been so rapid and intense that they have required imports from many partner countries, including East Asian neighbors, and have contributed to favorable macroeconomic performance over a wide area.

3.4 Asia in the 21st Century – China and India as the New Players for the 'New Asian Miracle'

Looking ahead to the future developments in Asia, China and India are emerging as two increasingly important regional and eventually global economic powers. They are relatively the fastest-growing (with respective GDP growth rates of 8–10 percent for China and 6–7 percent p. a. for India in the last ten years) with dynamic and open economies, at least with respect to trade flows. These two countries appear fully poised to be the new players in the 'New Asian Miracle', if we may modify a much-worn label. The important question from our perspective is: how much are these countries going to benefit from the lessons learned from the recent financial crises around the world? No doubt, the open economies of these countries will make them vulnerable to external shocks. They need to be ready with robust financial institutions, willingness to adopt sound macroeconomic policies and of course, have a viable social safety net, just in case.

Specifically, China's case is important from many points of view. China, of course, has been growing tremendously fast since reform in 1978 and is already a dominant part of future economic prosperity of the region. However, its openness in terms of trade flows makes it vulnerable to crises. In the face of prospective openness of capital account, China has a long-standing policy of minimal variations in the exchange rate despite international reserves that are projected to reach $1 trillion in 2007. Thus, China is at the center of the debate about the appropriate exchange rate and the capital controls policies to adopt. These are issues that have been an intimate part of the financial crisis experience. China is also an obviously important player through its trade and direct investment links to the region. Thus, focusing on China is only natural.

However, we know that some people have expressed a degree of skepticism about the veracity of China's growth statistics. This is an aspect of the Chinese economy that is of interest to us. Besides addressing the question of China's 'true' growth rate, we are also interested in exploring what role China may have played – a stabilizing or a destabilizing one – during the 1997–98 Asian Crisis. The major question, of course, is whether we have learned enough from the previous crises so that we can more confidently determine the optimal degree of openness of a country's capital and exchange rate markets.

In terms of the specific situation that India finds itself in, there is certainly a historic change afoot in this country. India is another emerging Asian 'giant', side by side with China. Both these countries have enjoyed strong growth in the real sector (GDP) although they reached high growth in unique fashion – China's has been a case of growth led now by exports of manufactured goods, while India's growth has been fueled by growth of service sector activity (especially in the information technology [IT], financial and health sectors). While each of these countries have exhibited impressive rates of GDP growth in recent years, there are significant financial sector issues such as stock and bond market reform, greater transparency and better corporate governance that still need attention. Even though India appears ahead in terms of financial market efficiency and institution-building for now, much work remains. Also, China is apparently making financial sector reforms as its high priority too. In any event, it is clear that going forward, financial sector and capital market reforms will be necessary for the continued success of these countries while keeping in mind some of the important ways – political and structural – in which these countries differ from each other. However, the important point is that, as evidently the new players on the growth playing field, so to speak, these countries' reliance on open trade and foreign direct investment flows make them vulnerable to financial crises. It is useful to watch to see whether lessons from the recent crises were learned well. During the crisis period, neighbors and other competitors blamed China for stealing their export markets. Now they enjoy China's import appetite. As for India, advanced countries blame 'white collar' unemployment problems on India's burgeoning service sector, but should be benefiting from reduced operating costs in the near future.

4 FINANCIAL CRISIS, POVERTY AND INCOME DISTRIBUTION

What happens to the poor as a result of economic downturns induced by financial crises? This is an important question, in part, because it is often the developing countries with their disproportionate share of the poor that are vulnerable to financial crises. However, relative to studies of the impact of financial crises in terms of output or financial loss, there are few studies of the societal cost of such crises in terms of effects on poverty and income inequality.[12] Some of the important questions in this regard are:

- What are the mechanisms through which financial crises affect poverty and income distribution?
- What are the magnitudes of the above effects?
- What relevant policy implications arise in this context?

Theoretically, financial crises are expected to worsen poverty (or slow down the rate of poverty alleviation) and worsen inequality for a number of reasons:

1. *Worsening labor market conditions*. The financial crises bring in their wake high-level job loss, lower wage rates, forced transition into informal sector activities with poorer labor market prospects and increased job insecurity.
2. *Relative price change*. The relative price of tradables increases due to currency depreciation causing decrease in relative wage rates in the non-tradable sector, which may additionally suffer because depreciation-induced export growth bolsters employment prospects relatively in the export sector.

   Large currency depreciations also lead to an increase in domestic inflation rates that hurt the relatively poor who have few assets to fall back on. To the extent food may be imported this also hurts the relatively poor who spend proportionately more of their budget on food.

3. *Post-crisis tight fiscal and monetary policy.* As a result of the crisis, the governments invariably feel pressure in terms of fiscal budgets. Often this means that public expenditure on health, education and the various transfer and social sector programs will be cut back in the countries beset by a financial crisis, thus hurting the poor. The situation is worsened as, generally speaking, tight fiscal policies are accompanied by tight monetary policies undertaken to stem capital flight or other stabilization goals.
4. *Regional and ethnic distress.* Financial crises and resulting economic downturns invariably exacerbate the various political, regional and ethnic tensions in a country. Regrettably, tolerance is an easy victim during such periods of turmoil and it is usually the 'have-nots' who end up paying the price of such societal disruption.

Baldacci et al. (2002) examine the relationship between currency crises and poverty across a number of developing countries during 1960–98. Compared with a standardized control group that did not suffer any such crises, the study reports that besides increases in inflation rates 'by nearly 62 percent relative to the pre-crisis year' and an increase in unemployment by 1.1 percent in crisis years relative to pre-crisis years, the inequality increases as well as poverty worsens in the group of countries that suffer currency crises. A decline in average income of a country is accompanied by a more than proportionate decline in income of the lowest and second lowest quintiles, which worsens income inequality as well as increases incidence of poverty, as households in the lower quintiles are more likely to have income below the poverty line. Further, government cutbacks in expenditure on social programs, health and education are associated with falling incomes of the poorest. In the case of Mexico, the study finds that the 'poverty rate spiked to nearly 17 percent of the population in 1996, from nearly 11 percent in 1994, reversing the gains made in 1992–94'.

Thus, as discussed above, occurrence of financial crisis can be expected generally to have an impact on the incidence of poverty as well as the income distribution in the country. In fact, such crises will also have broader effects on the living standards of the affected countries. We will discuss these issues in turn mainly for the case of the 'Affected Five' countries of East Asia in the context of the 1997–98 Financial Crisis.

4.1 Impact on the Incidence of Poverty

Generally speaking, poverty worsens at the onset of a financial or currency crisis and, in many instances, such an ill effect is relatively long-lived. Table 1.6 presents the data for selected countries that have recently suffered

Table 1.6 Incidence of poverty in selected countries

Country and Type of Crisis	Incidence of Poverty as Percentage (year in parentheses)		
	Before crisis	Year of crisis	After crisis
Argentina, hyperinflation and currency	25.2 (1987)	47.3 (1989)	33.7 (1990)
Argentina, contagion	16.8 (1993)	24.8 (1995)	26.0 (1997)
Indonesia, contagion and financial	11.3 (1996)	18.9 (1998)	11.7 (1999)
Mexico, currency and financial	36.0 (1994)	nd	43.0 (1996)
Russian Federation, financial	21.9 (1996)	32.7 (1998)	nd
Thailand, currency and financial	11.4 (1996)	12.9 (1998)	nd

Note: Based on national poverty lines and per capita household income except for Indonesia (per capita expenditure), Mexico (household income), and Russia (household expenditure per equivalent adult). Data for Argentina refer to Greater Buenos Aires. nd = no data available.

Source: World Bank (2000), p. 163.

a financial crisis. For instance, poverty rose by almost 50 percent in Indonesia as a result of the 1997 Asian Crisis and, in the case of Russia, the incidence of poverty rose from 21.9 percent to 32.7 percent between 1996 and 1998. While in the East Asian case, poverty fell as the economies recovered; in Russia as well as Latin American countries that experienced a financial crisis, the incidence of poverty remained relatively elevated compared with its pre-crisis levels even several years later.

4.2 Impact on Income Inequality

The available empirical evidence suggests that, in general, inequality rises or, at best, stays constant *during* a crisis. As reported in the *World Development Report* of 2000–01 (World Bank, 2000), for Latin American countries, inequality (as measured by the Gini coefficient) increased in 15 of 20 crisis episodes for which there are data available. For the East Asian countries, on the other hand, the pattern was somewhat more complex. While during the crisis year or very soon after it (that is, 1997 or 1998), the Gini coefficient was virtually unchanged, it often increased (signaling worsening inequality) in the years following the onset of the crisis. However, in some cases, the Gini coefficient has dropped as economies have recovered (for instance, Thailand).

Table 1.7 has pre- and post-crisis data for the Gini coefficient (column 1) for several of the East Asian countries affected by the 1997 crisis – Malaysia,

Table 1.7 Gini coefficients, headcount index and mean consumption/month for selected East Asian countries

	Gini Coefficient (Scale: 0–100)	Headcount Index (%) $2/day	Mean Consumption (1993 PPP $/month)
Malaysia			
1990	46.2	18.5	195.32
1992	47.7	17.6	219.48
1995	48.5	14.0	253.64
1996	48.5	13.1	261.87
1997	49.1	8.8	315.95
1998	49.1	12.9	269.00
1999	49.1	12.6	271.52
2000	49.1	9.8	303.31
2001	49.1	9.8	303.46
2002	49.1	9.6	305.14
2003	49.1	8.7	316.58
2004	49.1	7.9	328.80
Korea			
1990	42.9	<0.5	301.09
1993	43.3	<0.5	330.38
1994	43.7	<0.5	362.09
1995	44.1	<0.5	383.03
1996	44.5	<0.5	411.09
1997	45.0	<0.5	440.03
1998	45.5	<0.5	480.46
1999	46.0	<0.5	483.84
2000	46.4	<0.5	400.86
2001	46.9	<0.5	450.06
2002	47.3	<0.5	478.67
2003	47.6	<0.5	492.54
2004	48.0	<0.5	535.38
Thailand			
1990	43.8	47.0	102.88
1992	46.2	37.5	129.75
1996	43.4	28.2	143.92
1998	40.6	34.1	121.73
1999	40.7	33.6	123.50
2000	43.2	35.6	125.42
2001	42.4	32.0	131.21
2002	42.2	27.7	139.40
2003	41.4	23.7	147.03
2004	41.4	21.4	153.97

Table 1.7 (continued)

	Gini Coefficient (Scale: 0–100)	Headcount Index (%) $2/day	Mean Consumption (1993 PPP $/month)
Indonesia			
1990	28.9	71.1	61.58
1993	31.7	61.6	68.54
1996	36.5	50.5	86.62
1999	31.0	65.1	66.80
2000	32.2	59.5	72.53
2001	32.1	58.7	73.44
2002	34.3	53.5	81.72
2003	34.8	50.1	85.88
2004	35.4	48.1	88.82
Philippines			
1990	40.7	55.6	82.77
1991	43.8	53.5	90.32
1994	43.8	55.0	87.75
1996	42.9	53.1	89.10
1997	46.2	46.5	107.15
1998	46.0	45.2	110.21
1999	46.7	46.6	108.77
2000	46.2	46.9	107.2
2001	46.2	47.1	107.03
2002	46.0	45.3	110.61
2003	45.9	44.1	113.32
2004	45.9	41.8	118.10

Note:
The poverty lines in Table 1.7 are set at $2.15 per person per day (in 1993 PPP $) for all countries. For most countries, 1993 World Bank PPP (purchasing power parity) estimates are used. The PPP for the Philippines is from the Penn World Tables. Estimates for all countries except Malaysia are based on surveys of household consumption. The estimates for Malaysia use income surveys. These poverty estimates differ from those commonly found in national poverty assessments for two main reasons. First, country assessments use national poverty lines that differ from the uniform international poverty lines used here. Second, national poverty lines also typically allow for spatial cost-of-living differentials within countries, but such adjustments are omitted here to maintain a consistent methodology across countries. For instance, in the case of Thailand, these differences explain why the above estimates indicate a small increase in poverty between 1998 and 2000 (in spite of adjusting the CPI by the change in the national poverty lines over this period), while national poverty line-based estimates indicate a decline. Also for Thailand, the 2002 estimate is based on a longer consumption module, which could lead to a small overestimation of consumption relative to 2000.

Korea, Thailand, Indonesia and the Philippines. It is worthwhile looking at the pattern of the changes in Gini coefficient in each of these selected countries.

In Malaysia's case, the Gini coefficient increased from 48.5 in 1996 to 49.1 in 1997, yet after this initial increase in inequality during the crisis year, the Gini coefficient has virtually stayed constant (at 49.1) since then.

In the case of South Korea, the Gini coefficient registered a slight increase from 44.5 in 1996 to 45.0 in 1997. However, the Gini coefficient has steadily increased since then signifying a steady trend towards deteriorating income inequality.

In Thailand's case, the Gini coefficient started at 43.4 in 1996. While the relevant statistic for 1997 is not available, the Gini coefficient's value for 1998 was 40.6; which surprisingly showed an improvement in income equality during the year of crisis. For the longer run, however, the Gini coefficient has shown a mixed pattern – worsening in 2000, 2001 and 2002 relative to 1998 or 1999 before starting to improve of late.

In Indonesia, the Gini coefficient stood at 31.7 in 1993 – four years prior to the 1997 crisis, while its value was equal to 31.0 in 1999 two years after the crisis – thus, it would seem that income inequality was virtually unchanged during the crisis. However, the 1996 Gini coefficient value of 36.5 would appear to tell a different story. If we are willing to set aside 1996 as an 'outlier', the trend appears to be one of increasing inequality since 1990, which certainly accelerated after 1999.

In the case of the Philippines, the Gini coefficient jumped in 1997 to 46.2 from 42.9 in the previous year – a significant increase in income inequality during the year of the crisis. This elevated level of income inequality has pretty much persisted over the longer run as evidenced by the values of the Gini coefficient hovering quite close to 46.

When crises are accompanied by increasing inequality, economic downturns can impede or even reverse previous gains in poverty reductions and also adversely affect standards of living. Let us look at this issue for the East Asian countries affected by the 1997 crisis.

Also, in Table 1.6, we will measure poverty reduction by declines in 'Headcount Index (%) $2/day', which measures the percentage of the population living below $2/day (column 2) and standard of living by 'Mean Consumption (1993 PPP $/month)' which is given in column 3.

In the case of Malaysia, the headcount index had been steadily declining before the 1997 crisis. However, in 1998, this index jumped almost 25 percent from 8.8 in 1997 to 12.9 in 1998 and even though significant improvements were evident after 1999, it took several more years (until 2003) for poverty reduction to attain the level of 8.7, which approximated the situation in 1997. Thus, once again, we see that a crisis accompanied by even a very slight worsening income inequality between 1996 and 1997 meant reversals in poverty alleviation in Malaysia.

Similarly, the mean consumption in Malaysia that had steadily risen from 195.32 in 1990 to 315.95 in 1997, dropped to 269.00 in 1998 although it picked up rather smartly soon after that, perhaps, in part, due to the fact that inequality measures were nearly constant after 1997, the year of the crisis. If inequality would have worsened significantly after the crisis, it is very likely that Malaysia's mean consumption would have stayed depressed for a considerably longer period of time.

In the Korean case, while income inequality increased after the crisis, such a trend had been in place even before the crisis. Thus it would appear that there were structural factors unique to the Korean economy that were prompting an increasing trend in Gini coefficient values independent of the 1997 crisis. Nevertheless, the data indicate that any such pre-crisis trend may have been exacerbated as a result of the crisis. Further, in terms of the status of poverty reduction in Korea, the headcount index has stayed constant at a relatively low level (<0.5 percent) since 1990 and the mean consumption series also seems to have been little affected by the incidence of the 1997 crisis. The most likely reason for this pattern is the fact that in the Korean case, relatively speaking, the recovery from the crisis was the fastest of all the affected countries (the 'V'-shaped pattern of recovery), thus the previous trends were little disturbed. Korea, in other words, has fared the best by not suffering any major ill effects of the 1997 crisis in terms of possible reversals in poverty reduction.

Thailand was the 'classic' case where the 1997 crisis led to immediate reversals in poverty reduction trends. Prior to the crisis, Thailand had been making remarkable progress in poverty reduction as can be noted from the fact that, by 1996, the headcount index had dropped to 28.2 from a high of 47.0 in 1990. However, one year after the crisis, the index had jumped significantly to 34.1 (in 1998) relative to 28.2 in 1996. However, economic recovery by 2002 meant that the pace of poverty reduction had been restored. The headcount index was 27.7 in 2002 and, it has, in fact, continued to drop since then.

The mean consumption pattern in Thailand as of 1990 has followed a pattern similar to that of the headcount index for the country. The mean consumption increased from a level of 102.88 in 1990 to a peak of 143.92 in 1996 only to drop precipitously to 121.73 in 1998 on account of the financial and economic crisis. The previous peak of 1996 was regained only in 2003 when the mean consumption level rose to 147.03.

Similarly, for Indonesia, the mean consumption had been steadily increasing before the 1997 crisis (61.58 in 1990 to 86.62 in 1996). However, this figure tumbled to 66.80 in 1999 compared with its value of 86.62 in

1999, and it took several years of slow recovery to come close to the 1999 level, when in 2003, the mean consumption climbed back to 85.88. Thus, standard of living, as measured by mean consumption was significantly adversely affected due to the crisis and it recovered only after almost six years.

The situation in Indonesia was similar to that of Malaysia. Indonesia had been making significant gains by way of poverty reduction as headcount index had dropped from 71.1 percent in 1990 to 50.5 percent in 1996. However, it jumped back up to 65.1 percent in 1999. It was only several years later in 2003 that the poverty reduction level attained in 1996 was regained.

In the case of the Philippines, the trend in poverty reduction witnessed in terms of a secular trend in lower headcount index values continued unabated through the 1997 crisis year and after. Similarly, for the Philippines, the mean consumption continued to show a steady upward trend through the 1990s and into the early 2000s. In some sense, this result for the Philippines may appear at odds with the results for similar measures for say, Indonesia or Malaysia. However, for one, this may be due to the fact that the Philippines had been a 'latecomer' to the economic growth era dubbed 'The Asian Miracle' and thus had 'less to lose'. For another, IMF- and later, World Bank-inspired safety net programs and redistributive policies of the Philippines' government, may have cushioned the blow even in the face of worsening income inequality.

4.3 Impact on Living Standards

The full impact of financial or economic crises on the living standards in the affected countries goes beyond their impact on measures of poverty and inequality. As measured by social indicators of health and schooling enrollments, the living standards take a turn for the worse. As a result of the crisis, typically, such social indicators either deteriorate or improve only at a slower pace with their long-term implications for reducing earnings potential of the poor (Table 1.8).

As can be seen from the Table 1.8, in Mexico, on account of the debt crisis, the infant and pre-school mortality due to nutritional deficiency rose in the 1980s (reversing a beneficial trend) and such infant mortality rose again in 1995 on the heels of the peso crisis. In Indonesia, the percentage of women with body mass index in a range vulnerable for illnesses and death increased by a quarter in 1998. Also, the average weight of babies under age three years declined.

Besides the specifics noted in the above table, it may be mentioned here that in Latin America, overall, the infant mortality rates increased only at

Table 1.8 Societal impact of economic crises in selected countries

	Main Crisis Indicators	Health Indicators	Education Indicators
Mexico 1995	• Per capita GDP fell 7.8%	• Among children under age one, mortality from anemia increased from 6.3 deaths per 100 000 live births in 1993 to 7.9 in 1995	• Gross primary enrollment increased 0.44% in 1994, but fell 0.09% in 1995
	• Per capita private consumption fell 11.1%	• Among children aged one to four, the mortality rate from anemia rose from 1.7 to 2.2 per 100 000	
Indonesia 1998	• Per capita GDP fell 14.6%	• The share of women whose body mass index is below the level at which risks of illness and death increase rose 25%	• The dropout rate for children in the poorest fourth of the population rose from 1.3% in 1997 to 7.5% in 1998 for those aged 7–12 and from 14.2% to 25.5% for those aged 13–19. In both cohorts the poorest fifth experienced the largest increase
	• Per capita private consumption fell 5.1%	• Most indicators of child nutritional status remained stable. The exception may be the weight (conditional on height) of children under age three, suggesting that families may be investing in some members at the expense of others	• The share of children in the poorest fourth of the population not enrolled in school rose from 4.9% in 1997 to 10.7% in 1998 for those aged 7–12 and from 42.5% to 58.4% for those aged 13–19. In both cohorts the poorest fourth experienced the largest increase

Source: World Bank (2000), p. 164.

a relatively lower rate in the 1980s compared with the earlier decade. Thus, we can see that financial crisis adversely affect the state of the social indicators of health either by slowing down their progress or even causing an absolute decline in them.

Similarly, broad indicators of human capital investments such as school attendance, enrollment and literacy were also adversely affected during crises. It may also be noted that, in Mexico, the proportion of each graduating high school class that went on to the next level declined during the 1980s debt crisis. Also, primary school enrollment dropped too in the 1980s. There was a similar drop (of almost 1 percent) in 1995 on the eve of the peso crisis.

The adverse impact of financial and macroeconomic crises on human capital accumulation and health improvements are the channels through which such crises have secular impact on poverty and potential earnings of the affected populace, especially the poor who are disproportionately affected. According to the *World Development Report 2000–2001* World Bank (2000), for Indonesia, the dropout rate in the lowest fourth of income distributions rose from 1.3 percent in 1997 to 7.5 percent in 1998 among children aged 7–12 and from 14.2 percent to 25.5 percent among ages 13–19. At the same time, the proportion of poor children not enrolled in school more than doubled from 4.9 percent to 10.7 percent.

In conclusion, it needs to be emphasized that the social costs of the Asian Crisis were substantial, and a disproportionate burden fell on the poor or the 'near poor'. In each of the 'Affected Five' countries, the 1997–98 crisis led to higher incidence of poverty, and the living standards in general were adversely affected in these countries. Also, by and large, the income inequities were often exacerbated on account of the crisis.

4.4 Policy Implications

The above analysis, in sections 4.1–4.3, clearly implies the kind of public policies that are needed to ameliorate the situation precipitated by financial crises. There is an obvious need to provide a better social security net that should be 'targeted' to the support groups most affected by the crisis, robust and put in place well in advance of the crisis. Policy-makers need to take concrete steps to protect pro-poor public spending in the wake of a financial crisis.

Finally, in an overarching sense, policy-makers should strive to balance the purely financial aspects of the policy response to a financial crisis against a meaningful concern for the societal costs of such measures. Thus, somewhat akin to the now commonplace 'environmental impact' study of any land development or economic growth project, there should be a social cost impact study of the feasible financial policies. The final choice should be based on the optimal policy net of its social costs.

5 CONCLUDING REMARKS

Since financial crises can be costly both in economic, as well as, societal terms, it is only natural to inquire whether such crises are predictable. Besides providing an overview of the various theories that motivate the specification of possible early warning systems, this chapter reviewed the performance of logit/probit as well as more recent Markov-switching models of currency crisis prediction. In this respect, we would like to conclude that while econometric predictive models can be very useful in identifying various indicators of 'vulnerability', such exercises are not a cure-all.

While formal econometric predictive models of currency crises are very useful tools, due to limitations related to convergence requirements and other technical matters, they can be too structured and thus restrict the scope of the discussion necessary to get a broad sense of the possible determinants of the vulnerabilities of economies to a currency crisis. In this chapter, we also examined the broad determinants of vulnerability or susceptibility to crisis of an economy. This enables us to think about the mechanisms that may be needed to monitor the economy as well as institute policies to reduce its susceptibility to a financial crisis.

Finally, it is also very important to explore the aftermath of a financial crisis. Since the after-effects of such crises are societal and not only economic, this chapter focuses on the income distributional consequences of the Asian Financial Crisis of 1997–98 as well as its impact on the poverty alleviation trends in the 'Affected Five' countries. Amongst the suggested policy implications is the need to put in place an early warning system and, at the same time, institute structural reforms to reduce the chances of recurrence of financial crises or soften their impact.[13] To deal with the societal aftermath of a crisis, we recommend robust safety nets targeted towards those in the economy that are most likely to be adversely impacted by a financial crisis.

NOTES

1. This discussion is based, in a significant fashion, on Shabbir's earlier joint work reported in Mariano et al. (2002).
2. See Berg and Pattillo (1999) for a skeptical viewpoint.
3. This discussion is drawn from Shabbir's earlier joint work reported in Mariano et al. (2003).
4. Also see, Chauvet and Dong (2004).
5. The significance of these indicators can be motivated analytically, however, in this chapter, we do not engage in such an exercise.
6. The discussion in this section has drawn on the analysis presented in Warr (2002).

7. For instance, Bhagwati (1998, p. 12) notes '[T]he only explanation that accounts for the massive net capital outflows is panic and herd behaviour: whether of domestic or foreign nationals' and Radelet and Sachs (1998, p. 43) infer that the 'crisis was triggered by dramatic swings in creditors' expectations about the behavior of other creditors, thereby creating a self-fulfilling – although possibly individually rational – financial panic'. On the other hand, as Dornbusch (1997, p. 21) notes, 'vulnerability means that if something goes wrong, then suddenly a lot goes wrong'. The 'something' that causes things to go wrong can be considered as a trigger, whereas the possibility of 'suddenly a lot going wrong' is conditional on existence of 'vulnerability'.
8. The list of indicators we have examined is certainly not an exhaustive one. Warr (2002), in a similar analysis of pre-1997 crisis determinants of vulnerability for Thailand, Indonesia and Korea, concludes that in these countries there had been a significant increase in fragility of the banking sector as measured by exposure to interest rate risk and deteriorating quality of loans (in the absence of data on non-performing loans, quality was indirectly proxied by an increasing ratio of total loans outstanding for the banking sector to GDP) as well as currency depreciation risk (measured by the ratio of foreign liabilities to total loans). Based on evidence provided by indicators such as 'reserves'/ 'Volatile' Capital Inflows, 'CA/FDI' and significant real exchange rate appreciation (as proxy of erosion in foreign competitiveness), Warr (2002) also demonstrates that, in general, these countries had become vulnerable to a currency crisis much before 1997. Ghosh and Ghosh (2003) come to a similar conclusion for 'deep' currency crises, however, see Berg and Pattillo (1999) for a somewhat skeptical viewpoint favoring contagion as the primary explanation.
9. See Barro (2001) for an early attempt at examining the pre- versus post-crisis situation in the same countries. Also, see Adams and Shabbir, Chapter 6 in this volume, for a more recent exploration of some analytical aspects of the pre- versus post-crisis comparisons.
10. Incidentally, Klein et al., Chapter 4 in the present volume, analyzes the macroeconomic consequences of the Malaysian capital controls policy more formally by means of a macroeconometric model and conclude that in the Malaysian case, the capital controls policy had, on average, beneficial effects in terms of post-crisis stabilization.
11. Interestingly, Warr (2002) maintains that the real exchange rates were overvalued for Indonesia, Thailand and Korea for reasons independent of China's exchange rate policy.
12. Some exceptions are Hyun and Lim (2003); Baldacci et al. (2002); Birdsall and Haggard (2000); Lee (1998) and Shabbir (1998).
13. The authors have discussed several reforms in the Introduction to this volume; additional details about relevant reforms may be noted in Klein (2004).

REFERENCES

Abiad, A.G. (2002), 'Early Warning Systems for Currency Crises: A Markov Switching Approach with Applications to Southeast Asia', PhD dissertation, Department of Economics, University of Pennsylvania, Philadelphia.

Alvarez-Plata, Patricia and Mechthild Schrooten (2003), 'The Argentinean Currency Crisis: A Markov-Switching Model Estimation', Discussion Paper, DIW Berlin.

Baldacci, Emanuele, Luiz de Mello and G. Inchauste (2002), 'Financial Crises, Poverty, and Income Distribution', *IMF Working Paper* 02/4.

Barro, Robert J. (2001), 'Economic Growth before and after the Financial Crisis', Working Paper 8330, Cambridge, MA: National Bureau of Economic Research.

Berg, A. and C. Pattillo (1999), 'Predicting Currency Crises: The Indicators Approach and an Alternative', *Journal of International Money and Finance*, **18**, 561–86.

Bhagwati, Jagdish (1998), 'Asian Financial Crisis Debate: Why? How Severe?', Paper presented at Managing the Asian Financial Crisis: Lessons and Challenges Conference, Asian Strategic Leadership Institute and Rating Agency, Kuala Lumpur, 2–3 November.

Birdsall, Nancy and S. Haggard (2000), *After the Crisis: The Social Contract and the Middle Class in East Asia*, Carnegie Endowment for International Peace.

Brunetti, C., R.S. Mariano, C. Scotti and A.H.H. Tan (2003), 'Markov Switching GARCH Models of Currency Crises in Southeast Asia', Working Paper 03-008, Philadelphia: Penn Institute of Economic Research, University of Pennsylvania. http://pier.econ.upenn.edu/Archive/03-008.pdf.

Chauvet, M. and F. Dong (2004), 'Leading Indicators of Country Risk and Currency Crises: The Asian Experience', *Economic Review*, Federal Reserve Bank of Atlanta,Q1, 25–37.

Demirgüç-Kunt, A. and E. Detragiache (1998), 'The Determinants of Banking Crises in Developing and Developed Countries', *IMF Staff Papers*, **45** (1), 81–109.

Dornbusch, R. (1997), 'A Thai–Mexico Primer: Lessons for Outmaneuvering a Financial Meltdown', *The International Economy*, September/October.

Eichengreen, B. and A. Rose (1998), 'Staying Afloat When the Wind Shifts: External Factors and Emerging-market Banking Crises', *NBER Working Paper* No. 6370, Cambridge, MA.

Ghosh, S.R. and A.R. Ghosh (2003), 'Structural Vulnerabilities and Currency Crises', *IMF Staff Papers*, **50** (3).

Hamilton, James B. (1994), *Time Series Analysis*, Princeton, NJ. Princeton University Press.

Hyan, Jin K. and B. Lim (2003), 'Financial Crises and Income Distribution in Korea', Working Paper, Korea Development Institute.

Inada, Yoshihisa, Lawrence R. Klein and J. Makino (2000), 'A Retrospective View of the Asian Financial Crisis: Special Reference to Exchange Rate Policy', in L. Klein and S. Ichimura (eds), *Econometric Modeling of China*, Singapore: World Scientific.

Kaminsky, G. and C. Reinhart (1998), 'Financial Crises in Asia and Latin America: Then and Now', *American Economic Review*, **88**, 444–8.

Kaminsky, G. and C. Reinhart (1999), 'The Twin Crises: The Causes of Banking and Balance of Payments Problems', *American Economic Review*, **89**, 473–500.

Kaminsky, G., S. Lizondo and C. Reinhart (1998), 'Leading Indicators of Currency Crises', *IMF Staff Papers*, **45** (1), 1–48.

Klein, Lawrence R. (2004), 'Financial Crises in Asia and Development Issues', mimeo, Department of Economics, University of Pennsylvania, Philadelphia.

Krugman, Paul (1979), 'A Model of Balance of Payments Crises', *Journal of Money, Credit and Banking*, **11**, 311–25.

Krugman, Paul (1994), 'The Myth of Asia's Miracle' , *Foreign Affairs*, November/December.

Kumar, M., U. Moorthy and W. Perraudin (2003), 'Predicting Emerging Market Currency Crashes', *Journal of Empirical Finance*, **10**, 427–54.

Lau, Lawrence J. (1995), 'LINK meeting presentation', Pretoria, South Africa.

Lee, Eddy (1998), *The Asian Financial Crisis: The Challenge for Social Policy*, Geneva: International Labour Office.

Mariano, R.S., A.G. Abiad, S. Özmucur, T. Shabbir and A.H.H. Tan (2003), 'Markov Chains in Predictive Models of Currency Crises – With Applications to Southeast Asia', *Taiwan Economic Review*, **31** (4), December.

Mariano, R.S., B.N. Gultekin, S. Özmucur, T. Shabbir and C.E. Alper (2002), 'Predictive Models of Economic Financial Crises (Final Report)', Report submitted to the Economic Research Forum (ERF) for the Arab countries, Iran and Turkey for ERF Research Project ERF99-US-4004, mimeo, Department of Economics, University of Pennsylvania, December.

Mariano, R.S., B.N. Gultekin, S. Özmucur, T. Shabbir and C.E. Alper (2004), 'Prediction of Currency Crises: Case of Turkey', *Review of Middle East Economics and Finance*, **2** (2).

Martinez-Peria, M.S. (1999), 'A Regime Switching Approach to Studying Speculative Attacks: A Focus on European Monetary System Crises', *World Bank Development Research Group Working Paper* 2132, June.

Masson, P. (1998), 'Contagion: Monsoonal Effects, Spillovers and Jumps between Multiple Equilibria', *IMF Working Paper* 98/142.

Obstfeld, M. (1994), 'The Logic of Currency Crises', *Cahiers Economiques et Monetaires*, **43**, 189–213.

Pérez, J. (2005), 'Empirical Identification of Currency Crises: Differences and Similarities between Indicators', *Applied Financial Economics Letters*, **1**, 41–6.

Radelet, S. and J. Sachs (1998), 'The East Asian Financial Crisis: Diagnosis, Remedies, Prospects', *Brookings Papers on Economic Activity*, **2**, 1–89.

Shabbir, T. (1998), 'The Social Costs of the Asian Financial Crisis', mimeo, Department of Economics, University of Pennsylvania, Philadelphia.

Warr, Peter (2002), 'Crisis Vulnerability', *Asian-Pacific Economic Literature*, **16** (1), 36–47, May.

World Bank (2000), *World Development Report (2000/2001), Attacking Poverty*, New York: Oxford University Press.

2. Indicators and analysis of vulnerability to currency crisis: Thailand*

Pranee Tinakorn

1 INTRODUCTION

Thailand was the first of the Asian developing countries to experience the financial crisis in 1997. The crisis started with a series of currency attacks during late 1996 and mid-1997, which eventually led to the collapse of Thailand's fixed exchange rate system on 2 July 1997. The consequent severe fall of around 40–108 percent in the baht value (from June 1997 average of 25.75 baht/$ to January 1998 average of 53.71 baht/$ before hovering around 36–45 baht/$ later) led to a tremendous increase in the liability side of the balance sheet for a significant number of enterprises that had borrowed heavily from international markets. Many financial institutions were faced with both liquidity and insolvency problems. The situation was aggravated by the contagion effect of currency depreciation that hit other Asian countries and had a further feedback effect on the Thai economy. In addition, since the Bank of Thailand (BOT) had used up almost all of the international reserves through the swap operation to defend the baht value in vain, resulting in a net reserve of only about 1 billion dollars in July 1997 (see Figure 2.1),[1] the country had to turn to the International Monetary Fund (IMF) for a stand-by credit of 17.2 billion dollars.

The IMF package required the country to cut fiscal expenditure and raise interest rates mainly to restore international confidence. This in effect dried up whatever little domestic liquidity there was and the economy inevitably headed into a deep recession. Thailand's real GDP in 1998 contracted by –10.4 percent and the unemployment rate increased more than three times the rate of 1997.

In fact, even without the IMF austerity package, Thailand had been heading for an economic downturn anyway as predicted by the composite leading indicator. Tinakorn (1998) constructs a composite leading economic indicator for Thailand and finds that the composite leading indicator had

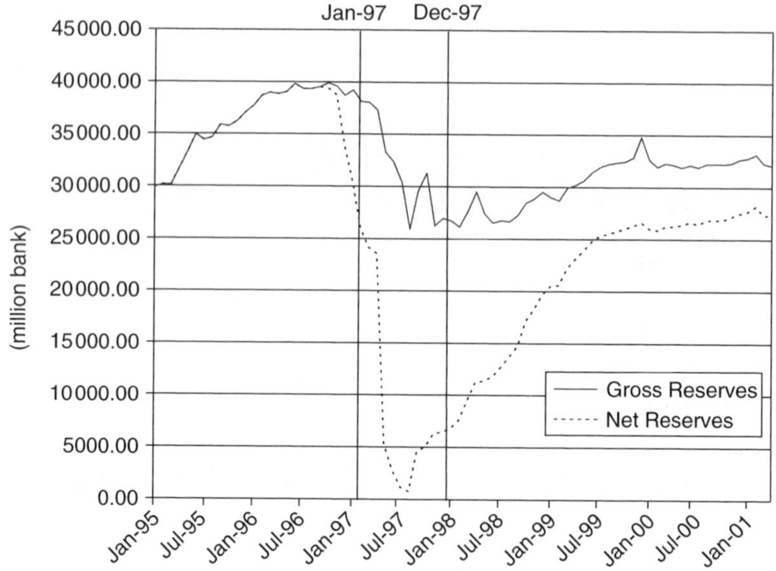

Figure 2.1 Thailand's international reserves: gross and net

been following a downward trend since early 1996, with a leading time of six months on average. Although Thailand needed the IMF stand-by credit badly, the Thai authorities might have negotiated for a less contractionary package if they had had prior knowledge about the leading indicator of the economy and where it was heading. Similarly, the IMF might have yielded to a less contractionary package if they had known that the economic downturn in Thailand would have occurred anyway and such downturn would have helped correct the current account deficits without a strong contractionary package initially imposed by the IMF.

Although the use of leading indicators as warning signals is widespread in most developed countries, especially those in the Organisation for Economic Co-operation and Development (OECD), the situation is quite different for Thailand where many leading indicators were simply not available and cannot be incorporated into the composite index. It is suggested that the concerned authorities should spend more efforts to gather the required data and try to improve the performance of the present composite leading indicator so that it can serve as a more reliable warning signal in the future. In addition to improving and monitoring leading economic indicators for the real sector activities, Thailand also needs some warning signals about the impending crisis in the financial sector and the balance of payments as well. Kaminsky and Reinhart (1999) found that problems in the banking sector typically precede a currency crisis and the currency crisis deepens the banking crisis. For example, the 1996 abrupt halt to Thailand's export growth[2] might not have caused such a severe attack on the baht value if Thailand had not already had troubles in its financial sector. The high ratios of non-performing loans (NPLs) among the Thai banks and financial institutions due to the sluggishness in the property sector must have created fear about their ability to repay debt. This unsurprisingly leads baht traders and speculators to have growing doubts about Thailand's debt servicing capacity and creditworthiness. While it would be desirable to study leading indicators for both the banking crisis and currency crisis for Thailand, due to time and data constraints this study is focused on analyzing warning signals for the currency crisis alone.

Since the banking crisis and currency crisis are found to have strong links, many studies on currency crises also found that overstretched financial variables provide warning signals to currency crisis. By including several indicators from the financial sectors in the analysis of currency crisis, it is hoped that they will provide warning signals not only to currency crisis but also to financial problems. While most studies on currency crisis use international cross-section data to look for signals of crisis, this study will use the time-series data on a monthly basis. Both non-parametric and parametric analysis will be explored. When a set of leading indicators are confirmed from statistical analysis, they can be used to assess future vulnerability of the Thai economy.

2 REVIEW OF SOME SELECTED STUDIES ON CURRENCY CRISIS

2.1 Theoretical Explanation of Currency Crisis

Prior to the Asian currency crisis in the late 1990s, there were basically two models explaining the onset of currency attacks. They are known as the first- and second-generation models. The former model focused on the balance-of-payments problems created mainly through seignorage; the latter model viewed currency crisis not as a result of bad policy but of a shift in expectation and the model was called 'self-fulfilling'. However, the causes of speculative attacks on Asian currencies, with the Thai currency being hit first, appeared to be different from those explained in the first- and second-generation models. Therefore, economists came up with a third-generation model to explain currency crisis. Kaminsky et al. (1998) provided a summary of the main explanation of speculative attacks and

Krugman (2001) provided a brief history of currency crisis modeling. The following summary draws heavily from both papers.

First-generation crisis models

Krugman (1979) explained that under a fixed exchange rate system, the expansion rate of domestic credit in excess of money demand growth led to persistent losses of international reserves, which ultimately led to speculative attacks on the currency. The root cause of the crisis appeared to be poor government policy, that is, excessive public sector deficit that becomes monetized under a fixed exchange rate system. The balance-of-payments crises or near-crisis events that took place in the 1970s[3] provided inspiration for the first-generation modeling.

Second-generation crisis models

The series of attacks on some European currencies under the European Monetary System (EMS) in 1992–93 could not be explained by the first-generation models. Seignorage was not an issue and it was not the depletion of reserves that led the authorities to abandon the parity. Rather, it was a matter of policy choice as they may have been concerned about the adverse consequences of policies needed to maintain the parity (for example, the effect of higher interest rates on employment). Obstfeld (1996) offered several variants but the main theme seemed to focus on macroeconomic trade-offs and decisions, and the existence of multiple equilibria. If speculators question the credibility of the peg, they may attack and the result can be a self-fulfilling crisis of confidence. Within the second-generation models, crises are no longer the result of irresponsible policy, but they occur because market participants expect them to.

Third-generation crisis models

The Asian Crisis in 1997 appeared to be the inspiration for several variant explanations in the third-generation crisis models. Krugman (2001) suggested that there were three versions: moral-hazard-driven investment, which leads to an excessive build-up of external debt and then to a collapse; bank-run; and balance-sheet implications of currency depreciation.

In addition to these three main reasons as explanation for currency crises, some papers also discuss 'contagion effects'. Gerlach and Smets (1995) explained that the devaluation by one country could lead its trading partners to devalue in order to avoid a loss of competitiveness. Other channels, such as financial linkages, can also serve as transmission of contagion effects (see Calvo and Reinhart, 1996 and Eichengreen et al., 1996 for further discussion). Since the growth in international bank lending to emerging markets and its sharp retrenchment was a remarkable feature of the East Asian Crisis, Jeanneau and Micu (2002) found evidence of several fundamental factors as determinants of international capital flows. Dodd (2001) pointed out that the 'carry trade', whereby foreign exchange forwards and swaps were used to hedge as well as speculate on the fixed exchange rate regimes while profiting from the interest rate differential between pegged currencies, was the major factor preceding and precipitating the Thai currency crisis in 1997. If authorities are not mindful of their activities, derivatives can make the economy more susceptible to financial crisis because they create conditions for entities to raise risk in relation to capital and to dodge prudential regulatory safeguards even though they play the useful role in hedging and risk management.

Krugman (2001) also conjectured about a future 'fourth-generation' crisis model, which may not be a currency crisis model, but may be a more general financial crisis model in which other asset prices play the major role.

2.2 Some Recent Empirical Studies on Currency Crisis Indicators

The theoretical explanation of currency crisis contained in the first- and second-generation models implies that there are some fundamental variables or indicators that should help us assess the vulnerability of an economy to currency attacks. If speculative attacks are due to the 'self-fulfilling' crisis of the second-generation model, the prospect of predicting its occurrence from various economic indicators is rather dim because attacks may occur against a fundamentally sound economy. The Mexican Crisis in 1994 and the Asian Crisis in 1997 revived academic interest in looking for indicators that can help predict currency crisis.

From the author's survey of literature published since 1997, the following studies are found and hereby summarized.[4] Goldfajn and Valdés (1997) used the logit model to estimate the probability of a crisis and found that lagged overvalued exchange rate was a statistically significant variable. Esquivel and Larrain (1998) used the probit model and found the following variables to be significant: change in reserve money as a percentage of GDP, real exchange rate misalignment, ratio of current account to GDP, ratio of money supply (M2) to international reserves, change in terms of trade, growth in GNP per capita and contagion effect. Kruger et al. (1998) also estimated the probit model and found three variables to be consistently linked to currency crises: a measure of lending booms, real exchange rate misalignment and the ratio of M2 over reserves. They also performed some sensitivity analysis and found that other macroeconomic variables did not have as robust a performance as these three.

The methodological approach used by Kaminsky et al. (1998) is different from the above three studies. Their 'signals' approach is a non-parametric method where leading indicators of currency crises are identified by their non-normal behavior, or the so-called 'signaling'. Their study found the following variables to be particularly useful: international reserves, real exchange rate, domestic credit, credit to the public sector and domestic inflation.

All the above-mentioned studies used cross-section data from different numbers of countries within the period 1970 to 1997. Their sample size differs as do their methodology and definition of currency crisis. Table 2.1 provides some major comparison of these four studies.

The 1997 currency crisis also stimulated academic interest on this issue in Thailand. Table 2.2 summarizes the two pieces of study on early warning indicators of currency crisis for Thailand. Engwatana (1999) used both monthly and quarterly data during 1990–98 while Poonpatpibul and Ittisupornrat (2001) used monthly data during 1990–2000. It is somewhat surprising that with the same methodology of probit analysis, they found different sets of significant indicators, except for one variable. This could be partly due to their different definitions of currency crisis. Engwatana (1999) used 'accumulated one month exchange rate change of 10% or more' or 'deviation of forward premium from its three-month moving average by more than 10% in one month'. Poonpatpibul and Itthisupornrat (2001) 'used an accumulated weakening of exchange rate of more than 15% in three months'.

It is also notable that the latter study did not find short-term foreign debt to be a significant indicator in both the signals approach and probit model even though in reality excessive short-term foreign debt was a prominent factor in Thailand's 1997 currency crisis. Besides, there appears to be some inconsistency in Poonpatpibul and Ittisupornrat's (2001) reporting of their sample data. They reported using monthly samples between January 1990 to December 1998 for probit analysis but their regression reported only 78 total observations instead of 108 observations. In addition, following their definition of a currency crisis, they reported having 16 observations of crisis (where the dependent variable was set to 1) but if one examines the exchange rate data, and using their definition, one will find only eight such observations (this can be verified by examining the data in Table 2.3).

Since the objective of this research study is to evaluate Thailand's future vulnerability to currency crisis, the author does not feel comfortable relying on the results found in other studies that still require data clarification. This study is an additional attempt in the pool of research work on Thailand's leading indicators of currency crises, in the hope that they can help to forewarn of such events in the future.

Perhaps, it should be noted here that after this research work was completed and while in the process of revision, the study on predicting currency crises by Mariano et al. (2002) was called to the author's attention. Mariano et al.

Table 2.1 Summary comparison of four studies on leading indicators of currency crises

	Goldfajn and Valdés (1997)	Esquivel and Larrain (1998)	Kaminsky et al. (1998)	Kruger et al. (1998)
1. Sample	26 countries May 1984–May 1997	30 countries 1975–96	20 countries 1970–95	19 countries 1977–93
2. Definition of currency crisis	This paper follows three alternative procedures as follows: 1. Devaluation is a crisis when it is larger than • 1.96 times the standard deviation of the country's nominal exchange rate, and • 2% plus 1.5 times the devaluation rate of the previous month. Crises are required to be two months apart 2. Given downward price rigidity, large jumps in the real exchange rate could be deemed to be a crisis	1. The accumulated three-month real exchange rate change is 15% or more or 2. One-month change in the real exchange rate is higher than 2.54 times country-specific standard deviation of real monthly growth rate, provided that it also exceeds 4%	The index of currency market turbulence is more than 3 standard deviations above the mean, where the index is a weighted average of monthly percentage changes in exchange rate and monthly percentage changes in gross international reserves	Exchange rate pressure index is 1.5 times standard deviations above mean, where the index is defined as a weighted average of percentage changes in the nominal exchange rate and the negative of percentage changes in international reserves

Table 2.1 (continued)

	Goldfajn and Valdés (1997)	Esquivel and Larrain (1998)	Kaminsky et al. (1998)	Kruger et al. (1998)
	3. The index of currency market turbulence is more than three standard deviations above mean, where the index is a weighted average of monthly percentage changes in gross international reserves			
3. Methodology	Logit model	Probit model with random effect	Signals approach	Probit model
4. Variables found to be significant indicators	1. Overvalued real exchange rate	1. Change in reserve money a percentage of GDP 2. Current account imbalance 3. Real exchange rate misalignment 4. Foreign exchange reserves 5. Terms of trade shock 6. Poor growth performance 7. Regional contagion	1. Real exchange rate. 2. Banking crises 3. Exports 4. Stock prices 5. M2/reserves 6. Output 7. Excess M1 balance 8. International reserves 9. M2 multiplier 10. Domestic credit/GDP 11. Real interest rate 12. Terms of trade 13. Real interest differential	1. M2/international reserves 2. Ratio of bank claims on private sector to GDP (a measure of lending boom) 3. Real exchange rate misalignment

Table 2.2 Summary of studies on currency crisis in Thailand

	Engwatana (1999)		Poonpatpibul and Ittisupornrat (2001)	
1. Sample	1990–98		1990–2000	
2. Definition of currency crisis	1. The accumulated one-month nominal exchange rate change is 10% or more; or 2. The forward premium deviates from its three-month moving average by more than 10% in one month		Accumulated three-month depreciation in nominal exchange rate is 15% or more	
3. Methodology	Probit model (monthy data)	Probit model (quarterly data)	Signals approach	Probit model
4. Variables found to be significant indicators	1. Excessive domestic credit creation 2. High ratio of M2 to international reserves 3. Low ratio of international reserves to monthly imports 4. Large domestic and foreign interest rate differentials 5. Real (effective) exchange rate overvaluation	1. High ratio of short-term foreign debt to international reserves 2. Large domestic and foreign interest rate differentials 3. Large current account deficit 4. Reversal of portfolio investment capital inflow	1. Export growth 2. Change in real exchange rate 3. Terms of trade 4. Spread between lending rate and deposit rate	1. Export growth 2. Ratio of M2 to international reserves 3. Percentage change in credits (private sector) 4. Inflation rate

Table 2.3 Monthly data on exchange rate and international reserves

	Exchange Rate		International Reserves		Net Forward	IMF Borr-owing	Net Reserves	
	Baht/US$	% change	Million US$	% change	Position (mill $)	(mill $)	(mill $)	% change
Dec-92	25.47		21 181.5		0.0	0.0	21 181.5	
Jan-93	25.53	0.24	21 937.0	3.57	0.0	0.0	21 937.0	3.57
Feb-93	25.49	−0.16	21 634.9	−1.38	0.0	0.0	21 634.9	−1.38
Mar-93	25.42	−0.27	22 239.4	2.79	0.0	0.0	22 239.4	2.79
Apr-93	25.23	−0.75	22 611.6	1.67	0.0	0.0	22 611.6	1.67
May-93	25.22	−0.04	23 114.7	2.22	0.0	0.0	23 114.7	2.22
Jun-93	25.21	−0.04	23 979.8	3.74	0.0	0.0	23 979.8	3.74
Jul-93	25.31	0.40	23 919.7	−0.25	0.0	0.0	23 919.7	−0.25
Aug-93	25.18	−0.51	24 222.8	1.27	0.0	0.0	24 222.8	1.27
Sep-93	25.19	0.04	25 225.3	4.14	0.0	0.0	25 225.3	4.14
Oct-93	25.26	0.28	25 544.4	1.26	0.0	0.0	25 544.4	1.26
Nov-93	25.36	0.40	25 206.1	−1.32	0.0	0.0	25 206.1	−1.32
Dec-93	25.45	0.35	25 438.8	0.92	0.0	0.0	25 438.8	0.92
Jan-94	25.53	0.31	25 359.3	−0.31	0.0	0.0	25 359.3	−0.31
Feb-94	25.38	−0.59	26 251.3	3.52	0.0	0.0	26 251.3	3.52
Mar-94	25.29	−0.35	26 672.6	1.60	0.0	0.0	26 672.6	1.60
Apr-94	25.25	−0.16	26 592.8	−0.30	0.0	0.0	26 592.8	−0.30
May-94	25.21	−0.16	27 512.8	3.46	0.0	0.0	27 512.8	3.46
Jun-94	25.14	−0.28	28 340.5	3.01	0.0	0.0	28 340.5	3.01
Jul-94	24.97	−0.68	28 588.3	0.87	0.0	0.0	28 588.3	0.87
Aug-94	25.02	0.20	29 064.0	1.66	0.0	0.0	29 064.0	1.66
Sep-94	24.98	−0.16	29 950.2	3.05	0.0	0.0	29 950.2	3.05
Oct-94	24.96	−0.08	29 851.7	−0.33	0.0	0.0	29 851.7	−0.33
Nov-94	24.98	0.08	29 743.2	−0.36	0.0	0.0	29 743.2	−0.36
Dec-94	25.10	0.48	30 279.0	1.80	0.0	0.0	30 279.0	1.80
Jan-95	25.07	−0.12	29 906.1	−1.23	0.0	0.0	29 906.1	−1.23
Feb-95	25.02	−0.20	30 135.6	0.77	0.0	0.0	30 135.6	0.77
Mar-95	24.76	−1.04	30 119.5	−0.05	0.0	0.0	30 119.5	−0.05
Apr-95	24.56	−0.81	31 727.1	5.34	0.0	0.0	31 727.1	5.34
May-95	24.66	0.41	33 272.4	4.87	0.0	0.0	33 272.4	4.87
Jun-95	24.67	0.04	34 958.3	5.07	0.0	0.0	34 958.3	5.07
Jul-95	24.74	0.28	34 415.7	−1.55	0.0	0.0	34 415.7	−1.55
Aug-95	24.95	0.85	34 629.1	0.62	0.0	0.0	34 629.1	0.62
Sep-95	25.12	0.68	35 866.1	3.57	0.0	0.0	35 866.1	3.57
Oct-95	25.11	−0.04	35 731.4	−0.38	0.0	0.0	35 731.4	−0.38
Nov-95	25.16	0.20	36 204.4	1.32	0.0	0.0	36 204.4	1.32
Dec-95	25.16	0.00	37 026.7	2.27	0.0	0.0	37 026.7	2.27
Jan-96	25.29	0.52	37 721.2	1.88	0.0	0.0	37 721.2	1.88
Feb-96	25.24	−0.20	38 694.2	2.58	0.0	0.0	38 694.2	2.58
Mar-96	25.23	−0.04	38 982.5	0.75	0.0	0.0	38 982.5	0.75
Apr-96	25.27	0.16	38 862.3	−0.31	0.0	0.0	38 862.3	−0.31

Table 2.3 (continued)

	Exchange Rate		International Reserves		Net Forward	IMF Borrowing	Net Reserves	
	Baht/US$	% change	Million US$	% change	Position (mill $)	(mill $)	(mill $)	% change
May-96	25.29	0.08	39 053.8	0.49	0.0	0.0	39 053.8	0.49
Jun-96	25.35	0.24	39 830.0	1.99	0.0	0.0	39 830.0	1.99
Jul-96	25.34	−0.04	39 360.6	−1.18	0.0	0.0	39 360.6	−1.18
Aug-96	25.27	−0.28	39 370.3	0.02	0.0	0.0	39 370.3	0.02
Sep-96	25.36	0.36	39 537.0	0.42	0.0	0.0	39 537.0	0.42
Oct-96	25.46	0.39	39 902.5	0.92	−500.0	0.0	39 402.5	−0.34
Nov-96	25.45	−0.04	39 613.3	−0.72	−850.0	0.0	38 763.3	−1.62
Dec-96	25.56	0.43	38 724.5	−2.24	−4 890.0	0.0	33 834.5	−12.72
Jan-97	*25.69*	*0.51*	*39 233.8*	*1.32*	*−8 860.0*	*0.0*	*30 373.8*	*−10.23*
Feb-97	*25.90*	*0.82*	*38 149.1*	*−2.76*	*−12 190.0*	*0.0*	*25 959.1*	*−14.53*
Mar-97	*25.92*	*0.08*	*38 065.6*	*−0.22*	*−13 960.0*	*0.0*	*24 105.6*	*−7.14*
Apr-97	*26.03*	*0.42*	*37 320.1*	*−1.96*	*−13 760.0*	*0.0*	*23 560.1*	*−2.26*
May-97	*25.84*	*−0.73*	*33 307.6*	*−10.75*	*−28 010.0*	*0.0*	*5 297.6*	*−77.51*
Jun-97	*25.75*	*−0.35*	*32 353.0*	*−2.87*	*−29 510.0*	*0.0*	*2 843.0*	*−46.33*
Jul-97	*30.16*	*17.13*	*30 424.2*	*−5.96*	*−29 280.0*	*0.0*	*1 144.2*	*−59.75*
Aug-97	*32.41*	*7.46*	*25 938.6*	*−14.74*	*−23 460.0*	*1 729.0*	*749.6*	*−34.49*
Sep-97	36.27	11.91	29 612.2	14.16	−23 380.0	1 644.2	4 588.0	512.10
Oct-97	37.55	3.53	31 287.2	5.66	−24 430.0	1 804.8	5 052.4	10.12
Nov-97	39.30	4.66	26 253.6	−16.09	−18 280.0	1 663.6	6 310.0	24.89
Dec-97	45.29	15.24	26 967.7	2.72	−18 010.0	2 534.0	6 423.7	1.80
Jan-98	53.71	18.59	26 724.3	−0.90	−17 420.0	2 491.8	6 812.5	6.05
Feb-98	46.30	−13.80	26 156.1	−2.13	−16 340.0	2 245.1	7 571.0	11.13
Mar-98	41.33	−10.73	27 680.0	5.83	−15 740.0	2 504.6	9 435.4	24.62
Apr-98	39.48	−4.48	29 530.5	6.69	−15 630.0	2 638.3	11 262.2	19.36
May-98	39.14	−0.87	27 450.5	−7.04	−13 370.0	2 740.6	11 339.9	0.69
Jun-98	42.36	8.25	26 571.7	−3.20	−12 010.0	2 793.2	11 768.5	3.78
Jul-98	41.19	−2.77	26 776.3	0.77	−11 330.0	2 763.6	12 682.7	7.77
Aug-98	41.58	0.94	26 678.8	−0.36	−10 170.0	2 840.9	13 667.9	7.77
Sep-98	40.41	−2.80	27 290.8	2.29	−9 700.0	2 928.1	14 662.7	7.28
Oct-98	38.14	−5.62	28 482.1	4.37	−8 400.0	2 981.5	17 100.6	16.63
Nov-98	36.46	−4.40	28 891.4	1.44	−7 600.0	3 000.8	18 290.6	6.96
Dec-98	36.25	−0.58	29 535.9	2.23	−6 600.0	3 277.0	19 658.9	7.48
Jan-99	36.59	0.94	29 013.1	−1.77	−5 300.0	3 215.3	20 497.8	4.27
Feb-99	37.06	1.28	28 721.4	−1.01	−5 000.0	3 166.5	20 554.9	0.28
Mar-99	37.51	1.21	29 936.1	4.23	−4 600.0	3 132.2	22 203.9	8.02
Apr-99	37.60	0.24	30 203.8	0.89	−3 900.0	3 207.6	23 096.2	4.02
May-99	37.02	−1.54	30 637.2	1.43	−3 500.0	3 230.7	23 906.5	3.51
Jun-99	36.91	−0.30	31 433.9	2.60	−3 300.0	3 336.7	24 797.2	3.73
Jul-99	37.11	0.54	31 928.8	1.57	−3 200.0	3 408.3	25 320.5	2.11
Aug-99	37.98	2.34	32 216.1	0.90	−3 200.0	3 453.3	25 562.8	0.96
Sep-99	39.88	5.00	32 360.2	0.45	−3 000.0	3 565.4	25 794.8	0.91

Table 2.3 (continued)

	Exchange Rate		International Reserves		Net Forward	IMF Borr-owing	Net Reserves	
	Baht/US$	% change	Million US$	% change	Position (mill $)	(mill $)	(mill $)	% change
Oct-99	39.47	−1.03	32438.1	0.24	−3000.0	3384.5	26053.6	1.00
Nov-99	38.77	−1.77	32842.1	1.25	−3100.0	3446.6	26295.5	0.93
Dec-99	38.18	−1.53	34780.6	5.90	−4800.0	3367.9	26612.7	1.21
Jan-00	37.35	−2.16	32630.2	−6.18	−3200.0	3394.9	26035.3	−2.17
Feb-00	37.71	0.96	31953.8	−2.07	−2700.0	3369.7	25884.1	−0.58
Mar-00	37.90	0.50	32283.9	1.03	−2700.0	3358.9	26225.0	1.32
Apr-00	37.97	0.18	32166.0	−0.37	−2600.0	3302.2	26263.8	0.15
May-00	38.95	2.58	31904.2	−0.81	−2200.0	3314.0	26390.2	0.48
Jun-00	39.06	0.28	32142.0	0.75	−2100.0	3348.5	26693.5	1.15
Jul-00	40.22	2.97	31929.6	−0.66	−2100.0	3383.8	26445.8	−0.93
Aug-00	40.87	1.62	32232.4	0.95	−2100.0	3262.7	26869.7	1.60
Sep-00	41.88	2.47	32249.8	0.05	−2100.0	3270.6	26879.2	0.04
Oct-00	43.21	3.18	32244.7	−0.02	−2100.0	3253.3	26891.4	0.05
Nov-00	43.73	1.20	32316.1	0.22	−2100.0	3022.9	27193.2	1.12
Dec-00	43.09	−1.46	32661.3	1.07	−2100.0	3074.4	27486.9	1.08
Jan-01	43.12	0.07	32795.0	0.41	−2100.0	3009.4	27685.6	0.72
Feb-01	42.64	−1.11	33153.9	1.09	−2100.0	2858.5	28195.4	1.84
Mar-01	43.90	2.95	32294.7	−2.59	−2200.0	2732.2	27362.5	−2.95
Apr-01	45.46	3.55	32095.9	−0.62	−2100.0	2694.5	27301.4	−0.22

Source: Bank of Thailand.

criticized the probit/logit and the signals approaches for possible misclassification error in the construction of crisis dummy variables. They pointed out several issues regarding these techniques: the need for a priori dating of crisis occurrence, the use of arbitrary thresholds and inadequate modeling of the dynamics in the systems, for example. The Markov-switching model of exchange rate fluctuations with time-varying transition probabilities was used as a predictive model of currency crises in their study.

3 DEFINITION OF CURRENCY CRISIS AND METHODOLOGIES FOR IDENTIFYING ITS LEADING INDICATORS

From the summary of previous studies presented in Tables 2.1 and 2.2, we can see that researchers use either the multivariate logit/probit model or the signals approach in analyzing crisis (except for the study by Mariano et al.). The most commonly used approach seemed to be the estimation of logit/probit models, and Kaminsky et al. (1998) are the first to use the signals approach. For this research study, both methodologies are employed. The sample period is restricted by the availability of monthly data needed for this study, and covers the period January 1992 to December 2000.[5]

3.1 Definition of Currency Crisis in this Study

The definition of currency crisis used in Engwatana (1999) and Poonpatpibul and Ittisupornrat (2001) focused on what happened to the value of currency (including its forward premium in Engwatana). It is the author's opinion that his definition is not broad enough as speculative attacks may not change the value of the currency by much if the monetary authority could defend it with their international reserves. Furthermore, depletion of international reserves could lead to many other economic problems including the crisis of confidence. Therefore, we should regard the huge reduction of international reserves as an indication of currency crisis as well. Kaminsky et al. (1998) defined a currency crisis as 'a situation in which an attack on the currency leads to a sharp depreciation of the currency, a large decline in international reserves, or a combination of the two'. From this definition, an index of exchange market pressure is constructed as a weighted average of monthly percentage changes in the exchange rate and the negative of monthly percentage changes in the gross international reserves.

In the case of Thailand, pressures on the exchange rate started around the end of 1996 and the Bank of Thailand (BOT) intervened to maintain the value of the baht. However, the amount of the BOT's selling of dollars to support the value of the baht in the market did not show up as a large depletion in the international reserves because it used the swap operation to buy back dollars (with an obligation to sell back dollars in the future). Some BOT officials argued that the swap operation helped ease the liquidity dry-up, which would have occurred without it. We can see from Table 2.3 that a series of speculative attacks in the first half of 1997 resulted in the BOT's swap obligation of a huge amount, from around 4.890 billion dollars in December 1996 with gross international reserves standing at 38.725 billion dollars to a swap obligation of 29.510 billion dollars in June 1997. The gross international reserves at the end of June 1997 stood at 32.353 billion dollars while the net international reserves stood at only 2.843 billion dollars. The depletion in gross reserves did not look as severe as that in the net reserves because the swap operation concealed the problem by postponing it into the future. Therefore, the crisis index in this study will be based on the movements in net reserves and exchange rates.

An index of currency market turbulence (I) for Thailand was constructed based on the formula:

$$I = \frac{\Delta e}{e} - \frac{\Delta R}{R} * \frac{\sigma_e}{\sigma_r} \quad (2.1)$$

where Δe = change in nominal exchange rate
ΔR = change in net international reserves
σ_e = standard deviation of $\Delta e/e$
σ_r = standard deviation of $\Delta R/R$

By defining a currency crisis as a situation when the index I exceeds its mean plus 2 standard deviations, the observations of crisis came to only 3. And if we receded to defining the threshold at mean plus 1.5 standard deviations, the observations on crisis still came to only 4. (See Appendix 2A, Table 2A.1: Index of currency market turbulence.) Such numbers may be adequate for the signals analysis but they are inadequate for the probit estimate which requires a minimum number of dependent variables not being equal to 0 (or $Y = 1.0$ when crisis occurs). Since either the severe fall in exchange rate or the excessive depletion of reserves can be a result of speculative attacks, it is decided that a currency crisis is a situation where one of the following situations takes place:

1. there is an accumulated three-month depreciation in exchange rate of 15 percent or more; or
2. there is an accumulated three-month depletion in net international reserves of 15 percent or more.

With the above definition, the Thai economy fell within the episode of currency crisis during January 1997 up to February 1998. This gives us a total of 14 monthly observations of crisis from our sample of 108 observations during January 1992 and December 2000. However, for some indicators their year-on-year changes are used as signals, which means the first 12 months of the sample are lost.

3.2 Set of Possible Leading Indicators

From a comprehensive survey of empirical studies on leading indicators of currency crises, Kaminsky et al. (1998) found a large variety of indicators used among those studies – as many as 105 indicators were used. However, not all of them passed the statistical significance test. The choice of variables used in this study was dictated not only by economic reasoning but also by data availability on a monthly basis in Thailand. The set of potential leading indicators with available monthly observations during our sample period may be grouped as follows:

- current account variables:
  export growth;
  import growth;
  trade balance (as a ratio to GDP);
  current account balance (as a ratio to GDP);
  terms of trade (growth);
  real exchange rate (deviation from past average or trend);
- capital account variables:
  spread between domestic and foreign interest rates;
  ratio of external debt to total debt of financial institutions;
  short-term external debt to international reserves;
  capital account balance (growth);
- financial variables:
  real deposit rate;
  spread between lending and deposit rates;
  ratio of M2 to international reserves (growth);
  ratio of domestic credit to GDP (growth);
  excess real M1 balance;
- real sector variables:
  fiscal balance (as a ratio to GDP);
  inflation rate;
  GDP growth;
  Change in stock prices (represented by SET index).

It should be pointed out that Thailand does not have monthly GDP data and the quarterly GDP data go back only to 1993. Since several indicators above should be measured as a ratio to GDP, we need to generate monthly GDP data from the quarterly data. This is done by making use of the quarterly relationship between GDP and other variables, which are themselves available in monthly series. The estimated quarterly relationship between GDP and exports, indirect taxes, government expenditures and electricity consumption is used to estimate monthly GDP from the monthly data of these variables. The estimated monthly GDP is adjusted so as to make the sum of the estimated monthly series equal to the actual quarterly data. The estimated monthly GDP series are also used to estimate the demand for money in order to calculate excess real

M1 balance. In addition, the short-term external debt is also available on a quarterly basis until 1999 when monthly data became available. The monthly short-term debt is estimated by interpolation between two adjacent quarters.

3.3 Methodology

There are two popular approaches in the analysis of leading indicators for currency crisis. The parametric approach utilizes the qualitative dependent variable regression models (probit, logit) to identify leading indicators. The non-parametric approach uses the signals analysis proposed by Kaminsky et al. (1998). This study applied both the signals analysis and the probit estimates to identify the leading indicators of currency crisis for Thailand.

The signals analysis starts with the 'signaling horizon' of 24 months as used in Kaminsky et al. (1998) and also performs a test on a 12-month signaling horizon to see if the results are sensitive to the choice of the horizon. The threshold value for each indicator is scanned between the 10–25 percentiles[6] of the indicator's distribution and the 'optimal' threshold is the one that minimizes the adjusted 'noise-to-signal' ratio where 'noise' and 'signal' can be defined in the following matrix.

	Event (within 12 or 24 months)	
	Crisis	No crisis
Signal is issued	A (good signal)	B (bad signal or noise)
No signal is issued	C	D

$$\text{Adjusted noise-to-signal ratio} = \frac{B/(B+D)}{A/(A+C)}$$

The parametric approach employed in this study is the probit estimates. One advantage of this approach is that it summarizes information from all significant variables in one useful number, the probability of a crisis. However, it also has some drawbacks as the estimates may have to exclude some important indicators due to multicollinearity problems. Its summary nature, on the other hand, makes it unclear which variables are sending out the alarm unless we keep a close watch on the movement of all significant variables.

4 EMPIRICAL RESULTS

4.1 Crisis Indicators from Signals Approach

Based on the signaling horizon of 24 months and the scan between the 10–25th percentiles, the optimal threshold for each indicator is found and presented in Table 2.4 together with its adjusted noise-to-signal ratio. A change of signaling horizon to 12 months is also performed to gauge the sensitivity of our indicators and the information is presented in Table 2.5. It can be seen that for most indicators, changing the signaling horizon does not significantly affect their threshold levels and the adjusted noise-to-signal

Table 2.4 Performance of indicators based on 24-month signaling horizon

Indicator	Threshold (%)	Adjusted Noise-to-signal Ratio
Current account		
• Import growth in US$ (%)	30.2	0.45
• Export growth in US$ (%)	−6.9	0.95
• Ratio of current account to GDP	−8.1	0.13
• Ratio of trade balance to GDP	−9.3	0.18
• Terms of trade growth	−8.6	0.26
• Real exchange rate misalignment (deviation from previous 60-month average)	−5.9	0.06
Capital account		
• Difference between domestic (MLR) and foreign interest rates (LIBOR in $)	7.8	0.48
• Ratio of private short-term external debt to international reserves	127.0	0.00
• Ratio of total short-term external debt to international reserves	126.0	0.04
Financial variables		
• Spread between lending and deposit rates	9.6	0.95
• Growth of M2/international reserves	11.4	0.53
• Growth of domestic credit/GDP	14.8	0.43
• Percentage excess real M1 balance	6.6	0.47
• Growth of money multiplier (M2)	8.5	1.18
Real sector		
• Real GDP growth	−1.0	1.05
• Ratio of fiscal balance to GDP	−3.4	1.01
• Growth of stock prices (SET index)	−42.5	0.29
• Inflation rate	6.5	0.42

Table 2.5 Performance of indicators based on 12-month signaling horizon

Indicator	Threshold (%)	Adjusted Noise-to-signal Ratio
Current account		
• Import growth in US$ (%)	*	*
• Export growth in US$ (%)	−3.8	0.55
• Ratio of current account to GDP	−8.3	0.42
• Ratio of trade balance to GDP	−8.5	0.52
• Terms of trade growth	−8.6	0.25
• Real exchange rate misalignment (deviation from previous 60-month average)	−5.3	0.85
Capital account		
• Difference between domestic (MLR) and foreign interest rates (LIBOR in $)	7.5	0.52
• Ratio of private short-term external debt to international reserves	138.0	0.05
• Ratio of total short-term external debt to international reserves	128.4	0.13
Financial variables		
• Spread between lending and deposit rates	9.6	0.51
• Growth of M2/international reserves	11.4	0.28
• Growth of domestic credit/GDP	15.0	0.42
• Percentage excess real M1 balance	3.6	0.69
• Growth of money multiplier (M2)	9.6	0.68
Real sector		
• Real GDP growth	−1.0	0.57
• Ratio of fiscal balance to GDP	−3.4	0.55
• Growth of stock prices (SET index)	−42.5	0.15
• Inflation rate	6.5	0.42

Note: * No signals were found between the 10–25th percentiles with the 12-month horizon for import growth.

ratios, with the exception of import growth M2 money multiplier, real GDP growth and the ratio of fiscal balance to GDP.

Since the performance of these indicators are indicated by their adjusted noise-to-signal ratio, Tables 2.6 and 2.7 rank these indicators from low to high ratios. It can be noticed that the ratio of trade balance to GDP is not present in these two tables because its effect is already included within the ratio of current account to GDP. The same goes for the ratio of private short-term external debt to international reserves, the effect of which is already included in the ratio of total short-term external debt to international

Table 2.6 Indicators ranked according to their performance (24-month horizon)

Rank	Threshold (%)	Adjusted Noise-to-signal Ratio
1. Ratio of total short-term external debt to international reserves	126.0	0.04
2. Real exchange rate misalignment	−5.9	0.06
3. Ratio of current account to GDP	−8.1	0.13
4. Terms of trade growth	−8.6	0.26
5. Growth of stock prices	−42.5	0.29
6. Inflation rate	6.5	0.42
7. Growth of domestic credit/GDP	14.8	0.43
8. Import growth (in US$)	30.2	0.45
9. Percentage excess real M1 balance	6.6	0.47
10. Difference between domestic and foreign interest rates (MLR/LIBOR in $)	7.8	0.48
11. Growth of M2/international reserves	11.4	0.53
12. Export growth (in US$)	−6.9	0.95
13. Spread between lending and deposit rates	9.6	0.95
14. Ratio of fiscal balance to GDP	−3.4	1.01
15. Real GDP growth rate	−1.0	1.05
16. Growth of money multiplier (M2)	8.5	1.18

Note: The indicators 'Trade balance/GDP' and 'Private short-term external debt/international reserves' are excluded from this table as their effect is implicit in 'Ratio of current account/GDP' and 'Ratio of total short-term external debt/international reserves' respectively.

reserves. In fact, during the period covered in this study the private short-term external debt is very close to the total short-term external debt because the public short-term external debt was insignificantly small in comparison to that of the private sector. It would be redundant to have duplicate measures of the same effect.

Comparing the rank and the adjusted noise-to-signal ratio of the indicators in Tables 2.6 and 2.7, we can see that there are a few indicators the performance of which is rather sensitive to the choice of signaling horizon. Based on an evaluation of the magnitude change in threshold levels and in the noise-to-signal ratio, the following two indicators appear to be rather sensitive to the choice of horizon: import growth and the growth of money multiplier. For import growth, no signals were found for the 12-month signaling horizon. For growth of the money multiplier, the threshold and the adjusted noise-to-signal ratio changed from 8.5 and 1.18 for the 24-month

Table 2.7 Indicators ranked according to their performance (12-month horizon)

Rank	Threshold (%)	Adjusted Noise-to-signal Ratio
1. Ratio of total short-term external debt to international reserves	128.4	0.13
2. Growth of stock prices	−42.5	0.15
3. Terms of trade growth	−8.6	0.25
4. Growth of M2/international reserves	11.4	0.28
5. Ratio of current account to GDP	−8.3	0.42
6. Growth of domestic credit to GDP	15.0	0.42
7. Inflation rate	6.5	0.42
8. Spread between lending and deposit rates	9.6	0.51
9. Difference between domestic and foreign interest rates (MLR/LIBOR in $)	7.8	0.52
10. Export growth (in US$)	−3.8	0.55
11. Ratio of fiscal balance to GDP	−3.4	0.55
12. Real GDP growth	−1.0	0.57
13. Growth of money multiplier (M2)	9.6	0.68
14. Percentage excess real M1 balance	3.6	0.69
15. Real exchange rate misalignment	−5.3	0.85
16. Import growth (in US$)	–	–

Note: The indicators 'Trade balance/GDP' and 'Private short-term external debt/international reserves' are excluded from this table as their effect is implicit in 'Ratio of current account/GDP' and 'Ratio of total short-term external debt/international reserves' respectively.

horizon to 9.6 and 0.68 for the 12-month horizon. The changes in thresholds and noise-to-signal ratios of other variables are not so large as to cause concern.

From the author's judgment, the following indicators appear to be least sensitive to the change of signaling horizon:

- the ratio of total short-term external debt to international reserves;
- terms of trade growth;
- growth of stock prices;
- inflation rate.

The remaining indicators appear to be sensitive but their sensitivity appears moderate and does not warrant as much concern as the import growth and the growth of money multiplier.

It is the opinion of the author that a signaling horizon of 24 months may be rather extended as an irregular movement over the threshold at a certain date to be read as a signal for crisis in the following 24 months. Signals obtained from a 12-month horizon analysis may be better if we take the viewpoint that the shorter time span between the occurrence of signals and a possible impending crisis may compel us to be more alert about tracking the monthly movement of these indicators. Therefore, the following discussion will be based on the results from the 12-month horizon.

Based on the 12-month signaling horizon we can see from Table 2.7 that there are 15 variables that can serve as leading indicators of currency crisis for Thailand. From historical experience they have issued relatively fewer bad signals (noise) than good ones as evidenced by their adjusted noise-to-signal ratio of less than 1. Their movement can be seen in Figures 2.2 and 2.3. However, upon detailed examination of the data's monthly movement, it was found that for some variables their signals were issued after July 1997. Such observation makes it unclear whether their abnormal behavior was in fact caused by the crisis and not vice versa. These are mainly some of the financial variables: spread between lending and deposit rates, difference between domestic and foreign interest rates, growth of money multiplier and excess real M1 balance. Eliminating these from the list of our leading indicators for currency crises, the remaining 11 indicators are deemed to have satisfactory performance. They are grouped here as indicators with positive and negative shocks.

Indicators with positive shocks are those whose increases over a threshold may lead to or add to the possibility of a currency crisis. From the signals analysis, there are four such indicators:

- ratio of total short-term external debt to international reserves;
- growth of M2/international reserves;
- growth of domestic credit/GDP;
- inflation rate.

The ratio of total short-term external debt to international reserves reflects a constraint on the country's liquidity in international transactions: the higher the ratio, the more likely the crisis. The threshold level for this ratio with minimum adjusted noise-to-signal ratio is 28.4 percent, found at the 21st percentile. So if the amount of total short-term external debt is 28.4 percent higher than reserves, it should trigger concern from the policy-maker. This indicator is very important from at least two perspectives: mismatch in maturity and mismatch in denomination of currencies. It is well known that financial institutions including commercial banks face the maturity mismatch of borrowing short and lending long. This creates a

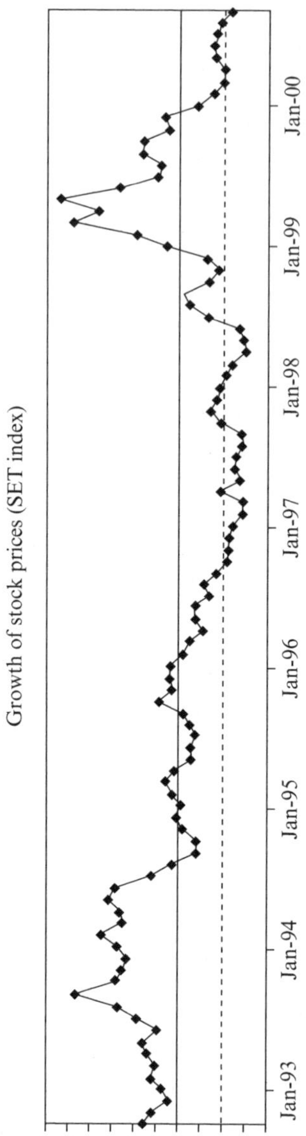
Growth of stock prices (SET index)
120
100
80
60
40
20
0
–20
–40
–60
–80
Jan-93
Jan-94
Jan-95
Jan-96
Jan-97
Jan-98
Jan-99
Jan-00

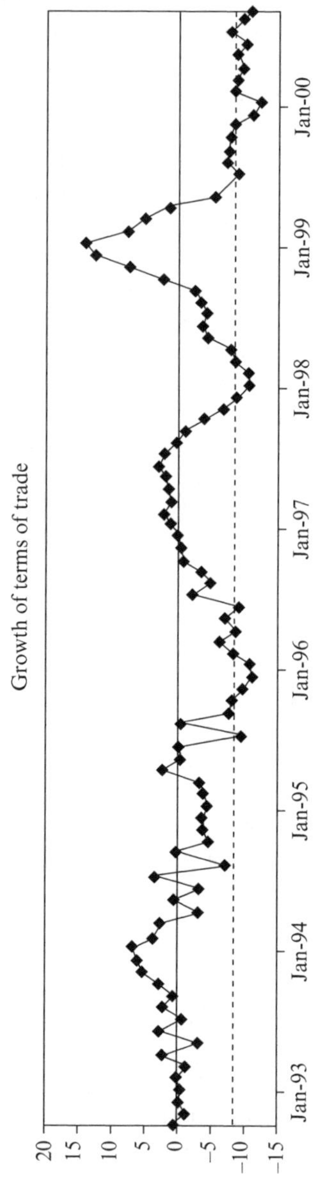
Growth of terms of trade
20
15
10
5
0
–5
–10
–15
Jan-93
Jan-94
Jan-95
Jan-96
Jan-97
Jan-98
Jan-99
Jan-00

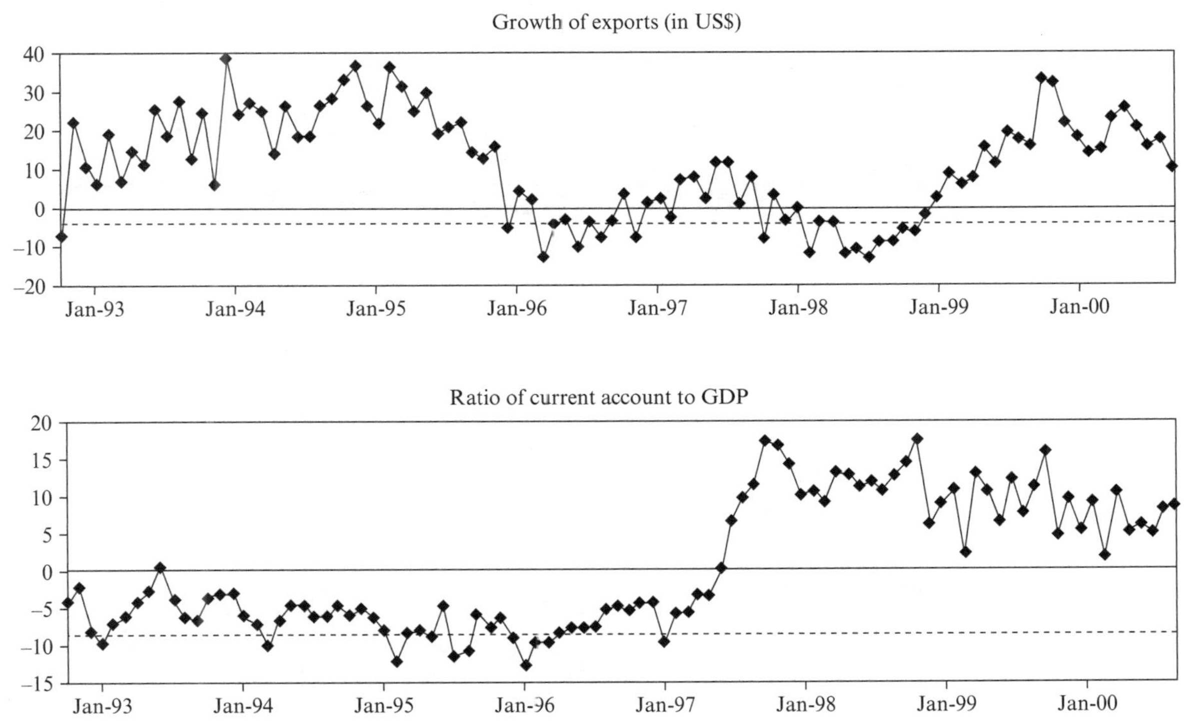

Figure 2.2 Movement of indicators with negative shocks (threshold from 12-month horizon)

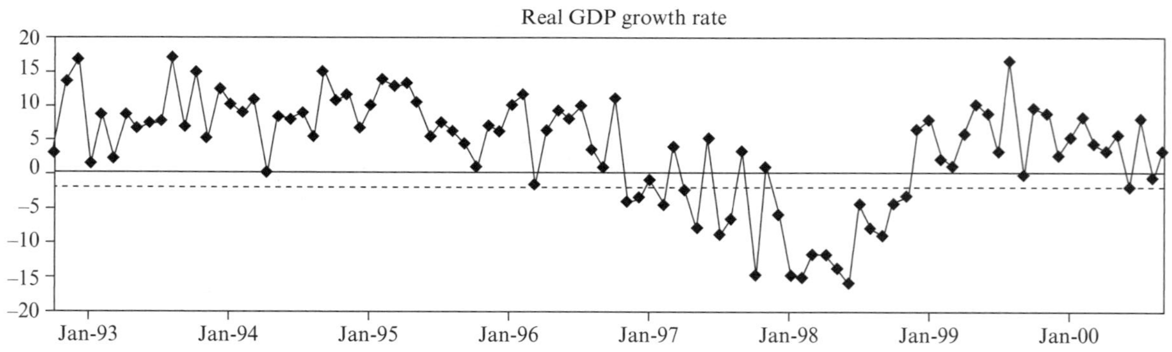
Real GDP growth rate
20
15
10
5
0
−5
−10
−15
−20
Jan-93
Jan-94
Jan-95
Jan-96
Jan-97
Jan-98
Jan-99
Jan-00

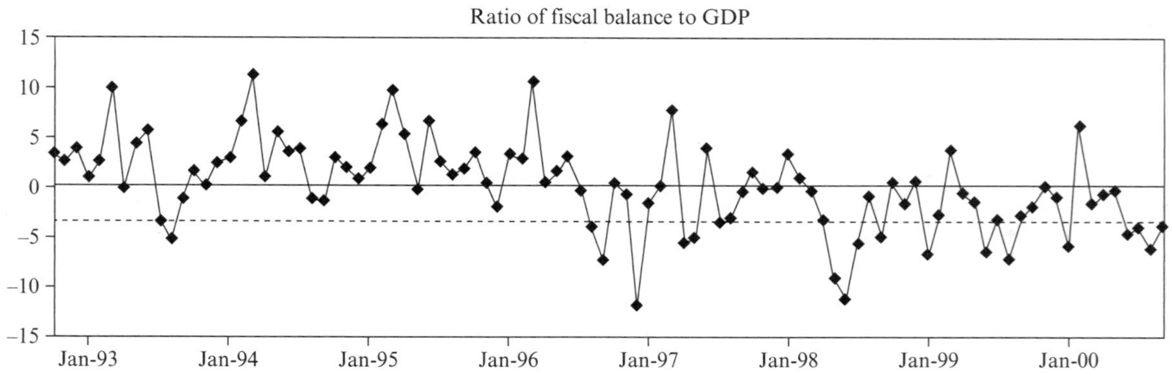
Ratio of fiscal balance to GDP
15
10
5
0
−5
−10
−15
Jan-93
Jan-94
Jan-95
Jan-96
Jan-97
Jan-98
Jan-99
Jan-00

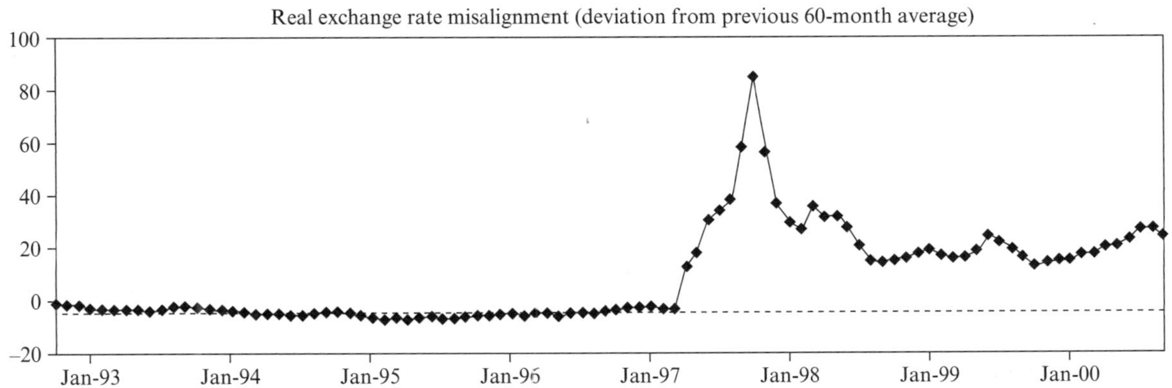

Figure 2.2 (continued)

Ratio of total short-term external debt to international reserves

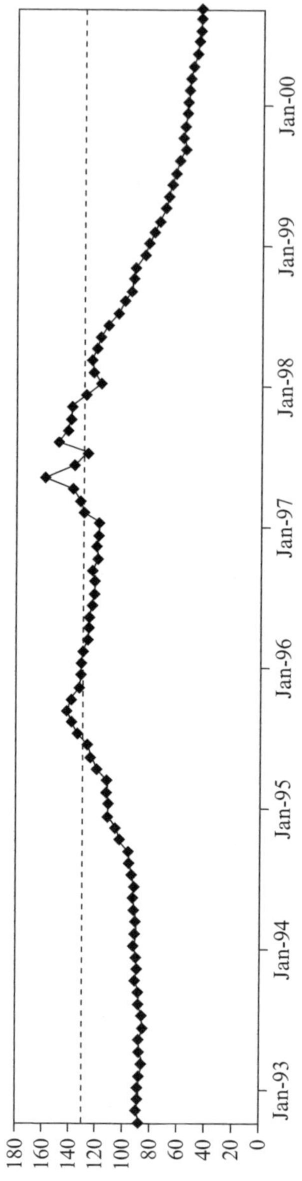

Growth of ratio of M2 to international reserves

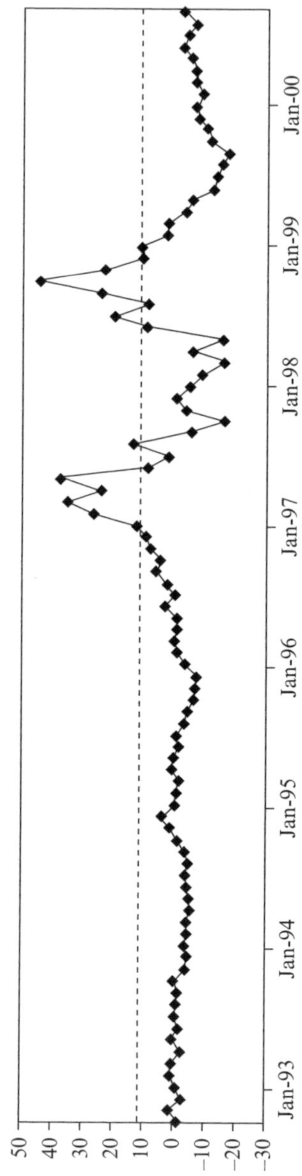

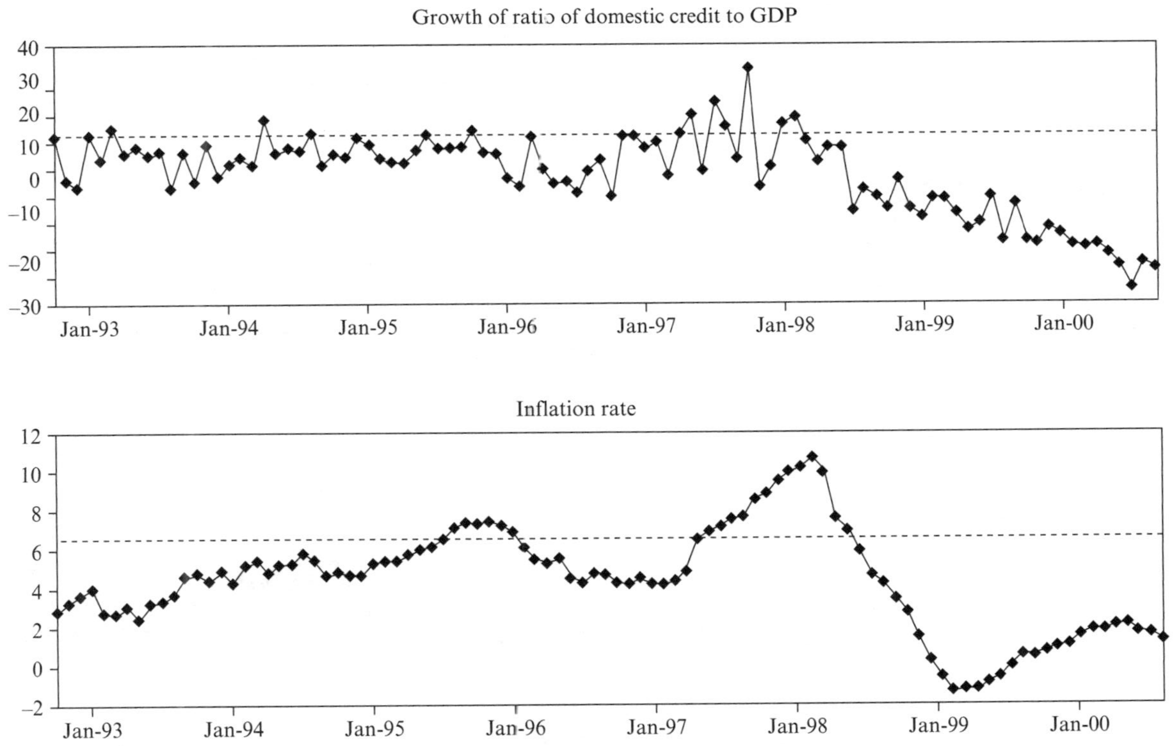

Figure 2.3 Movement of indicators with positive shocks (threshold from 12-month horizon)

Difference between domestic and foreign interest rate (MLR/LIBOR in US$)

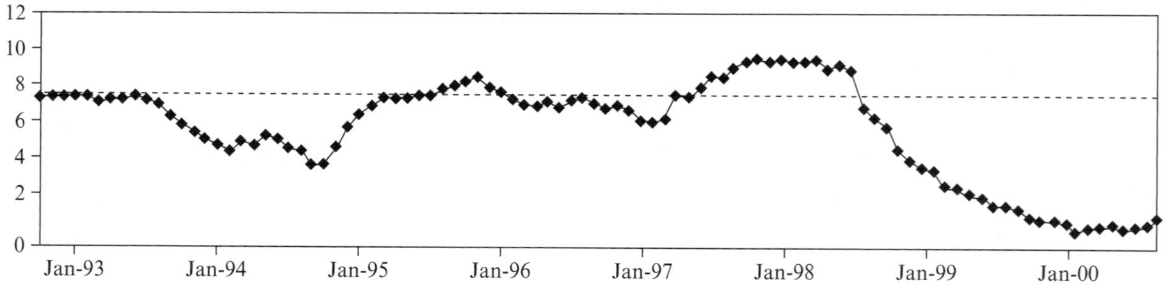

Spread between lending and deposit rates

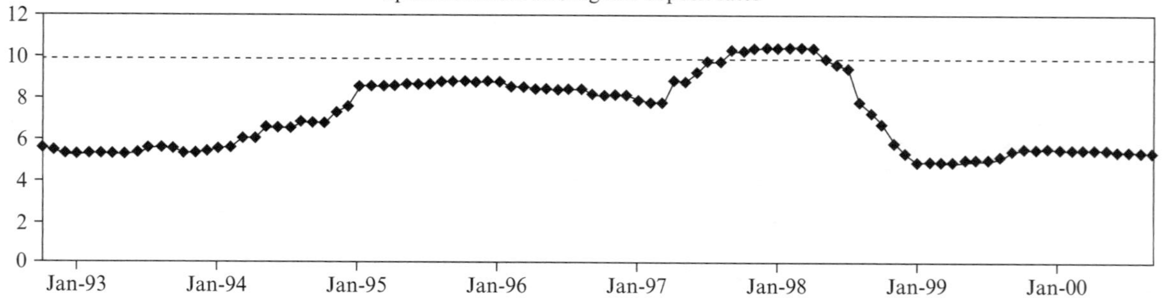

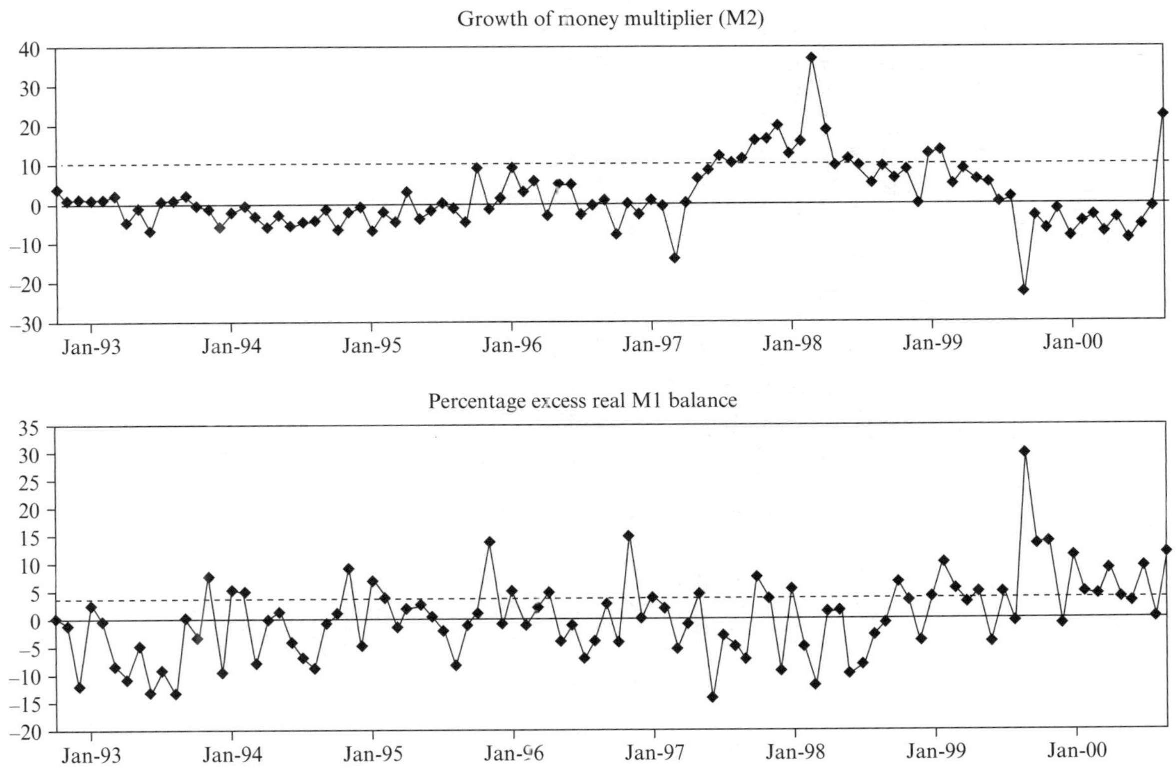

Figure 2.3 (continued)

liquidity problem when there is a bank-run even if banks are solvent. In addition, when the short-term debts are borrowed from foreign lenders the country inevitably faces the currency mismatch problem since developing countries are unable to borrow abroad in their own currencies. Therefore the high ratio of short-term external debt to international reserves erodes investors' confidence and incurs high probability of both banking crisis and currency crisis.

The growth of M2/international reserves indicates the rate of monetary expansion in the economy, which could create a harmful inflationary environment. This ratio could also grow due to the decline in foreign exchange reserves. The threshold level for the growth of this ratio with minimum adjusted noise-to-signal ratio is 11.4 percent, found at the 12th percentile.

The growth of domestic credit/GDP reflects the rate of credit expansion relative to real economic activities. If this growth is excessive, it can lead to bubbling asset prices and inflationary demand due to the wealth effect. The threshold with minimum adjusted noise-to-signal ratio of this growth rate is 15 percent, found at the 20th percentile.

The inflation rate may be a result of excessive expansionary policies, or a rapid increase in demand, or from higher imported prices of inputs. Whatever its cause, its excessive rate erodes the competitiveness of the country and increases the vulnerability to crisis. The threshold of inflation rate with minimum adjusted noise-to-signal ratio is 6.5 percent, found at the 24th percentile.

Indicators with negative shocks are those whose decreases below a threshold may lead to or add to the possibility of a currency crisis. There are seven such indicators:

- growth of stock prices;
- terms of trade growth;
- export growth;
- ratio of current account to GDP;
- real GDP growth rate;
- ratio of fiscal balance to GDP;
- real exchange rate misalignment.

The negative growth in stock prices reflects lower expectation of future earnings and lower confidence in the domestic economy. The stock prices as measured by the SET index is also found to be an important component of Thailand's composite leading indicator by Tinakorn (1998). The threshold with minimum adjusted noise-to-signal ratio for the SET index is –42.5 percent, found at the 18th percentile. This number appears to be of a rather large magnitude if the SET index hovers around 200–300 points as at present. But during the sample period, the range of the SET index was between 1528.83 (October 1994) and 214.3 (August 1998) and the rate of year-on-year decline went up to almost 60 percent for some months.

The terms of trade is the ratio of export price over import price. A decline in this ratio means imports are relatively more expensive than exports, which will have a negative impact on the trade and current account, and ceteris paribus, the balance of payments. In a cross-country study by Kaminsky and Reinhart (1999), it is found that crises are preceded, on average, by a deterioration of the terms of trade with an annual decline that is about 10 percent deeper than those observed in tranquil times before a balance-of-payments crisis. For the case of Thailand, the threshold of the annual decline in the terms of trade with the minimum adjusted noise-to-signal ratio is –8.6 percent, found at the 10th percentile.

Exports account for more than 50 percent of GDP in Thailand. Therefore its decline has grave implications for the real sector as well as the position of the current account and the balance of payments. The threshold with the minimum adjusted noise-to-signal ratio is the export growth at –3.8 percent,[7] found at the 20th percentile.

The current account includes the international exchange of both goods and services and the current account deficit has a negative impact on the foreign exchange earnings. This variable is measured as a ratio to GDP and its threshold with minimum adjusted noise-to-signal ratio is found to be –8.3 percent, at the 15th percentile meaning that current account deficit that runs in excess of 8.3 percent of GDP is a warning for increased vulnerability of the economy.

Both the real GDP growth rate and the ratio of fiscal balance to GDP are found to be rather sensitive to the choice of signaling horizon. Their performance improves when the 12-month horizon is used. The threshold for GDP growth rate is –1.0 percent, at the 25th percentile and that for the ratio of fiscal balance to GDP is –3.4 percent, at the 19th percentile. Although the deterioration in these two indicators increases the economy's vulnerability, it is also the case that these two indicators tend to deteriorate after the onset of crisis if the currency crisis evolves into economic crisis.

The evolution of real exchange rate has a significant implication for the country's competitiveness. Kaminsky and Reinhart (1999) found that during the year before the balance-of-payments and banking crises, the real exchange rate shows evidence of being overvalued. This is also the case for Thailand. In this study, the real exchange rate is measured in terms of baht per US dollar adjusted by the ratio of US consumer price index over Thai consumer price index. Therefore a decline in this variable means an appreciation of the baht, which will have a negative impact on export earnings and increase the vulnerability of the economy. The misalignment of the real exchange rate is measured as a deviation from its previous 60-month average. The threshold of this deviation with minimum adjusted noise-to-signal ratio is –5.3 percent, at the 25th percentile.

It should be remarked here that if it were not due to the limitation of data the exchange rate indicator to be used ought to be the real effective exchange rate. By using the real exchange rate of the baht vis-à-vis the US dollar only, one may lose information coming from the movement of other currencies. For example, the Chinese adjustment of their exchange rate regime in 1994 (by merging the official rate and the swap market rate to produce a single exchange rate) in effect created a devaluation in the renminbi from 5.8 yuan per US dollar to 8.45 yuan per US dollar. This must have put a lot of pressure on the competitiveness of Asian countries including Thailand. We can see in Figure 2.2 that Thailand's export growth began to decline since the beginning of 1995 and hit negative growth rates in many months of 1996 but the real exchange rate misalignment did not look as severe since it was based on the US dollar.

4.2 Composite Indicator and Probability of Crisis from Signals Approach

One way of combining the signals sent out by all the above 11 indicators is simply by counting the number of individual indicators that have crossed their threshold in a particular month as in equation (2.2):

$$I_t^{(1)} = \sum_{j=1}^{n} S_t^j \tag{2.2}$$

where $S_t^j = 1$ if variable j crosses the threshold in period t

$S_t^j = 0$, otherwise.

However, $I_t^{(1)}$ does not take into account the fact that each variable has different forecasting accuracy as depicted by its adjusted noise-to-signal ratio. For example, the low noise-to-signal ratio of 0.1 of a variable Z contains information that it has more forecasting accuracy than another variable Y with a noise-to-signal ratio of 0.5. Therefore, the composite indicator should give more weight to the signal sent out by Z than that by Y. This leads us to a weighted composite indicator based on the adjusted noise-to-signal ratio of each variable.

$$I_t^{(2)} = \sum_{t=1}^{n} S_t^j \cdot \frac{1}{w^j} \tag{2.3}$$

where w^j = the adjusted noise-to-signal ratio of variable j.

Kaminsky (1999) also experimented with two other composite indicators, and found the weighted composite indicator presented in equation (2.3) to perform the best when predicting both currency and banking crisis.[8] In this study, the weighted composite index ($I_t^{(2)}$) is computed and used to calculate the conditional probability of currency crises in the formula:

$$\text{Prob (crisis}/I = X) = \frac{\begin{array}{c}\text{(No. of months the composite index} = X \text{ and} \\ \text{currency crisis actually occurred within 12 months)}\end{array}}{\text{No. of months the composite index} = X}$$

where X is the value of the composite index. It was found that, in general, the increase in the composite indicator results in higher conditional probability of crisis. However, there were a few cases where the value of the composite index (X) was high but crisis did not actually occur within 12 months and vice versa. This can be seen in Figure 2.4 (a), which plots the conditional probability of a crisis, given the value of the composite index. To obtain a smoother increasing function of probability as the composite index increases requires some grouping of the composite index. It appears that a grouping with a range of six (Figure 2.4f) renders a smooth increasing function of probability as the composite index increases. The result of such grouping is presented in Table 2.8.

Based on the above conditional probability we may look at the value of the composite index computed from those 11 indicators and predict that the probability of a crisis in the next 12 months is about 0.61 if the value exceeds 12. And if the value of the composite index exceeds 18, it is most likely that a crisis is coming as the conditional probability is equal to one.

4.3 Probit Estimates

The set of indicators used as explanatory variables in the probit estimation is the same as that used for signals analysis. However, all of the indicators cannot be simultaneously put into an estimation as the presence of multicollinearity among some variables results in large variances and insignificant t-statistics. Two of the most acceptable sets of estimates are shown in Tables 2.10, and 2.11. These two models are chosen based on the signs of coefficients that conform to economic reasoning, and also on their statistical significance and predictive performance. There appears to be a common set of core variables that can explain the probability of crisis. Their coefficients have the correct (expected) signs and the coefficients are statistically significant at the 95 percent confidence level (one-tail test). These variables are summarized below in Table 2.9:

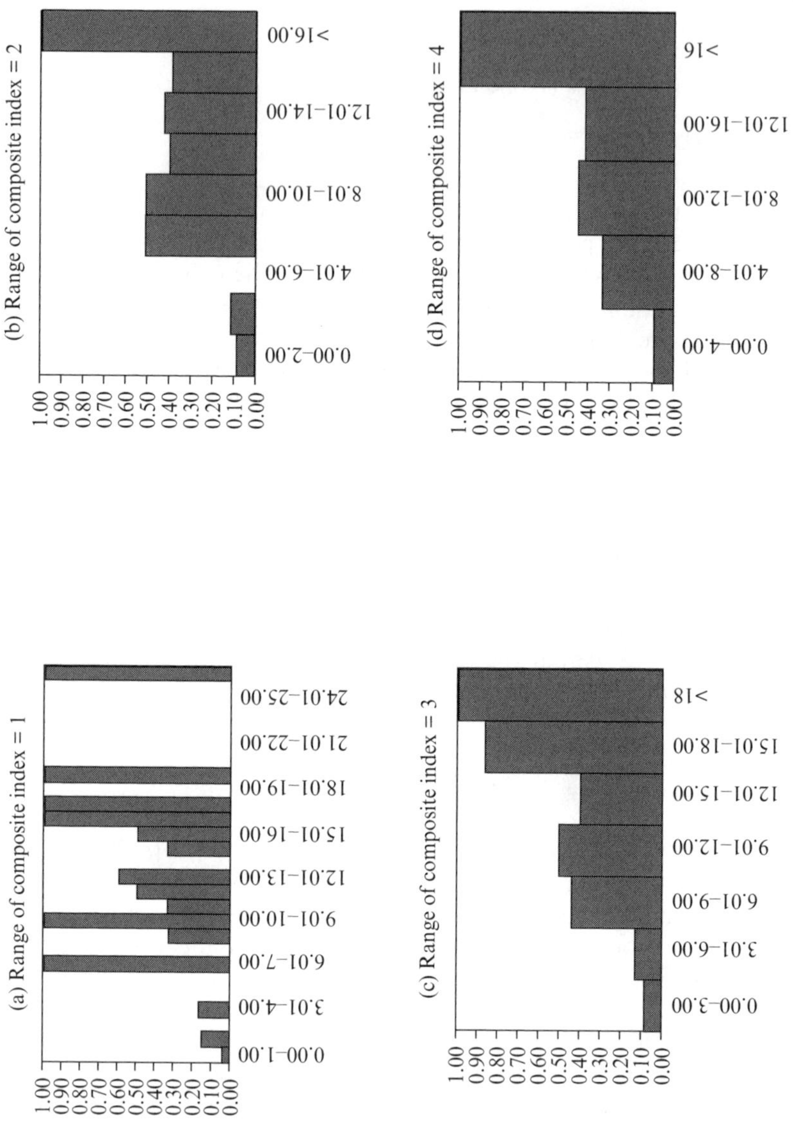
(a) Range of composite index = 1
1.00
0.90
0.80
0.70
0.60
0.50
0.40
0.30
0.20
0.10
0.00
0.00–1.00
3.01–4.00
6.01–7.00
9.01–10.00
12.01–13.00
15.01–16.00
18.01–19.00
21.01–22.00
24.01–25.00
(b) Range of composite index = 2
0.00–2.00
4.01–6.00
8.01–10.00
12.01–14.00
>16.00
(c) Range of composite index = 3
0.00–3.00
3.01–6.00
6.01–9.00
9.01–12.00
12.01–15.00
15.01–18.00
>18
(d) Range of composite index = 4
0.00–4.00
4.01–8.00
8.01–12.00
12.01–16.00
>16

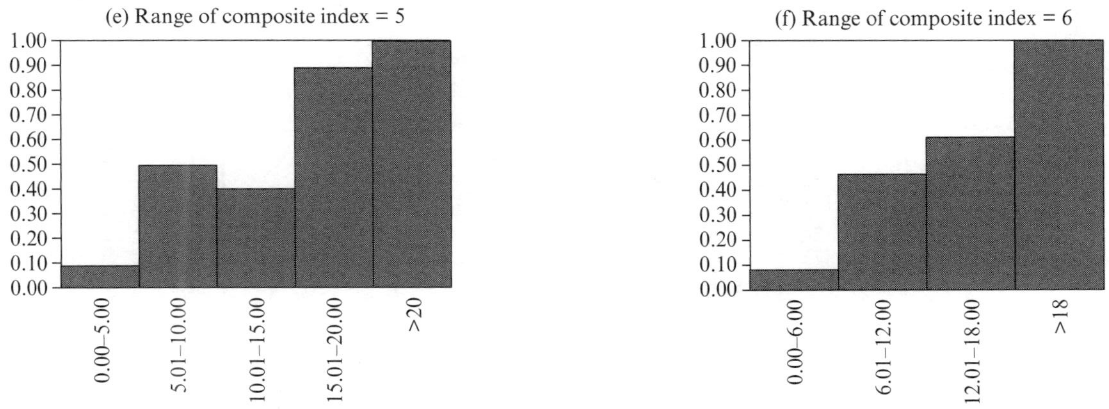

Figure 2.4 Plot of conditional probability of crisis given the value of the composite index

Table 2.8 Composite index and conditional probability of currency crisis

Value of Composite Index (X)	No. of Months the Index = X	No. of Months the Index = X and Currency Crisis Occurred within 12 Months	Conditional Probability of Currency Crisis
0.00–6.00	49	4	0.08
6.01–12.00	13	6	0.46
12.01–18.00	18	11	0.61
>18.00	4	4	1.00
*Quadratic probability score (QPS) = 0.266			

Note: * $\text{QPS} = \frac{1}{T}\sum_{t=1}^{T} 2(P_t - R_t)^2$

Where P_t = probability of crisis between t and $t+h$ conditional on information provided by the composite indicator
R_t = realization that equals 1 if a crisis occurs between t and $t+h$ and equals 0 otherwise
h = time horizon, for example, 12 months.

QPS ranges from 0 to 2, with a score of 0 corresponding to perfect accuracy. See Kaminsky (1999).

Table 2.9 Core variables

Significant Indicators	Model 1	Model 2
1. Growth rate of the ratio M2/reserves	√	√
2. Deviation of real exchange rate	√	√
3. Ratio of current account to GDP	√	√
4. Growth of stock price index	√	√
5. Growth of real GDP	√	–
6. Ratio of fiscal balance to GDP	√	√
7. Export growth	–	√

Even though these two models seem to be about equal on statistical grounds, the frequencies of actual and predicted outcomes appear to be in favor of Model 2. Based on a cut-off probability of 0.5, Model 2 made a correct prediction of 1's for 13 observations out of 14 outcomes during the crisis period and made an incorrect prediction of 1's for seven observations during the tranquil period. On the other hand, Model 1 made fewer numbers of correct predictions for crisis and more numbers of incorrect predictions during the tranquil time.

In the currency crisis literature, contagion effect has received considerable attention from academics. Kaminsky and Reinhart (2000) examined both trade links and financial sector links and found that susceptibility to contagion is highly non-linear. While it would be desirable to examine whether Thailand was affected by contagion, the available data do not permit us to test this in probit estimates. First of all, Thailand was among the primary countries to experience the 1997 currency crisis. Secondly, although contagion from the Tequila Crisis of 1994–95 was possible for Thailand through links with the United States, data conditions in probit models do not allow us to obtain a regression estimate with a contagion dummy.[9]

If we regard the probit prediction of 1 as a signal for crisis, then we can regard the incorrect signal as noise. With this perspective, the adjusted noise-to-signal ratio can be calculated for each model and the ratios are also presented in Tables 2.10 and 2.11. The adjusted noise-to-signal ratios of Models 1 and 2 are, respectively, 0.145 and 0.108. Therefore, the in-sample predictive performance appears to be in favor of Model 2. It should also be pointed out that during the crisis period, the probability of a crisis from probit estimation is very high and it is low during the non-crisis period. The plots of the probability of crisis from Models 1 and 2 are presented in Figure 2.5.

4.4 Assessment of Future Vulnerability

We can use both the signals analysis and the probit estimates to assess the future vulnerability of Thailand to currency crisis. However, the data requirements of these two methods are somewhat different. From the signals approach, we may use the present available data to compute the index of currency crisis and make use of the conditional probability in Table 2.8 to assess the likelihood of a crisis within the next 12 months. Forecasts by the probit estimation, on the other hand, can be made for only three months ahead since the lags of explanatory variables vary from three to 12 months. So for the probit estimate, we only check its out-of-sample predictive performance, given the data for 2001.

Table 2.12 presents the out-of-sample forecast for the probability of a crisis from probit models during 2001. It can be seen that both models predicted very low probability of a currency crisis during 2001. There appeared to be a rise in this probability during the months of July, September and October but the probability dropped afterwards. Overall, the probability predicted by probit models was low and there was no currency crisis in 2001. If we want to assess future vulnerability, then we must first forecast the values of the indicators in probit models, this is at present

Table 2.10 Probit estimate for currency crisis: Model 1 (1994.1–2000.12)

Variable	Coefficient (partial derivatives)	Std. Error	b/Std.Err	$P[\|Z\|>z]$	x-bar
M2RESG6	0.0072	0.0034	2.133	0.0329	0.7728
DRER603	−0.0137	0.0035	−3.905	0.0001	8.8105
CAGDP6	−0.0180	0.0082	−2.201	0.0277	0.3084
SETG6	−0.0026	0.0014	−1.796	0.0726	−2.3993
FBGDP12	−0.0217	0.0101	−2.145	0.0320	0.2302
RGDP6	−0.0253	0.0078	−3.226	0.0013	3.5784

Log-likelihood	−27.1393
Chi-squared	21.4158
Significance level	0.0007

Frequencies of actual and predicted outcomes (cut-off probability = 0.5)

Predicted	Actual		Total
	1 (Crisis)	0 (No crisis)	
1 (signal)	11	8	19
0 (no signal)	3	62	65
Total	14	70	84

Proportion of correct prediction = 0.869
Adjusted noise-to-signal ratio = 0.145

Definition of variables

M2RESG6 = growth in the ratio of M2 over reserves (lagged six months)
DRER603 = deviation of real exchange rate from previous 60-month average (lagged three months)
CAGDP6 = ratio of current account to GDP (lagged six months)
SETG6 = growth rate of stock price index (lagged six months)
FBGDP12 = ratio of fiscal balance to GDP (lagged 12 months)
RGDP6 = growth rate of real GDP (lagged six months)

beyond the scope of this report. But we can do it with the signals approach, given that the signals approach helps predict a crisis within the next 12 months (from ex post analysis). We can use the available data in December 2001 to say something about the prospect of a crisis up to December 2002.

Table 2.13 presents the composite index ($I^{(2)}$) of 11 variables found to be leading indicators of a currency crisis for Thailand in this study. The

Table 2.11 Probit estimate for currency crisis: Model 2 (1994.1–2000.12)

Variable	Coefficient (partial derivatives)	Std. Error	b/Std.Err	$P[\|Z\|>z]$	x-bar
M2RESG6	0.0059	0.0031	1.911	0.0560	0.7728
DRER603	−0.0097	0.0035	−2.788	0.0053	8.8105
CAGDP6	−0.0121	0.0069	−1.752	0.0798	0.3084
SETG3	−0.0030	0.0015	−1.950	0.0511	−4.3632
X$G6	−0.0136	0.0039	−3.438	0.0006	10.0784
FBGDP12	−0.0234	0.0104	−2.250	0.0244	0.2302
Log-likelihood	−19.28912				
Chi-squared	37.11604				
Significance level	0.0000				

Frequencies of actual and predicted outcomes (cut-off probability = 0.5)

Predicted	Actual		Total
	1 (Crisis)	0 (No crisis)	
1	13	7	20
0	1	63	64
Total	14	70	84

Proportion of correct prediction = 0.905
Adjusted noise-to-signal ratio = 0.108

Definition of variables
M2RESG6 = growth in the ratio of M2 over reserves (lagged six months)
DRER603 = deviation of real exchange rate from previous 60-month average (lagged three months)
CAGDP6 = ratio of current account to GDP (lagged six months)
SETG3 = growth rate of stock price index (lagged three months)
X$G6 = export growth (US$) (lagged six months)
FBGDP12 = ratio of fiscal balance to GDP (lagged 12 months)

composite index for 2001 lies between 1.82 and 7.64 with probability of a crisis between 0.08 and 0.46. Using 0.5 as a cut-off point, the composite index implies that a currency crisis is not likely in the next 12 months. Nevertheless, we should be watchful of these indicators because the terms of trade have had a negative growth in the past 12 months and export growth in dollar value has also continuously registered negative growth below its threshold value of –3.8 percent since July 2001. The fiscal balance

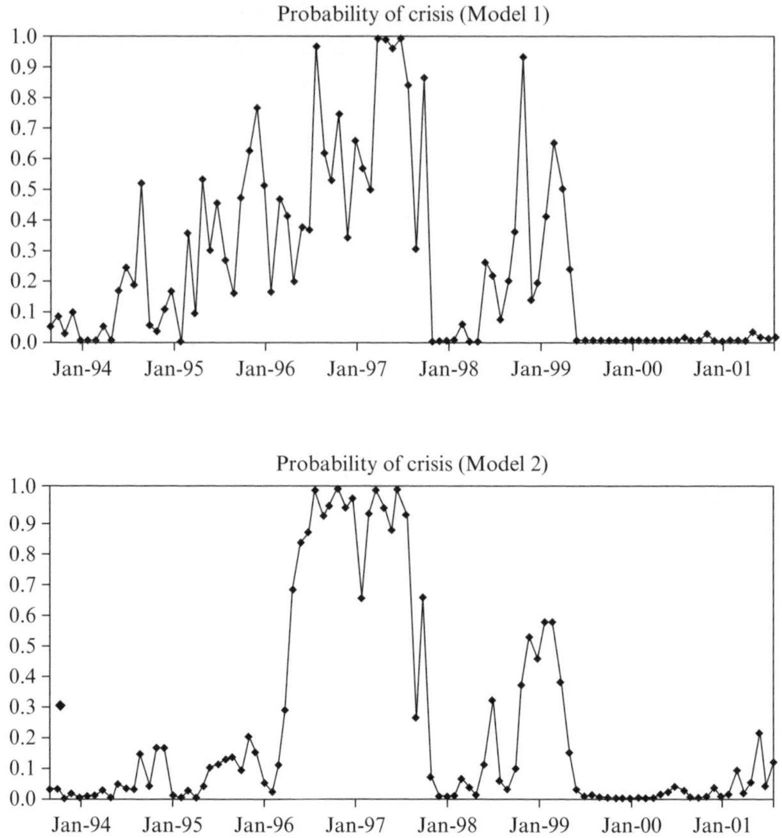

Figure 2.5 Plot of probability of currency crisis from probit estimates

has also been mostly in deficit due to the stimulative fiscal policy. As a consequence, the ratio of fiscal balance to GDP was running below its threshold value in the last four months of 2001. There also remain some structural problems in the financial and real sectors, and the high and rapidly rising public debt was a significant cause for concern.

5 SUMMARY AND CONCLUSION

Based on Thailand's available monthly data during 1992–2000, it is found in this study that there are several leading indicators of currency crisis that we should keep track of. The signals analysis based on the 12-month

Table 2.12 Probability of a currency crisis from probit estimates (out-of-sample forecast)

Year 2001	Model 1	Model 2
January	0.0001	0.0001
February	0.0001	0.0001
March	0.0202	0.0030
April	0.0018	0.0325
May	0.0003	0.0000
June	0.0018	0.0109
July	0.0002	0.0914
August	0.0003	0.0134
September	0.0244	0.0482
October	0.0137	0.2110
November	0.0084	0.0351
December	0.0104	0.1149

signaling horizon yielded 11 indicators that seem to have good performance. A subset of these indicators also performed well with probit estimates, which yielded high probability of crisis during the crisis period and very low probability otherwise. These variables can be grouped by sector as follows in Table 2.14.

In fact, these variables indicate the general health of the macroeconomy and they should be kept track of by the concerned authorities. One can notice that the above list is rather short in use of financial variables. Since there seems to be a vicious cycle in which currency crisis and banking crisis feed back on each other, an in-depth analysis of Thailand's banking troubles and their causes in the past is recommended.

There are some weaknesses in this study that should be pointed out to the readers. The first one is that the sample period included in this study actually covered only one episode of currency crisis, running continuously from January 1997 to early 1998. It would have been more desirable to cover another episode of currency crisis in 1984 when the baht had to be devalued by about 14.7 percent. However, several important indicators are not available on a monthly or even a quarterly basis before the 1990s. Therefore, the 1984 currency crisis episode can not be used with confidence in this study due to lack of data. Second, even when the sample period is restricted to the 1990s, there are still some important variables that are available only at the quarterly level. These are GDP and short-term external debt, and their quarterly data were used to estimate the monthly data as already explained in the text. Given the above-mentioned weaknesses, the results

Table 2.13 Composite index and conditional probability of a currency crisis within 12 months

	Total Short-term Debt/Reserves		SET Index		Terms of Trade		M2/Reserves	
	(Ratio)	Signal	(Growth)	Signal	(Growth)	Signal	(Growth)	Signal
Threshold	128.4		−42.5		−8.6		11.4	
Adj n-t-s	0.13		0.15		0.25		0.28	
Jan-01	44.47	0	−30.32	0	−12.76	1	−9.31	0
Feb-01	43.67	0	−13.12	0	−14.60	1	−10.38	0
Mar-01	44.50	0	−27.07	0	−13.80	1	−8.53	0
Apr-01	45.30	0	−22.99	0	−12.53	1	−10.70	0
May-01	45.97	0	−4.07	0	−11.81	1	−8.68	0
Jun-01	47.10	0	−0.96	0	−10.64	1	−6.35	0
Jul-01	45.82	0	4.57	0	−7.97	0	−6.21	0
Aug-01	43.99	0	9.01	0	−6.45	0	−5.05	0
Sep-01	43.08	0	−0.09	0	−4.75	0	−1.74	0
Oct-01	41.55	0	1.20	0	−6.01	0	−2.20	0
Nov-01	40.37	0	8.89	0	−6.95	0	0.00	0
Dec-01	39.73	0	12.88	0	−6.09	0	1.06	0

	Domestic Credit/ GDP		Deviation of RER From 60 Months		Current Account/GDP		Inflation	
	(Growth)	Signal	(%)	Signal	(Ratio)	Signal	(Own level)	Signal
Threshold	15.0		−5.3		−8.3		6.5	
Adj n-t-s	0.42		0.85		0.42		0.42	
Jan-01	−22.32	0	23.67	0	2.79	0	1.31	0
Feb-01	−17.29	0	21.20	0	8.68	0	1.46	0
Mar-01	−17.54	0	24.15	0	2.77	0	1.39	0
Apr-01	−19.70	0	27.00	0	1.61	0	2.55	0
May-01	−21.44	0	26.03	0	3.95	0	2.78	0
Jun-01	−20.49	0	24.93	0	5.59	0	2.31	0
Jul-01	−25.67	0	24.50	0	3.50	0	2.15	0
Aug-01	−23.48	0	21.72	0	10.53	0	1.38	0
Sep-01	−0.30	0	19.32	0	3.65	0	1.37	0
Oct-01	−14.86	0	19.53	0	5.13	0	1.38	0
Nov-01	−10.70	0	17.83	0	5.59	0	0.99	0
Dec-01	−10.06	0	15.47	0	11.05	0	0.77	0

Table 2.13 (continued)

	Exports (US$)		Real GDP		Fiscal Balance/ GDP		Composite Index of Currency Crisis	Conditional Probability of Currency Crisis
	(Growth)	Signal	(Growth)	Signal	(Ratio)	Signal		
Threshold	−3.8		−1.0		−3.4			
Adj n-t-s	0.55		0.57		0.55			
Jan-01	−3.91	1	5.35	0	−3.18	0	5.82	0.08
Feb-01	−3.70	0	−0.86	0	−2.65	0	4.00	0.08
Mar-01	3.59	0	0.66	0	−2.56	0	4.00	0.08
Apr-01	−8.02	1	1.61	0	−5.00	1	7.64	0.46
May-01	6.81	0	2.92	0	5.19	0	4.00	0.08
Jun-01	−0.96	0	0.94	0	2.67	0	4.00	0.08
Jul-01	−14.18	1	7.60	0	−1.75	0	1.82	0.08
Aug-01	−7.59	1	5.70	0	1.13	0	1.82	0.08
Sep-01	−11.38	1	−8.18	1	−5.94	1	5.39	0.08
Oct-01	−14.16	1	6.09	0	−10.09	1	3.64	0.08
Nov-01	−12.30	1	0.86	0	−5.00	1	3.64	0.08
Dec-01	−13.70	1	−0.70	0	−3.72	1	3.64	0.08

Table 2.14 Leading indicators

	Signals Approach	Probit Estimates
External sector variables		
Terms of trade growth	√	
Export growth	√	√
Ratio of current account to GDP	√	√
Real exchange rate misalignment	√	√
Ratio of short-term external debt to international reserves	√	
Financial variables		
Growth of M2/international reserves	√	√
Growth of domestic credit/GDP	√	
Real sector variables		
Ratio of fiscal balance to GDP	√	√
Inflation rate	√	
Real GDP growth rate	√	√
Change in stock prices	√	√

from both the signals analysis and probit estimates conducted in this study appear quite satisfactory on both theoretical and statistical grounds.

The 1997 crisis in Thailand and its phenomenal spread has spawned a large body of literature on its analysis and its lessons. This chapter is just a humble attempt to use the available data in Thailand to study their leading or signaling nature. The study finds many statistically significant indicators. It also finds that many important indicators are lacking due to inadequate collection and dissemination. For example, the data on non-performing loans are not available before June 1998 and the series are simply not long enough to establish a reliable statistical pattern. At present, the data collection and dissemination by public authorities have improved a great deal since the 1997 crisis. Although Thailand joined the IMF Special Data Dissemination Standard (SDDS) since 1996, it was not until May 2000 that it could meet the SDDS specifications for coverage, periodicity, timeliness and advance release calendars. Also the present effort by the National Economic and Social Development Board to track the short-term movement of the economy by the Current Quarter Model (CQM) should provide a better opportunity to observe some of the early warning signals.

In hindsight, the fact that there were signals for and high probability of a currency crisis for the 1997 event indicated that there were some fundamental problems with the Thai economy that led speculators to attack the baht. The fact that the concerned authorities were not mindful of the early warning signs and decided to defend the baht almost at all costs makes ordinary citizens shudder. Now with faster reporting of data, greater transparency and improved information and indicators to monitor the economic conditions, we can hope that monetary authorities will quickly realize an imminent crisis and put out remedial measures before things get out of hand.

NOTES

* This chapter is a result of the East Asian Development Network (EADN) research project in 2002 to evaluate vulnerabilities to economic crises of East Asian countries and to learn from the 1997–98 economic crisis that severely affected most economies in the region. Since the project was finished in 2002, the data in this chapter are only up to December 2001. The author thanks Professor Lawrence R. Klein and Professor Tayyeb Shabbir, both of the University of Pennsylvania, and Dr Chalongphob Sussangkarn of Thailand Development Research Institute for their valuable comments and Miss Sanpichit Songpaisan for her research assistance.

1. Ministry of Finance (1998). In the document, it was pointed out that Thailand's net international reserves decreased from 33.8 billion dollars in December 1996 to around 1 billion dollars in July 1997. Such a huge loss was concealed by the swap operation and did not show up in the gross reserves as can be seen in the plots of Thailand's gross and net international reserves in Figure 2.1.

2. The growth of exports (in millions of US$) during 1994–95 was 21.7 percent and 24.9 percent, respectively. It went down to –1.4 percent in 1996 before picking up to 4.3 percent in 1997.
3. For instance in Argentina, Chile, Malaysia and Mexico, etc. See Kaminsky and Reinhart (1999).
4. The year 1997 was chosen just for being a convenient cut-off point. Otherwise, there is a significant amount of related literature to be reviewed. Interested readers can see a comprehensive review of earlier literature in Kaminsky et al. (1998).
5. However, for GDP, there are only quarterly data starting from the first quarter of 1993 and the monthly GDP data have to be estimated from a quarterly relationship of GDP and other variables.
6. The 10–25th percentile range may appear arbitrary but it may be looked upon as the probability of rejecting the null hypothesis when it is true, or Type I error. We may regard the normal or tranquil period as our null hypothesis and take the export growth as our indicator, for example. If we find that 10 percent of the observations post an export growth below 1 percent, we then regard any export growth below 1 percent as a signal. Such reading of the indicator may be wrong if the null hypothesis (tranquility) is true. Therefore, setting the maximum 25th percentile as the upper limit implies that we are willing to accept one-fourth probability of calling a crisis when it is not true. It is found in this study that for some indicators the percentile at which the adjusted noise-to-signal ratio is minimum is far below the 25th percentile. See more details on methodology in Kaminsky and Reinhart (1999).
7. It is notable that this number is quite different from the threshold of 5.6 found in Poonpatpibul and Ittisupornrat (2001), who used the same signals approach. Such a difference cannot be attributed to their using a 24-month horizon because in this study the threshold from the 24-month horizon for export growth is –6.9.
8. The other two composite indicators considered by Kaminsky (1999) are the following cases: a) Extreme signals are given more weight than mild signals. b) A time horizon of eight months is taken into account when adding up signals because not all indicators issue signals jointly in the same month. See more details in Kaminsky (1999).
9. The criterion for dummy variables in probit estimates is that there must be observations for which the left-hand-side variable takes both values 0 and 1 in both groups of the observations for the right-hand-side dummy variable. See Greene (1995, p. 416).

REFERENCES

Calvo, G. and C. Reinhart (1996), 'Capital Flows to Latin America: Is there Evidence of Contagion Effects?', in G.A. Calvo, M. Goldstein and Eduard Hochreiter (eds), *Private Capital Flows to Emerging Markets*, Washington, DC: Institute for International Economics, pp. 151–71.

Dodd, R. (2001), 'The Role of Derivatives in the East Asian Financial Crisis', Special Policy Report 1, Derivatives Study Center.

Eichengreen, B., A. Rose and C. Wyplosz (1996), 'Contagious Currency Crisis', Centre for Economic Policy Research Discussion Paper No. 1453, August.

Engwatana, Pipat (1999), 'Early Warning Indicators of Currency Crisis: A Case Study of Thailand', MA: Thesis, Faculty of Economics, Thammasat University.

Esquivel, Gerardo and Felipe Larrain (1998), 'Explaining Currency Crises', *Development Discussion Paper*, No. 666, Massachusetts: Harvard Institute for International Development, November.

Gerlach, S. and F. Smets (1995), 'Contagious Speculative Attacks', *European Journal of Political Economy*, **11**, 45–63.

Goldfajn, Ilan and Rodrigo O. Valdés (1997), 'Are Currency Crises Predictable?', *IMF Working Paper* WP/97/159, December.
Greene, W.H. (1995), *LIMDEP Version 7.0 User's Manual*, Econometric Software, Inc. New York.
Jeanneau, S. and M. Micu (2002), 'International Bank Lending to Emerging Market Countries: Explaining the 1990s Roller Coaster', *BIS Quarterly Review*, March, 52–64.
Kaminsky, G.L. (1999), 'Currency and Banking Crises: The Early Warnings of Distress', *IMF Working Paper* WP/99/178, December.
Kaminsky, G.L. and C.M. Reinhart (1999), 'The Twin Crises: The Causes of Banking and Balance-of-payments Problems', *American Economic Review*, **89** (3), June.
Kaminsky, G.L. and C.M. Reinhart (2000), 'On Crises, Contagion, and Confusion', *Journal of International Economics*, **51**, 145–68.
Kaminsky, G.L., S. Lizondo and C.M. Reinhart (1998), 'Leading Indicators of Currency Crisis', *IMF Staff Papers*, **45** (1), March, 1–48.
Kruger, M., P.N. Osakwe and J. Page (1998), 'Fundamentals, Contagion and Currency Crises: An Empirical Analysis', *Bank of Canada Working Paper* WP/97/159, December.
Krugman, P. (1979), 'A Model of Balance of Payments Crisis', *Journal of Money, Credit and Banking*, **11**, August, 311–25.
Krugman, P. (2001), 'Crises: The Next Generation?', Paper prepared for the Razin Conference, Tel Aviv University, March.
Mariano, R.S., A.G. Abiad, B. Gultekin, T. Shabbir and A.H.H. Tan (2002), 'Markov Chains in Predictive Models of Currency Crises – With Applications to Southeast Asia', *PIER Working Paper* No. 02-013, University of Pennsylvania.
Ministry of Finance (1998), 'Directions of Monetary and Fiscal Measures to Solve Economic Problems', a mimeograph, July (in Thai).
Obstfeld, M. (1996), 'Model of Currency Crises with Self-fulfilling Features', *European Economic Review*, **40** (3–5), April, 1037–47.
Poonpatpibul, Chaipat and Anotai Ittisupornrat (2001), 'Early Warning System', *BOT Working Paper* WP/05/2001, June (in Thai).
Tinakorn, Pranee (1998), 'Analysis of Leading Economic Indicators for Thailand', a TDRI research report in the project Short-Term Economic Model and Forecast, financed by the National Economic and Social Development Board, September (in Thai).

APPENDIX 2A

Table 2A.1 Index of currency market turbulence

	Exchange Rate		International Reserves		Index of Currency Market Turbulence				
		% change		% change	I	I+ 2sd	I>I + 2sd	I+ 1.5sd	I>I + 1.5sd
Jan-93	25.53	0.24	21 937.00	3.57	−3.60	12.60	0	9.47	0
Feb-93	25.49	−0.16	21 634.90	−1.38	1.33	12.60	0	9.47	0
Mar-93	25.42	−0.27	22 239.40	2.79	−3.28	12.60	0	9.47	0
Apr-93	25.23	−0.75	22 611.60	1.67	−2.55	12.60	0	9.47	0
May-93	25.22	−0.04	23 114.70	2.22	−2.43	12.60	0	9.47	0
Jun-93	25.21	−0.04	23 979.80	3.74	−4.07	12.60	0	9.47	0
Jul-93	25.31	0.40	23 919.70	−0.25	0.67	12.60	0	9.47	0
Aug-93	25.18	−0.51	24 222.80	1.27	−1.88	12.60	0	9.47	0
Sep-93	25.19	0.04	25 225.30	4.14	−4.41	12.60	0	9.47	0
Oct-93	25.26	0.28	25 544.40	1.26	−1.08	12.60	0	9.47	0
Nov-93	25.36	0.40	25 206.10	−1.32	1.82	12.60	0	9.47	0
Dec-93	25.45	0.35	25 438.80	0.92	−0.64	12.60	0	9.47	0
Jan-94	25.53	0.31	25 359.30	−0.31	0.65	12.60	0	9.47	0
Feb-94	25.38	−0.59	26 251.30	3.52	−4.37	12.60	0	9.47	0
Mar-94	25.29	−0.35	26 672.60	1.60	−2.08	12.60	0	9.47	0
Apr-94	25.25	−0.16	26 592.80	−0.30	0.16	12.60	0	9.47	0
May-94	25.21	−0.16	27 512.80	3.46	−3.88	12.60	0	9.47	0
Jun-94	25.14	−0.28	28 340.50	3.01	−3.51	12.60	0	9.47	0
Jul-94	24.97	−0.68	28 588.30	0.87	−1.62	12.60	0	9.47	0
Aug-94	25.02	0.20	29 064.00	1.66	−1.59	12.60	0	9.47	0
Sep-94	24.98	−0.16	29 950.20	3.05	−3.44	12.60	0	9.47	0
Oct-94	24.96	−0.08	29 851.70	−0.33	0.27	12.60	0	9.47	0
Nov-94	24.98	0.08	29 743.20	−0.36	0.47	12.60	0	9.47	0
Dec-94	25.10	0.48	30 279.00	1.80	−1.46	12.60	0	9.47	0
Jan-95	25.07	−0.12	29 906.10	−1.23	1.21	12.60	0	9.47	0
Feb-95	25.02	−0.20	30 135.60	0.77	−1.03	12.60	0	9.47	0
Mar-95	24.76	−1.04	30 119.50	−0.05	−0.98	12.60	0	9.47	0
Apr-95	24.56	−0.81	31 727.10	5.34	−6.55	12.60	0	9.47	0
May-95	24.66	0.41	33 272.40	4.87	−4.83	12.60	0	9.47	0
Jun-95	24.67	0.04	34 958.30	5.07	−5.41	12.60	0	9.47	0
Jul-95	24.74	0.28	34 415.70	−1.55	1.95	12.60	0	9.47	0
Aug-95	24.95	0.85	34 629.10	0.62	0.18	12.60	0	9.47	0
Sep-95	25.12	0.68	35 866.10	3.57	−3.16	12.60	0	9.47	0
Oct-95	25.11	−0.04	35 731.40	−0.38	0.36	12.60	0	9.47	0
Nov-95	25.16	0.20	36 204.40	1.32	−1.23	12.60	0	9.47	0
Dec-95	25.16	0.00	37 026.70	2.27	−2.44	12.60	0	9.47	0
Jan-96	25.29	0.52	37 721.20	1.88	−1.50	12.60	0	9.47	0
Feb-96	25.24	−0.20	38 694.20	2.58	−2.97	12.60	0	9.47	0
Mar-96	25.23	−0.04	38 982.50	0.75	−0.84	12.60	0	9.47	0
Apr-96	25.27	0.16	38 862.30	−0.31	0.49	12.60	0	9.47	0

Table 2A.1 (continued)

	Exchange Rate		International Reserves		Index of Currency Market Turbulence				
		% change		% change	I	I+ 2sd	I>I +2sd	I+ 1.5sd	I>I +1.5sd
May-96	25.29	0.08	39053.80	0.49	−0.45	12.60	0	9.47	0
Jun-96	25.35	0.24	39830.00	1.99	−1.90	12.60	0	9.47	0
Jul-96	25.34	−0.04	39360.60	−1.18	1.23	12.60	0	9.47	0
Aug-96	25.27	−0.28	39370.30	0.02	−0.30	12.60	0	9.47	0
Sep-96	25.36	0.36	39537.00	0.42	−0.10	12.60	0	9.47	0
Oct-96	25.46	0.39	39902.50	0.92	−0.60	12.60	0	9.47	0
Nov-96	25.45	−0.04	39613.30	−0.72	0.74	12.60	0	9.47	0
Dec-96	25.56	0.43	38724.50	−2.24	2.85	12.60	0	9.47	0
Jan-97	25.69	0.51	39233.80	1.32	−0.91	12.60	0	9.47	0
Feb-97	25.90	0.82	38149.10	−2.76	3.79	12.60	0	9.47	0
Mar-97	25.92	0.08	38065.60	−0.22	0.31	12.60	0	9.47	0
Apr-97	26.03	0.42	37320.10	−1.96	2.53	12.60	0	9.47	0
May-97	25.84	−0.73	33307.60	−10.75	10.84	12.60	0	9.47	1
Jun-97	25.75	−0.35	32353.00	−2.87	2.74	12.60	0	9.47	0
Jul-97	30.16	17.13	30424.20	−5.96	23.54	12.60	1	9.47	1
Aug-97	32.41	7.46	25938.60	−14.74	23.32	12.60	1	9.47	1
Sep-97	36.27	11.91	29612.20	14.16	−3.33	12.60	0	9.47	0
Oct-97	37.55	3.53	31287.20	5.66	−2.56	12.60	0	9.47	0
Nov-97	39.30	4.66	26253.60	−16.09	21.97	12.60	1	9.47	1
Dec-97	45.29	15.24	26967.70	2.72	12.31	12.60	0	9.47	1
Jan-98	53.71	18.59	26724.30	−0.90	19.56	12.60	1	9.47	1
Feb-98	46.30	−13.80	26156.10	−2.13	−11.51	12.60	0	9.47	0
Mar-98	41.33	−10.73	27680.00	5.83	−17.00	12.60	0	9.47	0
Apr-98	39.48	−4.48	29530.50	6.69	−11.67	12.60	0	9.47	0
May-98	39.14	−0.87	27450.50	−7.04	6.71	12.60	0	9.47	0
Jun-98	42.36	8.25	26571.70	−3.20	11.69	12.60	0	9.47	1
Jul-98	41.19	−2.77	26776.30	0.77	−3.60	12.60	0	9.47	0
Aug-98	41.58	0.94	26678.80	−0.36	1.33	12.60	0	9.47	0
Sep-98	40.41	−2.80	27290.80	2.29	−5.27	12.60	0	9.47	0
Oct-98	38.14	−5.62	28482.10	4.37	−10.31	12.60	0	9.47	0
Nov-98	36.46	−4.40	28891.40	1.44	−5.95	12.60	0	9.47	0
Dec-98	36.25	−0.58	29535.90	2.23	−2.98	12.60	0	9.47	0
Jan-99	36.59	0.94	29013.10	−1.77	2.84	12.60	0	9.47	0
Feb-99	37.06	1.28	28721.40	−1.01	2.37	12.60	0	9.47	0
Mar-99	37.51	1.21	29936.10	4.23	−3.34	12.60	0	9.47	0
Apr-99	37.60	0.24	30203.80	0.89	−0.72	12.60	0	9.47	0
May-99	37.02	−1.54	30637.20	1.43	−3.09	12.60	0	9.47	0
Jun-99	36.91	−0.30	31433.90	2.60	−3.10	12.60	0	9.47	0
Jul-99	37.11	0.54	31928.80	1.57	−1.15	12.60	0	9.47	0
Aug-99	37.98	2.34	32216.10	0.90	1.38	12.60	0	9.47	0
Sep-99	39.88	5.00	32360.20	0.45	4.52	12.60	0	9.47	0
Oct-99	39.47	−1.03	32438.10	0.24	−1.29	12.60	0	9.47	0

Table 2A.1 (continued)

	Exchange Rate		International Reserves		Index of Currency Market Turbulence				
		% change		% change	I	I+ 2sd	I>I +2sd	I+ 1.5sd	I>I +1.5sd
Nov-99	38.77	−1.77	32 842.10	1.25	−3.11	12.60	0	9.47	0
Dec-99	38.18	−1.53	34 780.60	5.90	−7.88	12.60	0	9.47	0
Jan-00	37.35	−2.16	32 630.20	−6.18	4.49	12.60	0	9.47	0
Feb-00	37.71	0.96	31 953.80	−2.07	3.19	12.60	0	9.47	0
Mar-00	37.90	0.50	32 283.90	1.03	−0.61	12.60	0	9.47	0
Apr-00	37.97	0.18	32 166.00	−0.37	0.58	12.60	0	9.47	0
May-00	38.95	2.58	31 904.20	−0.81	3.46	12.60	0	9.47	0
Jun-00	39.06	0.28	32 142.00	0.75	−0.52	12.60	0	9.47	0
Jul-00	40.22	2.97	31 929.60	−0.66	3.68	12.60	0	9.47	0
Aug-00	40.87	1.62	32 232.40	0.95	0.60	12.60	0	9.47	0
Sep-00	41.88	2.47	32 249.80	0.05	2.41	12.60	0	9.47	0
Oct-00	43.21	3.18	32 244.70	−0.02	3.19	12.60	0	9.47	0
Nov-00	43.73	1.20	32 316.10	0.22	0.97	12.60	0	9.47	0
Dec-00	43.09	−1.46	32 661.30	1.07	−2.61	12.60	0	9.47	0
Mean	31.43	0.63	31 050.33	0.53	0.06				
SD	7.46	4.13	4 835.86	3.84	6.27				

PART II

Cures and Reforms

3. The next financial crisis[1]

Barry Eichengreen

There has been considerable water under the bridge since early 1998 when then US Treasury Secretary Rubin faced the problem of financial instability made so evident by the Asian Crisis. In reality, these efforts long predate Rubin's speech. Some would trace them to the Mexican Crisis of 1994–95, which then IMF Managing Director Michel Camdessus referred to as 'the first financial crisis of the 21st century' on the grounds that financial structure and markets had played such a prominent role in its development.[2] Other observers would place the inauguration of this effort even earlier, perhaps at the time of the 1982 Mexican Crisis, out of which developed the Brady Plan, or the 1974 Herstatt Crisis that provided the impetus for the Basel Capital Accord, or even the global financial crisis of the 1930s that prompted the creation of the Bretton Woods Institutions.

So what makes this an appropriate time for stock taking? As I write, in the spring of 2005, all the ingredients are in place for a classic emerging market crisis.[3] We have come to the end of a long period when the Federal Reserve has kept interest rates low.[4] Partly in response to the FED's earlier policies, spreads on emerging market debt have fallen to very low levels. Now US policy rates are rising, and rising US rates are a traditional trigger for financial problems in emerging markets. Market participants see this coming: we have already seen a significant widening of spreads in the first half of 2005. And there are growing worries about a disorderly correction of the US current account deficit. On top of this, oil prices are rising, creating additional difficulties for emerging markets that are not energy exporters. The OECD estimates that China and India are two to three times more intensive in the use of energy than the developed countries and that an increase of $10 in the cost of a barrel of oil shaves 0.8 percent off China's rate of GDP growth.[5]

Global economic growth of course is entirely dependent on two engines: the United States and China. This makes the specter of a hard landing in China as policy-makers attempt to cool down an overheated economy, and of a dollar crash in the United States if the problem of twin deficits finally comes home to roost, particularly alarming for emerging markets. The US is the single most important market for exports of consumer goods by emerging markets, while China is far and away the most rapidly growing market for both consumer and producer goods. If either engine begins to sputter, the result could be very serious problems for emerging markets that are heavily dependent on exports for both growth and debt sustainability. And if growth slows simultaneously in both countries, the consequences could be serious indeed.

Thus, it is striking that this potentially fatal cocktail of rising US interest rates, higher oil prices and growing uncertainty about Chinese policy has not yet produced serious difficulties. One response to this observation is 'just be patient'. Give it more time, and the financial ambulance chasers among us will eventually acquire a new set of clients. But another response is that considerable progress has in fact been made in strengthening the international financial architecture. Reforms of international financial institutions and markets have strengthened the global financial system, while significant reforms in emerging market economies themselves have made these countries more resilient to mounting strains.

There is at least a kernel of truth in this point of view. Specifically, I would point to ten important reforms that have helped to make the world a safer financial place. However, these reforms have come at a cost. Each of them has had unintended consequences that are not entirely salutary from the point of view of either emerging markets or the international system.

First, emerging markets have grown more cautious since 1994, and especially since 1997, about cross-border bank borrowing as a way of accessing external finance. Less reliance on short-term finance, and less reliance on cross-border bank finance in particular, has reduced an important source of financial vulnerability. Foreign banks, for their part, have grown more cautious about cross-border lending, having been reminded of the risks of international financial intermediation by earlier crises.[6] New net flows through money markets and new bond flotations have also fallen, albeit by less than cross-border bank lending and less in Asia than Latin America.[7] Be that as it may, the point is that emerging markets have taken valuable steps to lengthen the maturity structure of their debts.[8]

Second, emerging markets have become more prudent about running current account deficits. The Institute of International Finance, at latest report, forecasts that emerging Asia will run a current account surplus of $113 billion in 2005, down only slightly from its surplus of $120 billion in 2004.[9] Latin America as a whole is running a balanced current account. Of the principal Latin countries, only Ecuador has a noticeable deficit. But elsewhere the notorious problem of current account reversals – what happens when funding for the flow deficit suddenly dries up – has been very considerably ameliorated. The one place where this is not the case is emerging Europe – that is, in countries like Hungary, Romania and Turkey.[10]

The problem with these solutions to the problem of financial instability, if we may call them that, is that they imply foregoing many of the benefits of capital mobility. In Asia we have the anomalous situation of low-income developing countries and middle-income emerging markets financing the deficits of a high-income country, the United States, and subsidizing the consumption of its residents. This is not how the international financial system is supposed to work. The growth of foreign direct investment is one thing, but portfolio capital continues to flow upstream from the developing to the developed world. Thus, this 'solution' to the problem of financial volatility comes at significant cost.

A third stabilizing development is the massive accumulation of foreign reserves by emerging markets.[11] Reserves provide insurance against financial shocks. Even if external debt cannot be rolled over, reserves are still available to service it. But they provide insurance at a cost, in the short run because the yield on US treasury bonds is less than the opportunity cost of funds, and in the long run because the twin deficits problem in the United States implies capital losses on dollar-denominated assets. Reserve accumulation is therefore a sign that net capital transfer from rich to poor countries is even less than meets the eye. And reserve accumulation in dollars exposes emerging markets to very considerable capital losses if the US currency falls.

Fourth, there is the fact of greater exchange rate flexibility. I regard this as one of the most significant reforms of the international financial architecture. Greater flexibility has reduced the temptation for governments to stick with unsustainable policies. It gives them additional capacity to use macroeconomic policy in stabilizing ways. It creates two-way bets for speculators, removing a focal point for destabilizing financial dynamics.

Except for Ecuador and Venezuela, all of the principal Latin American countries have now adopted flexible exchange rates. But while the Mexican peso now floats freely and the Brazilian real has been allowed to fall by about 9 percent since financial market participants began contemplating rising US interest rates, other emerging markets remain reluctant to let their currencies move. Asian countries, China in particular, fear the implications for export growth. Latin American countries fear the financial consequences, given the extent of exchange-rate-linked debt.[12]

Fifth, stronger fiscal policies in emerging markets have reduced the risk of old-fashioned 'first-generation' crises.[13] In Latin America, improvements in fiscal discipline were long overdue, and in the short term their implications for financial stability were strongly positive. The problem is the inability of governments to pursue their social agendas, which raises questions about the durability of political support and therefore about the sustainability of the policies. Running primary surpluses to pay off the debt also leaves a smaller share of tax revenues for investment in infrastructure and education, with negative implications for growth. In Turkey, impressive fiscal consolidation has come at the expense of education spending, which raises questions about future growth and therefore about debt sustainability. The commitment to primary surpluses also means that fiscal policy is dangerously procyclical, since the worse the country's economic performance, the larger its surplus must become.

Sixth, leverage in the international financial system has been reduced, moderating one important threat to systemic stability. Following the Long-term Capital Management Crisis in 1998, banks curtailed the amount of credit that they made available to hedge funds.[14] The 'macro funds' that were the most voracious consumers of leverage have since gone out of business or changed their investment styles. This raises hopes that if an unexpectedly rapid rise in US policy rates unleashes a flight to quality and causes sudden deleveraging, the impact on the international system will be lessened. The only problem is that recent data suggest that the use of leverage has been growing again.[15]

Seventh, multilateral surveillance of financial systems has been strengthened. I can remember visiting the IMF's Capital Markets Division in 1995 when it occupied a small bank of offices in one of the Fund's satellite buildings. Now the Capital Markets Division occupies the better part of a floor in the Fund's headquarters. The IMF issues a *Global Financial Stability Report* twice annually. There are regular reviews of prudential supervision and regulation in the context of the Financial Sector Assessment Program. But there remains the problem that IMF expertise is still heavily dominated by the macroeconomic side. The IMF continues to hire new PhD's in economics, as opposed to people with experience in bank supervision and securities market regulation. And the Capital Markets Division spends too much time writing the equivalent of low-level investment bank newsletters for internal consumption while doing too little analytical work.

Eighth, there is the effort to promulgate standards and codes designed to enhance transparency and strengthen market discipline, backed up by the Bank and Fund's Reviews of the Observance of Standards and Codes (ROSCs). While it is still early, there are some indications that the markets take these efforts seriously and reward countries that subscribe to the SDDS (Special Data Dissemination Standard) or adhere to the international financial community's other standards and codes with lower borrowing costs and improved credit ratings.[16] The problem is that the benefits may turn out to be less than meets the eye if public information crowds out private information. At least one study suggests that when countries subscribe to the SDDS or adopt internationally recognized accounting standards, there is a decline in the number of private analysts following the country, since investing in private information generation and acquisition become less profitable. The increase in the accuracy of information produced by the improvement in public information is partly offset by the reduction in the accuracy of privately generated information associated with the fall in analyst following.[17]

Ninth, there is the addition of collective action clauses (CACs) to debt securities governed by New York law. Since 2003 this contractual innovation, which was long dismissed as infeasible, has become the norm. (In the latter part of 2003 and early part of 2004, sovereign bonds containing CACs constituted more than 75 percent of the total value of total new issues.)[18] There is reason to hope that the addition of majority consent provisions to sovereign debt instruments will ease holdout problems and facilitate orderly restructuring. The prospect of less painful restructuring gives grounds for expecting that the IMF will be able to stand aside and let events run their course when countries have unsustainable debts. There will be fewer cases like Argentina in August 2001, in other words, when the Fund feels compelled to run to the rescue of a bankrupt country in order to avert fears that doing otherwise will destabilize the global financial system. This will reduce the moral hazard associated by the expectation of bailouts, in turn strengthening market discipline.

But it will take until the end of the present decade, or longer, until CACs dominate the stock of emerging market debt securities. In addition, issue-specific majority voting rules do little to facilitate coordination among the holders of different bond issues, a problem whose importance is apparent in Argentina's default. So long as coordination remains difficult, restructuring will remain difficult. It is not yet certain, in other words, that collective action clauses will make a difference.

Tenth and finally, the IMF has become more transparent. Stanley Fischer has referred with some justification to the revolution in IMF transparency that occurred on his watch.[19] The IMF now posts so much information on its website that it is difficult for its critics to keep up. Some would say that this is precisely the point. Seriously, making policy in the light of day forces the Fund to justify and defend its decisions. It enhances the institution's ability to make credible commitments. In principle, it also makes it more difficult for the Fund's principal shareholders, like the United States, to use the institution as a vehicle for advancing its foreign policy goals as opposed to addressing problems of financial instability.

But while the IMF has become more transparent, questions can still be asked about whether it has become more accountable.[20] The representativeness of its managing board can be questioned. The procedure used for selecting its managing director is hardly open, even-handed and merit-based. These problems undermine the legitimacy of the institution and hence the credibility of its commitments. Clearly, while there has been progress in the direction of greater transparency and openness, there is still an accountability problem.

This brings me to the agenda for the future. What key reforms remain incomplete? What are the most important tasks going forward? How can we continue to strengthen the international financial system while minimizing corollary damage to emerging markets?

The first item on my list, while the least exciting, is at the same time the most important. It is more business as usual. I mean redoubling efforts to strengthen banking systems, enhance shareholder rights, improve the effectiveness of corporate governance and heighten the transparency and efficiency of financial markets. This effort to improve the structure, regulation and efficiency of financial markets, first and foremost at the national level, has been the touchstone of recent efforts to strengthen the international financial architecture. There has been progress, but much remains to be done. While this observation is commonplace, it is no less important for that fact.

The second item is to create a credit culture in emerging markets. When cheap credit becomes available, it flows in large amounts into the property market and other speculative investments, with too little attention to the decline in credit quality that occurs with the pursuit of higher risk projects. More investment means faster growth, at least temporarily, which attracts more foreign investors impressed by the improvement in economic performance. The result is self-reinforcing, procyclical and dangerously unstable dynamics.

The solution to this problem is to price credit risk more efficiently. Doing so is the job of bond markets.[21] The implication is that emerging markets need better bond markets. Developing them will have a number of corollary benefits, including reducing dependence on bank finance and limiting currency and maturity mismatches. While I have doubts about the efficacy of some fashionable initiatives in this area – the Asian Bond Fund, for example – I nonetheless regard the objective, domestic bond market development, as a high priority.[22]

The third priority item should be to move to still more flexible exchange rates as a way of discouraging procyclical capital flows and permitting the authorities to provide better tailoring of credit conditions to meet local needs. China is the current poster boy for this argument, but it is only the latest example of a country that would benefit from a more flexible rate.[23] Emerging markets as a class would benefit from greater exchange rate flexibility and less fear of floating. Getting there will require putting in place the prerequisites for flexible inflation targeting – an independent central bank, sound fiscal policies and market-determined interest rates – in countries where they do not already exist. It will require moving away from outdated commitments to export-led growth in countries like Taiwan and South Korea where the export sector is no longer the exclusive locus of learning effects and productivity spillovers, and where educating and retaining knowledge workers will require a better balance of investment between traded and non-traded goods sectors.[24] In Latin America, it will require measures to reduce liability dollarization and to help countries acquire the capacity to borrow abroad in local currency.

This brings me to the fourth priority, namely measures to address the inability of emerging markets to borrow abroad in their own currencies. The evidence is overwhelming that institutional and policy reform at the national level, by themselves, will not solve this problem anytime soon.[25] Stronger policies and institutions help to solve many problems, to be sure, but not obviously this one. Chile has admirably strong policies and institutions, but it still cannot borrow abroad in its own currency. This suggests that the problem resides at least in part in the structure of international financial markets. International investors reap limited diversification benefits from adding a variety of currencies to their portfolios while incurring significant transactions costs from managing positions in relatively small, illiquid markets. The smaller a country, the greater the difficulty it has in getting its currency added to the global portfolio.[26]

Part of the solution is for the World Bank and regional development banks to borrow and lend in these currencies. Their AAA credit rating permits them to do so with relative ease. The issuance of World Bank debt denominated in pesos will supply the high-quality benchmark asset that investors need in order to price riskier credits. It will increase the installed base of local currency denominated securities. It will enhance market liquidity. In turn, this will make positions in assets denominated in these currencies more attractive to international investors. From this point of view, the decision of the Asian Development Bank to issue in Chinese yuan, Thai baht and Indian rupees is an important step. So was the decision of the Inter-American Development Bank to include a local currency conversion clause in a $300 million loan to Mexico in May of 2005. These are valuable precedents; the World Bank and other regional development banks need to respond in kind.

The fifth and final priority should be to address governance problems at the Bretton Woods Institutions. Admittedly, it is easier to advocate reform of IMF governance than to specify exactly what steps should be taken. (If nothing else, this is a salutary reminder to high-income countries urging developing economies to strengthen corporate governance that moving from statements of high policy to implementation is easier said than done.) Clearly, recommendations for the reform of IMF governance should start with a statement of which objectives of governance are most poorly achieved. My own view is that the key problems are those of stakeholder representation and management accountability. Seats and votes in the IMF reflect historical circumstances, specifically what was the disproportionate weight of a few high-income countries, notably the United States, in the much less multi-polar world economy that existed when the Fund was created at the end of World War II. The countries with seats and votes disproportionate to their place in the world economy and their stake in the IMF have naturally resisted suggestions for reforms that reduce their power. This leads to the under-representation of Asian countries that are some of the fastest-growing members of the international economy and that loom increasingly large in the operation of the international system and the African countries that are the subject of the bulk of IMF programs. The 85 per cent of IMF members that are not advanced industrial countries have only 50 per cent of the seats on the executive board. The 46 sub-Saharan African countries that are chronic users of IMF resources are represented by just two executive directors. The result is complaints that inappropriate policies are being foisted on crisis economies by the governments of the United States and other high-income countries that dominate decision-making in the IMF. Even if conditionality and lending decisions were little different in a more representative Fund, giving other members more voice in the formulation of such policies would enhance their legitimacy and thereby 'ownership' of programs by the crisis countries. Ultimately, it would enhance the effectiveness of IMF policy.

On the question of accountability, the IMF is both inadequately accountable to governments and other stakeholders in general and excessively accountable to the advanced industrial countries and the United States in particular. The opacity of IMF decision-making and the multidimensional nature of the institution's objective function make it hard to hold those responsible for the policies of the institution accountable for their actions. Who remembers who was fired in the wake of the Argentine fiasco? The answer is not the managing director (or those responsible for international economic policy at the US Treasury, which pushed for the August 2001 loan) but the head of the Latin American department. Arguably, differences in board composition and voting shares in the Fund would have led to different consequences and greater accountability.

Hence, my recommendations for the reform of IMF governance would be addressed at these aspects of governance. They would include addressing problems of representativeness by increasing the share of basic votes and restoring the principal of universality that was acknowledged when the institution was originally established. At present, each country has 250 basic votes plus one additional vote for each part of its quota equivalent to

100 000 Special Drawing Rights, on which basis both its contribution and ability to draw resources are calibrated, while quotas are calculated on the basis of a complicated set of formulas that in practice place substantial weight on country size and current account volatility. Quotas have been increased in the course of 11 reviews in order to reflect better the growth of countries and their balances of payments, but without also increasing basic votes. Consequently, the share of basic votes has fallen from 11 percent in 1945 and 14 percent in 1955, by which time additional members had been admitted, to only 2 percent today. Increasing the share of basic votes would go some way toward restoring the principle of universality and enhance the representation of the poor countries that are frequently the subject of IMF programs. In addition, using GDP at purchasing power parity rather than GDP at market exchange rate prices in quota calculations would enhance the voice of rapidly growing countries like those of Asia that are chronically under-represented in the Fund.

I would also favor appointing a single executive director for the European Union. Rationalizing Europe's board representation in this way will free up chairs on the Executive Board for under-represented countries. The majority of EU members have a single currency. Hence, there is no more possibility of balance-of-payments problems among them than there is scope for balance-of-payments problems between US states. If a financial crisis develops in an EU member state, the bailout, for better or worse, will be extended by its partners in the European Union and not by the IMF. In addition, the Fund should rely more heavily on the International Monetary and Financial Committee for defining the objectives and strategies of the institution (including meetings of IMFC heads of state, which can substitute for G7/8 summits). This will be possible insofar as the composition of the IMFC becomes more representative as quotas and constituencies are adjusted.

It should also be possible to strengthen the frankness of staff surveillance by creating a presumption that staff studies written for Article IV consultations will be published. Staff performance assessments could be revised to give greater weight to ability to make independent, candid judgments, and a presumption could be established that reports of the IMF's own Independent Evaluation Office would be published. By further enhancing transparency, these steps will strengthen the accountability of the institution. They will enhance the efficiency of IMF governance by limiting doubts that political pressures, both internal to the Fund and from national sources, are unduly influencing staff assessments. They will reassure those who worry that, in the absence of adequate transparency and accountability, a handful of advanced economies have disproportionate influence in the Fund as a result of their personal, political and intellectual connections.

Finally, selection of the managing director and deputy managing directors should be based on considerations of technical qualification rather than nationality. The current arrangement whereby European governments get to nominate the managing director of the Fund and the US government gets to pick the first deputy managing director de-legitimizes the institution in the eyes of many governments and NGOs. An open competition would be more likely to lead to selection of the best man or woman for the job.

Given such a lengthy list of incomplete reforms, how immediate is the residual crisis risk? Under what circumstances might a crisis arise? Might we be on the verge of one now, given the rise in US interest rates and global oil prices? If so, which countries will be affected?

As will be evident from the preceding, policies and institutions have been strengthened significantly in the last 11 years, particularly since the Asian Crisis of 1997–98. This means that a large shock would be required to destabilize a major emerging market, much less the international financial system. Such a shock is not inconceivable. Specifically, one can imagine simultaneous slowdowns in the US and China, removing the two locomotives that have been also exclusively responsible for global growth.[27] This might occur if international investors lost faith in US policies and abruptly stopped financing its current account deficit, and if the revaluation of the Chinese yuan was bungled.[28] The effects would be particularly disruptive if it turned out that one or more major financial institutions in the advanced countries had large positions in derivatives that left them exposed to the subsequent change in relative prices. This is clearly on the minds of Federal Reserve officials such as Timothy Geithner (2004) and Alan Greenspan (2005).

While this is not the most likely scenario, neither can we rule it out. If growth slowed significantly in both the US and China, the demand for the exports of emerging markets would fall. Global interest rates would rise sharply as the FED found it necessary to raise interest rates faster than currently expected in response to the collapse of the dollar and its inflationary consequences. Doubts about the stability of major financial institutions and markets in the face of these rapid changes would cause a flight to quality that further curtailed capital flows to emerging markets. This in turn would force the sudden compression of current account deficits where these had been allowed to reach high levels. And the reallocation of resources necessary to effect that shift would require major changes in exchange rates, specifically significant depreciation where current account deficits had been allowed to widen, which could cause distress for banks and firms with currency and maturity mismatches on their balance sheets. All this will sound disturbingly familiar to those who remember the Asian Crisis.

What countries are we talking about? The answer this time around is the emerging markets of Central and Eastern Europe that have allowed large current account deficits to develop and that are financing them mostly or entirely with portfolio capital inflows. Specifically, I mean Hungary, Romania and Turkey, which have current account deficits in the order of 6 to 8 percent of GDP at the time of writing. These countries are widely regarded as 'convergence plays', the assumption that their interest rates will come down to Western European levels as a result of their recent or imminent accession to the European Union and the consequent 'Europeanization' of their policies.[29] But if capital flows turn around, growth will slow, budget deficits will widen and the stability of financial systems will be undermined. Again, this will sound alarmingly familiar to those who recall the Asian Crisis. Some say that this time is different – that, unlike previous episodes, rising US policy rates and tightening global credit conditions will not precipitate a crisis in emerging markets. I am not so sure.

NOTES

1. This chapter is a considerable revision of a speech given on 'Economics Day' at the University of Pennsylvania in May 2005. The chapter also draws on my plenary address to the 3rd Annual PECC Finance Conference, Santiago, in June 2004 and the 50th anniversary conference of Seoul National University, Seoul 2005. I thank participants in all these meetings for their comments and reactions.
2. See Camdessus (1995).
3. The parallels with previous crisis periods are unmistakable; see Eichengreen and Fishlow (1998).
4. In the early 1990s the reason was to cope with the Savings & Loan Crisis in the United States. This time around, the rationale was fear of deflation.
5. And 1 percent off India's.
6. To be sure, international banks are even more active in emerging markets than was the case ten years ago. But they now fund most of their lending activities in those markets out of local deposits. However much their presence enhances the efficiency of international financial intermediation, this does not make foreign banks a source of external finance.
7. After peaking at $150 billion in 1995, net private debt flows to developing countries fell steadily for three years, approaching zero in 1999. Net bond-related flows fell by half, from $49 billion in 1996 to $19 billion in 2001, while bank loans fell even more dramatically, from $51 billion in 1998 to negative levels the following year. In 2000 net debt flows to developing countries were negative; in 2001 and 2002 they were barely positive. If one limits one's attention to the subgroup of developing countries classified by the Institute of International Finance as emerging markets – supposedly the leading destinations for capital flows – the picture is essentially the same.
8. Turkey and Brazil are cases in point. The maturity of the debt lengthened from an average of 7.7 months in January 2001 to 15.3 months in June 2004. Fixed rate debt has been raised from 25 percent of total domestic debt in 2002 to 38 percent today. And foreign-currency indexed or denominated debt has declined from 32 percent of domestic debt in 2002 to 19 percent today. In Brazil, the average maturity of the domestic debt has risen to some 20 months from little more than five at the time of the 1998–99 crisis.
9. See IIF (2006).
10. I will come back to this.
11. Most obviously in Asia but in Latin America as well.

12. Fear of floating, as this phenomenon is labeled by Calvo and Reinhart (2000), is still a problem, in other words.
13. First-generation crises as modeled by Krugman (1979) and Flood and Garber (1984) are crises where a deterioration in domestic policies leads to a speculative attack that collapses the exchange rate ex post. This is in contrast with second-generation models where the speculative attack on the exchange rate leads to the deterioration of domestic policies that validates the attack ex post (for example, Obstfeld, 1986). I claim the credit – or the blame – for coining this terminology (in Eichengreen et al., 1995).
14. See Eichengreen and Park (2002).
15. At least so far as we can tell, given that information on the still largely unregulated hedge fund industry is thin on the ground.
16. See for example Cady (2004); Christofides et al., (2003); Gelos and Wei (2002); and Glennerster and Shin (2003).
17. See Tong (2004).
18. See IMF (2004).
19. See Fischer (2001).
20. Many of the same questions apply to the World Bank.
21. See Xie (2004) for a more elaborate discussion of this point. Banks, in contrast, tend to be too easily influenced by their customers – and the government – and in any case they operate in the less transparent, more information-impacted segments of the economy.
22. See Eichengreen (2004a) for some of these doubts.
23. Eichengreen (2004b) elaborates this argument. Currently, when the Chinese authorities attempt to clamp down on the provision of bank credit to reduce property market speculation and the danger of overheating, capital simply flows in from abroad and enters the property market through non-bank channels. This is the classic 'trilemma' of not being able to have an independent monetary policy when the exchange rate is pegged and the capital account is increasingly porous (whether the authorities like it or not). A more flexible exchange rate would go a considerable way toward squaring this circle.
24. That is to say, more investment in universities and housing.
25. For evidence on this see Eichengreen and Hausmann (2005).
26. For evidence, see Eichengreen et al. (2003).
27. This is the scenario in Goldstein (2005).
28. Which might not in fact be two independent events.
29. Hungary became a member of the EU in 2004. Romania will join at the beginning of 2007 while Turkey's (presumably lengthy) accession negotiations are underway.

REFERENCES

Cady, John (2004), 'Does SDDS Subscription Reduce Borrowing Costs for Emerging Market Economies', *IMF Working Paper* No. 04/58, April, www.imf.org.

Calvo, Guillermo and Carmen Reinhart (2000), 'Fear of Floating', *Quarterly Journal of Economics*, **117**, 379–408.

Camdessus, Michel (1995), 'Drawing Lessons from the Mexican Crisis: Preventing and Resolving Financial Crises – the Role of the IMF', Address at the 25th Washington Conference of the Council of the Americas, Washington, DC, 22 May, www.imf.org.

Christofides, Charis, Christian Mulder and Andrew Tiffin (2003), 'The Link between Adherence to International Standards of Good Practice, Foreign Exchange Spreads, and Ratings', *IMF Working Paper* No. 03/74.

Eichengreen, Barry (2004a), 'The Unintended Consequences of the Asian Bond Fund', unpublished manuscript, University of California, Berkeley.

Eichengreen, Barry (2004b), 'Is a Change in the Renminbi Exchange Rate in China's Interest?', *Asian Economic Papers*, **4**, 40–75.

Eichengreen, Barry and Albert Fishlow (1998), 'Contending with Capital Flows: What is Different About the 1990s?', Occasional paper, Council on Foreign Relations.

Eichengreen, Barry and Ricardo Hausmann (eds) (2005), *Other People's Money: Debt Denomination and Financial Instability in Emerging Market Economies*, Chicago: University of Chicago Press.

Eichengreen, Barry and Bokyeong Park (2002), 'Hedge Fund Leverage Before and After the Crisis', *Journal of Economic Integration*, **17**, 1–20.

Eichengreen, Barry, Ricardo Hausmann and Ugo Panizza (2003), 'Currency Mismatches, Debt Intolerance and Original Sin: Why They Are Not the Same and Why It Matters', *NBER Working Paper* (December).

Eichengreen, Barry, Andrew Rose and Charles Wyplosz (1995), 'Exchange Market Mayhem: The Antecedents and Aftermath of Speculative Attacks', *Economic Policy*, **21**, 249–312.

Fischer, Stanley (2001), 'Farewell to the IMF Executive Board', 30 August, http://www.imf.org/external/np/speeches/2001/083001.htm.

Flood, Robert and Peter Garber (1984), 'Collapsing Exchange Rate Regimes: Some Linear Examples', *Journal of International Economics*, **17**, 1–13.

Geithner, Timothy (2004), 'Perspectives on the U.S. Financial System', Speech to the Economic Club of New York, 27 May, http://www.newyorkted.org/newsevents/speeches/2004/gei040527.htm.

Gelos, Gaston and Shang-Jin Wei (2002), 'Transparency and International Investor Behavior', *IMF Working Paper* No. 02/174.

Glennerster, Rachel and Tongseok Shin (2003), 'Is Transparency Good for You, and Can the IMF Help?', *IMF Working Paper* No. 03/132.

Goldstein, Morris (2005), 'What Might the Next Emerging-market Financial Crisis Look Like?', unpublished manuscript, Institute for International Economics (April).

Greenspan, Alan (2005), 'Risk Transfer and Financial Stability', Speech to the Federal Reserve Bank of Chicago's 41st Annual Conference on Bank Structure, Chicago, Illinois, 5 May, www.federalreserve.gov/boarddocs/speeches/2005/20050505/.

Institute of International Finance (IIF) (2006), 'Capital Flows to Emerging Market Economies', Washington, DC: Institute of International Finance (15 September).

International Monetary Fund (IMF) (2004), 'Progress Report to the International Monetary and Financial Committee on Crisis Resolution', 20 April, www.imf.org.

Krugman, Paul (1979), 'A Model of Balance of Payments Crises', *Journal of Money, Banking and Credit*, **11**, 311–25.

Obstfeld, Maurice (1986), 'Rational and Self-fulfilling Balance of Payments Crises', *European Economic Review Papers and Proceedings*, **76**, 72–81.

Tong, Hui (2004), 'Transparency Standards and Financial Market Efficiency', unpublished manuscript, University of California, Berkeley.

Xie, Andy (2004), 'The Calm before the Storm', *Morgan Stanley Global Economic Forum* (26 May).

4. Capital controls, financial crises and cures: simulations with an econometric model for Malaysia*

Lawrence R. Klein, Roberto S. Mariano and Süleyman Özmucur

1 INTRODUCTION

Capital flows to developing countries grew substantially during the post-1990 period. With liberalization of the capital account a country becomes more vulnerable to outside effects. Domestic policy-makers have a problem in controlling their economy as seen in many countries (Mariano et al., 2002). Controls have been advocated to deal with financial crises. They help to slow down capital flight and depletion of international reserves. Krugman (1998) indicated that countries facing major crisis may benefit from temporary imposition of controls, by giving time to lower domestic interest rates and adopt a growth package. The reaction to the imposition of controls may be negative in international financial markets. There is a delicate balance between liberalization and controls. As Tobin (2001) concluded 'Integration of finance throughout the world can be of benefit to developing, emerging, and transition economies, but not without some limits.' The 'Tobin Tax' gained considerable popularity among many international economists as a way to raise liquid funds, but Tobin often said that his intent was 'to put sand in the wheels' in order to slow down crises in early stages of trouble.

Effects of capital controls, especially on economic growth, are highly debated (among others Calvo, 1998; Edison et al., 2002; Goldstein et al., 2000; IMF, 1998a, 1998b; Kahler, 1998; Kaminsky and Reinhart, 1998, 1999, 2000; Klein, 1998; Krugman, 1979, 1998; Rodrik, 2001; and Salvatore, 1998). There are cross-country studies, as well as case studies using different methodologies. This chapter offers another method to study possible effects of capital controls, which takes feedback mechanisms in the economy into consideration. The proposed approach is the use of a macro-econometric model for Malaysia. A simultaneous equation model has the advantage of incorporating various aspects of the economy, and analyzing possible effects on many variables as well as on the growth, which is generally the focus of attention.

The major conclusion of the chapter is that capital controls in Malaysia had many desired effects on growth, inflation and balance of payments, without doing much harm to the attraction of foreign direct investment, in the medium run.

The chapter is in four sections. Section 2 is devoted to a very brief review of earlier studies. Main characteristics of the macroeconometric model are summarized in the third section. Simulation results are given in section 4, and major conclusions are stated in the final section.

2 A BRIEF REVIEW OF STUDIES ON CAPITAL CONTROLS AND FINANCIAL CRISES

It is argued that with liberalization of the capital account a country becomes more vulnerable to outside effects. The instability caused by liberalization can be compensated by a higher growth rate to follow, largely due to greater availability of capital (Summers, 2000). Stiglitz (2000) draws attention to the need for the distinction between various forms of capital flows, and advocates the flow of foreign direct investment [FDI]). Singh (2003) argues that 'even FDI, if unregulated, may do more harm than good to many countries'.

Edison et al. (2002) survey the effects of capital account and stock market liberalization on economic growth, and conclude that there is support for a positive effect of capital account liberalization on growth, especially for developing countries.

Eichengreen and Leblang (2003) state that capital controls influence macroeconomic performance through two channels, directly with a positive impact on resource allocation and efficiency and indirectly by limiting the disruptive effects of crises. There are significant flows of capital toward sectors where the rate of return is high, provided financial markets are working well. In that case, liberalization leads to a more efficient allocation of resources and to faster economic growth. If there are problems in domestic and/or international financial markets, the consequences can be less favorable. They also demonstrate the ability of controls to neutralize the disruptive effects of crises. Since vulnerability to crises varies across countries and with the structure and performance of the international financial system, 'the effects of capital account liberalization on growth are contingent and context specific'. They present empirical results using a panel of 21 countries covering a longer period of 1980–97, and a wider panel for the post-1971 period to support their arguments.

Kaplan and Rodrik (2001) study how Malaysia performed compared with Thailand and Korea when they were all undergoing IMF programs. The reason for making that comparison was their view on Malaysian policies in the summer of 1998, which seemed to be unsustainable. They argue that pressure against the ringgit was building up, and the economic decline was not about to be reversed on its own. Controls were introduced to contain the joint effects of crisis, stabilization and especially contagion to others in the region. They use difference-in-differences method and monthly and quarterly data to show that Malaysian policies including capital controls produced faster economic recovery compared with its neighbors.

Edison and Reinhart (2000) use monthly and daily data to study effectiveness of capital controls in Malaysia, Thailand, Philippines and South Korea. Their GARCH(1,1) models using daily data indicate that capital controls were significant in reducing volatility in daily interest rates and daily changes in interest rates in Malaysia, and increasing volatility in daily stock returns in Thailand. They conclude that controls led to a greater stability in interest rates and exchange rates in Malaysia, but not in Thailand. A possible explanation given for the difference was the existence of offshore banking centers that provided leakages and arbitrage opportunities in Thailand. Attention was drawn to differences between experiences of Thailand and Malaysia. First, Thailand was undergoing speculative attacks when they tried to use capital controls as a defense mechanism; Malaysia was not. Second, Malaysian controls were quite broad and aimed to eliminate all loopholes and speculations, while controls in Thailand were not as comprehensive.

Mariano et al. (2002) constructed a Markov-switching autoregressive model that allows intercepts, lag coefficients and error variances to switch stochastically over time according to the value taken by a latent Markov chain describing the vulnerability of the country's currency to speculative attacks. Estimates of Markov-switching models for Indonesia, Malaysia, the Philippines and Thailand were obtained using monthly data from 1974 to 1998. The estimated models are mean-switching and variance-switching models of month-to-month percentage changes in nominal exchange rates, with transition probabilities in the Markov chain depending on deviations of real effective exchange rates from trend (REER), year-on-year percentage changes in the ratio of money supply (M2) to gross international reserves, and year-on-year percentage changes in real domestic credit. Real exchange rate overvaluation (relative to trend) is an important explanatory variable for predicting a switch from normal periods to vulnerable periods. The two other early warning variables, growth in real domestic credit and M2/reserves, showed only moderate importance, entering into the final specifications only in selected countries. There is good evidence for the importance of non-performing loans in crisis prediction. However, differences in definitions and treatment of these loans among countries render the use of it difficult. After the Asian Crisis, there have been efforts for standardization of the definition of non-performing loans, which will eventually enable researchers to use it as one of the critical indicators.

For all four countries, one regime is a normal period with zero mean and low volatility in exchange rate percentage changes. The other regime is a financially vulnerable period with positive mean and high volatility in the dependent variable. Forecast probabilities of a vulnerable period, given past information, are calculated from the estimated model. Such forecast probabilities rise substantially for Malaysia and Thailand in early 1997 – before the start of the Asian Crisis in July 1997 – but do not send strong signals for Indonesia and the Philippines.

3 MAIN CHARACTERISTICS OF THE MACROECONOMETRIC MODEL

The model is a simultaneous equations system designed to address the needs in short-term and medium-term forecasting and in scenario and policy analysis (Klein et al., 2002). The model covers all the major sectors of Malaysia's economy and the feedback linkages among them. It serves as a quantitative tool of Bank Negara in forecasting economic variables at a disaggregated level, in analyzing the macroeconomic impact of policy measures, and in simulating scenarios of interest to the Bank. There is a very detailed treatment of balance of payments, public sector and the financial sector.

The macroeconometric model contains 438 equations in seven blocks. Of these equations, 259 are stochastic, and 179 are identities. There are 607 variables, of which 438 are endogenous, and 169 are exogenous. The relatively large size of the model is a direct result of the need for capturing basic features of the Malaysian economy. These features may be summarized as the openness of the economy, diversity of exports ranging from agricultural commodities to semiconductors, diversity in the banking sector, and the significance of the public sector in the production as well as in the decision-making process.

There are ten production and employment sectors. These sectors are agriculture, mining, manufacturing, electricity, construction, wholesale and retail trade, transportation and communication, finance, government services, and other services. In addition, production of major commodities in agriculture and mining are also treated as endogenous variables. These commodities are rubber, saw logs, palm oil, kernel oil, cocoa, crude oil, tin and natural gas. Industrial production indexes for major manufacturing sub-categories are also estimated in the model. There are five private investment categories, namely, agriculture, manufacturing, mining, construction and other.

There is a very detailed section on the export component of the balance of payments. The capital account is also treated as endogenous. Both foreign direct investment and portfolio investment are treated endogenously in the model. Interest rates, exchange rates and equity prices are explained within the model.

Because of the public sector's significance, the model has a detailed public sector block. Public revenues are determined within the model, using the appropriate base for the revenue being considered. Current expenditures are also treated as endogenous. Development expenditures are treated as exogenous. Non-financial public enterprises, state and local governments' accounts are also studied in detail. The financial sector is also treated in detail. Monetary base and money supply are determined by the net claims of the government, net claims of the private sector, and net claims of the external sector. Money demand equations are estimated, assuming equilibrium in the money market. Banking sector balance sheets are treated in detail.

The in-sample forecasting performance of the model is assessed through static and dynamic simulations of the model over the period 1990–2001. The one-period simulation indicates that the major macroeconomic variables can be predicted within reasonable error margins (in terms of mean absolute percentage error or MAPE): GDP with 6 percent, private consumption with 5.1 percent, total investment with 5.2 percent, and prices (CPI and the implicit GDP deflator) with 1.5 percent and 3 percent, respectively. For the unemployment rate and the interest rate, the relevant performance indicator is either mean absolute error (MAE) or root mean square error (RMSE). The mean absolute errors are 124 basis points for the unemployment rate. These errors are rather low when compared with those from other models; the model is relatively successful in tracking historical values.

4 SIMULATIONS WITH THE MODEL

The model was solved (dynamic solution) for the 1997–2005 period for a baseline solution. The scenario of 'no capital controls' was the alternative (simulation). In the model, there is a capital control dummy that is equal to 1 in 1994, 1998 and 1999, and 0 for other years.[1] This dummy variable is set to 0 (no controls) for the period 1997–2005 to obtain the alternative solution. The difference (or the percentage difference) between the simulation and the baseline were calculated to see the possible effects of the 'no capital controls' policy. The results are obtained for all endogenous variables, but for brevity, results for only selected variables are provided here.

The real GDP would have been 0.08 percent higher in 1998 without controls (Figure 4.1). This effect turns to negative 0.01 percent in 1999, negative 0.12 percent in 2000 and 0.02 percent in 2001. The overall effect is negative, indicating that GDP would have been lower without capital controls. The GDP deflator would have been 0.04 percent higher in 1998, and 0.03 percent higher in 1999. The percentage differences are negative, but quite small in magnitude, after 1999. The overall effect is positive, indicating that GDP deflator would have been higher without capital controls.

The real exports of goods and services would have been 0.15 percent higher in 1998 without controls (Figure 4.1). This effect turns to negative 0.01 percent in 1999, negative 0.22 percent in 2000, and 0.02 percent in 2001. The overall effect is negative, indicating that real exports of goods and services would have been lower without capital controls. The real imports of goods and services would have been 0.10 percent higher in 1998 without controls. This effect turns to negative 0.01 percent in 1999, negative 0.12 percent in 2000, and 0.02 percent in 2001. The overall effect is negative, indicating that real imports of goods and services would have been lower without capital controls.

The real private consumption expenditures would have been 0.08 percent higher in 1998 without controls. This effect turns to negative 0.01 percent in 1999, negative 0.11 percent in 2000 and 0.01 percent in 2001. The overall effect is negative, indicating that real private consumption expenditures would have been lower without capital controls. The real private fixed investment would have been 0.23 percent higher in 1998 without controls. This effect turns to negative 0.01 percent in 1999, negative 0.28 percent in 2000 and 0.02 percent in 2001. The overall effect is negative, indicating that real private fixed investment would have been lower without capital controls.

The real government consumption expenditures would have been 0.028 percent lower in 1998, and 0.022 percent lower in 1999 without controls. This effect turns to 0.02 percent in 2001, 0.005 percent in 2001 and 0.01 percent in 2002. The overall effect is negative, indicating that real government consumption expenditures would have been lower without capital controls. The real government fixed investment would have been 0.010 percent lower in 1998, and 0.008 percent lower in 1999 without controls. This effect turns to 0.006 percent in 2001, 0.002 percent in 2002. The overall effect is negative, indicating that real government fixed investment would have been lower without capital controls.

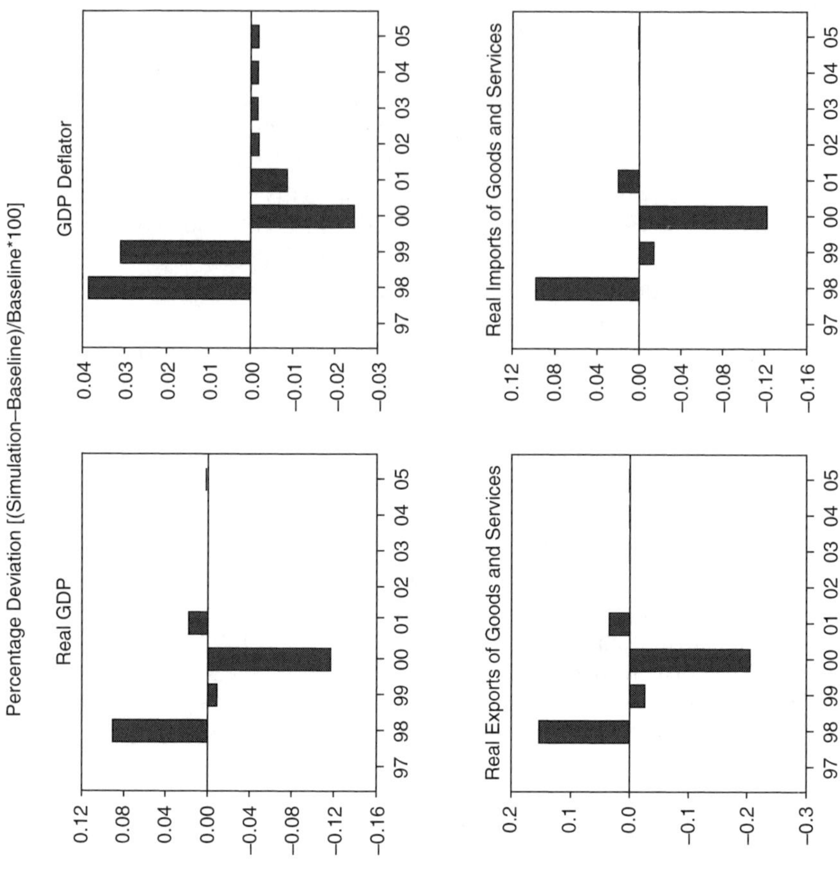

Percentage Deviation [(Simulation–Baseline)/Baseline*100]
Real GDP
GDP Deflator
Real Exports of Goods and Services
Real Imports of Goods and Services

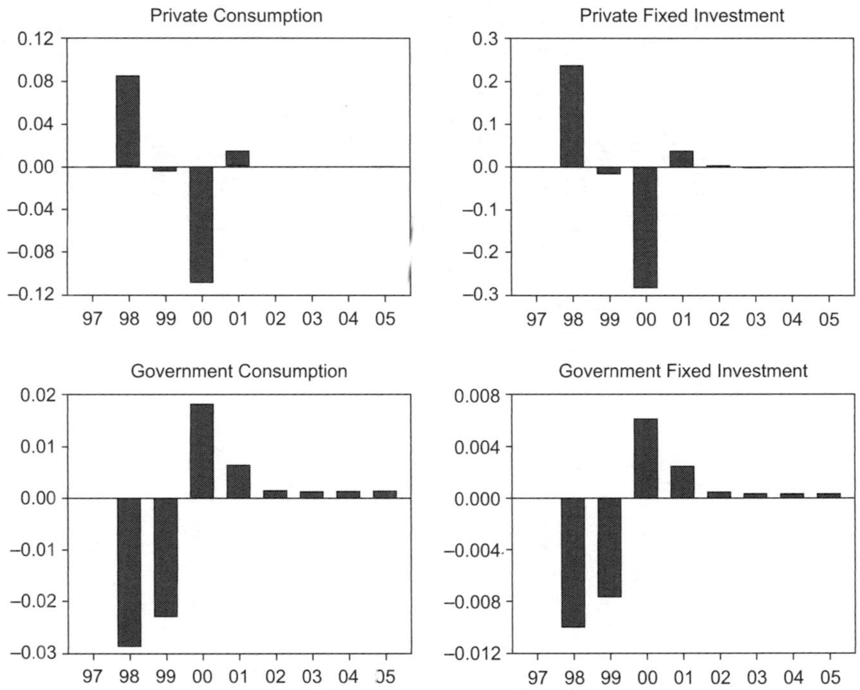

Figure 4.1 Effects of capital controls on real indicators and the GDP deflator

The government's total tax revenues would have been 0.08 percent higher in 1998, and 0.10 percent higher in 1999 without controls (Figure 4.2). This effect turns to negative 0.08 percent in 2000, and negative 0.12 percent in 2001. The overall effect is a small negative, indicating that government tax revenues would have been lower without capital controls. Similar results are obtained for total revenues of the government. The federal budget balance would have been about 50 million ringgits higher both in 1998 in 1999 without controls. This effect turns to negative 60 million in 2000, and negative 80 million in 2001. The overall effect is negative, indicating that federal government budget balance would have been lower without capital controls. The federal government debt would have been 40 million ringgits lower in 1998, 90 million lower in 1999 and 40 million lower in 2000 without controls. This effect turns to 30 million in 2001, and remains in the neighborhood of 10 million until 2005. The overall effect is negative, indicating that federal government debt would have been lower without capital controls. It should be noted that this is largely driven by domestic debt.

The effect of capital controls on net private capital flows is of special interest. The net effect on long-term private capital flows is negative, but very small in magnitude (Figure 4.3). The effect on the short-term capital flows is also small in magnitude and negative. The net private short-term capital flows would have been 200 million higher in 1999. The figure turns to be negative 300 in 2000, and negative 280 in 2001, and positive 400 in 2002. The net effect is very small, especially when these are compared with the effects on the current account and the balance of payments. There is a significant effect on the current account, and hence the basic balance and the overall balance of payments. The balance of payments could have been 2500 million lower in 1998 and 2800 million lower in 1999. The effects are much smaller in following years. The corresponding figures for the basic balance were 2600 million in 1998 and 3200 million in 1999. The major determinant of the change in the basic balance is the change in the current account balance.

The initial effect on interest rates would have been higher in 1998, but generally smaller in 1999 and 2000 if there were no capital controls (Figure 4.4). The overall effect on interest rates and exchange rates is quite small. However, since the model is an annual one it is not possible to study another interesting question, namely the volatility of interest rates, and stock prices as done by Edison and Reinhart (2000).

All in all, temporary controls of capital flows in Malaysia achieved intended goals of keeping inflation under control, and resuming growth without much distortion in foreign exchange and financial markets. A coordinated stabilization policy was the key to a successful outcome.

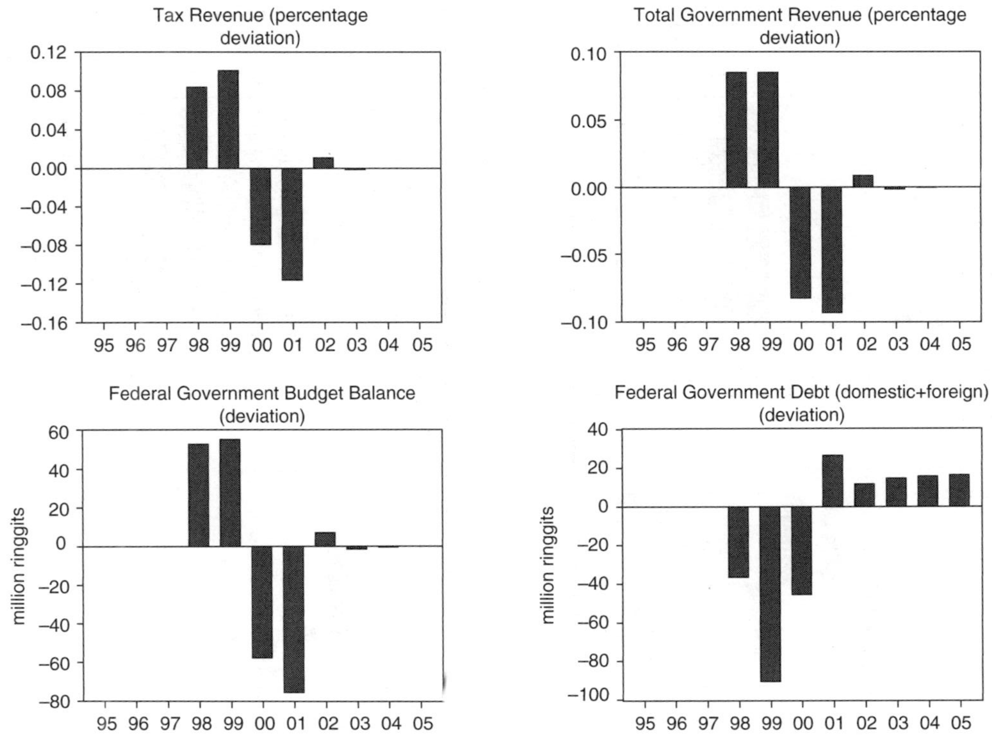

Figure 4.2 Effects of capital controls on government revenues, balance and debt

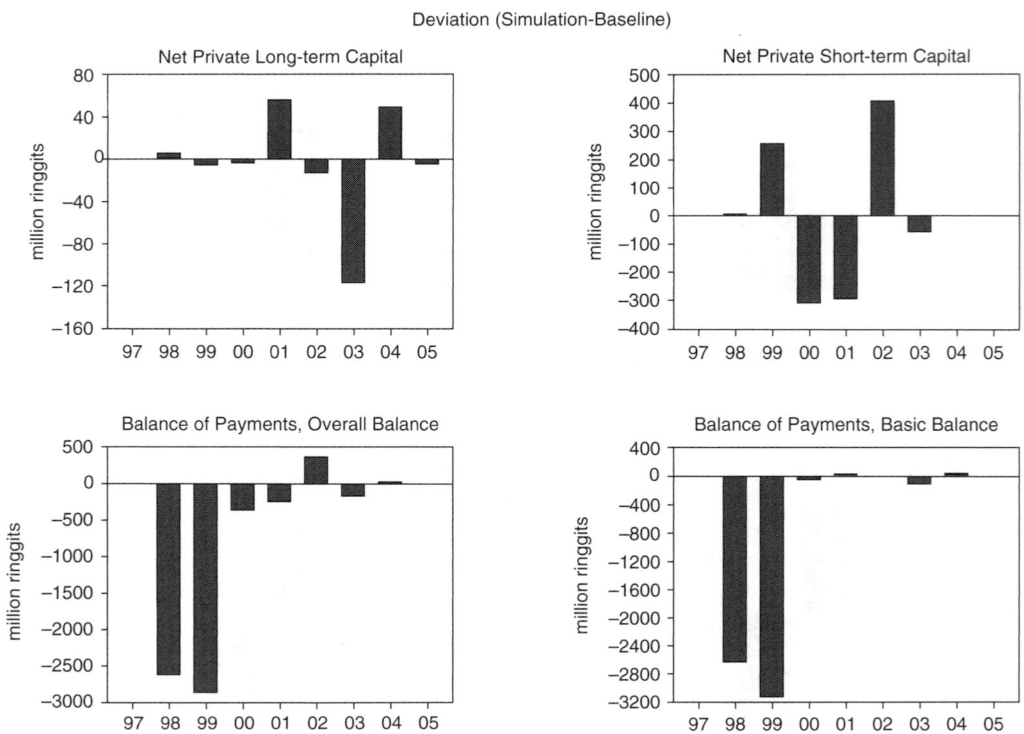

Figure 4.3 Effects of capital controls on balance of payments

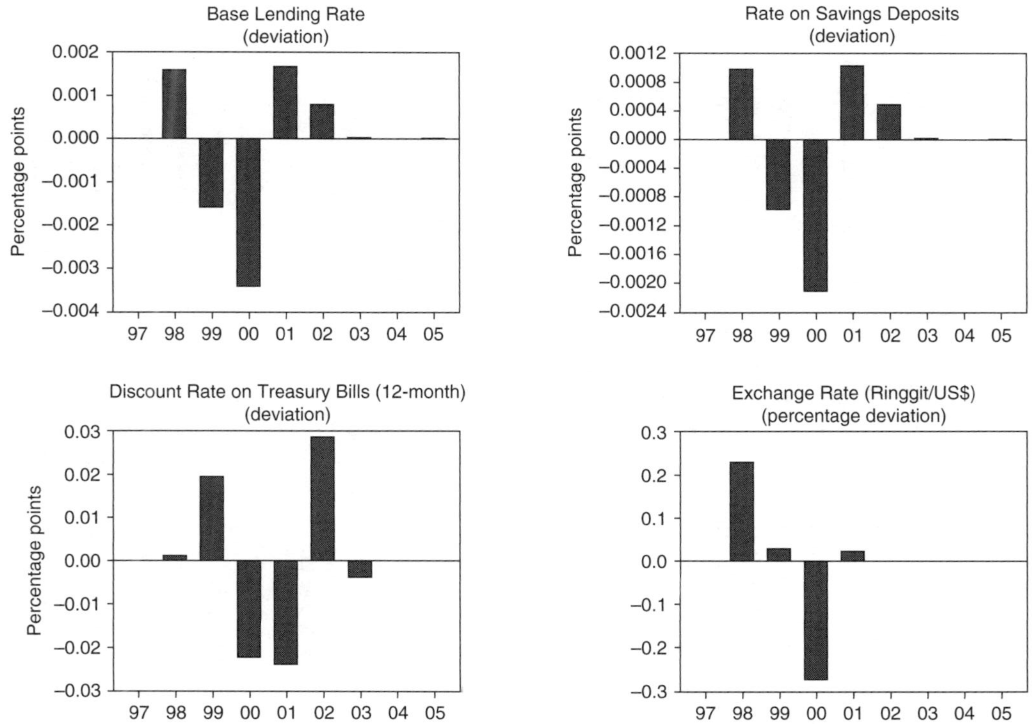

Figure 4.4 *Effects of capital controls on interest rates and exchange rates*

5 CONCLUSION

Results based on alternative methods indicate that capital controls worked well in Malaysia, but not in Thailand. The timing, the dosage, degree of commitment to and the duration of a policy as well as initial conditions are critical determinants of the success of a policy. Controls over capital flows are no exception to this general rule.

A simultaneous equation macroeconometric model is used to study possible effects of capital controls. Simulation results indicate that controls improved the performance of the Malaysian economy. A probable channel is the reduction of the level of uncertainty surrounding the key prices such as the exchange rate and the interest rate.

There are lessons to be learned from the Malaysian experience. Probably, the first requirement is to have the house in order. This is a necessary but not a sufficient condition. A small open economy is always vulnerable to external shocks, and policy making is always more difficult in such an open economy because of lack of control over most of the policy instruments usually employed. There is definitely a need for early warning indicators of financial vulnerability such as real exchange rate overvaluation, growth in real domestic credit and ratio of money supply to reserves.

NOTES

* The views expressed in this chapter are those of the authors and do not necessarily represent those of the Central Bank of Malaysia.

1. Using a dummy variable indicates the existence of controls, but not the intensity of controls. There are attempts to measure the intensity to alleviate the limitation of using a dummy variable. See Edison and Warnock (2002).

REFERENCES

Calvo, G. (1998), 'Capital Flows and Capital Market Crises: The Simple Economics of Sudden Stops', *Journal of Applied Economics*, **1** (1), 35–54.

Edison, H.J. and C.M. Reinhart (2000), 'Capital Controls During Financial Crises: The Case of Malaysia and Thailand', Board of Governors of the Federal Reserve System International Finance Discussion Papers No. 662, Washington, DC, March (mimeo).

Edison, H.J. and F.E. Warnock (2002), 'A Simple Measure of the Intensity of Capital Controls', Board of Governors of the Federal Reserve System International Finance Discussion Papers No. 708, Washington, DC, October (mimeo).

Edison, H.J., M. Klein, L. Ricci and T. Slok (2002), 'Capital Account Liberalization and Economic Performance: A Review of Literature', *IMF Working Paper* 02/120, Washington, DC.

Eichengreen, B. and D. Leblang (2003), 'Capital Account Liberalization and Growth: Was Mr Mahathir Right?', *NBER Working Paper* No. 9427, January.

Goldstein, M., G. Kaminsky and C.M. Reinhart (2000), *Assessing Financial Vulnerability: An Early Warning System for Emerging Markets*, Institute for International Economics, Washington, DC (June).

IMF (1998a), *International Financial Markets*, Washington, DC.

IMF (1998b), *World Economic Outlook*, Washington, DC.

Kahler, M. (ed.) (1998), *Capital Flows and Financial Crises*, Ithaca: Cornell University Press.

Kaminsky, G.L. and C.M. Reinhart (1998), 'Financial Crises in Asia and Latin America: Then and Now', *American Economic Review*, **88** (2), 444–8, May.

Kaminsky, G.L. and C.M. Reinhart (1999), 'The Twin Crises: The Causes of Banking and Balance of Payments Problems', *American Economic Review*, **89** (3), 473–500.

Kaminsky, G. and C.M. Reinhart (2000), 'On Crises, Contagion, and Confusion', *Journal of International Economics*, **51** (1), June, 145–68.

Kaplan, E. and D. Rodrik (2001), 'Did the Malaysian Capital Controls Work?', *NBER Working Paper* No. 8142, Cambridge, MA, February.

Klein, L.R. (1998), 'Financial Crises in Asia and Development Issues', Department of Economics, University of Pennsylvania, Philadelphia, PA (mimeo).

Klein, L.R., R.S. Mariano and S. Özmucur (2002), 'BNM Macroeconometric Model of Malaysia', Bank Negara Malaysia, Kuala Lumpur, July (mimeo).

Krugman, P. (1979), 'A Model of Balance of Payments Crises', *Journal of Money, Credit, and Banking*, **11** (August), 311–25.

Krugman, Paul (1998), 'Saving Asia: It's Time to Get Radical', *Fortune*, 8 September.

Mariano, R.S., B.N. Gultekin, S. Özmucur, T. Shabbir and C.E. Alper (2002), 'Predictive Models of Economic Financial Crises', Report for the Economic Research Forum (ERF) for the Arab countries, Iran and Turkey, December (mimeo).

Rodrik, D. (2001), *Has Globalization Gone Too Far?*, Institute for International Economics, Washington, DC.

Salvatore, D. (1998), 'Capital Flows, Current Account Deficits, and Financial Crises in Emerging Market Economies', *International Trade Journal*, **12** (1), 5–22, Spring.

Singh, A. (2003), 'Capital Account Liberalization, Free Long-term Capital Flows, Financial Crises and Economic Development', *Eastern Economic Journal*, Spring, **29** (2), 191–216.

Stiglitz, J.E. (2000), 'Capital Market Liberalization, Economic Growth, and Instability', *World Development*, **28** (6), 1075–86.

Summers, L. (2000), 'International Financial Crises: Causes, Prevention and Cures', *American Economic Review Papers and Proceedings*, May, **90** (2), 1–16.

Tobin, J. (2001), 'International Trade and Financial Markets', *Japan and the World Economy*, **13**, 499–502.

5. The case of the missing market: the bond market and why it matters for financial development

Richard J. Herring and Nathporn Chatusripitak

1 INTRODUCTION

Over the last decade, interest in the role of finance in economic growth has revived. Building from the pioneering work of Goldsmith (1965) and the insights of Shaw (1973) and McKinnon (1973), the more recent work examines the role of financial institutions and financial markets in corporate governance and the consequent implications for economic growth and development. Levine (1997) and Stulz (2000) have provided excellent reviews of this literature and Allen and Gale (2000) have extended it by developing a framework for comparing bank-based financial systems with market-based financial systems.[1] Although the literature addresses 'capital markets', on closer inspection the main focus is really equity markets. Bond markets are almost completely overlooked.[2]

Although the omission of the bond market is not defended in the literature, one could argue that it does little violence to reality. As Table 5.1 shows, in most emerging economies in Asia, bond markets are very small relative to the banking system or equity markets.[3] Moreover, the most striking theoretical results flow from a comparison of debt contracts with equity contracts and at a high level of abstraction bank lending can proxy for all debt. In any event, data are much more readily available for equity markets and the banking system than for bond markets, even in the United States.

In contrast to the academic literature, however, policy-makers have become increasingly concerned about the absence of broad, deep, resilient bond markets in Asia. The World Bank (Dalla et al., 1995, p. 8) has published a study of emerging Asian bond markets urging that Asian economies 'accelerate development of domestic . . . bond markets', and has launched another major study aimed at helping countries develop more efficient bond markets. Along with Malaysia, Hong Kong has led the way. Hong Kong has succeeded in fostering development of an active fixed-income market in

Table 5.1 The size of bond versus equity and loan markets (as a percentage of GDP, average 1990–97)

	Bank Credit	Stock Market Capitalization	Bonds Outstanding
Hong Kong	140.7	193.2	11.3
Indonesia	46.0	18.4	1.8
Malaysia	103.2	197.0	68.5
Philippines	33.2	51.6	33.1
Singapore	96.6	137.5	28.4
South Korea	96.7	35.2	40.3
Thailand	87.4	57.3	9.9
Canada	92.4	57.3	81.8
Japan	176.5	77.1	90.1
United States	111.9	79.2	138.2
Euro-area	86.0	33.5	83.9
Non-euro EU	105.4	93.0	67.6

Source: World Bank Financial Structure and Economic Development Database.

exchange fund bills and notes even though the government has not run significant deficits (Sheng, 1994 and Yam, 1997). In 1998, the Asia-Pacific Economic Cooperation (APEC 1999) formed a study group to identify best practices and promote the development of Asian bond markets. Much of this official concern stems from the perception that the absence of bond markets made several Asian economies more vulnerable to financial crisis. The Governor of the Bank of Thailand (Sonakul, 2000) reflected this view when he observed, 'If I [could] turn back the clock and have a wish [list] . . . high in its ranking would be a well-functioning Thai baht bond market'. (In the concluding section we will discuss not only Thailand's efforts to nurture a bond market, but also the broader initiatives of the Executives' Meeting of East Asia-Pacific Central Banks [EMEAP].)

In this chapter, we consider why bond markets are so underdeveloped relative to equity markets and the banking sector. In addition, we investigate what the absence of a well-functioning bond market may imply for savings, the quality and quantity of investment and for risk management. Our analysis leads us to conclude that the absence of a bond market may render an economy less efficient and significantly more vulnerable to financial crisis.

If a government wishes to enhance efficiency and financial stability by nurturing the development of a bond market, what are the appropriate policy remedies? We review the key requirements for developing a broad, deep, resilient bond market and conclude with an analysis of recent financial development in Thailand, which is broadly representative of the wide range of countries that have highly developed equity markets and a large banking sector, but until very recently, only the most rudimentary bond market.

2 OVERVIEW OF THE FINANCIAL SECTOR AND FLOW OF FUNDS ANALYSIS

The impact of the financial sector on the real economy is subtle and complex. What distinguishes financial institutions from other firms is the relatively small share of real assets on their balance sheets. Thus, the *direct* impact of financial institutions on the real economy is relatively minor. Nonetheless, the *indirect* impact of financial markets and institutions on economic performance is extraordinarily important. The financial sector mobilizes savings and allocates credit across space and time. It provides not only payment services, but more importantly products that enable firms and households to cope with economic uncertainties by hedging, pooling, sharing and pricing risks. An efficient financial sector reduces the cost and risk of producing and trading goods and services and thus makes an important contribution to raising standards of living.

The structure of financial flows can be captured in flow of funds analysis, a useful analytical tool for tracing the flow of funds through an economy. This device has been used for evaluating the interaction between the financial and real aspects of the economy for nearly half a century (Copeland, 1955 and Goldsmith, 1965, 1985). The basic building block is a statement of the sources and uses of resources for each economic unit over some period of time, usually a year.

Our analysis of the relationship between the financial sector and economic performance will proceed in stages. In the first stage, we consider how an economy would perform without a financial sector in order to provide a clear benchmark for comparison. The second stage introduces direct financial claims in an environment with severe information asymmetries. The third stage considers financial intermediaries that transform the direct obligations of investors into indirect obligations of financial intermediaries that have attributes that savers prefer. The fourth stage introduces the government sector and the international sector.

2.1 Savings and Investment without Financial Markets or Institutions

In order to understand the role of the financial sector in enhancing economic performance, it is useful to begin with a primitive economy in which

Table 5.2 Sources and uses of funds for the household sector

Uses (U) Flows	Sources (S) Flows
• Real assets	• Net worth (savings)
• *Equity*	• *Financial liabilities*
• *Direct financial assets*	• *Foreign financial liabilities*
• *Indirect financial assets*	
• *Claims on government*	
• *Foreign financial assets*	
• Total assets	• Total liabilities and net worth

there is no financial sector. Without financial instruments, each household would necessarily be self-financing and would make autonomous savings and investment decisions without regard for the opportunity cost of using those resources elsewhere in society.

In this case households are the fundamental economic unit of analysis and the sources and uses of resources accounts (Table 5.2) reflect the changes in each household's balance sheet over the year. Since, at this point financial instruments do not exist, all assets are real and there are no liabilities. (Other categories of financial instruments that will be introduced later are in italics.) Changes in real assets, here the accumulation of goods, reflect savings or changes in net worth; dissaving results in corresponding declines in real assets.

The fundamental decisions that influence economic performance – (1) how much to consume and save; (2) how to allocate the flow of savings; and (3) how to allocate the existing stock of wealth – depend on each autonomous household's opportunities, present and expected future income, tastes, health, family composition, the costs of goods and services and confidence in the future. Although barter transactions among households would permit some specialization in production, the extent of specialization would be severely limited by the necessity for each household to be self-financing.

By aggregating sources and uses of accounts for each economic unit, a matrix of flows of funds can be constructed for the entire economy. For illustrative purposes, we present a primitive economy with two households in Table 5.3. Although other sectors are listed, they are irrelevant at this stage of the analysis because we have assumed that there are no financial instruments that can link one sector to another. These parts of the matrix (which will be introduced later) are in italics.

In this example, we have inserted arbitrary entries for each household. Household 1 is saving 80 units of current income, while household 2 saves

Table 5.3 The flow of funds matrix for an economy without a financial sector

Sectors	Household 1		Household 2		Non-financial Firms		Financial Institutions		Rest of World		Total	
Flows of Real Income	U	S	U	S	U	S	U	S	U	S	U	S
Savings		80		40								120
Real Assets	80		40								120	
Financial Flows												
Equity												
Fixed Income Instruments												
Indirect Financial Instruments												
Financial Instruments Issued by Foreign Residents												
Totals	80	80	40	40							120	120

only 40. If productive opportunities were fortuitously distributed across households in such a way that each household earned precisely the same rate of return on its stock of real assets, this economy could prosper without a financial sector. Such an outcome is highly unlikely, however, because investment opportunities and desired savings are apt to differ markedly across households. Moreover, there is no assurance that households with high savings have commensurately greater or more profitable real investment opportunities.

If, for example, household 2's desired investment exceeded its current savings, its investment would have to be postponed until it could accumulate sufficient savings. This would be true even if its investment opportunities offer substantially higher returns than the investment opportunities available to household 1. Assume further that household 1's investment opportunities are less productive than household 2's. Since household 1 does not have access to the superior investment opportunities of household 2, it may undertake inferior investment projects or save less. Society's flow of savings is inefficiently allocated and the stock of investment is less productive than it might otherwise be. Both the quality of capital formation and the quantity of future output suffer, and the standard of living in this society is less than it would be if household 1 could be induced to transfer some of its resources to household 2 in exchange for a financial claim.

A 'financial claim' is a contractual agreement entitling the holder to a future pay-off from some other economic entity. Unlike a real asset, it does not provide its owner with a stream of physical services. Rather it is valued for the stream of pay-offs it is expected to return over time. The financial claim is both a store of value and a way of redistributing income over time, which may be much more attractive to savers than the stream of services that savers could anticipate from their own investment opportunities in real assets.

Given the assumptions in our simple case, it is conceivable that a bargain could be arranged between household 1 and household 2. In exchange for household 1's real assets, household 2 could issue a financial claim to household 1 that would promise a more attractive pattern of pay-offs than the investment opportunities available to household 1. This reallocation of assets between household 1 and household 2 could increase the return on capital formation for this society. Indeed, the possibility of investing in financial claims that are more attractive than household 1's own real investment opportunities might even increase the savings of household 1 and thus increase the total quantity as well as the quality of capital formation.[4]

2.2 Flows with Direct Financial Claims but no Secondary Market

To examine how a financial sector affects the economy, we will introduce the direct financial claims suggested above. The exposition is further simplified by introducing a second sector in the economy. Assume that firms specialize in investing in real assets financed by issuance of direct financial claims, while households specialize in saving and investing in these direct financial claims. Financial claims are reflected in the flow of funds accounts as *sources* of funds for firms and as *uses* of funds for households. Households continue to hold real assets, but most real assets appear on the balance sheets of firms. At this stage, we will assume that direct claims cannot be traded in well-organized secondary markets. Issues of direct claims are, in effect, private placements that will be held by households until they mature or the firm is liquidated.

The flow of funds matrix in Table 5.4 illustrates such a system and reflects the sort of qualitative changes that occur when an economy first begins to specialize in production. It differs from the flow of funds matrix in Table 5.3 in

Table 5.4 The flow of funds matrix for an economy with private placement of direct claims

Sectors	Household 1		Household 2		Non-financial Institutions		Financial Institutions*		Rest of World*		Total	
Flows of Real Income	U	S	U	S	U	S	U	S	U	S	U	S
Savings		87		43		10						140
Real Assets	7		2		131						140	
Financial Flows												
Equity	60		31			91					91	91
Fixed Income Instruments	20		10			30					30	30
Indirect Financial Assets												
Financial Instruments Issued by Foreign Residents												
Totals	87	87	43	43	131	131					261	261

Note: * Entries for these columns are developed in later tables.

three respects: (1) firms hold most of the real assets; (2) households hold direct financial claims on firms in lieu of most of their previous holdings of real assets; and (3) household savings have increased by (an arbitrary) ten units to reflect the enhanced level of income that could be gained from reallocating real assets to more productive uses. Generally, the higher an economy's per capita income, the higher the ratio of financial assets to real assets.

What makes this reallocation of resources possible? What induces households to exchange real assets for direct financial claims on firms? The simple answer is that the direct financial claims that firms offer, promise more attractive rates of return than households could expect to earn from investing in real assets themselves. In short, they shift from real investment to the purchase of financial claims because they expect it to be profitable to do so. But this superficial answer ignores several important obstacles that must be overcome in order to induce savers to give up real assets in exchange for direct financial claims.

The fundamental problem is that, once savers no longer invest in real assets directly, they must worry about the performance of those who act as their agents and undertake the real investments to determine the returns on their financial investments. Households are confronted with a principal/agent problem in which they must deal with the possibility of hidden actions and hidden information (Arrow, 1979). They must be concerned about 'adverse selection' – the possibility that they may inadvertently invest in incompetent firms with poor prospects instead of competent firms with good productive opportunities. And they must be concerned with 'moral hazard' – the possibility that firms may not honor their commitments once they have received resources from investors. In order to protect against adverse selection and moral hazard, households must spend resources in deciding how to allocate savings. The activities involved include: (a) collecting and analyzing information about firms; (b) negotiating a contract that will limit the firm's opportunities for taking advantage of the saver; (c) monitoring the firm's performance; and, if necessary, (d) enforcing the contract. In the absence of strong accounting standards, good disclosure practices, strong legal protections for holders of direct claims and an efficient judiciary and enforcement function, the information and transactions costs may be so great that direct financing is not feasible.

In economies where the financial infrastructure – accounting and disclosure practices, the legal framework and clearing and settlement arrangements – is not sufficiently well developed to support arms-length direct financial transactions, other non-market mechanisms for allocating savings are likely to arise. Households may be linked together with firms through family groups rather than in the marketplace.

Family ties may substitute for a strong financial infrastructure in two ways. In the absence of strong accounting and disclosure practices, information is likely to flow more readily within families than between unrelated parties. Moreover, reputation within the family may substitute for information. Thus, the adverse selection problem is likely to be mitigated for investment in direct claims within the family group. Moreover, in the absence of strong legal protections for creditors and minority shareholders, families have enforcement mechanisms such as the threat of disinheritance, withholding of affection, or expulsion from the family that may mitigate moral hazard.

In the absence of efficient capital markets, family groups may serve as a quasi-financial system, pooling the savings of several related households to finance a family-controlled firm in which the governance structure of the family substitutes for capital market discipline. As the family enterprise succeeds, it will accumulate retained earnings that can be used to finance new family enterprises. To some extent, the growth of family-controlled industrial conglomerates in emerging economies can be viewed as an adaptation to the absence of efficient capital markets. In several of the emerging markets of Asia, more than 50 percent of publicly traded corporations are family-controlled (Claessens et al., 1998a).

This mode of allocating capital has several potential disadvantages relative to that which would take place in a well-functioning capital market. Firms are not confronted with the true opportunity cost of funds in the economy, so investment may be too great or too small. Similarly, firms lose the aggregation of information that takes place in a well-organized capital market and may pursue inefficient investment projects far too long in the absence of market discipline. Finally, the economy's reliance on financial flows within family groups raises high barriers to entry by unaffiliated firms, which may have more attractive investment opportunities.[5]

As the family financial conglomerate grows in complexity, it is likely to form an enterprise that will coordinate financial flows within the group. This financial enterprise may also offer services to non-family members and become a bank.

2.3 The Financial Sector with Financial Intermediaries

Banks and other financial intermediaries purchase direct financial claims and issue their own liabilities; in essence, they transform direct claims into indirect claims. The fundamental economic rationale for such institutions is that they can intermediate more cheaply than the difference between what the ultimate borrowers would pay and the ultimate saver would receive in a direct transaction. Financial intermediaries enhance the efficiency of the financial system if the indirect claim is more attractive to the ultimate saver and/or if the ultimate borrower is able to sell a direct claim at a more attractive price to the financial intermediary than to ultimate savers.

A comparison of the flow of funds matrix for an economy with only direct financial claims (Table 5.4) with the flow of funds matrix for an economy with both direct and indirect financial claims (Table 5.5) reveals a more complex pattern of financing,[6] characteristic of the financial deepening that usually accompanies economic development (Goldsmith, 1965). The household sector has substituted much of its holdings of direct financial claims for 'indirect financial claims' on financial firms. Correspondingly, financial firms hold most of the direct financial claims on non-financial firms. Also, the household sector has a better opportunity to borrow from financial institutions because the scale of borrowing by individual households seldom warrants the heavy fixed costs of issuing a direct financial claim.

But how can financial institutions link some savers and investors more efficiently than direct market transactions between the household sector and non-financial firms? Several factors may explain the relatively greater

Table 5.5 The flow of funds matrix for an economy with private placement and financial institutions

Sectors	Households		Non-financial Firms		Financial Institutions		Govern-ment*		Rest of World*		Total	
Flow of Real Income	U	S	U	S	U	S	U	S	U	S	U	S
Savings		145		12		5					0	162
Real Assets	12		148		2						162	0
Financial Flows												
Equity	10			34	28	4					38	38
Fixed Income Instruments	25	7		105	87						112	112
Indirect Financial Instruments	105		3			108					108	108
Financial Instruments Issued by Foreign Residents												
Totals	152	152	151	151	117	117					418	418

Note: * Entries for these columns are developed later.

efficiency of financial intermediaries. First, financial intermediaries may be able to collect and evaluate information regarding creditworthiness at lower cost and with greater expertise than the household sector. And, when some information regarding creditworthiness is confidential or proprietary, the borrower may prefer to deal with a financial intermediary rather than disclose information to a rating agency or to a large number of individual lenders in the market at large.

Second, transactions costs of negotiating, monitoring and enforcing a financial contract may be lower for a financial intermediary than for the household sector since there are likely to be economies of scale that can be realized from investment in the fixed costs of maintaining a specialized staff of loan monitors and legal and workout experts. In addition, by handling other aspects of the borrower's financial dealings, the financial intermediary may be in a better position to monitor changes in the borrower's creditworthiness.

Third, the financial intermediary can often transform a direct financial claim with attributes that the borrower prefers into an indirect claim with attributes that savers prefer. Borrowers typically need large amounts for relatively long periods of time, while savers prefer to hold smaller-denomination claims for shorter periods of time. By pooling the resources of many savers, the financial intermediary may be able to accommodate the preferences of both the borrower and savers.

Fourth, the financial intermediary often has a relative advantage in reducing and hedging risk. By purchasing a number of direct claims on different borrowers whose prospects are less than perfectly correlated, the financial intermediary is able to reduce fluctuations in the value of the portfolio of direct claims, given the expected return, relative to holdings of any one of the direct claims with the same expected return. Diversification reduces the financial intermediary's net exposure to a variety of risks and thus reduces the cost of hedging.

The upshot is that the introduction of bank deposits is likely to mobilize additional savings that can be used to finance investment, since some households will now substitute bank deposits for holdings of precious metal, jewelry and other durable assets that are traditionally used as a store of wealth. The increase in the pool of savings available to finance investment and the reduction in transactions costs in linking ultimate savers and investors will lead to an increase in the quantity of investment. Improved evaluation and monitoring of loans made possible by the specialization of banks may lead to better screening and implementation of investment projects and thus improve the return on investment. These changes are reflected in Table 5.5 where both household sector savings and real assets have risen. Total household savings have risen from 130 units to 145 units and retained earnings have risen from 10 units to 17 units.

Although the bank loans introduced in this section and the private placements introduced in the preceding section are forms of debt, it is important to note that they have strikingly different properties than marketable debt securities. A 'pure loan' is a credit contract between a borrower and a single lender. The contract is custom-tailored to meet the borrower's financial requirements and the lender's need for assurances regarding the borrower's creditworthiness. Because the contract involves only one lender, it may be renegotiated at relatively low cost should the borrower's circumstances change. Often the lender has specialized expertise regarding the business of the borrower that enables the lender to monitor the borrower's performance at relatively low cost. The 'pure loan' is usually part of a relationship between the borrower and lender in which the borrower may draw down and repay loans over time, the lender monitors the activities of the borrower, and the borrower may purchase other services from the lender. A pure loan is likely to be an illiquid asset because, relative to a pure security of equal maturity, only a small percentage of the full market value of the asset can be realized if it is sold at short notice. The fundamental problem is that it is difficult for a potential buyer to evaluate the credit standing of the debtor. Moreover, the transactions costs of finding a counterparty and executing a transaction are likely to be very high because the idiosyncratic features of a 'pure loan' preclude the development of dealer markets.

A 'pure security', in contrast, is a contract between the borrower and many investors who may be unknown to the borrower and need have no other relationship to the borrower. The investor need not have any specialized knowledge of the borrower's business. Each investor is issued an identical type of claim on the borrower, which is readily transferable. A 'pure securities' contract is much simpler than a loan agreement, containing fewer covenants and contingent clauses, because after the security is issued, it is impractical to renegotiate terms of the contract with the borrower; the costs of coordinating collective action among a large number of (often anonymous) investors are prohibitive.

A 'pure security' of a given maturity is likely to have a much more liquid secondary market than a 'pure loan' of equal maturity. The issuance of securities in primary markets is directed to many investors, all of whom hold identical claims and none of whom is necessarily privy to information about the borrower not available to the others. The standardization of claims facilitates the development of dealer markets and leads to lower transactions costs in selling securities. Since buyers in the secondary market need not fear that sellers know more than they do about securities being offered in the market, buyers can safely ignore the identity of the seller. In contrast, loan contracts may be highly idiosyncratic, and the originating lender may have information about the borrower, or specialized expertise about the borrower's business, not available to potential buyers. The loan contract may also have contemplated some degree of monitoring by the lender that the purchaser would be obliged to perform unless the loan were serviced by the seller. These features severely limit the marketability of conventional loans. Unless a buyer receives a full guarantee from the original lender or some trusted third party, the buyer must make the same investment in information that the original lender made, and/or monitor the loan agreement, perhaps without the expertise of the original lender.

2.4 The Government and International Sector

In order to complete the flow of funds matrix, we need to introduce two additional sectors. First, the government sector affects the flow of funds in two distinct ways. It issues direct claims to banks that serve as the reserve base for the money supply. It also issues direct claims to finance its own spending when desired government expenditures for purchases of goods and services and the redistribution of income exceed current tax revenues.

Table 5.6 shows the flow of funds matrix that incorporates the government sector. The government is shown with a deficit of 33 units that causes a corresponding reduction in net savings for the economy. Some economists argue that current deficits lead to a one-for-one increase in household savings in anticipation of higher future tax burdens (Barro, 1974). Other economists regard this view as too extreme in light of the empirical evidence (Hausman and Poterba, 1987). Table 5.6 depicts a case in which households make a partial response to the government deficit: household savings rise from 145 units to 150 units. The government issues 45 units of financial liabilities to fund its current and capital expenditures as well as its subsidies to favored private sector borrowers. In our example, real sector investment declines in spite of subsidies from the government to the private sector. Total real sector

Table 5.6 The flow of funds matrix for a closed economy with a government sector

Sectors	Households		Non-financial Firms		Financial Institutions		Govern-ment		Rest of World*		Total	
Flows of Real Income	U	S	U	S	U	S	U	S	U	S	U	S
Savings		150		12		5	33				33	167
Real Assets	7		118		2		7				134	0
Financial Flows												
Equity	10			34	28	4					38	38
Fixed Income Instruments	30	10		77	97		5	45			132	132
Indirect Financial Assets	113		5			118					118	118
Financial Instruments Issued by Foreign Residents												
Totals	160	160	101	101	127	127	45	45			423	423

Note: * Entries for these columns are developed later.

assets decline from 162 units in Table 5.5 to 134 units in Table 5.6, indicative of the 'crowding out' of private sector investment by government funding demands.

Second, to complete the flow of funds, we add the international sector. As national economies have become increasingly interdependent, cross-border financial transactions of all kinds have become commonplace. Opening a country to trade in financial assets offers advantages similar to those that we observed in introducing financial instruments in the primitive economy. World savings may be allocated more efficiently so that national income in all countries is increased. International specialization on the basis of comparative advantage in financial services, like international specialization in production, is likely to enhance efficiency. Competition from foreign institutions also stimulates innovations to cut costs and expand the range of products. Moreover, the broader range of financial instruments available enhances the scope for diversification to reduce country-specific risks.

Table 5.7 shows the complete flow of funds matrix. In this example the national economy is running a current account deficit of 28 units. This deficit is financed by net financial inflows that provide both debt and equity

Table 5.7 The flow of funds matrix for an open economy

Sectors	Households		Non-financial Firms		Financial Institutions		Govern-ment		Rest of World		Total	
Flows of Real Income	U	S	U	S	U	S	U	S	U	S	U	S
Savings		155					33			28	33	183
Real Assets	7		134		2		7				150	0
Financial Flows												
Equity	13			41	28	5			5		46	46
Fixed Income Instruments	27	10		98	81		5	45	40		153	153
Indirect Financial Assets	116		5			136			15		136	136
Financial Instruments Issued by Foreign Residents	2				30					32	32	32
Totals	165	165	139	139	141	141	45	45	60	60	550	550

investment to the domestic economy and by drawing down some of the domestic economy's holdings of foreign assets. Household savings reflect the benefits of opening the economy to the world capital market by increasing to 155 units. The non-financial sector also benefits from the net inflow of capital. Net domestic real investment increases from 134 in Table 5.6 to 150 in Table 5.7.

3 THE ROLE OF FINANCIAL INFRASTRUCTURE AND EFFICIENT FINANCIAL MARKETS

The economy that we have sketched in the preceding section has a banking system, but only a rudimentary capital market. The absence of an adequate financial infrastructure meant that direct claims tended to be allocated through extended families rather than through arm's-length transactions in the marketplace. Most corporate borrowing was in the form of bank loans.

The underdevelopment of capital markets in this economy limits risk-pooling and risk-sharing opportunities for both households and firms. It also robs the economy of a crucial source of information that helps coordinate decentralized decisions throughout the economy. Interest rates and equity prices should be used by households in allocating income between consumption and savings and in allocating their stock of wealth. And firms should rely on financial markets for information about which investment projects to select and how such projects should be financed (Merton, 1989). Efficient financial markets help to allocate, transfer and deploy economic resources across time and space in an uncertain environment (Merton, 1990). Without efficient financial markets, these functions are likely to be performed less well and living standards will be lower than they might otherwise have been.

The infrastructure to support a corporate bond market includes an appropriate legal framework including reliable enforcement of bankruptcy and foreclosure laws, strong accounting and disclosure standards, and efficient and reliable clearing and settlement arrangements. It is also useful to have a community of bond analysts and ratings agencies who can help investors evaluate bonds. And, as we will emphasize in section 4, it is essential to develop a broad, deep, resilient secondary market.

In order for potential investors to be willing to accept a claim on future cash flows for the repayment of principal and interest, they must be confident that their rights to collect the promised debt payments are well defined and enforceable. La Porta et al. (1998) have identified six measures of creditor rights that are shown in Table 5.8a for countries in Table 5.1 along with a measure of contract enforceability. The measures focus on creditors' rights in the event of a default and include reorganization procedures, priority rules and the scope for autonomous action by managers to evade creditors. Based on data before the Asian Financial Crisis, on average, the four industrialized countries score better on these indices of creditor rights than do the eight Asian emerging economies.

La Porta et al. have also identified five indicators of the effectiveness of the judiciary system since, in principle, strong enforcement by the courts could compensate for weak laws. These measures (shown in Table 5.8b) include proxies for the efficiency of the judicial system, and commitment to the rule of law as well as indicators of the government's attitude toward business. Kane (2000a) also includes a measure of the quality of a country's bureaucracy since administrative efficiency may also affect the speed with which rights are enforced. Again, on average, the four industrialized countries score better on these measures of the effectiveness of the judicial system than do the eight Asian emerging economies.

In addition to assurances regarding the legal right to the promised cash flows and the enforceability of such rights in the event of default, a potential investor will need to form an estimate of the probability of default and the expected recovery in the event of default. This depends on the availability of reliable and relevant data about the firm's current condition and prospects as well as the availability of expert advice. La Porta et al. (1998) have identified an index of accounting standards, which is reported in Table 5.8c. In addition, Kane (2000b) has identified an index of restrictions on the press as an indication of the openness of the society and the scope for manipulating flows of information. Again, on average, the four industrialized countries have much better scores than the eight Asian emerging economies, although the average masks wide variations across the eight countries.

Finally, a potential investor must have confidence in arrangements for the clearing and settlement of bond trades. Creditor rights, judicial efficiency and good information will be of little use if the investor cannot be certain of receiving the bond when payment is made. Ideally, the clearing and settlement system should offer delivery against payment. Many of the emerging markets in Asia are adopting such systems.

Generally, countries that rate higher on indices of creditor rights, judicial efficiency, and quality of information have larger bond markets. As we will see in section 4, there are many useful things that a government can do to nurture development of a strong bond market, but these indices measure issues of fundamental importance. Indeed, Kane (2000a) has suggested that the official international financial institutions should help countries improve their rankings on such indices and that the managers of these official international financial institutions should be evaluated and compensated on the basis of their success in encouraging such improvements.

Table 5.8a, b and c Indicators of the quality of the financial infrastructure

5.8a Creditor rights

	Contract Enforceability	No Automatic Stay on Secured Assets	Secured Creditors Paid First	Restrictions on Autonomous Reorganization	Management Does Not Stay in Reorganization	Creditor Rights	Legal Reserves Required to Continue Operation
Hong Kong	N/A	1	1	1	1	4	0
Indonesia	1.76	1	1	1	1	4	0
South Korea	2.19	1	1	0	1	3	0.5
Malaysia	2.26	1	1	1	1	4	0
Philippines	1.75	0	0	0	0	0	0
Singapore	3.22	1	1	1	1	4	0
Taiwan	N/A	1	1	0	0	2	1
Thailand	2.23	1	1	0	1	3	0.1
Average	2.24	0.88	0.88	0.5	0.75	3	0.2
Australia	3.04	0	1	0	0	1	0
Japan	3.16	0	1	0	1	2	0.25
UK	3.43	1	1	1	1	4	0
US	3.55	0	1	0	0	1	0
Average	3.30	0.25	1	0.25	0.5	2	0.06

Notes and sources:

Contract enforceability: Measures the 'relative degree to which contractual agreements are honored and complications presented by language and mentality differences'. Scored 0–4, with higher scores for superior quality. *Source:* Business Environmental Risk Intelligence and Kane (2000b).

No automatic stay on secured assets: Equals 1 if the reorganization procedure *does not* impose an automatic stay on the assets of the firm upon filing the reorganization petition. Automatic stay prevents secured creditors from gaining possession of their security. It equals 0 if such restriction *does* exist in the law. *Source:* Bankruptcy and Reorganization Laws and LaPorta et al. (1998).

Table 5.8a, b and c (continued)

Secured creditors paid first: Equals 1 if secured creditors are ranked first in the distribution of the proceeds that result from the disposition of the assets of a bankrupt firm. Equals 0 in non-secured creditors, such as the government and workers are given absolute priority. *Source:* Bankruptcy and Reorganization Laws and LaPorta et al. (1998).

Restrictions on autonomous reorganization: Equals 1 if the reorganization procedure imposes restrictions such as creditors' consent to file for reorganization. It equals 0 if there are no such restrictions. *Source:* Bankruptcy and Reorganization Laws and LaPorta et al. (1998).

Management does not stay in reorganization: Equals 1 when an official appointed by the court, or by the creditors, is responsible for the operation of the business during reorganization. Equivalently, this variable equals 1 if the debtor does not keep the administration of its property pending the resolution of the reorganization process, and 0 otherwise. *Source:* Bankruptcy and Reorganization Laws and LaPorta et al. (1998).

Creditor rights: An index aggregating different creditor rights. The index is formed by adding 1 when: (1) the country imposes restrictions such as creditors' consent or minimum dividends to file for reorganization; (2) secured creditors are able to gain possession of their security once the reorganization petition has been approved (no automatic stay); (3) secured creditors are ranked first in the distribution of the proceeds that result from the disposition of the assets of a bankrupt firm; and (4) the debtor does not retain the administration of its property pending the resolution of the reorganization. The index ranges from 0 to 4. *Source:* Bankruptcy and Reorganization Laws and LaPorta et al. (1998).

Legal reserves required to continue operation: It is the minimum percentage of total share capital mandated by Corporate Law to avoid the dissolution of an existing firm. It takes a value of 0 for countries without such restrictions. *Source:* Company Law or Commercial Code and LaPorta et al. (1998).

Table 5.8a, b and c (continued)

5.8b Effectiveness of judicial system

	Efficiency of Judicial System	Rule of Law	Corruption	Bureaucratic Quality	Risk of Expropriation	Risk of Contract Repudiation
Hong Kong	10.0	8.22	8.52	4.14	8.29	8.82
Indonesia	2.50	3.98	2.15	1.50	7.16	6.09
South Korea	6.00	5.35	5.30	4.18	8.31	8.59
Malaysia	9.00	6.78	7.38	3.54	7.95	7.43
Philippines	4.75	2.73	2.92	1.46	5.22	4.80
Singapore	10.00	8.57	8.22	5.11	9.30	8.86
Taiwan	6.75	8.52	6.85	N/A	9.12	9.16
Thailand	3.25	6.25	5.18	4.39	7.42	7.57
Average	6.53	6.3	5.82	3.47	7.85	7.67
Australia	10.00	10.00	8.52	6.00	9.27	8.71
Japan	10.00	8.98	8.52	5.89	9.67	9.69
UK	10.00	8.57	9.10	6.00	9.71	9.63
US	10.00	10.00	8.63	6.00	9.98	9.00
Average	10	9.39	8.69	5.97	9.66	9.26

Notes and sources:
Efficiency of judicial system: Assessment of the 'efficiency and integrity of the legal environment as it affects business, particularly foreign firms' produced by the country risk-taking agency Corporation for International Business. It 'may be taken to represent investors' assessments of conditions in the country in question'. Average between 1980–83. Scale from 0 to 10, with lower scores for low efficiency levels. *Source:* LaPorta et al. (1998).

Rule of law: Assessment of the law and order tradition in the country produced by the country-risk rating agency International Country Risk (ICR). Average of the months of April and October of the monthly index between 1982 and 1995. Scale from 0 to 10, with lower scores for less tradition for law and order. *Source:* *International Country Risk Guide* (*ICRG*) and LaPorta et al. (1998).

Corruption: ICR's assessment of corruption in government. Lower scores indicate 'high government officials are likely to demand special payments' and 'illegal payments are generally expected throughout the lower levels of government' in the form of 'bribes connected with import and export licenses, exchange controls, tax, assessment, policy protection, or loans'. Scale runs from 0 to 6, with lower scores indicating higher levels of corruption. *Source:* *ICRG* and LaPorta et al. (1998).

Bureaucratic quality: Average of 'bureaucratic quality' assessment values assigned by *ICRG* between 1982–1995. Scored 0–6, with higher scores for superior quality. *Source:* Kane, (2000b).

Risk of expropriation: ICR's assessment of the risk of 'outright confiscation' or 'forced nationalization'. Average of the months of April and October of the monthly index between 1982 and 1995. Scale from 0 to 10, with lower scores for higher risks. *Source:* LaPorta et al. (1998).

Risk of contract repudiation: ICR's assessment of the 'risk of modification in a contract taking the form of a repudiation postponement, or scaling down' due to 'budget cutbacks, indigenization pressure, a change in government, or a change in government economic and social priorities'. Average of the month of April and October of the monthly index between 1982 and 1995. Scale from 0 to 10, with lower scores for higher risks. *Source:* LaPorta et al. (1998).

Table 5.8a, b and c (continued)

5.8c Quality of economic information

	Accounting Standards	Index of Restrictions on the Press
Hong Kong	73	32.75
Indonesia	N/A	71.40
South Korea	68	26.40
Malaysia	79	61.00
Philippines	64	44.60
Singapore	79	63.60
Taiwan	58	28.40
Thailand	66	39.80
Average	69.6	45.99
Australia	80	8.80
Japan	71	20.20
UK	85	22.20
US	76	12.80
Average	78	16

Notes and sources:
Accounting standards: Index created by examining and rating companies' 1993 annual reports on their inclusion or omission of 85 items. These items fall into seven categories (general information, income statement, balance sheet, funds flow statement, accounting policies, stockholders' information and supplementary information). A minimum of five companies in each country was studied. There are 1000 industrial companies from 41 countries. The companies represent a cross-section of various industry groups. Scores are from 0–100. Higher scores indicate better accounting standards. *Source:* Center for International Financial Analysis and Research Inc.(1995), *International Accounting & Auditing Trends*, 4th edn.

Index of restrictions on the press: Assessment of repressive actions and laws, regulations, controls and political pressures that influence media content. Score reported is the average index assigned by Freedom House staff *Annual Press Freedom Reports*, 1994–98. Scale runs from 0 to 100, with lower scores indicating greater freedom. *Source:* Kane (2000b).

3.1 Why Equity Markets May Exist Where Bond Markets Fail to Thrive

What are the main obstacles to developing an efficient bond market? Why, in environments with weak financial infrastructures, which discourage all external finance to some extent, do equity markets appear to flourish relative to bond markets? Part of the answer is inherent in the difference between debt and equity contracts. Debt claims promise repayment of principal and interest, while equity claims promise payment of a pro rata share of profits and usually convey a proportionate vote in important corporate governance matters.

The maximum return on a bond[7] purchased at par value is the promised interest payments. But the downside may include loss of the principal amount as well as promised interest payments. The bond contract defines the obligations of the borrower and remedies in the event of default. Usually, the key remedy in the event of default is that the bondholders may seize collateral or control of the enterprise from its owners. This remedy may be of little value, however, if bankruptcy and foreclosure laws are weak and enforcement is ineffectual.

The main challenge in pricing a bond is setting an interest rate that will compensate for the opportunity cost of funds, default, purchasing power and liquidity risk as well as whatever idiosyncratic features the bond may have such as a call option or sinking fund. In the absence of an active secondary market in risk-free debt of a comparable maturity, it will be difficult to identify the appropriate opportunity cost of funds. Estimating the probability of default and the expected recovery from the liquidation or sale of the firm in the event of default will also prove difficult in an economy with a weak financial infrastructure where the ability to enforce a collateral agreement is questionable. In the absence of credible accounting practices, good disclosure practices or reliable bond ratings, it may be very difficult to estimate a probability of default or expected loss in the event of default. This challenge is still more difficult in the absence of clear laws setting out the bondholder's rights in the event of default, or an efficient judiciary that will oversee enforcement of such rights and a reliable enforcement mechanism. If households are concerned about a high probability of default or the expected loss in the event of default, it may not be possible to establish a viable bond market. Borrowers may not be able to offer credibly a sufficiently high interest rate to compensate for the perceived risk of loss (Stiglitz and Weiss, 1981).

In contrast to a bond in which the upside is limited by the promised interest rate, an equity claim has an unlimited upside return, which can compensate for the perceived riskiness of the claim. Although minority shareholders will experience the same frustrations as bondholders in evaluating a firm's current condition and its earnings prospects, they can take comfort in the fact that they share an interest with the controlling shareholders (who are often also the managers in emerging market firms) in a rising share price.[8] Thus, if there is an active secondary market and reliable clearing and settlement procedures for buying and selling equity claims, an active market may develop for a firm's equity even though investors would not be willing to buy its debt.

What are the consequences of operating a financial system with a banking sector and equity market, but no bond market? The implications are profound and far-ranging. We will analyze the impact on other markets, savers, investors, banks and financial development more broadly.

3.2 Absence of Bond Markets: Implications for Other Markets

In the absence of a bond market, the economy will lack a market-determined term structure of interest rates that accurately reflects the opportunity cost of funds at each maturity. Without a term structure of interest rates, it will be difficult to develop efficient derivatives markets that enable economic agents to manage financial risks. Forward markets trade forward contracts that obligate the owner to buy a given asset on a specific date at a price specified at the origination of the contract. Since market participants always have the option of buying the asset on the spot market and holding it until the maturity of the forward contract, the forward price is linked to the current price by the interest cost of holding the asset until the forward contract matures. In the case of forward foreign exchange contracts, the relationship is a bit more complex because it involves both foreign and domestic interest rates. The forward foreign exchange rate is related to the spot foreign exchange rate by the ratio of (1 +) the home country interest rate relative to (1 +) the foreign interest rate, both corresponding to the maturity of the forward contract. If there is no market-determined domestic interest rate, it may still be possible to buy a forward contract, but the market will be very thin and transactions costs will be heavy because market-makers will not be able to hedge their positions using the bond market.

Futures markets trade futures contracts that obligate the owner to purchase a specified asset at a specified exercise price on the contract maturity date. Futures markets differ from forward markets in that changes in the value of a futures contract are settled day by day as they occur rather than at the maturity of the contract. Thus Black (1976) has described futures contracts as a series of forward contracts that are settled day by day. Again, however, a key link between spot and futures prices is the interest rate corresponding to the maturity of the contract. Futures contracts are exchange-traded instruments that require a significant volume of trading to warrant the substantial fixed costs of organizing and running an exchange. Countries without a bond market are unlikely to generate enough activity to support development of an active futures exchange. Although Hong Kong, Singapore, Malaysia, the Philippines, and China all have futures exchanges, active trading has been confined mainly to Singapore's International Monetary Exchange (SIMEX).

Swap contracts obligate two parties to exchange, or swap, some specified cash flows at specific intervals. The most common form is an interest rate swap in which cash flows are determined by the two different interest rates specified in the swap agreement. But, the swap contract can be decomposed into a portfolio of forward contracts (Smith et al.,1986) in which, at each settlement date throughout the term of the swap contract, part of the change in value is transferred between the counterparties. In contrast to the forward contract, in which the change in value is transferred between the counterparties at the maturity of the contract or the futures contract, in which the change in value is transferred between the counterparties day by day over the term of the contract, part of the value of the change in a swap contract is conveyed between the counterparties at each settlement date specified in the swap contract. Again, the key link between spot and forward rates is the corresponding interest rate.

In contrast to the owners of forward, futures or swap contracts who have an *obligation* to perform as specified in the contract, the owner of an option contract has the *right*, but not the obligation to perform as specified in the contract. Just as futures and swaps can be viewed as a portfolio of forward contracts, options can be viewed as portfolios of forward contracts and risk-free bonds. Black and Scholes (1973) have shown that a dynamic portfolio of forward contracts on the underlying asset and riskless bonds can replicate a call option. As the price of the asset rises, the call-option-equivalent portfolio contains an increasing proportion of forward contracts on the asset. As the price of the asset falls, the replicating portfolio contains a decreasing proportion of forward contracts on the asset. Like the forward, futures and swap markets, the options market depends critically on the bond market for pricing and hedging positions.

In the absence of a well-functioning bond market, it may be possible to obtain forward, swaps and options contracts that are specially tailored for a client. But they will be very expensive relative to what they would cost in an economy with a well-functioning bond market because they cannot be hedged as efficiently. The consequence is that market participants will be exposed to more financial risk than they would choose to accept if they had access to well-functioning derivatives markets. The events of 1997 showed that many market participants had accepted excessive exposures to foreign exchange risk.

The absence of a risk-free[9] term structure of interest rates also makes it difficult to price credit risk by comparing a risky asset with a risk-free asset that is alike in all other characteristics. Although inefficiencies caused by mispricing credit risk may be second order relative to inefficiencies that result from mispricing the risk-free rate, they nonetheless cause distortions in the economy. Without a government bond market that establishes benchmark risk-free rates at critical maturities, it will be very difficult to establish a corporate bond market, much less a market for high-yield debt or securitized assets. Partly, this is a consequence of the microeconomics of market-making. It is easier to start a new market if the activity must cover only the marginal cost of the new market rather than the full costs of setting up and maintaining a market. If institutions have already invested in trading in government bonds, then the marginal cost of introducing another fixed income market will be relatively slight.

The absence of a broad, deep, resilient bond market also causes a loss of information to society. The differential yield between a risky bond and a risk-free bond that is alike in all other characteristics, reflects a market consensus about the appropriate credit risk (and possibly liquidity risk) premium. This market information can be used to price comparable bank loans and it is likely to extend the range of credit risk that can be priced in the market rather than quantity rationed.

Although, as noted above, an equity market may flourish in the absence of the bond market, it may not be very efficient in the sense of aligning prices with fundamental economic values. Ideally, share prices should reflect the present discounted value of expected future earnings. But in economies that lack the infrastructure to support a bond market, investors are likely to have considerable doubt about what past earnings have been and what current earnings are, much less what expected future earnings will be. Moreover, in the absence of a bond market it is not clear how the appropriate discount rate should be determined. Thus shares are likely to be priced on the basis of expectations that are often shallowly held and subject to considerable volatility and the usefulness of share prices in allocating resources and corporate governance is correspondingly vitiated.

3.3 Absence of Bond Markets: Implications for Savers

Without a well-functioning bond market, savers face a diminished array of assets. They will hold more substitute assets such as bank deposits and possibly, but less likely, equity and probably more non-financial assets such as gold or jewelry that reduce the supply of savings that can be mobilized for productive investment. They will be forced to accept a lower return for any given level of risk or a higher level of risk for a given level of return relative to an economy with a well-functioning bond market. As Hakansson (1999) has argued with respect to the corporate bond market, 'we can expect that a large number of these securities will be such that we will be unable to find *any* portfolio of other securities in the market which can replicate their payoff patterns across contingencies or states'. Applying his earlier theoretical work Hakansson (1982, 1992) compared equilibria with and without a well-developed bond market, and concluded that under fairly general conditions 'the financial market richer in bonds will constitute a Pareto-improvement over the financial market in which banks do most of the lending'.

In the absence of a well-functioning bond market, specialized financial institutions with long-term liabilities such as life insurance companies and pension funds will find it more difficult to acquire long-term assets that match the maturity of their liabilities. And consequently, the insurance they provide against future contingencies will be more costly.

3.4 Absence of Bond Markets: Implications for Investors

Without a well-functioning bond market, firms will lack a clear measure of the opportunity cost of funds. From society's perspective this may lead to overinvestment if the firm's internal rate is too low or underinvestment, if the firm's internal rate is too high. Evidence from the mid-1990s in several dynamic Asian economies suggests that the internal discount rate may have often been too low because returns on investment fell markedly.

Firms will be entirely reliant on banks for debt financing. The same weaknesses in the financial infrastructure that impede development of a bond market – inadequate accounting and auditing, weak disclosure laws and uncertain enforcement of contracts – also lead banks to prefer short-term credit. As Diamond (1991) has shown, short-term credit is an important way to control borrowers when there are hidden action and hidden information problems since it limits the time an opportunistic firm can exploit its creditors without being in default.

Since banks typically lend for periods much shorter than the maturity of long-term bonds, this may affect the firm's preferred leverage. Any given leverage structure will be riskier the shorter the maturity of the debt outstanding. Firms may attempt to compensate for this risk by attempting to control the bank lender. As noted earlier, corporate conglomerates will attempt to affiliate with a bank in part to form an internal capital market that will substitute for the absence of an external capital market. If the subsequent loans should go bad, this sort of relationship can give rise to the charge of crony capitalism.

Another consequence of the reliance on short-term bank lending may be a bias in firms' investment decisions. Based on Hart and Moore (1995), Caprio and Demirgüç-Kunt, (1997) have argued that firms will tend to match the maturity of their assets and liabilities. This tendency has been documented in the United States and Caprio and Demirgüç-Kunt (1997) report on World Bank studies that affirm the pattern of matching maturities of assets and liabilities holds for developing countries as well. This suggests that reliance on short-term bank lending will bias investment toward short-term assets. As a result, there may be too little investment in longer-term assets such as infrastructure, public utilities, housing and capital-intensive industries.

Exclusive reliance on bank lending may bias investment in another more subtle way. Access to the bond market may play a role in encouraging entrepreneurial ventures by limiting the ability of banks to extract rents from successful ventures. Black and Gilson (1998) have argued that a dynamic venture capital sector will not thrive in a bank-based financial system because successful venture capitalists need the option of exiting from the project through issue of bonds or equity.

Some recent evidence for the bank-centered Japanese system (Weinstein and Yafeh, 1998) suggests banks do extract rents from their dependent corporate customers. The consequence is that the effective cost of funds is higher than it would have been if the firm had access to a well-functioning bond market.

The largest, best-known firms may attempt to compensate for the lack of a domestic bond market by issuing bonds in the international market. Table 5.9 shows corporate issues outstanding as a percentage of GDP in 1998 for several Asian economies and a benchmark group of high-income economies. In general, reliance on international issuance of bonds was higher in this group of Asian economies than in the benchmark group (apart from the United Kingdom, which may be a special case because it is the locus of the

Table 5.9 Corporate borrowings in domestic and international markets (year-end, 1998)

	Domestic Corporate Debt Securities Outstanding (% GDP)	International Corporate Debt Securities Outstanding (% GDP)
Hong Kong	1.2	8.9
Indonesia	N/A	13.5
South Korea	32.2	5.7
Malaysia	33.7	15.3
Philippines	0.0	9.4
Singapore	2.5	4.7
Taiwan	1.5	2.5
Thailand	3.8*	5.2
Average	10.7	8.2
Australia	15.9	4.7
Japan	17.9	4.2
UK	8.2	9.1
US	27.4	3.2
Average	17.4	5.3

Note: * Includes data for financial institutions.

Source: IMF *International Financial Statistics*, IMF World Economic Outlook Database, Bank for International Settlements.

largest concentration of international bond market activity). While this behavior is easily explained as an accommodation to the inadequacies of domestic bond markets, it subjects the borrowers to a heavy potential cost.

In general, issues on international bond markets are denominated in foreign currency, usually US dollars or euros. Thus, to the extent that borrowing firms use this source of financing to fund activities that will have returns in the domestic currency, they will be increasing their exposure to foreign exchange risk. As already noted, opportunities for hedging this risk in derivatives markets are limited and generally quite expensive.

3.5 Absence of Bond Markets: Implications for Banks

Without competition from the bond market, the banking sector will be larger than it would otherwise be. Banks will have more deposits at lower cost because their customers will have very few other alternative fixed-income investments and they will have more corporate loans because their borrowers will have few other sources of debt financing. If the banking market were highly competitive, the distortions from bank dominance of debt finance might be relatively slight, but in most countries without a bond market the banking system is highly concentrated. The deposit rate is not likely to reflect the true opportunity cost of funds for the economy because of cartel pricing in some countries and because in most countries, banks benefit from access to an implicit, if not an explicit safety net. The perception that claims on the bank will receive some degree of protection from the government, means that depositors will not be an effective source of discipline on bank risk-taking.

It is generally argued that bank monitoring of a borrower is superior to monitoring by bondholders because bank lenders have lower costs of collective action and can renegotiate a loan contract at lower cost in the event that the borrower cannot meet the original repayment schedule. This may be true in general, but recent experience has shown that if a bank is weakly capitalized so that it cannot take a write-down in a loan renegotiation without violating capital adequacy standards, the bank may let the borrower continue negative present value projects by funding these activities to avoid declaration of default (Herring, 1989). In this circumstance, monitoring by bondholders may be preferable since they will have no motive to sustain uneconomic activity.

The absence of a bond market precludes banks from issuing bonds, which might reduce their exposure to liquidity risk and provide another source of market discipline.[10] The virtual absence of market discipline from debt markets places a heavier burden on bank supervisors to curb risk-taking. Like their counterparts in the industrialized world, however, bank supervisors in emerging markets have seldom been up to the challenge. Thus, the main restraint must come from shareholders of the bank. But in a world of implicit deposit guarantees, they have an incentive to take greater risks. This tendency is exacerbated if the bank is controlled by interests who are also heavy borrowers from the bank.

Even without this distortion of the incentives for risk-taking, a bank that operates in an economy without bond markets has a diminished capacity to manage risks. The thinness of derivatives markets means that most hedging activities must involve transactions on the balance sheet. It will be particularly challenging to deal with concentrations of credit risk, since in the absence of a well-developed bond market, it will be difficult to sell or securitize loans or negotiate credit derivatives. And without access to a liquid bond market, banks will be more vulnerable to a liquidity shock because they will not have the option of selling bonds in a liquid secondary market and thus are more likely to be obliged to accept fire-sale losses on the liquidation of bank loans.

Viewed from a broader perspective, the economy is at risk of crisis due to excessive reliance on bank lending. Because banks are highly leveraged institutions, the economy is much more vulnerable to a financial crisis than if more corporate borrowing had taken place in the bond market and the claims were held in well-diversified portfolios. In the event of a shock that cripples the banking system, there will be an enormous impact on economic activity because borrowers will not be able to substitute issuance of bonds for bank borrowing. Instability in the banking system can halt investment projects and reduce aggregate demand. Economic activity may be depressed until the banking system can be recapitalized. As experience in Asia since 1997 has shown, this can be a very painful process.

The absence of bond markets also inhibits efforts to clean up bank balance sheets in the wake of a crisis. From Scandinavia to the United States, Japan and several emerging economies in Asia, governments have issued debt in exchange for non-performing loans. In the absence of well-organized bond markets, the government debt issued is less liquid and therefore less useful in resuscitating bank lending. More importantly, in the absence of an active fixed-income market, it is more difficult to securitize non-performing loans so that resources can be redeployed as rapidly as possible to restructure the economy.

3.6 Absence of Bond Markets: Summary

An economy that relies exclusively on banks for debt financing faces several major costs. First is the loss of information that is contained in market-determined interest rates. This impedes the development of derivatives markets and may lead to inefficiencies in the pricing of equities. Without a clear measure of the opportunity cost of capital firms may invest too little or too much and the allocation of capital will be less efficient than if the economy had the advantage of a well-functioning bond market.

Second is the loss of welfare to savers who are less well off than they would be with the option of investing in a well-functioning bond market. Because financial investment is less attractive than it would otherwise be, fewer savings may be mobilized in the financial system to fund investment.

Third, firms may face a higher effective cost of funds than if they had access to the bond market and their investment policies may be biased in favor of short-term assets and away from entrepreneurial ventures. If firms attempt to compensate for the lack of a domestic bond market by borrowing in international bond markets, they may be obliged to accept excessive exposure to foreign exchange risk. In any event, the underdevelopment of domestic derivatives market will make it more difficult to manage financial risks.

Fourth, the banking sector will be larger than it would otherwise be. Since banks are highly leveraged, this may render the economy more vulnerable to crisis. Certainly, in the event that a banking crisis occurs, the damage to the real economy will be much greater than if investors had access to a well-functioning bond market and the financial restructuring process will be more difficult.

If the economy would be better off with a well-functioning bond market, what can the government do to nurture it? What policies will facilitate development of a bond market? We turn to that topic in the next section.

4 THE ROLE OF GOVERNMENT AS ISSUER

The first major bond market to develop is usually the market in government obligations. In many countries, the government has the largest stock of issues outstanding. In general, it is easier for bond traders to price government issues where credit risk is not an important consideration. Government bond prices can then serve as a basis for pricing the issues of other borrowers who are subject to credit risk.

In most countries, governments issue debt to fund the gap between tax receipts and current expenditures, and sometimes to finance some extraordinary current expenditure. (See Table 5.10 that shows government borrowing and government borrowing relative to borrowing by other issuers in the eight Asian emerging economies and the four industrialized countries.) The US bond market took flight after the issuance of Liberty Bonds to finance US participation in World War I. Rajan and Zingales (1999) note

Table 5.10 Public and total borrowings in domestic and international markets (year-end, 1998)

	Domestic Debt Securities Outstanding (% GDP)		International Debt Securities Outstanding (% GDP)	
	Public	All issuers	Public	All issuers
Hong Kong	3.3	17.4	4.7	19.5
Indonesia	N/A	1.5	0.7	18.2
South Korea	16.2	75.7	7.2	16.8
Malaysia	31.3	85.4	1.4	17.5
Philippines	32.3	32.3	3.7	16.6
Singapore	20.8	23.3	0.1	6.5
Taiwan	11.7	13.2	0.0	2.8
Thailand	16.5	20.3	2.0	12.7
Australia	25.2	68.3	8.0	25.0
Germany	40.3	93.3	0.6	23.4
Japan	97.2	136.9	0.7	8.3
UK	33.1	60.8	0.9	25.8
US	88.8	159.5	1.5	9.6

Source: IMF *International Financial Statistics*, IMF World Economic Outlook Database, Bank for International Settlements.

that people who would otherwise not buy a financial security, bought these bonds for patriotic reasons. The favorable experience investors had with these bonds left them willing to invest in securities issued by corporations. This gave liquidity to the corporate securities market and made possible the significant expansion of these markets during the 1920s.

Does this mean that fiscally conservative governments that do not run deficits cannot nurture a robust bond market? Hong Kong has shown that this need not be true. After all, it is *gross* debt that matters for the development of the market, not the *net* debtor position of the government. Hong Kong developed a benchmark yield curve in Hong Kong dollars through issues of exchange fund bills and notes, the proceeds of which are used primarily to invest in international markets, not to fund government spending.

If the government's objective is the nurture of a robust bond market, then it should aim at establishing a benchmark yield curve that can serve as the risk-free rate for the pricing of other securities. This means committing to a program of regular issues at the appropriate maturities – usually three months, six months, one year, three years, five years and ultimately ten years. It must be recognized at the outset that the goal of developing a robust bond market may conflict with the goal of minimizing the cost of government borrowing.[11]

The design of government securities should be as simple as possible without complicated covenants and the design should be consistent across the maturities that comprise the benchmark yield curve. This will facilitate pricing of the risk-free rate without the complication of special features such as sinking funds, call options or other features.

It is crucial that the interest rate on government bonds be market-determined, not administratively determined. If the government attempts to manipulate the bond market to reduce the cost of government borrowing, important information will be lost, which may lead to distortions in the allocation of capital. This means that the government should not require certain institutions to hold its debt or devise special tax treatment of government debt that differs from that for other securities. Here again there is a natural tension between the objectives of nurturing the development of a robust bond market and minimizing the cost of government borrowing.

Generally, the price discovery process is enhanced by combining competitive auctions of new issues with issuance through a set of primary dealers who act as underwriters. It is useful to invite foreign firms to become primary dealers on the same basis as domestic firms. This is likely to speed the adoption of world-class best practices in the local bond market and enhance the access of domestic borrowers to longer-term foreign sources of funds. Primary dealers should be required to make markets in the issues by continuously quoting a bid-asked spread and standing ready to buy or sell at the stated rates.

Although the government will find a natural constituency for its longer-term issues in the portfolios of institutions with longer-term liabilities, such placements will not facilitate the development of a liquid secondary market because these institutions are likely to buy and hold bonds until they mature. Thus, it is important to attract other investors who will have a trading orientation. Mutual funds, for example, should be encouraged to enter the market.

4.1 Nurturing a Strong Secondary Market

The liquidity of an asset is enhanced if it is traded in a liquid secondary market. Even if the asset is not sold, the liquidity of the secondary market increases its value as collateral for a loan because its worth can be more easily verified. Liquid secondary markets also raise the value of primary securities.[12] Confidence in the liquidity of secondary markets provides a valuable option to investors. Even if the investor does not plan to sell the primary claim before maturity, the investor's future portfolio allocation preferences are inevitably subject to uncertainty and thus the availability of a deep, broad, secondary market enhances the investor's willingness to buy the initial, primary claim.

Empirical evidence suggests that this option may be very valuable indeed. Pratt (1989) reports comparisons of the value of letter stocks that are identical in all respects to the freely traded stock of public companies except that they are restricted from trading on the open market for a specified period.[13] Pratt (1989, p. 241) concludes that 'compared to their free-trading counterparts, the discounts on the letter stocks were the least for NYSE-listed stocks, and increased in order for AMEX-listed stock, OTC reporting companies, and OTC nonreporting companies'. This ranking of discounts corresponds roughly to perceptions of the liquidity of these secondary markets. Using the midpoints of the discount range for letter stocks relative to their freely traded counterparts, Pratt found that the discount was 25.8 percent.[14]

The 'liquidity of a secondary market' is usually described in terms of its depth and breadth. 'Depth' connotes the quantity that can be sold without moving prices against the seller. 'Breadth' connotes the diversity of participants and the heterogeneity of their responses to new information. Both qualities are usually positively correlated with the size of the secondary market. Deep, broad markets are generally more resilient against disturbances of any given size than thin, narrow markets; they tend to display greater price stability in response to a shock of a given magnitude.

Liquid secondary markets are also 'transactionally efficient' in the sense that the cost of a round-trip (the bid-asked spread) is low (Guttentag and Herring, 1986). Dealer markets are usually regarded as especially transactionally efficient because in addition to providing information and matching buyers and sellers, dealers also provide immediacy by buying and selling from inventory. The bid-asked spread charged by dealers in secondary markets must cover the opportunity cost of maintaining an inventory of securities, operating costs and the risk of holding an inventory of securities. Greater price stability, which is associated with deep, broad markets, reduces the risk of inventorying securities and thus reduces transactions costs.

A government can track its progress in fostering a liquid secondary market by tracking the spreads quoted by dealers. The smaller the spread and the larger the size of the transaction that dealers are willing to undertake at the quoted spread, the more liquid the secondary market.

The liquidity of an asset also depends on the reliability of arrangements for exchanging the asset for cash. Heightened perception of 'settlement risk' – the risk that one party in a transaction will fulfill its settlement obligation while the counterparty does not – can undermine the liquidity of an asset. In these respects the liquidity of an asset depends on the liquidity of its secondary market. In this instance emerging markets may have an advantage over some well-established markets with legacy clearing and settlement systems. They have the opportunity to leapfrog traditional arrangement by adopting modern technology to facilitate clearing and settlement of secondary market trading. Hong Kong, for example, has established a computerized book-entry system for bonds to reduce clearing and settlement risk. This book-entry system is linked to a real time gross settlement payment system so that it can provide real time delivery against payment for Hong Kong dollar debt securities.

While there are many measures a government can implement to enhance the liquidity of its secondary markets, the scope for success is inherently constrained by the size of the economy. Most European economies have not been of sufficient size to foster broad, deep, resilient bond markets like those found in the United States. Early experience within the euro area, however, indicates that the combined bond market denominated in euros may indeed grow to rival US-dollar-denominated markets. This raises the interesting question of whether Asia might be able to achieve similar gains through the development of a regional bond market.

5 CONCLUDING COMMENT: THE EXAMPLE OF THAILAND

The Thai economy is illustrative of both the problems we identified in section 3 and the solutions we outlined in section 4. Before the crisis of 1997, Thailand had a highly developed banking sector and a buoyant stock market, but a moribund bond market. (See italic figures in Table 5.11 that show the amount of the bonds outstanding when the crisis erupted.)

The underdevelopment of the Thai bond market can be attributed to several causes (see Figure 5.1). First is the lack of a benchmark, market-determined yield curve. Until the crisis, the Thai government had a tradition, dating from 1988, of fiscal surpluses. Since the government viewed issuance of bonds solely as a means of financing deficits rather than as a way of nurturing the development of a bond market, no government bonds were issued from June 1990 until 1998, when the government was forced to run significant series of deficits to recapitalize the financial system and boost aggregate demand.

Second, the Thai government had constructed a captive market for its securities. Banks and finance companies were required to hold substantial reserves in the form of national government securities and often chose to hold more bonds than required. These securities were usually held to

Table 5.11 Size of Thai financial markets

	Bank Loans	Stock Market Capitalization	Bond Outstanding (domestic)	GDP
1992	2161.9	1485.0	*215.1*	2830.9
1993	2665.2	3325.4	*262.0*	3170.3
1994	3430.5	3300.8	*339.0*	3634.5
1995	4230.5	3564.6	*424.4*	4192.7
1996	4825.1	2559.6	*519.3*	4622.8
1997	6037.5	1133.3	*546.8*	4732.6

Note: Unit = billion baht.

Source: Thai Bond Dealing Center.

maturity so that they need not be marked to market. This discouraged secondary market trading and meant that the interest rate did not necessarily reflect the true opportunity cost of funds.

Third, tax laws impeded the development of the secondary market. Until 1995, Thailand imposed a stamp duty on transfers of bond ownership. Although the rate was low, approximately 0.1 percent of the value of the bond,[15] it was a powerful deterrent to secondary market trading.

Fourth, a weak legal infrastructure created doubts about creditor rights in the event of default. Although Thailand ranked relatively well in terms of creditor rights (see Table 5.8a), it ranked poorly in terms of judicial effectiveness. Thailand has made a concerted effort to improve its legal infrastructure, but survey data from a sample of local law firms and bankruptcy judges in each country, reported in *Doing Business in 2004* (World Bank, 2004) show that Thailand appears to lag behind six other middle income countries in two important respects. Table 5.12 provides data for four Asian countries and three other middle income countries, all of which have recently undertaken structural reforms. Based on the specified bankruptcy scenario, the time to go through insolvency in Thailand (2.6 years) is exceeded only by Indonesia (6.0 years) and Argentina (2.8 years). Moreover, the costs of going through insolvency in Thailand (38 percent of the bankruptcy estate) are markedly higher than in the six other countries.

Fifth, weak accounting and disclosure standards impeded the evaluation of credit risk and made it difficult for external investors to value risky debt. Table 5.8c shows that accounting standards in Thailand ranked below average among the eight Asian emerging economies. Again, there have been recent efforts to correct this weakness. Based on a study funded by the Asian Development Bank, Thailand launched its first credit rating agency,

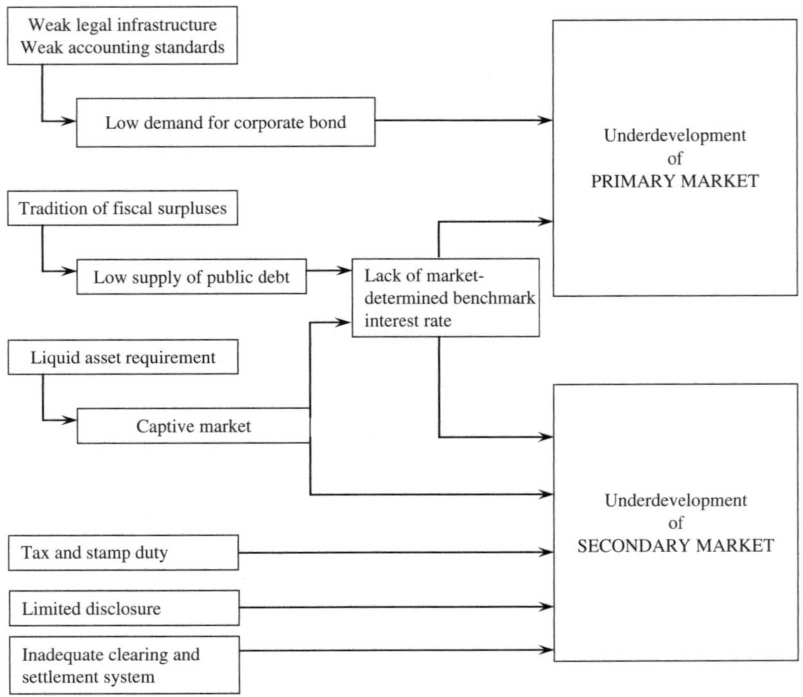

Figure 5.1 Thailand's structural problems and consequences for the development of the bond market

Table 5.12 Bankruptcy infrastructure: closing a business in seven emerging markets

	Thailand	South Korea	Malaysia	Indonesia	Turkey	Mexico	Argentina
Time to Go Through Insolvency (years)	2.6	1.47	2.2	6.0	1.8	2.0	2.8
Cost to Go Through Insolvency (% estate)	38	4	18	18	8	18	18
Absolute Priority Preserved	67	100	100	67	67	33	67
Efficient Outcome Achieved	1	1	0	0	0	1	0
Goals-of-Insolvency Index	62	91	52	35	51	61	43
Court-Powers Index	33	67	33	100	67	67	67

Source and notes: *Doing Business in 2004, Understanding Regulation* (World Bank, 2004). Based on responses to a questionnaire filled out by local law firms and bankruptcy judges specifying the details of the insolvency in which the business runs a hotel in downtown real estate, its only asset. The business is assumed to default on principal and interest 2 January, 2003. The measure for preservation of absolute priority is on a scale of 100. A score of 100 means that secured creditors are paid before labor, tax claims and shareholders. A score of 67 means that secured creditors get paid second. The efficient outcome measure takes on the value 1 if the insolvency process results in either foreclosure or liquidation with a going-concern sale or in a successful rehabilitation with new management. A 0 indicates the efficient outcome was not achieved. The Goals-of-Insolvency Index goes from 0 to 100 and is the simple average of the time of insolvency and cost of insolvency (each rescaled from 0 to 100) and the observance of absolute priority. The Court-Powers Index is a measure of the degree to which the court drives insolvency proceedings and is the average of three indicators: whether the court appoints and replaces the insolvency administrator with no restrictions imposed by law, whether the reports of the administrator are accessible only to the court and not the creditors, and whether the court decides on the adoption of the rehabilitation plan. The index is scaled from 0 to 100, with higher values indicating more court involvement. South Korea, Malaysia and Indonesia are included because they experienced crises more or less simultaneously with Thailand. Argentina, Mexico and Turkey are included because they are middle income countries that have also undertaken structural reforms.

Table 5.13 Deteriorating corporate performance of Thai firms

	Profits Over Interest Expenses	No. of Firms with Profits < Interest Expenses (%)	Loans of Firms with Profits < Interest Expenses (%)	Profits Over Liabilities (%)	Leverage
1997: Q4	1.49	32.0	36.4	7.3	2.95
1997: Q3	2.59	23.3	30.8	10.2	2.95
1997: Q2	3.18	19.9	18.4	NA	2.12
1997: Q1	3.66	15.3	16.2	NA	2.01
1996: Q4	3.11	13.8	11.8	14.9	1.90
1995: Q4	4.01	9.6	7.6	18.1	1.67
1994: Q4	5.78	5.1	1.4	24.0	1.50

Note: Profit is defined as earnings before interest, taxes, depreciation and amortization (EBITDA). Leverage is debt over equity.

Source: Alba et al. (1998).

the Thai Rating and Information Services Company Limited (TRIS) in 1993. TRIS rates both debt securities and companies. All public debt offerings with a maturity greater than one year require a rating from TRIS.[16]

The underdevelopment of the bond market may have caused serious distortions in the Thai economy. Without a market-determined interest rate that reflected true opportunity cost of funds, and with bank loan rates marked-up over deposit rates that were administratively determined, there was a tendency for Thai firms to overinvest. As a result, the efficiency of investment declined. Claessens et al. (1998b) report that the median return on assets for Thai firms declined steadily from 11.7 percent in 1990 to 7.4 percent in 1996. Alba et al.(1998) report four indicators of enterprise performance, using data for all firms listed on the Stock Exchange of Thailand, that indicate Thai corporate performance had been deteriorating well before the 1997 financial crisis (see Table 5.13).

The inadequacies of the bond market may have contributed to the heavy reliance of Thai firms on family group corporate structures. Claessens et al. (1998) documented that 46.85 percent of Thai firms were affiliated with corporate groups in 1996.

In the absence of an efficient bond market, firms relied heavily on foreign borrowing. Table 5.14 shows the evolution of foreign debt of the Thai private sector from 1987–99. Between 1988–95 it grew at rates ranging from 20 to 65 percent per annum. With limited access to relevant derivatives markets and risk management tools, foreign borrowing led to excessive

Table 5.14 Foreign debt of Thai private sector

	Long-term	Short-term	Total	Growth
1987	3175	2894	6069	−2.7%
1988	3282	4492	7774	28.1%
1989	4966	5777	10743	38.2%
1990	7633	10160	17793	65.6%
1991	10382	14686	25068	40.9%
1992	12189	18364	30553	21.9%
1993	15302	22634	37936	24.2%
1994	20153	28999	49152	29.6%
1995	25155	41011	66166	34.6%
1996	36172	37559	73731	11.4%
1997	34855	34238	69093	−6.3%
1998	31293	23373	54666	−20.9%
1999	25506	13546	39052	−28.6%

Note: Unit = $ million.

Source: Bank of Thailand.

build up of foreign exchange risk that contributed to the 1997 financial crisis.

One consequence of the underdeveloped state of the bond market was that the Thai economy was heavily reliant on bank lending. The year before the crisis, bank lending accounted for nearly all the external funding of Thai corporations. Banks financed about one-third of the change in gross fixed capital formation, while new issues of equity financed about 6 percent and net issues of bonds, a mere 2 percent.[17] (See Table 5.15.)

The consequence of this dependence on bank lending was catastrophic for the economy. When the banks suffered heavy losses, new lending ceased and firms were forced to halt investment projects. The result was a prolonged and painful economic contraction.

The Thai authorities have learned a costly lesson about the dangers of over-reliance on banks. They have begun to implement reforms designed to stimulate development of both the primary and secondary bond markets. The Bank of Thailand, acting as agent and advisor to the Ministry of Finance, has made an effort to introduce a quarter-ahead calendar of regular issuance of government bonds in the primary market, and with the government taking on responsibility for many of the costs of financial sector restructuring, there has been no shortage of supply. The Bank of

Table 5.15 The dominance of bank lending in the external financing of Thai corporations, 1996

Domestic Credit Provided by Banking Sector		Stock Market Capitalization		Domestic Corporate Debt Securities	
Amount (% GDP)	Change (% GCF)	Total (% GDP)	Equity raised (% GCF)	Outstanding (% GDP)	Net issues (% GCF)
100.0	31.3	65.8	6.0	3.9*	1.9

Notes and sources: Includes financial institution bonds. 1996, end of year data. The banking sector includes monetary authorities, deposit money banks, and other banking institutions for which data are available (including institutions that do not accept transferable deposits but do incur such liabilities as time and savings deposits). Examples of other banking institutions include savings and mortgage loan institutions and building and loan associations. The data are as reported on line 32d in the IMF *International Financial Statistics* (*IFS*). GDP is the gross domestic product as reported on line 99b in the *IFS*. GCF is the gross fixed capital formation as reported on line 93e in the *IFS*. Corporate debt securities are debt securities that were issued in domestic currency by residents of the country indicated, including short-term paper (for example, commercial paper).

Thailand has succeeded in developing a yield curve for government bonds that extends from less than one year out to 15 years.

In June 1999, the Bank of Thailand allowed financial institutions to conduct securities borrowing and lending business, which has helped promote risk management and market liquidity. The Thai Bond Dealing Center (BDC) was granted a Bond Exchange license from the Thai Securities and Exchange Commission to act as self-regulatory organization, institute a code of conduct for market participants and settle any disagreements between participants in the secondary market.

The Bank of Thailand has developed a primary dealership system to facilitate the conduct of open market operations. Primary dealers are also obliged to submit reference yields on government securities to the BDC at the conclusion of each business day to refresh information about the benchmark yield curve.

The Bank of Thailand has launched a fully automated delivery versus payment (DVP) settlement system. It has been supplemented by the intraday liquidity facilities and queuing mechanism, employing digital signature technology to ensure secure and smooth delivery and payments transactions, but is not yet available on a real time basis. Clearing and settlement for corporate bonds has been centralized at the Thailand Securities Depository Corporation (TSD). Clearing and settlement of government bonds is being shifted from the Bank of Thailand to the TSD as well.

These changes have markedly improved the liquidity of the government bond market. As the turnover data in Figure 5.2 show, the volume trading is substantially higher than at the end of the 1990s. While the volume of trading in corporate bonds is substantially lower, it is also trending upwards.

In addition to measures aimed directly at improving the functioning of local currency bond markets, the Thai government has also placed emphasis on upgrading accounting and disclosure standards and improving corporate governance. New accounting standards have been introduced since the crisis and implemented. Now all companies listed on the Stock Exchange of Thailand (SET) have audit committees in place. And the Institute of Directors has provided training to large numbers of corporate directors. But corporate governance practices in Thailand still fall short of world standards in some regards. Although Thailand has not yet adopted the OECD Code of Good Corporate Governance, the SET has adopted a Code of Best Practices for Directors of Listed Companies. The Institute of Directors released its second benchmarking survey on corporate governance practices of the 234 listed corporations with regard to the SET's 'Principles of Good Corporate Governance'. Relative to 2001 the survey showed improvement with regard to five standards and deterioration with regard to one (Controlling System and Internal Audit).[18] A cross-border survey of corporate governance practices, conducted by CLSA Asia-Pacific Markets,[19] shows that Thai practices compare favorably with those in China, the Philippines and Indonesia, but fall short of those in Malaysia, Korea and India.[20] Thailand earned particularly low ratings with regard to 'committed and effective enforcement of rules and regulations', 'the political and regulatory environment affecting corporate governance and the ability of companies to maximize value without arbitrary restrictions', and 'the adoption of International Generally Accepted Accounting Principles', although in each case the rankings showed improvement from 2002 to 2003.

The Thai authorities have also been active participants in regional initiatives to strengthen Asian bond markets. For example, Thai officials worked with the Asian Policy Forum (2001) to improve corporate bond markets in the region.[21] The proposal recognized that bond market development requires that governments make a number of policy trade-offs. Instead of borrowing only when a fiscal deficit arises and market conditions appear favorable, a government must borrow at regular intervals whether it needs the money or not. Instead of minimizing the cost of debt through requiring some institutions to hold the debt, a government must submit to a market determination of the interest rate. Similarly, rather than attempting to minimize the cost of the debt by playing the yield curve – which usually means borrowing at the short end – a government must issue regularly at

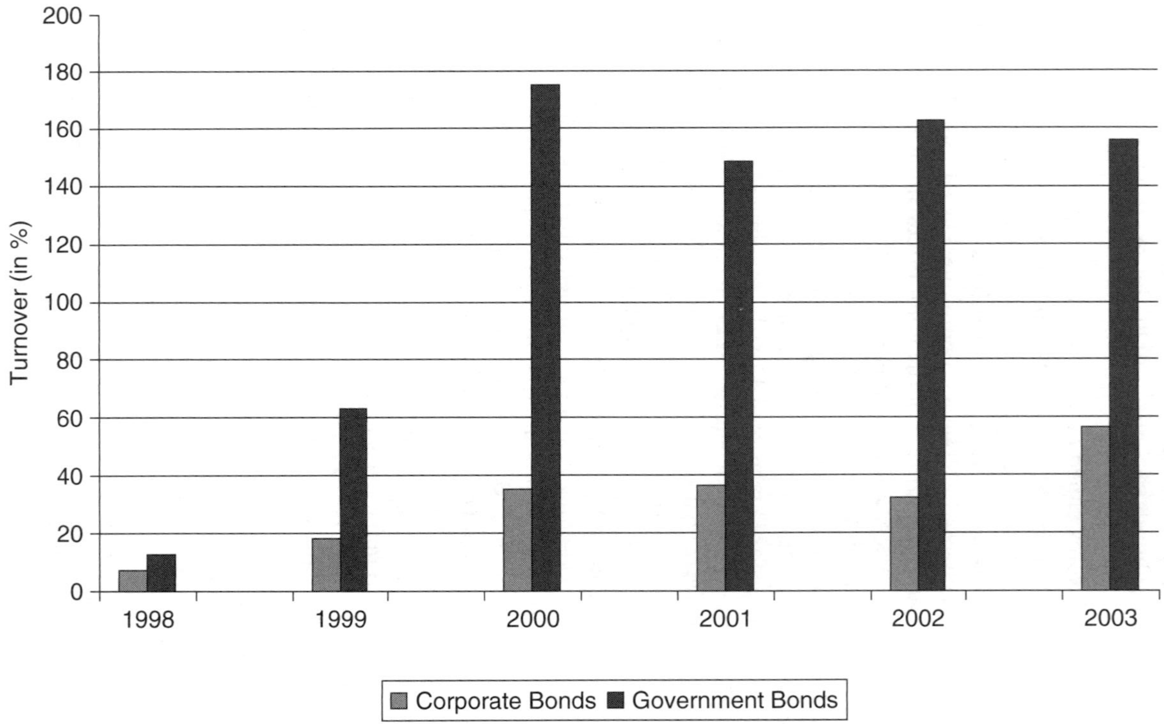

Source: Thai Bond Dealing Center.

Figure 5.2 Trading volume in Thai bond markets

each maturity interval. And, instead of raising revenue through taxing bond transactions, which discourages trading, the government must remove stamp taxes. Indeed, the Asian Policy Forum proposal even contemplated positive tax incentives.

More recently, along with ten[22] other Asian central banks, the Thai Central Bank formed the Executives' Meeting of East Asia-Pacific Central Banks (EMEAP) to consider ways to overcome the limitations inherent in the small size of most of the existing national markets and to work toward greater integration of these markets to form a regional market. This group established an Asian Bond Fund 1 (ABF 1) on 2 June, 2003 to invest about $1 billion in reserve assets in Asian bonds. On 16 December, 2004, a second fund was launched to invest in the local currency bonds of eight EMEAP members including Thailand. ABF 2 allocated about $2 billion to a Pan-Asia Bond Index Fund and a Fund of Bond Funds. ABF 2 is designed to encourage investment by public investors outside the EMEAP region and by private sector investors both in Asia and from around the world in local currency bonds of the EMEAP group.[23] The Thai government has also opened its market to issuance of local currency-denominated bonds by international financial institutions and borrowers from several other countries to further encourage the cross-border supply and trading of bonds.

The success of these efforts can be seen in the growth of bond markets in Asia. Relative to the pre-crisis situation, Table 5.16 shows that six of the

Table 5.16 The size of bond markets (as a % of GDP, average 1990–97 versus 2003)

	Bonds outstanding 1990–97	Bonds outstanding 2003
Hong Kong	11.3	28.7
Indonesia	1.8	27.5
Malaysia	68.5	95.1
Philippines	33.1	30.7
Singapore	28.4	63.2
South Korea	40.3	73.6
Thailand	9.9	39.7
Canada	81.8	81.4
Japan	90.1	181.8
United States	138.2	160.5
Euro Area	83.9	102.5
Non-euro EU	67.6	83.9

Source: World Bank Financial Structure and Economic Development Database.

Asian economies (the exception being the Philippines) have made substantial progress in developing their bond markets. The Thai bond market is more than four times larger, relative to GDP, than before the crisis.

As the Thai example has shown, bond markets do matter for financial development. Certainly, an economy can grow rapidly without an active bond market. But the cost is an increased vulnerability to a financial crisis and a loss of information to guide savings and investment decisions. Heavy reliance on banks means a correspondingly heavy exposure to banking crises. And the consequence can be catastrophic for the real economy. But the example of Thailand also shows that it may be possible to rebuild the financial system with an expanded role for the bond market.

NOTES

1. Hoontrakul (1996) provides a case study for Thailand.
2. Exceptions include Boot and Thakor (1997) and Hakansson (1999). Eichengreen, Chapter 3, this volume, also highlights the importance of bond markets.
3. Malaysia and South Korea appear to be exceptions to this generalization, but upon closer inspection neither country's bond market was as robust as these aggregate data indicate. The Malaysian market was dominated by issues of Malaysian government securities, which were placed in a, 'captive market' in which most financial intemediaries faced mandatory investment requirements (Harun, 2002). Until 2000, private issuance of bonds was deemed 'deposit taking' and subject to strict control by the Bank Negara Malaysia (Dalla et al., 1995, p. 81). The Korean bond market at this time also had an active corporate sector, but it was dominated by 'guaranteed' corporate bonds, for which the principal and interest were guaranteed by financial institutions that were assumed to be fully backed by the government. At that time, moreover, the financial sector held about four-fifths of the bonds and turnover was very low (Kim, 2000).
4. Higher returns on financial instruments may encourage saving; but higher returns also enable savers to achieve a target stock of wealth with a lower rate of saving. Thus in theory the impact of expected returns on the overall savings rate is ambiguous. Empirical studies across a number of countries have not been able to resolve the question. Nonetheless, higher returns on financial instruments will induce households to allocate more savings to financial instruments than to real assets such as jewelry and precious metals that do not contribute to productive investment (and, in an open economy, to shift from foreign to domestic assets). Efficient financial markets will allocate financial claims to projects that offer the highest, risk-adjusted returns and so income and total savings are likely to rise even though the savings rate may not.
5. Rajan and Zingales (1999) suggest that family groups may oppose financial development because improvements in capital markets would undermine the value of entrenched positions and increase competition.
6. Yet much of the complexity is obscured by the convention of aggregating flows by sector. Financial flows among financial firms are often very large relative to flows vis-à-vis other sectors. For example, interbank trading in the foreign exchange markets is roughly 90 percent of total volume and interbank transactions in the eurocurrency markets are virtually two-thirds of the total.
7. We shall use the term 'bond' in the broadest sense to include all tradable fixed income instruments such as bills and commercial paper (usually with maturities of less than one year), notes (with maturities of one to five years) and bonds (usually with maturities greater than five years).

8. Note that when the principal owners are the managers of the firm, the usual arguments about the disciplinary role of debt in constraining agency problems between the owner principal and manager agents do not apply.
9. Technically, it is not essential that the term structure be default risk-free. It is necessary, however, that the benchmark bonds that price the term structure share the same risk of default. In most markets, government issues, which are approximately default risk-free in domestic currency terms, provide the benchmarks for estimating the term structure of interest rates.
10. See, for example, the recent proposal by the Shadow Financial Regulatory Committee to require that all internationally active banks be required to issue subordinated debt (Calomiris et al., 2000).
11. The US, for example, is currently reducing the effective maturity of its outstanding debt. Because the US has a highly developed bond market with abundant issues by government-sponsored enterprises that serve as close substitutes for government debt, it may be able to reduce gross debt without undermining the efficiency of the bond market. This would not be a wise policy in an emerging market, however.
12. When Citibank introduced the Certificate of Deposit, it was careful to make arrangements with dealers to establish active secondary markets in which CDs could be traded.
13. Publicly traded corporations issue letter stock frequently in making acquisitions or raising capital when the time and cost of registering the new stock with the SEC (Securities and Exchange Commission) would make the transaction impractical. Even though such stock cannot be sold to the public on the open market, it may be sold in private transactions under certain circumstances. Such transactions must be reported to the SEC where they become a matter of public record Pratt (1989, p. 240).
14. Fernando and Herring (2002) have shown how liquidity depends on the diversity of market participants and provide evidence from a natural experiment in which the secondary market for perpetual floating rate notes collapsed and prices fell from 15 to 30 percent even though the credit standing of the issuers had not changed.
15. Emery (1997).
16. In 1999, the Securities and Exchange Commission passed a resolution requiring private placement debt of more than 100 million baht to be rated.
17. Retained earnings, of course, financed the remainder of the change in gross fixed capital formation.
18. *Thailand: Economic Monitor*, World Bank Thailand Office (2003), p. 33, Table 8.
19. CLSA Asia-Pacific Markets is a provider of brokerage and investment banking services, headquartered in Hong Kong.
20. *Thailand: Economic Monitor*, World Bank Thailand Office (2003), p. 34.
21. See also Yoshitomi and Shirai (2001) for an extensive discussion of many of the issues that underlie the proposals.
22. The other nine include the Reserve Bank of Australia, People's Bank of China, Hong Kong Monetary Authority, Bank of Indonesia, Bank of Japan, Bank of Korea, Bank Negara Malaysia, Reserve Bank of New Zealand, Bangko Sentral ng Pilipinas, and the Monetary Authority of Singapore.
23. For additional discussion, see *Asia Bond Monitor*, April 2005, Asian Development Bank.

REFERENCES

Alba, Pedro, Stijn Claessens and Simeon Djankov (1998), 'Thailand's Corporate Financing and Governance Structures: Impact on Firms' Competitiveness', Paper for the World Bank Conference on Thailand's Dynamic Economic Recovery and Competitiveness.

Allen, Franklin and Douglas Gale (2000), *Comparing Financial Systems*, Cambridge, MA: The MIT Press.

APEC (1999), *Compendium of Sound Practices, Guidelines to Facilitate the Development of Domestic Bond Markets in APEC Member Economies*, Report of the Collaborative Initiative on Development of Domestic Bond Markets.

Arrow, Kenneth (1979), 'Pareto Efficiency With Costly Transfers', *Economic Forum*, **10**, 1–13.

Asian Development Bank (1999), 'Governance in Thailand: Challenges, Issues and Prospects', http://www.adb.org/Work/Governance/thailand.pdf, April.

Asian Policy Forum (2001), 'Policy Recommendations for Designing New and Balanced Financial Market Structures in Post-crisis Asia, Proposals on How to Foster Bond Markets through Strengthening the Banking Sector', Asian Development Bank Institute, Forum Secretariat, October.

Bank for International Settlements, *International Financial Statistics*, http://www.bis.org/statistics.

Barro, Robert (1974), 'Are Government Bonds Net Wealth?', *Journal of Political Economy*, November/December, 1095–117.

Black, Bernard and Ronald Gilson (1998), 'Venture Capital and the Structure of Capital Markets: Banks Versus Stock Markets', *Journal of Financial Economics*, **47**, 243–77.

Black, Fischer (1976), 'The Pricing of Commodity Contracts', *Journal of Financial Economics*, **3**.

Black, Fischer and Myron Scholes (1973), 'The Pricing of Options and Corporate Liabilities', *Journal of Political Economy*, **81**, 637–59.

Boot, Arnoud and Anjan Thakor (1997), 'Financial System Architecture', *Review of Financial Studies*, **10** (3), 693–733.

Calomiris, Charles et al. (2000), *Reforming Bank Capital Regulation*, Proposal by the US Shadow Financial Regulatory Committee, Washington DC: American Enterprise Institute.

Caprio, Gerard, Jr and Aslï Demirgüç-Kunt (1997), 'The Role of Long Term Finance: Theory and Evidence', World Bank Working Paper, February.

Claessens, Stijn, Simeon Djankov and Larry H.P. Lang (1998a), 'Who Controls East Asian Corporations?', Working paper, World Bank.

Claessens, Stijn, Simeon Djankov and Larry H.P. Lang (1998b), 'East Asian Corporates: Growth, Financing and Risks over the Last Decade', Working paper, World Bank.

Claessens, Stijn, Simeon Djankov, Joseph P.H. Fan and Larry H.P. Lang (1998), 'Corporate Diversification in East Asia: The Role of Ultimate Ownership and Group Affiliation', Working paper, World Bank.

Copeland, Morris (1955), *A Study of Money Flows in the United States*, New York: National Bureau of Economic Research.

Dalla, Ismail, Deena Khatdhate, D.C. Rao, Kali Kondury, Lwang Jun and Terry Chuppe (1995), *The Emerging Asian Bond Market*, Washington DC: The World Bank.

Diamond, Douglas (1991), 'Debt, Maturity and Liquidity Risk', *Quarterly Journal of Economics*, **106**, 709–37.

Emery, Robert F. (1997), *The Bond Markets of Developing East Asia*, Boulder, Colorado: Westview Press.

Fernando, Chitru and Richard Herring (2002), 'Commonality in Liquidity and Market Collapse: Theory and Application to the Market for Perps', Working paper, Wharton Financial Institutions Center, The Wharton School, University of Pennsylvania.

Goldsmith, Raymond (1965), *The Flow of Capital Funds in the Postwar Economy*, New York: National Bureau of Economic Research, Chapter 2.

Goldsmith, Raymond (1985), *Comparative National Balance Sheets: A Study of Twenty Countries, 1688–1978*, Chicago: University of Chicago Press.

Guttentag, Jack M. and Richard J. Herring (1986), 'Financial Innovations to Stabilize Credit Flows to Developing Countries', *Studies in Banking and Finance*, **3**.

Hakansson, Nils H. (1982), 'Changes in Financial Markets: Welfare and Price Effects and the Basic Theories of Value Conservation', *Journal of Finance*, **37** (4), September, 977–1005.

Hakansson, Nils H. (1992), 'Welfare Economics of Financial Markets', in *The New Palgrave Dictionary of Money and Finance*, John Eatwell, Murray Milgate and Peter Newman (eds), London: MacMillan Press, pp. 790–96.

Hakansson, Nils H. (1999), 'The Role of a Corporate Bond Market in an Economy – and in Avoiding Crises', *China Accounting and Finance Review*, **1** (1), March.

Hart, Oliver and John Moore (1995), 'Debt and Seniority: An Analysis of the Role of Hard Claims in Constraining Management', *American Economic Journal*, June, 567–85.

Harun, Dato' Salleh (2002), 'The Development of Debt Markets in Malaysia', *BIS Papers No.11*, Bank for International Settlements, 147–50

Hoontrakul, Pongsak (1996), 'Should Thailand Have Bank Based or Stock Market Based Financial Systems?', Discussion paper, Sasin-GIBA.

Hausman, Jerry A. and James M. Poterba (1987), 'Household Behavior and the Tax Reform Act of 1986', *Economic Perspectives*, **1** (1), summer, 101–19.

Herring, Richard (1989), 'The Economics of Workout Lending', *Journal of Money, Credit and Banking*, **21**, February, 1–15.

International Monetary Fund (1999), *International Financial Statistics Yearbook*.

International Monetary Fund (2005), *Global Financial Stability Review*, April.

Kane, Edward J. (2000a), 'Architecture of Supra-governmental International Financial Regulation', Working paper, Boston College.

Kane, Edward J. (2000b), 'Designing Financial Safety Nets to Fit Country Circumstances', Working paper, Boston College.

Kim, Yongbeom (2000), 'Korea's Bond Market Following the Onset of Financial Crisis', *Building Local Bond Markets: An Asian Perspective*, International Finance Corporation, pp. 63–83.

La Porta, Rafael, Florencio Lopez-de-Silanes, Andrei Shleifer and Robert Vishny (1998), 'Law and Finance', *Journal of Political Economy*, **106**, 1113–55.

Levine, Ross (1997), 'Financial Development and Economic Growth: Views and Agenda', *Journal of Economic Literature*, **36**, 688–726.

McKinnon, Ronald (1973), *Money and Capital in Economic Development*, Washington: Brookings Institution.

Merton, Robert (1989), 'On the Application of the Continuous-time Theory of Finance to Financial Intermediation and Insurance', *The Geneva Papers on Risk and Insurance*, **14** (52), July, 225–61.

Merton, Robert (1990), 'The Financial System and Economic Performance', *Journal of Financial Services Research*, **4**, December, 263–300.

Pratt, Shannon P. (1989), *Valuing a Business, The Analysis and Appraisal of Closely Held Companies*, Homewood: Dow Jones-Irwin, 2nd Edition.

Rajan, Raghuram and Luigi Zingales (1999), 'The Politics of Financial Development', Working paper, University of Chicago.
Shaw, Edward (1973), *Financial Deepening in Economic Development*, New York: Oxford University Press.
Sheng, Andrew (1994), 'Future Directions for Hong Kong's Debt Market', Speech at the First Annual Pan-Asia Bonds Summit 29–30 November.
Smith, Clifford, Jr, Charles Smithson and Lee Wakeman (1986), 'The Evolving Market for Swaps', *Midland Corporate Finance Journal*, winter.
Sonakul, M.R. Chatu Mongol (2000), 'Keynote Address on the Occasion of the ADB Conference on Government Bond Market and Financial Sector Development in Developing Asian Economies', Manila, 28–30 March.
Stiglitz, Joseph E. and Andrew Weiss (1981), 'Credit Rationing in Markets with Imperfect Information', *American Economic Review*, **LXXXI** (3), June, 393–410.
Stulz, René (2000), 'Does Financial Structure Matter for Economic Growth? A Corporate Finance Perspective', Working paper, 24 January.
Thai Bond Dealing Center, http://www.thaibdc.or.th.
Weinstein, D.E. and Y. Yafeh (1998), 'On the Costs of a Bank Centered Financial System: Evidence from the Changing Main Bank Relations in Japan', *Journal of Finance*, **53** (2), 635–72.
World Bank (2004), *Doing Business in 2004: Understanding Regulation*, Washington: The International Bank for Reconstruction and Development/The World Bank.
World Bank (2005), Financial Structure and Economic Development Database, http://www.worldbank.org/research/projects/finstructure/database.htm.
World Bank Thailand Office (2003), *Thailand: Economic Monitor*, October, http://siteresources.worldbank.org/INTTHAILAND/Resources/Economic-Monitor/2003oct.pdf.
Yam, Joseph (1997), 'Development of the Debt Market, Keynote Address at the Asian Debt Conference', http://www.info.gov.hk/hkma/eng/speeches/speechs/joseph/speech_140797b.htm, 14 July.
Yoshitomi, Masaru and Sayuri Shirai (2001), 'Designing a Financial Market Structure in Post-crisis Asia', ADB Institute Working Paper 15, 27 March.

PART III

Analytical Issues Pertaining to the Recent Crises

6. Investment, growth and productivity during the East Asian Financial Crisis

F. Gerard Adams and Tayyeb Shabbir

1 INTRODUCTION

Almost ten years have passed since the East Asian Financial Crisis so rudely interrupted the rapid expansion of the East Asian economies. Most scholars have sought to evaluate the crisis phenomenon and its impact in terms of financial flows, international exchange exposure, contagion, etc. All of these factors seem to have had some relevance (Corsetti et al., 1998a and 1998b; Radelet and Sachs, 1998). Comparatively, little analysis has been devoted to the crisis from a production input/factor productivity perspective. Such a view has important implications for the growth prospects of the East Asian countries.

In this chapter, we will consider the East Asian Crisis from the perspective of macroeconomic performance, its impact on investment, growth and productivity. First, we discuss the East Asian growth process and its relationship to underlying growth forces. Then, we look at developments from an empirical perspective, computing total factor productivity and testing various explanations for it. Finally, we will speculate about the long-run implications for future development in East Asia.

2 ECONOMIC DEVELOPMENT, GROWTH AND THE FINANCIAL CRISIS

East Asian growth has been a process of transformation, turning low income subsistence agriculture countries into export industry powerhouses. Traditional development theory sees East Asian growth as export-led industrialization (Herrick and Kindleberger, 1983). High rates of domestic investment and capital inflows, improved production competence, and, often, international entrepreneurship enabled these countries, one after the other, to use their comparative advantage in low labor costs to compete effectively in world markets. Rising living standards then contributed to a growing domestic market that has also benefited East Asian industry.

The economic development of East Asia has sometimes been described as a sequential growth pattern followed by the countries in the region. Akamatsu (1961, 1962) pioneered the concept of the 'Flying Geese Pattern' (Kojima, 2000), an idea that has often been interpreted as a sequence of policy steps following the leader country, presumably Japan. But Akamatsu's early work already pointed to a rationale based on the changing patterns of comparative advantage as countries advance along the development ladder (Adams, 1998). The basic notion assumes that relatively low wages and favorable exchange rates initially provide comparative advantage in labor-intensive products like apparel and consumer electronics exports to the world market. As development advances, rising wage levels and appreciating exchange rates reduce comparative advantage in labor-intensive products. At this stage of development, production of traditional products is shifted to countries that still have lower costs and the more advanced East Asian countries turn to more sophisticated and, typically, more capital- and technology-intensive products. As the required technology comes closer to the technological frontier, growth is somewhat slower. Finally, we can envision a still more advanced stage of development with emphasis on sophisticated services like finance, management and high technology. The essential ingredient during the transition period is the shift of production toward industrial output and the acquisition of knowledge and experience (and capital) that makes possible the production of items that are competitive in the world market. High rates of investment, redirection of economic activity toward industrial products for domestic and export markets, and direct foreign investment appear to be important in facilitating these developments.

Another perspective on East Asian growth that we will emphasize, is the role of inputs and of total factor productivity (TFP), a term that summarizes structural changes and economies of scale, as well as technological change. The growth accounting framework has been applied to examine East Asian growth in a number of earlier papers (Collins and Bosworth, 1996; Crafts, 1999). The principal issue in these papers is to explain East Asia's rapid growth, specifically the explanation for East Asian growth as 'accumulation versus assimilation'[1] and to evaluate whether there remains substantial room for a productivity catch-up. The magnitude of an unexplained total factor productivity growth component in East Asian growth is a matter of controversy (World Bank, 1993) ever since empirical economists (Krugman, 1994; Young, 1995) have reported that, for some East Asian countries, rapid growth has been primarily a matter of more intensive input use rather than increased Total Factor Productivity (TFP).[2] By and large, the later empirical work suggests that while a large share of the growth in the region is attributable to growth of inputs, there remains substantial room for productivity catch-up (Timmer and Szirmai, 1997; Lau, 1998).

The growth accounting papers have used the traditional production function approach and then have attempted to explain the unexplained residual in terms of a number of general and country-specific variables. Some of these variables relate to the quality of inputs, for example, mean years of schooling acquired by labor, but others relate to macroeconomic issues like the exchange rate and the government budget deficit. Interestingly, these studies have not taken into account the impact of the business cycle, despite the fact that business fluctuations are known to be an important variable in explaining short-term variations in productivity in the industrial countries.[3]

Being aware of the sometimes heated debate that can involve the concept of total factor productivity (TFP), we would like to note that we intend to use the TFP concept non-judgmentally, that is, only as a mechanical way for summarizing growth that is not directly the result of increased factor inputs and not associate any one *specific* interpretation to this residual. Then we will try to explain computed TFP in terms of variables that relate to the speed of growth, industrialization and exports. An important aspect of our explanation will be the impact of the fluctuation in real output that was associated with the 1997 financial crisis. We stress that an emphasis on real output and productivity does not necessarily contradict the linkages between the rate and patterns of development and international financial considerations like capital flows, exchange rates, competitiveness and expectations that lie behind traditional explanations of the East Asian Crisis.

3 THE FINANCIAL CRISIS AND THE GROWTH RECORD

As is well known, the rapid development of East Asia was interrupted in the late 1990s by the East Asian Financial Crisis, introducing a sharp reversal in output growth and investment throughout the region. The impact was uneven with little apparent influence on China but with serious recessionary effect on the domestic economies of some countries, particularly Thailand, South Korea and Indonesia. Rapid growth of exports, in part, a result of financial crisis-induced exchange rate readjustments and a gradual return to higher rates of investment (though not as a share of GDP) have enabled most East Asian countries to resume their rapid growth in recent years.

Let us start by looking here at the East Asian growth record (Figure 6.1). The 1997 and 1998 period shows a severe interruption of real growth at the

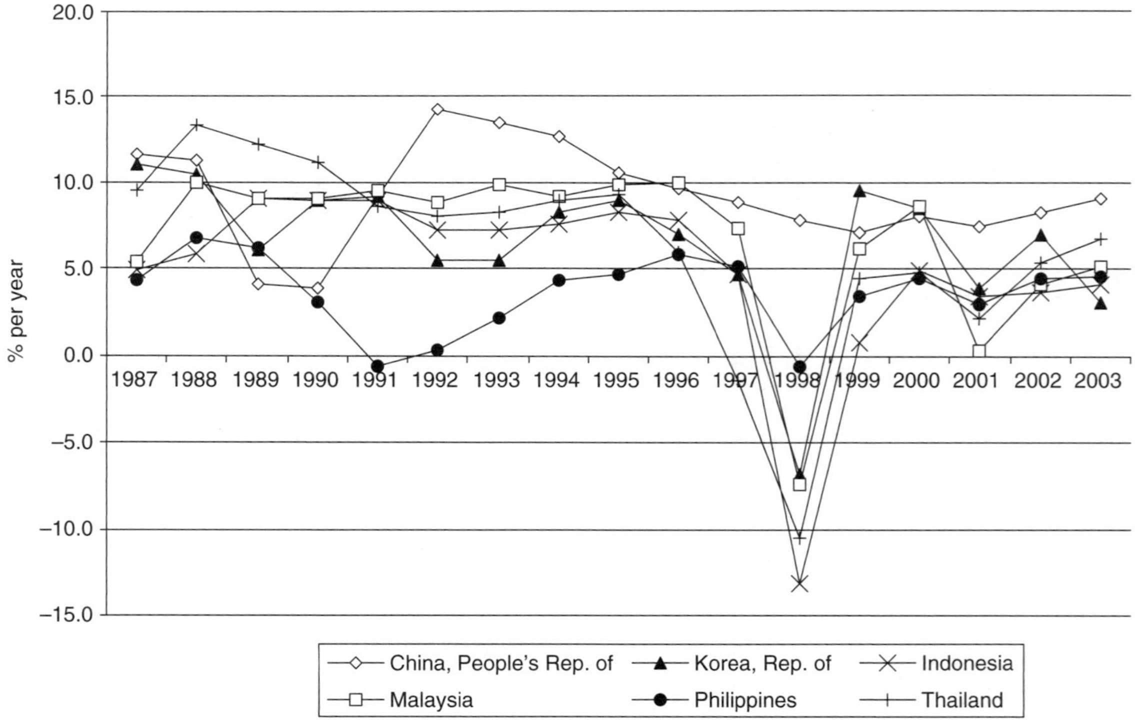

Figure 6.1 GDP growth rates

Table 6.1 Growth of real GDP, pre- and post-crisis (% per year)

	Pre-crisis Period		Financial Crisis Period			Post-crisis	Post vs. Pre-crisis
	1987–91	1991–96	1997	1998	1999	1999–2003	Difference*
China, People's Rep.	8.0	12.1	8.8	7.8	7.1	8.2	−3.9
Hong Kong, China	6.6	5.3	5.1	−5.0	3.4	3.9	−1.4
Korea, Rep. of	9.1	7.0	4.7	−6.9	9.5	5.6	−1.4
Indonesia	7.5	7.6	4.7	−13.1	0.8	4.0	−3.6
Malaysia	8.6	9.6	7.3	−7.4	6.1	4.5	−5.1
Philippines	3.9	3.5	5.2	−0.6	3.4	4.1	0.6
Singapore	9.3	9.3	8.6	−0.9	6.9	2.8	−6.5
Thailand	10.9	8.1	−1.4	−10.5	4.4	4.8	−3.3
Taipei	8.4	6.8	6.7	4.6	5.4	2.6	−4.2

Note: * (1999–2003) minus (1991–96).

Source: Asian Development Bank.

time of the East Asian Financial Crisis for all the East Asian countries except China. We show the relevant averages in Table 6.1 for the pre-crisis period, for the time of the financial crisis – 1997, 1998 and 1999 – and for a post-crisis period. Before the crisis, the growth rates are extraordinarily high in all the countries except the late-blooming Philippines, ranging from 6.8 percent in Taipei to 12.1 percent in China. The crisis-induced downswing is clearly apparent in 1997–98 particularly in Indonesia, Thailand, Malaysia and South Korea. The period 1998–99 is a time that marks the start of the recovery. The post-crisis period shows renewed growth but, with the exception of the Philippines, at substantially lower growth rates than in the pre-crisis period.

Now let us examine labor productivity which provides a simple way to measure improvements in a nation's productive power. Figure 6.2 and Table 6.2 show the movement of labor productivity in East Asia. For most countries, except China, the rate of productivity growth shows fluctuations, in relation particularly to the 1997–98 crisis. There appears to be a downward trend, with growth in the post-crisis period substantially lower than in the years that preceded the crisis.

The 1997–98 crisis is dominated by a huge swing in the share of fixed investment in GDP (Table 6.3, Figure 6.3). Before the crisis, gross fixed capital formation had risen to high levels relative to GDP, between 30 and 40 percent, in all the East Asian countries, except Thailand and the

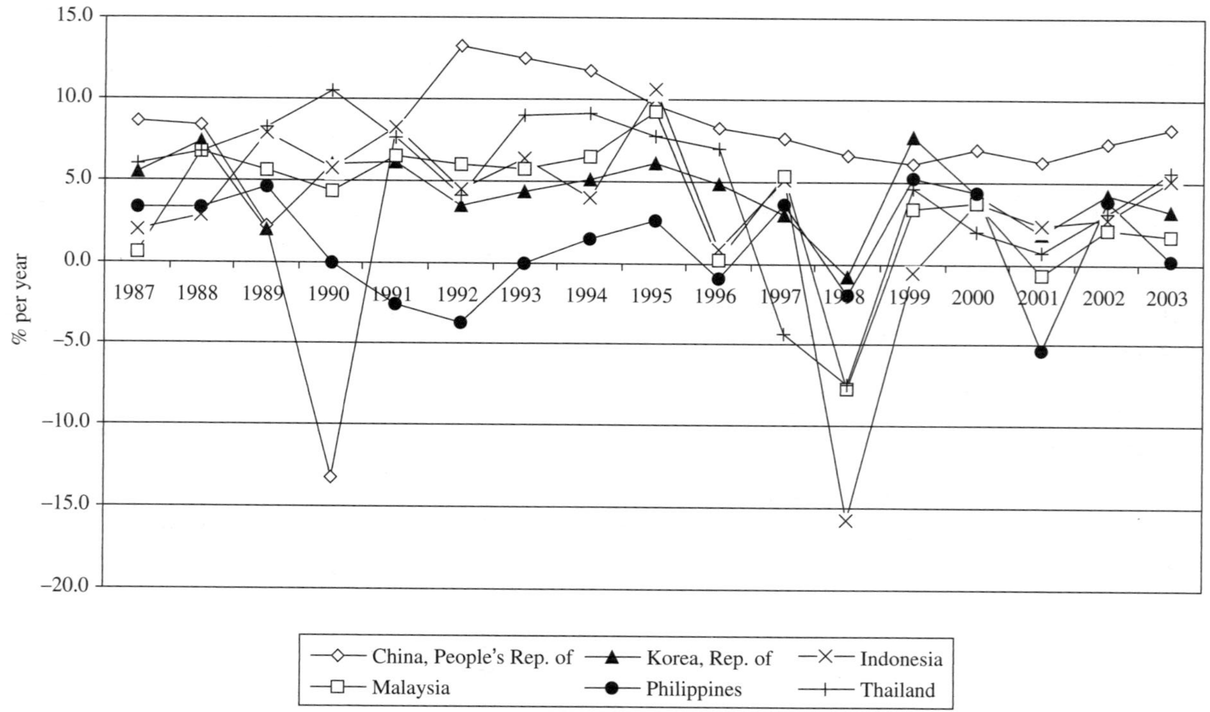

Figure 6.2 Labour productivity growth

Table 6.2 Improvement of labor productivity, pre- and post-crisis (% per year)

	Pre-crisis Period					Post-crisis Period	
	1987–91	1991–96	1997	1998	1999	2000–03	Difference*
China, People's Rep. of	2.8	11.1	7.6	6.6	6.1	7.2	−3.9
Hong Kong, China	5.6	3.1	2.1	−3.7	3.7	3.0	0.0
Korea, Rep. of	5.4	4.8	2.9	−0.8	7.7	3.4	−1.4
Indonesia	5.3	5.2	5.0	−15.8	−0.5	3.5	−1.8
Malaysia	4.7	5.5	5.3	−7.7	3.4	1.7	−3.7
Philippines	1.7	−0.2	3.6	−1.9	5.2	0.8	0.9
Singapore	4.7	6.5	3.9	−3.1	6.0	0.7	−5.8
Thailand	7.8	7.4	−4.3	−7.4	4.6	2.8	−4.6
Taipei	6.6	5.4	5.5	3.3	4.4	2.1	−3.3

Note: * (2000–2003) minus (1991–96).

Source: Asian Development Bank.

Table 6.3 Investment as share of GDP: pre- and post-crisis (% of GDP)

	Pre-crisis				Post-crisis	
	1986–90	1991–96	1997	1998	1999–2003	Difference*
China, People's Rep. of	36.3	39.3	38.2	37.7	39.4	0.1
Hong Kong, China	26.7	30.3	34.5	29.2	25.1	−5.2
Korea, Rep. of	30.4	31.3	31.8	16.8	15.4	−15.9
Indonesia	32.4	37.6	36.0	25.0	29.6	−8.0
Malaysia	27.5	39.8	43.0	26.7	23.8	−16.0
Philippines	19.4	22.7	24.8	20.3	19.7	−3.0
Singapore	36.1	35.1	39.2	32.3	24.7	−10.4
Thailand	21.7	24.8	24.2	24.9	19.6	−5.2
Taipei, China	32.6	41.2	33.7	20.4	23.3	−17.9

Note: * (1999–2003) minus (1991–96).

Source: Asian Development Bank.

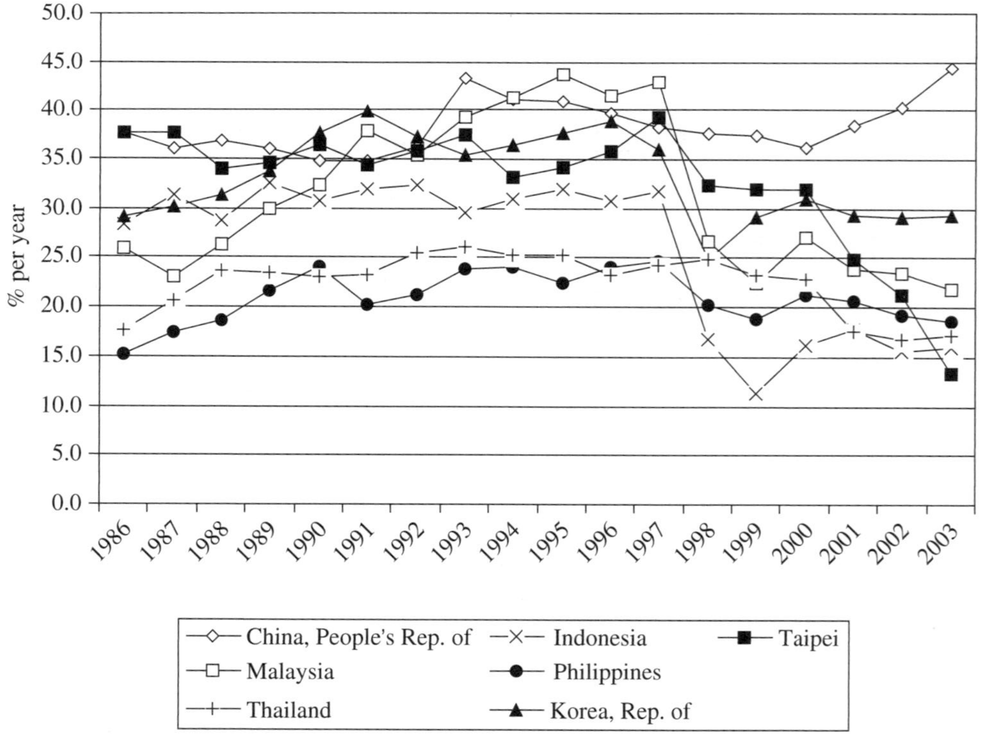

Figure 6.3 Gross domestic fixed investments as % of GDP

*Table 6.4 Growth of capital stock:** pre- and post-crisis (% per year)*

	Pre-crisis					Post-crisis	
	1986–91	1991–96	1997	1998	1999	1999–2003	Difference*
China, People's Rep. of	9.30	9.60	10.10	9.40	9.00	8.80	−0.90
Hong Kong, China	4.70	5.50	7.00	7.60	5.90	3.80	−1.80
Korea, Rep. of	7.30	9.20	12.10	9.90	5.40	5.90	−3.30
Indonesia	3.00	6.90	8.70	8.70	3.40	2.50	−4.40
Malaysia	5.70	11.50	12.80	12.20	3.80	3.80	−7.80
Philippines	2.30	3.00	4.20	4.80	3.30	3.30	0.30
Singapore	7.40	8.20	10.70	10.70	8.30	5.80	−2.30
Thailand	8.70	10.70	10.10	5.90	0.70	0.80	−9.90
Taipei	2.70	5.50	5.70	6.20	6.40	4.60	−0.90

Notes:
* (1991–96) minus (1999–2003).
** Computed from investment, an initial capital output ratio of 3 and an assumed depreciation rate of 0.05 per year.

Source: Asian Development Bank.

Philippines. This represents an extremely high rate since it implies an estimated increase in capital stock and, in capital, on the basis of our estimates, of almost 10 percent annually (Table 6.4). This rate of capital accumulation was maintained even in 1997 but dropped sharply in 1998 except in China. In fact, the post-crisis period shows relatively small recovery of the investment/GDP ratio. As compared with the pre-crisis period, capital investment in all East Asian countries has been accounting for a substantially lower share of GDP post-crisis with the glaring exception of China. Also, the rate of capital stock accumulations has been substantially lower post-crisis in all East Asian countries except the Philippines (Table 6.4).

Remarkably, the mostly adverse swing in investment was not matched by a similar swing in domestic saving, which remained comparatively stable as a share of GDP, so that post-crisis domestic saving greatly exceeded domestic investment in some East Asian countries, particularly in Malaysia and Singapore (Figure 6.4). The reconciling figures were, obviously, capital flows – foreign inflows turned sharply to outflows after the financial crisis.

Finally, note that export growth declined sharply in advance of and during the crisis (Figure 6.5, Table 6.5). In fact, it has been argued that the lag in the performance of export markets as early as in 1996, was one of the

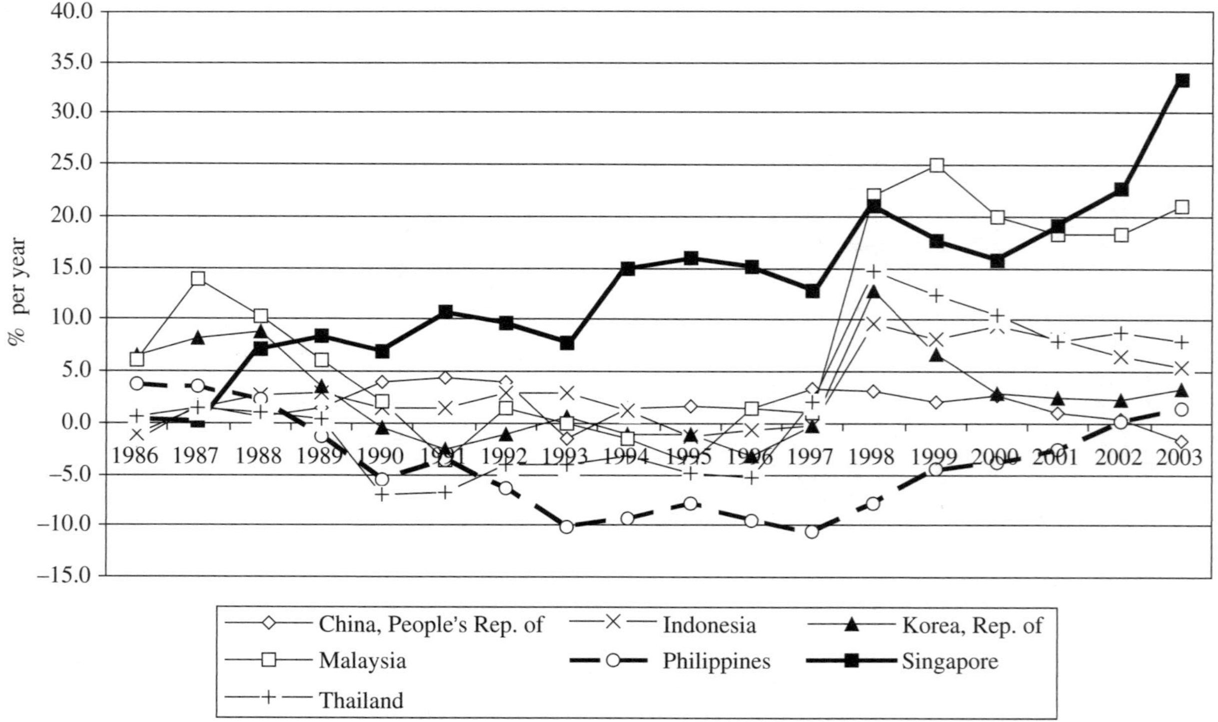

Figure 6.4 Domestic saving less domestic investment (% of GDP)

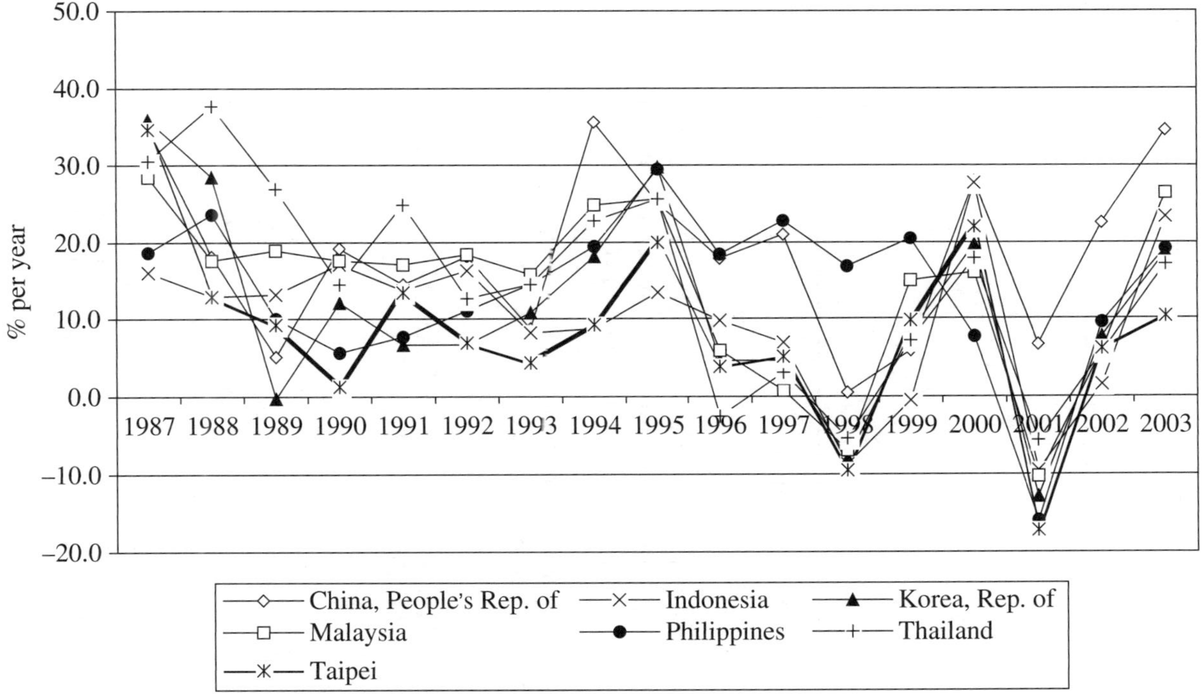

Figure 6.5 East Asian export growth (in US$)

Table 6.5 Growth of exports: pre- and post-crisis (In US $, % change per year)

	Pre-crisis						Post-crisis	
	1986–91	1991–95	1996	1997	1998	1999	1999–2003	Difference*
China	18.4	21.8	17.9	20.9	0.5	6.1	22.9	1.1
Hong Kong	23.0	15.2	4.0	4.1	−7.5	0.1	6.9	−8.4
Indonesia	14.5	11.8	9.8	7.1	−8.6	−0.4	10.7	−1.0
Korea	16.6	16.4	4.6	4.8	−7.9	8.2	8.3	−8.1
Malaysia	19.8	21.1	6.1	0.9	−6.9	15.1	9.5	−11.5
Philippines	13.2	18.6	18.3	22.8	16.9	20.3	5.1	−13.5
Singapore	21.7	19.2	5.9	0.2	−12.3	4.4	6.6	−12.6
Thailand	26.8	18.8	−2.5	3.3	−5.3	7.3	8.8	−10.1
Taiwan	14.3	10.2	3.8	5.3	−9.4	10.0	5.4	−4.8

Note: * (1999–2003) minus (1991–95).

Source: Asian Development Bank.

major contributing factors to the onset of the 1997 crisis (Adams, 1998). The recovery of exports after devaluation provided an important offset to the lower investment share in the post-crisis period, but export growth in the post-crisis period has been lower than before the crisis. China is, again, a glaring exception. The importance of exports here is that export production is hypothesized to contribute to the growth of productivity.

4 DISENTANGLING EAST ASIAN GROWTH: AN INPUT/TOTAL FACTOR PRODUCTIVITY APPROACH

In view of the complex interactions between the various forces to which the East Asian Crisis can be attributed, it is helpful to look at the phenomenon from the perspective of the underlying forces influencing the production potential of the region's economies. For this purpose, we take an input/total factor productivity view of the developments. Growth of output can be disentangled into that attributable to increased inputs and the residual factor, often termed 'total factor productivity'. (Denison, 1974; Solow, 1956).

Following Solow, the residual represents the difference between the growth of total output and a weighted sum of growth in labor and capital inputs:

$$\text{\% change of TFP} = \text{\% change of GDP} - (w_l * \text{\% change of labor} + w_k * \text{\% change of capital}).$$

The weights w_l and w_k correspond to factor shares assuming perfect competition and constant returns to scale.[4]

This decomposition analysis represents a very simple yet quite useful way to characterize the growth process. With standard assumptions about the weighting of the inputs and returns to scale, it provides a framework for empirical analysis. Crafts (1999) and Collins and Bosworth (1996) consider the possibilities for appropriate coefficients at some length. A range of weights for the capital component, from 0.3 to 0.4 is considered, with the suggestion that the elasticity of output with respect to capital might be on the high end of the range in East Asia. We have assumed $w_k = 0.4$ and $w_l = 0.6$.[5] The impact of the coefficient assumptions that underlie the calculation was validated with a sensitivity analysis.[6] As noted earlier, we are interpreting the meaning of the residual in a limited sense since it includes all elements that have not been taken into account in the computation of the growth of inputs. In addition to technological change, these include such factors as possible economies of scale, the composition of output, the role of exports, and, importantly, the cyclical position of the economy.[7] It is possible to hypothesize about the forces that might influence TFP, some closely related to industrial growth and consequent shifting from inefficient to efficient sectors, and others representing technical or managerial change that is associated with development of science and production techniques and which is more difficult to measure. In summary, we can define unexplained change in TFP as the remaining effect unaccounted for in such 'systematic' influences as business cycle effects as well as industrial composition and export effects. Thus:

Unexplained change of TFP = change of TFP – business cycle effect – industrial composition minus export effect.

Unexplained TFP then includes interaction effects, increasing returns and pure technical change.

Statistics on estimated total labor and capital inputs are presented in Figure 6.6 and, on a pre-crisis and post-crisis basis in Table 6.6 and corresponding figures for the residual growth factor are shown in Figure 6.7 and Table 6.7. The financial crisis period shows a sharp decline in the weighted sum of the growth rate of factor inputs in all countries except China and Taipei. Notable is the fact that input growth remains lower in all East Asian countries post-crisis than in the pre-crisis period, particularly in Indonesia, Malaysia and Thailand.

The growth of the residual (TFP) shows considerable variability from year to year and, particularly, over the financial crisis period. This reflects changes in efficiency of capital and labor use during the cycle. Capital stock

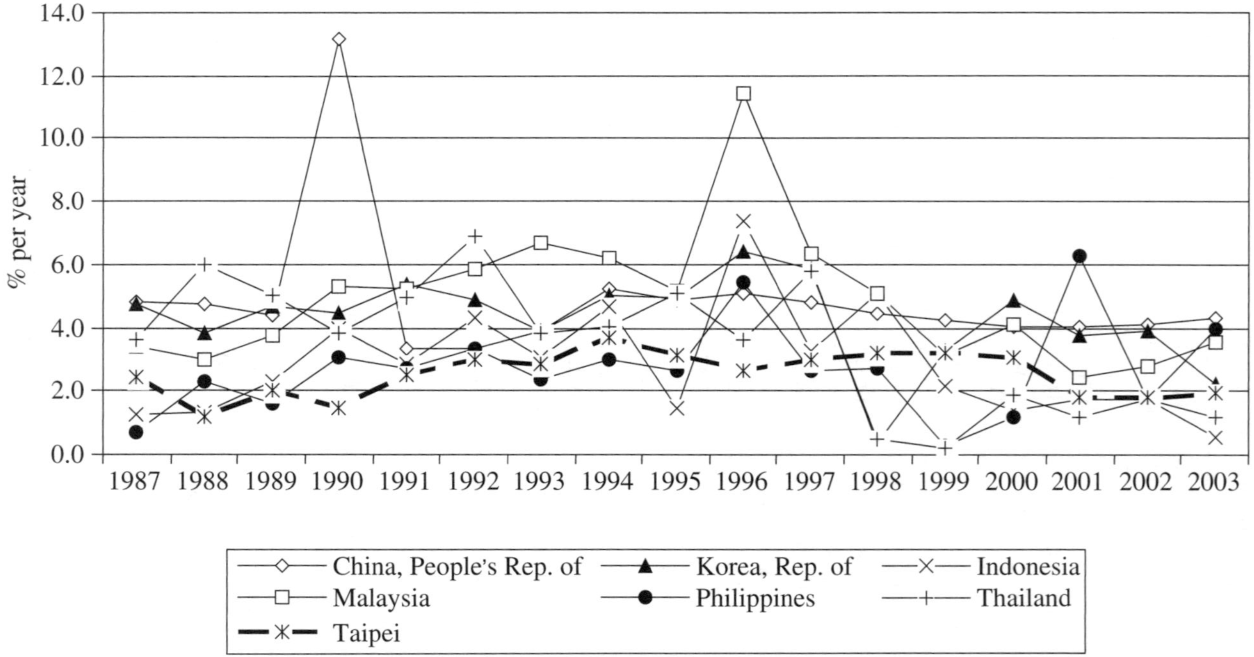

Figure 6.6 Growth of East Asian inputs of labor and capital (% per year, w_k *= 0.6 and* w_k *= 0.4)*

Table 6.6 Growth of capital and labor inputs in East Asia: pre-crisis and post-crisis (% per year assuming $w_k = 0.4$ *and* $w_l = 0.6$*)*

	Pre-crisis					Post-crisis	
	1987–91	1991–96	1997	1998	1999	1999–2003	Difference*
China, People's Rep. of	6.1	4.5	4.8	4.5	4.2	4.1	−0.3
Hong Kong, China	2.1	3.5	4.5	2.3	2.1	2.0	−1.5
Korea, Rep. of	4.6	5.0	5.9	0.4	3.2	3.7	−1.3
Indonesia	2.3	4.2	3.3	5.1	2.2	1.3	−2.8
Malaysia	4.1	7.1	6.3	5.1	3.2	3.2	−3.9
Philippines	2.1	3.4	2.7	2.7	0.3	3.3	−0.1
Singapore	5.2	4.9	7.1	5.6	3.9	3.6	−1.4
Thailand	4.7	4.7	5.8	0.5	0.2	1.5	−3.2
Taipei, China	1.9	3.1	3.0	3.2	3.2	2.1	−0.9

Note: Computed. *(1999–2003) minus (1991–96).

continues to grow during the first years of the financial crisis (note the estimates in Table 6.4) but output declines. Similarly, procyclical variation of labor productivity is well-known – employers delay hiring during the upswing and postpone layoffs during the downswing, producing cyclical variations in labor productivity over the cycle. In the post-crisis period, TFP growth is considerably lower than in pre-crisis China, Singapore and Taipei, but not in the other East Asian countries. In China, this may reflect statistical changes towards a 'norm', given the astonishingly high rate recorded earlier. In Taipei and Singapore, the decline in TFP growth may be a result of the fact that these countries are approaching the technological frontier in their high-tech industries.

5 STATISTICAL ANALYSIS OF 'DETERMINANTS' OF TFP

We proceed next to a statistical analysis of factors associated with the growth of TFP. As noted, TFP is measured as a residual from the standard growth accounting relationship and may encompass a number of factors – systematic as well as stochastic. Moreover, technical change is difficult to measure directly, since changes in production methods are difficult to pin down numerically. We test a number of factors suggested in our discussion

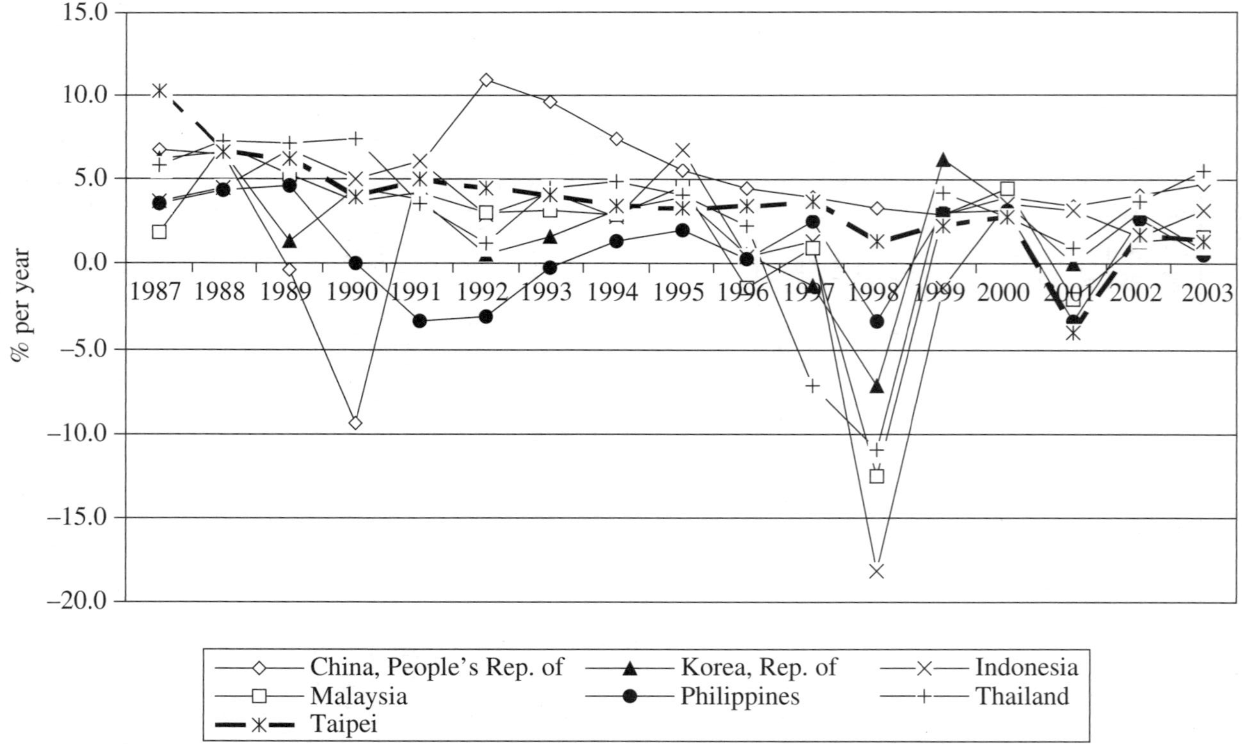

Figure 6.7 East Asian total factor productivity 1987–2003

Table 6.7 Total factor productivity growth in East Asia: pre-crisis and post-crisis (% per year assuming $w_k = 0.4$ *and* $w_l = 0.6$*)*

	Pre-crisis					Post-crisis	
	1987–91	1991–96	1997	1998	1999	1999–2003	Difference*
China, People's Rep. of	1.9	7.6	4.1	3.4	2.9	4.1	−3.5
Hong Kong, China	4.5	1.8	0.5	−7.2	1.3	1.9	0.1
Korea, Rep. of	4.5	2.0	−1.2	−7.2	6.2	1.9	−0.1
Indonesia	5.2	3.4	1.4	−18.2	−1.4	2.9	−0.5
Malaysia	4.4	2.5	1.0	−12.5	3.0	1.3	−1.2
Philippines	1.9	0.1	2.5	−3.3	3.1	0.8	0.7
Singapore	4.1	4.4	1.4	−6.5	3.0	−0.8	−5.2
Thailand	6.3	3.4	−7.1	−11.0	4.2	3.3	−0.1
Taipei, China	6.4	3.8	3.7	1.3	2.2	0.5	−3.3

Note: Computed. * (1999–2003) minus (1991–96).

above that might affect TFP, either by moving businesses away from the historical production path, such as in the financial crisis or shifts into new industries, or that might move the productivity path such as technical change incorporated in investment.

5.1 Financial Crisis Impacts

The 1997 financial crisis is the sharpest and most pervasive business fluctuation episode that affected the East Asian countries during the past two decades. As we have noted, there were severe declines in real output in most East Asian countries in 1997–98. We have examined the effect of these events on productivity using regressions linking TFP to a series of dummy variables covering the 1997–2001 period (Table 6.8). The significant coefficients for 1997 and 1998, amounting to 1 percent in 1997 (largely the effect on Thailand) and 9 percent for 1998, show that declines in production have clear impacts on TFP, probably through underutilization of capital and labor. Note that these effects are in addition to effects related to use of less labor and slower growth of capital that have been incorporated into inputs.

A closely related question is whether the impact of the crisis was symmetrical, in the sense that the loss in productivity suffered in 1997–98 was made up at a later point. That does not appear to be the case. With reference to Equation 2, the regression showing dummies for 1997, 1998 and

Table 6.8 Financial crisis impact on TFP

Equation 1			
	Coefficient	Standard error	Significance
Dependent variable			
% change TFP			
Independent variables			
Dummy 1997	−2.516	1.155	Significant
Dummy 1998	−10.022	1.155	Significant
Dummy 1999	−0.474	1.155	Non-significant
Constant	3.213	0.298	
Adjusted R^2	0.343		
Equation 2			
Dependent variable			
% change TFP			
Independent variables			
Dummy 1997	−3.096	1.136	Significant
Dummy 1998	−10.602	1.136	Significant
Dummy 1999	−1.055	1.136	Non-significant
Dummy 2000–03	−2.031	0.640	Significant
Constant	3.793	0.343	
Adjusted R^2	0.385		
Equation 3			
Dependent variable			
% change TFP			
Independent variables			
Time	−0.313	0.113	Significant
Dummy 1997	−1.371	1.274	Marginal
Dummy 1998	−8.563	1.333	Significant
Dummy 1999	1.297	1.399	Non-significant
Dummy 2000–03	1.105	1.294	Non-significant
Constant	5.518	0.707	
Adjusted R^2	0.416		

2000–03 shows negative coefficients, significant for 2000–03. A time trend, Equation 3, is significantly negative, suggesting that productivity growth is slowing over a longer period. In this case, the coefficients of the 1999 and the 2000–03 dummies are positive but not significant. In any case, the decline in TFP as a result of the financial crisis in 1997 and 1998, amounting to more than 10 percent was not made up in the recovery period.

Table 6.9 Regression test on residual factor

Equation 4	Coefficient	Standard error	Significance
Dependent variable			
% change TFP			
Independent variables			
China dummy	0.501	1.037	Non-significant
Dummy 1997	−1.109	0.871	Marginal
Dummy 1998	−4.169	1.066	Significant
Dummy 2000–03	−0.282	0.575	Non-significant
Income pc. ppp basis	−2.735E−06	3.500E−05	Non-significant
Industry share	−0.035	0.032	Marginal
Change of ind. share	−1.426	0.254	Significant
FDI/employment	2.163E−05	3.382E−05	Non-significant
Investment/GDP	−0.055	0.035	Marginal
% change exports	5.895	2.076	Significant
% change industrial output	49.774	5.729	Significant
Constant	1.870	1.805	
Adjusted R^2	0.683		

5.2 Impact of Industrial Production, Exports and Investment

The question is whether other variables like increasing exports, share of investment, or industrialization contribute to explaining the productivity (TFP) residual. Our fundamental hypothesis is that much of East Asian growth can be explained in terms of inputs and growth of production of industrial products and particularly products directed at the export market that involve greater productivity than traditional goods and services. We have tested numerous variables that might explain the unexplained part of growth of productivity in East Asia. In each case, we have included dummy variables to account for the productivity changes associated with the financial crisis. The computations are pooled time series/cross-section regressions covering eight East Asian countries over the period 1987–2003. The coefficients for the country dummies were not significantly different from zero.

A number of variables that might relate to the residual were tested separately and in combination. (Table 6.9). As anticipated, change in industrial output and change in exports make significant contributions to residual productivity change, 0.5 percent for each 1 percent increase in industrial production and 0.05 percent for each 1 percent change in exports.

Investment change has already been taken into account as an input, prior to the computation of the residual productivity change and it does not yield a significant result in the form of investment as a share of GDP. Notable are the results for industry as a share of GDP. The effects of the industry share variable are negative, though with only marginal significance. This suggests, that countries that already have a high level of industrialization are less likely to show technical change-based productivity change. More puzzling, however, is the result for change in the share of industry, since here also there is a negative coefficient and it is statistically significant. Given the level of industrial development, an increase in the share of industry appears to have a negative impact on TFP. Again, this may reflect the lessened potential for productivity change as high income countries shift further resources into industry. On the other hand, the income per capita variable does not show significant effects.

We also hypothesized that foreign direct investment would influence changes in TFP. It is difficult, however, to measure FDI across the East Asian countries since some, like Taipei, show negative values for FDI, while others benefit from positive values. In any case, we were not able to show a significant positive effect, though that may have been incorporated into the significant effect of export growth, many of which are produced by firms benefiting at some stage from foreign investment or management. The dummy variable for 1998 is significantly negative, the dummy for 1997 is only marginally significant. The dummy for China and the dummy for 2000–03 did not show significant effects.

The variables that showed statistically significant effects were combined into the regression shown in Table 6.10 and the differences between actual and predicted values are shown for the pre- and post-crisis periods in Table 6.11. Much of the variation in TFP can be explained in terms of growth of industrial output and exports (adjusted R-squared of 0.67) that appear to be associated with high TFP growth in the East Asian countries. Presumably, the resources employed in the new industries have a higher level of productivity than that prevailing elsewhere in the economy, causing TFP to increase with industrial and export growth.

The unexplained element of TFP growth (difference between actual TFP growth and the estimated value) can be said to indicate pure technical progress as well as interactions and possible increasing returns to scale. It is relatively small, accounting for less than a third of the variance of calculated TFP and a much smaller share of the total variance of productivity, for most countries throughout the entire estimation period. This is in accord with the results noted in earlier growth accounting studies. While there is no comprehensive evidence of a change in unexplained TFP growth, some countries are clearly doing better recently in this respect than

Table 6.10 Basic equation explaining TFP

Equation 5			
	Coefficient	Standard error	Significance
Dependent variable			
% change TFP			
Independent variables			
Dummy 1997	−1.237	0.828	Marginally significant
Dummy 1998	−4.123	0.957	Significant
% change exports ($)	−6.458	1.945	Significant
% change industrial output	45.783	4.819	Significant
Change in industrial share	−1.379	0.234	Significant
Constant	−0.833	0.405	
Adjusted R^2	0.674		

Table 6.11 Difference between actual and estimated TFP, pre-crisis and post-crisis

	Pre-crisis					Post-crisis	
	1987–91*	1992–96*	1997	1998	1999	2000–03	Difference*
China, Rep. of	0.2	1.9	0.9	4.4	0.1	−0.1	−1.9
Hong Kong, China	1.5	0.9	1.8	0.2	1.0	1.5	0.5
Korea, Rep. of	0.2	−1.3	−1.5	1.8	2.3	−0.6	0.7
Indonesia	1.6	−0.4	1.0	−6.7	−1.5	1.3	1.8
Malaysia	0.1	−2.2	−0.1	−4.0	0.7	−0.5	1.7
Philippines	0.0	−1.8	0.8	0.8	1.2	−0.9	1.0
Singapore	−0.7	−0.1	−0.4	−0.3	0.5	−1.8	−1.7
Thailand	0.3	−0.4	−4.8	−1.1	2.8	1.5	1.9
Taipei	2.2	0.8	2.3	4.8	0.0	−0.2	−1.0

Note: * Omitting outlier values for 1990 (China) and 1995 (Korea) (2000–03) minus (1992–96).

others. China shows almost zero unexplained TFP since the mid-1990s, meaning that all of its growth reflects either an increase in inputs or is closely associated with the expansion of industrial production and exports. Of course, one possible explanation of this phenomenon may lie in the fact that China has proven, in a systemic or institutional sense, to be a much sought-after destination for foreign direct investment and the resulting relatively large FDI inflows may have reduced China's imperative to worry about ways to improve productivity per se. Again, while the financial crisis had significant negative impacts on productivity growth, there is little evidence to suggest that the unexplained component of productivity growth is structurally different in the post-crisis period than in earlier years; it is lower in Taiwan and Singapore, where it may reflect the increasing difficulty of these relatively advanced countries in catching up with advanced technology. It is also lower in China, where it may reflect statistical problems, but it is higher in Indonesia, Malaysia and Thailand.

6 CONCLUDING REMARKS

The object of this study was to examine the effect of the East Asian Crisis on the growth of productivity change in East Asia. Our approach has been one based on measurement of inputs and explanation of total factor productivity (TFP), associating it with the cyclical impact of the financial crisis and growth in industrial production and exports. These considerations had statistically significant explanatory power. The coefficient estimates for other measured factors, including FDI and investment, did not show up statistically significant in the regressions.

As has also been shown by earlier empirical work, our calculations suggest that rapid growth in East Asia depends greatly on the expansion of inputs of labor and capital. Productivity growth also appears to be closely related to expansion of industrial production and exports and to vary considerably with cycles in business activity. A relatively small share of TFP remains unexplained and that may be associated with increasing returns and technological change.

The impact of the financial crisis is clearly apparent in 1997 and 1998. The loss in productivity growth associated with this period is not made up in later years. In the post-crisis years, investment is lower as a share of GDP and growth of total inputs is slower, except in the Philippines, than before the crisis. Moreover, in China, Singapore and Taipei, TFP is substantially lower in the post-crisis than in the pre-crisis period. In these countries, this reduction is also apparent in the unexplained part of TFP, though in other parts of East Asia, the unexplained part of TFP is somewhat higher post-crisis than before. Lower growth of unexplained TFP in the most advanced countries, Taipei and Singapore, suggests that they are finding it increasingly difficult to shift their production functions to take advantage of new technology. The reduced unexplained TFP element in China, which reflects a downward trend from an extraordinarily high pre-crisis rate of unexplained productivity growth, calls for further study.

NOTES

1. The subtitle of the Collins and Bosworth paper.
2. For instance, with particular reference to Singapore, Krugman comments that the country's rapid growth was a matter of 'perspiration rather than inspiration'. He then went on to suggest that diminishing returns will limit further growth as in the Soviet Union!
3. Since Collins and Bosworth work with data through 1994, before the East Asian Crisis, this may be understandable, but Crafts (1999) who is specifically concerned with before and after the crisis periods does not take this factor into account either.
4. More recent work also includes a factor for the development of human capital (H), that is, the production function assumes $Y = f(K, H, L)$. The difficulty with introducing H here is that, with the exception of high-tech industries, the human capital constraint has not been effective in East Asia as workers have moved from simple agricultural work to simple industrial tasks. Moreover, the aggregate level of educational attainment, years of schooling, as used by Collins and Bosworth, provides little information on the current growth of productive abilities.
5. The depreciation rate for capital is another necessary assumption. We have assumed that real depreciation of capital is at an annual rate of 0.05. The World Bank's capital stock statistics assume a depreciation rate of 0.04.
6. A sensitivity analysis postulating various values of the relevant coefficients showed that choice of the coefficients did not greatly affect the pattern of values produced.
7. Modern growth theory would also note the interaction between technical change and the rate of growth as well as the possibility of increasing returns to scale (Romer, 1986).

REFERENCES

Adams, F.G. (1998), 'The East Asian Development Ladder: Virtuous Circles and Linkages in East Asian Economic Development', in F.G. Adams and S. Ichimura, (eds), *East Asian Development*, Westport, CN: Praeger, pp. 3–18.

Akamatsu, K. (1961), 'A Theory of Unbalanced Growth in the World Economy', *Weltwirtschaftliches Archiv*, **86**, 195–213.

Akamatsu, K. (1962), 'Historical Pattern of Economic Growth in Developing Countries', *The Developing Economies*, **1**, 3–25.

Collins, Susan M. and Barry P. Bosworth (1996), 'Economic Growth in East Asia: Accumulation Versus Assimilation' *Brookings Papers*, Washington: Brookings Institution, http://www.brookings.edu/=views/articles/collins/19960828.htm.

Corsetti, G., P. Pesenti and N. Roubini (1998a), 'What Caused the Asian Currency and Financial Crisis? Part I: A Macroeconomic Overview', *NBER Working Paper*, W 6833, Cambridge, MA: NBER.

Corsetti, G., P. Pesenti and N. Roubini (1998b), 'What Caused the Asian Currency and Financial Crisis? Part II: The Policy Debate', *NBER Working Paper*, W 6834, Cambridge, MA: NBER.

Crafts, Nicholas (1999), 'East Asian Growth Before and After the Crisis', *IMF Staff Papers*, **46** (2) 139–66.

Denison, Edward F. (1974), *Accounting for United States Economic Growth, 1929–1969*, Washington: Brookings.

Herrick, Bruce and Charles P. Kindleberger (1983), *Economic Development*, New York: McGraw-Hill.

Kojima, K. (2000) 'The "Flying Geese" Model of Asian Economic Development: Origin, Theoretical Extensions, and Regional Policy Implications', *Journal of Asian Economics*, **11**, 375–401.

Krugman, Paul (1994), 'The Myth of East Asia's Miracle', *Foreign Affairs*, **73**, 62–78.

Lau, Lawrence (1998), 'The Sources of East Asian Economic Growth', in F.G. Adams and S. Ichimura (eds), *East Asian Development*, Westport: Praeger, pp. 41–68.

Radelet, Steven and Jeffrey D. Sachs (1998), 'The East Asian Financial Crisis: Diagnosis, Remedies, Prospects', *Brookings Papers on Economic Activity*, **1**, 1–90.

Romer, Paul (1986), 'Increasing Returns and Long Run Growth', *Journal of Political, Economy*, **94** (5), 1002–37.

Solow, Robert M. (1956), 'A Contribution to the Theory of Economic Growth', *Review of Economics and Statistics*, **70**, 65–94.

Timmer, M.R., and A. Szirmai (1997), 'Growth and Divergence in Manufacturing Performance in South and East Asia', Discussion paper GD37, Groningen: University of Groningen Growth Center.

World Bank (1993), *The East Asian Miracle: Economic Growth and Public Policy*, New York: Oxford University Press.

Young, A. (1995), 'The Tyranny of Numbers: Confronting the Statistical Realities of the East Asian Growth Experience', *Journal of Political Economy*, **110**, 641–80.

7. What really happened to Thai wage rates during the East Asian Financial Crisis?*

Jere R. Behrman, Anil B. Deolalikar and Pranee Tinakorn

1 INTRODUCTION

For most members of developing countries that experience negative macro shocks, such as the East Asian Financial Crisis of the late 1990s or the 'Lost Decade' of the 1980s in much of Latin America and Africa, the most important manifestations of the macro shocks are through the labor market. This is the case because the most important earning asset of most members of such societies – particularly for the poorer members of these societies – is their labor. Therefore, it is important to understand the effects of economic crises on the price of that asset, namely the real wage rate. What happens to this price is important because it directly affects marginal time allocation decisions, directly affects the income of many members of society, and is an important consideration for the design of effective anti-poverty and safety net policies. In this study we explore what happened to real wage rates for the particular case of Thailand during the East Asian Financial Crisis. Thailand was the first of the Asian developing economies to experience the financial crisis of the second half of the 1990s.[1] Indeed, the East Asian Financial Crisis is often said to have begun with events in Thailand in 1997. In part for this reason, the Thai experience has been viewed as particularly interesting and has been investigated in a number of studies. While our empirical analysis is for Thailand, the questions we address about what happened to real wage rates due to the macro crisis are of relevance for other developing countries that experience such macro shocks.

Most of the previous literature claims that real wage rates declined a fair amount in Thailand due to the crisis, as well as in various degrees in the other Asian economies most afflicted by the crisis. The most prominent and visible of these studies for Thailand is World Bank (2000). This study uses a methodology that other analysts have used as well for other studies of the Thai experience and of the experience of other countries (for example, Betcherman and Islam, 2000; also see Fallon and Lucas, 2000; Horton and Mazumdar, 1999; Mahmoud and Aryah, 1999). In this approach, the percentage change in the number of employed workers between the pre- and post-crisis period[2] is subtracted from the percentage change in aggregate real wage earnings between the pre- and post-crisis period to obtain the percentage change in the real wage rate due to the crisis. Using this methodology, the World Bank estimates that the Thai real wage rate fell by 4.6 percent and Betcherman and Islam estimate that real wages fell by –1.1 percent in Malaysia, –9.3 percent in Korea and –41.0 percent in Indonesia (Table 7.1). But we argue that the methodology used in these and other studies is subject to at least four possibly important limitations:

1. First, it assumes that percentage changes in overall employment are the same as percentage changes in the employment of wage workers.
2. Second, it attributes changes in hours worked to changes in real wage rates.
3. Third, rather than weighting each wage worker equally, it weights wage rates differentially across wage workers depending on how many hours they work.
4. Fourth, it ignores important compositional changes in wage recipients with regard to gender, age and schooling, as well as other possibly related factors such as ability and motivation.

Table 7.1 Percentage year-on-year changes in employment, real wages, real wage labor earnings and GDP, 1997–98 (% ratio to % change in GDP in parentheses)

Country	% Change In			
	Employment	Real wages	Real wage labor earnings	GDP
Indonesia	2.7 (−20)	−41.0 (299)	−38.3 (280)	−13.7
South Korea	−5.3 (91)	−9.3 (160)	−14.6 (252)	−5.8
Malaysia	−2.7 (36)	−1.1 (15)	−3.8 (51)	−7.5
Thailand	−3.0 (30)	−4.6 (46)	−7.6 (76)	−10.0

Sources: World Bank (2000, Table 1). Figures for Thailand calculated from Labor Force Survey data, and represent data for the first and third quarters of 1998. Figures for other countries obtained from Betcherman and Islam (2000), and refer to the full 1998 year.

While these may seem to be dry technical points, they may make a considerable difference in our understanding of the answer to the important empirical question of what did happen to real wage rates and what the implications are for policy.

We demonstrate that, indeed, in the Thai case, these four methodological aspects of the approach used by the World Bank and others each make differences in estimates of what happened to real wage rates. These differences are particularly large in the Thai case for the second and the fourth of these methodological limitations, resulting in absolute biases in measured real wage declines of 5.5 and 9.8 percentage points, respectively. In the particular case of Thailand, these biases are partially offsetting. Even so, we estimate that for the combination of these four reasons, the World Bank (2000) overestimates the decline in real wage rates by about 40 percent. Our preferred estimate, using the same data and, except for these four aspects of methodology, the same assumptions as the World Bank is that the Thai aggregate real wage rate declined by 7.8 percent due to the crisis.

In our judgment, these individual biases and their combined impact on the estimated decline in real wage rates due to the crisis are NOT small differences that should be relegated to a footnote in a country evaluation of the impact of the crisis. Such differences might significantly affect how analysts think about the impact of the crisis and what policy responses seem appropriate. Therefore, we claim that how one calculates the real wage rate is important in the Thai case, and quite possibly in other cases.

Finally, the method that we use to obtain our preferred estimates also permits us to investigate the frequent claim that the more vulnerable and poorer members of the work force suffered the largest real wage declines in the crisis: females, those with less schooling, and the young and the old. Our examination of this question suggests that the usual characterization is partially, but only partially, correct. Those who had limited schooling and the young did experience relative declines in real wage rates. But so did those with university schooling. And females and older wage earners experienced relative increases in their real wages in comparison with others.

This chapter is organized as follows. Section 2 reviews the previous studies on what happened to aggregate Thai real wage rates due to the crisis, with emphasis on World Bank (2000) because that is the most prominent study and the one that is clearest about the procedures followed to obtain the estimates. Section 3 presents estimates of the extent of the four biases noted above in World Bank (2000) estimates for the Thai case, presents our preferred estimates of the change in aggregate real wage rates due to the financial crisis, and presents our estimates of what happened to real wage rates for some of the more vulnerable workers. Section 4 concludes.

2 SUMMARY OF PREVIOUS LITERATURE ON REAL WAGE DECLINES DUE TO THE THAI CRISIS

Studies by other authors on the impact of the crisis on Thai labor markets have suggested – and in most cases stated explicitly – that wage rates fell considerably in the immediate aftermath of the crisis, though in some cases there is some ambiguity about whether wage *rates* or wage *earnings* are being discussed. We begin by summarizing the results of World Bank (2000) because, as noted, that is the most visible and the clearest on the methodology used among the available studies. We then summarize more briefly five other studies.

2.1 World Bank (2000) Estimates of Thai Real Wage Declines

As noted in the introduction, the World Bank (2000) estimates that the Thai real wage rate fell by 4.6 percent due to the crisis by subtracting the percentage change in the number of employed workers between the pre- and post-crisis period from the percentage change in aggregate real wage earnings between the pre- and post-crisis period. The pre-crisis period that is used is the average over three Labor Force Survey (LFS) rounds prior to the crisis (that is, the first and third quarters of 1996 and the first quarter of 1997). The post-crisis period that is used is the average over three survey rounds after the initiation of the crisis (that is, the first and third quarters of 1998 and the first quarter of 1999). Both periods cover five quarters, or 1.25 years, ending about six months before and starting about six months after, respectively, the July 1997 date that is often referred to as the start of the crisis period. For comparability, both are for the same duration and both include the same combination of seasonal peak and slack LFSs. Monthly wage earnings were calculated from wages reported for other reporting periods (for example, hourly, daily, weekly) by multiplying by standard factors that assume full-time work.[3] Then other monetary benefits were added and the resulting total monthly wage earnings were deflated by the consumer price index (CPI) to obtain the total real monthly wage earnings.

2.2 Other Studies on Thai Real Wage Rate Declines in Response to the Crisis

We summarize here more briefly several other studies. They all are based on pre- and post-crisis comparisons with LFS data and they all convey the impression that the empirical evidence suggests that Thai real wage rates declined due to the crisis. But they present a range of estimates, refer to somewhat different periods and in most cases are not very clear about their procedures. So it is not possible to determine why they differ in some respects from the World Bank (2000) estimates, nor whether they are subject to some or all of the same biases.

1. *Kittiprapas and Intaravitak (2000, Appendix 1)* define real monthly wages by translating wages reported for other periods (for example, hourly, daily, weekly) into monthly wages using: (a) hourly wages × hours worked per week × 30/7, (b) daily wages × days of work per week × 30/7, and (c) weekly wage × 30/7, respectively for the payment periods used in the reports in the LFS. In all cases, the monetary value of monthly bonuses plus overtime plus other monetary fringe benefits then were added, and the total deflated by the CPI. Their calculations suggest significant declines of 4.6 percent and 3.9 percent in real wage earnings for Rounds 1 and 3, respectively, of the LFS in 1998 as compared with 1997.
2. *Mahmood and Aryah (1999)* state: 'The crisis lowered real wage growth in 1997 to 1 percent, and then cut the real wage by over 7 percent in 1998. The cut in the real wage is expected to persist over 1999 [p. 4] . . . Again Labor Force data shows that between February 1997 and February 1998, the nominal wage dropped by 6 percent, while the real wage rate dropped by 4 percent' [p. 16].[4] We note that it is not clear whether the first statement refers to wage earnings or wage rates, but the second explicitly refers to wage rates.
3. *Siamwalla (2000)* states: '[N]ominal wages among the males in the educated group fell by about 6–8 percent between August 1997 and August 1998, and among females by about 4–7 percent. Among the less educated, the fall was less than 2 percent' [p. 27]. The fall in real wages, of course, would be almost 8 percent greater (given the 7.8 percent increase in the CPI between 1997 and 1998).
4. *Kakwani (1998)* presents in Table 6 in his paper, data on 'wage earnings' that indicate that they fell from 6273 baht per month in the first quarter of 1997 to 5825 baht per month in the first quarter of 1998, a decline of 7.1 percent.
5. *Pongsapich and Brimble (1999, section 3.2)* state: 'Wages fell back to near 1996 levels. The total nominal wage bill in the private sector in 1998 was about 1 1/4 billion baht lower than in 1997, falling back to little more than the levels of 1996. The loss of real income per income earner reached 21 percent by the wet season of 1998, declining further from the fall of 17 percent in the previous dry season.'

3 RE-EXAMINATIONS OF THAI REAL WAGE RATE CHANGES DUE TO CRISIS

We have questions, as we note above, about four aspects of the World Bank (2000) estimates of real wage rate decline of 4.6 percent due to the crisis. In this section we first consider each of these four aspects in turn and what they imply for the estimated change in real wages. We then consider what our estimates imply for what happened to the real wage rates for selected 'more vulnerable' groups.

3.1 Possible Biases in the World Bank (2000) Procedure and Our Preferred Estimates of Aggregate Thai Real Wage Rate Changes due to Crisis

The essence of the World Bank procedure about which we have questions can be summarized as follows. The World Bank calculates the change in real wage rates between the pre- and post-crisis periods as:

$$\% \text{ change in } W_m^w = \% \text{ change in } Y_m - \% \text{ change in } N, \qquad (7.1)$$

where $W_m{}^w$ is the real wage rate (with the superscript 'w' referring to the World Bank 2000 estimate), Y_m is the total real wage earnings based on all wage earners ($= \Sigma Y_i$, where i is summed over all wage recipients), N_m is the total number of employees, and the subscript 'm' denotes means). Relation (7.1) is consistent with the real wage rate being defined in each period as:

$$W_m^w = Y_m/(H_m E) = Y_m/(H_m aN), \qquad (7.2)$$

where H_m is the average hours worked per pay period by wage recipients, E is the number of wage recipients in each period and 'a' is the ratio between the number of wage recipients in each period E and the total number of employees in that period N, and both H_m and a are assumed to be constant across periods.

We argue that the best available estimate is to calculate for each period the average wage rate for individuals who are observably the same as:[5]

$$W_m = (\Sigma W_i)/E = (\Sigma(Y_i/H_i))/E, \qquad (7.3)$$

where W_i is the real hourly wage rate for the i-th wage recipient that is calculated by dividing real wage earnings Y_i for each wage recipient by the hours worked per pay period H_i for each wage recipient. We then calculate the percentage change in W_m between the pre- and the post-crisis periods.

Before we turn to why we think that our procedure is preferable and the empirical importance of each of the four differences between what we argue is the preferred procedure and the procedure that the World Bank utilized, we wish to emphasize that we are not disagreeing with a number of other important aspects of the World Bank estimates – the definition of the pre- and post-crisis periods, the use of the LFS and of particular rounds of the LFS, the deflation procedure, the definition of real wage compensation, the definition of wage recipients, the definition of who is employed – so we are following exactly the same procedures as the World Bank with regard to all these aspects of the estimates. Therefore, the differences on which we focus below are NOT due to other differences in the calculations.

3.1.1 Number of wage recipients are a fixed share of total employment

The World Bank use of the total numbers employed (*N*) instead of the total number of wage recipients (*E*) in relation (7.1) is fine as long as the share of wage recipients among all those employed (the parameter '*a*' in relation (7.2)) is constant across periods. The problem is that share may not be constant between the pre- and the post-crisis period. The World Bank (2000, Table 1) estimates that employment declined by 3 percent, but the composition of employment shifted from wage to non-wage workers, so the wage employment declined by 5.5 percent. This by itself causes a bias of 2.5 percentage points (= 5.5 – 3.0) in the World Bank estimates. That is, if this bias alone is corrected, the World Bank estimate of a decline in the real wage rate of 4.6 percent would change to a decline of 2.1 percent.

3.1.2 Hours worked are constant

The World Bank treatment (or non-treatment) of hours worked is fine if average hours worked did not change between the pre- and the post-crisis period. The problem is that mean hours worked did change, and in fact declined by 5.5 percent. This by itself causes a bias of 5.5 percentage points in the World Bank estimates. That is, if this bias alone is corrected, the World Bank estimate of a decline in the real wage rate of 4.6 percent would change to an *increase* of 0.9 percent. If both of these first two biases are corrected, the World Bank estimate would change to an *increase* of 3.4 percent.

3.1.3 Average of wage rates across wage recipients with these individuals weighted proportional to their hours worked

A more subtle difference between our preferred approach and that of the World Bank is how individuals are weighted when wages or wage rates are summed across individuals in relation (7.2) versus relation (7.3). The World Bank effectively weights wage recipients proportionately to their hours worked in relation (7.2) while we think that it is more appropriate to weight individuals equally to obtain the mean wage rates across wage recipients in relation (7.3). We think that for characterizing the changes in the average of the wage rates faced by wage recipients, each individual wage recipient should be weighted the same. We also note that treating each individual as an observation (rather than each hour worked as is implicit in relation (7.2)) is consistent with standard practices for the estimation of micro wage rate and other labor market relations (some of which we utilize below). Our estimate is that this by itself causes a bias of 1.4 percentage points in the World Bank estimates. That is, if this bias alone is corrected, the World Bank estimate of a decline in the real wage rate of 4.6 percent would change to a decrease of 6.0 percent. If all three of these first three biases are corrected, the World Bank estimate would change to an *increase* of 2.0 percent.

The result from correcting the first three sources of biases (or the first two, for that matter) that the change in real hourly wage compensation rate due to the financial crisis was positive is striking and puzzling. It contrasts sharply with previous suggestions that are summarized in sections 1 and 2 that real wage rate *declines* were an important aspect of the adjustment process, as well as with causal observations and the implications of most models of labor market outcomes given a negative macro shock. We have therefore examined our estimates very carefully. Figure 7.1 plots the real hourly wage rate over the 1987–99 period for which we have comparable data. Generally, this figure suggests a secular upward trend in real wage rates that continued after the crisis and that is consistent with an increase in the reported real wage rate after the initiation of the crisis, with the exception of a blip in the third quarter of 1997 (the first quarter after the usual dating of the start of the financial crisis).[6] For the three included survey periods subsequent to this blip, the real hourly compensation rate was decreasing,[7] but the average over these three periods exceeded the average over comparable periods before the blip.

3.1.4 No change in composition of wage recipients between pre- and post-crisis periods

The World Bank (2000) procedure compares the real wages obtained from all wage recipients in the pre-crisis period with the real wages obtained by all wage recipients in the post-crisis period. This comparison is fine if the composition of wage recipients remained the same in both periods. But this would be surprising. As noted above, the number of wage recipients declined by 5.5 percent between the two periods. Standard analysis of hiring and labor supply decisions suggests that this decline is likely to have been selective, not random. It is possible, and even likely, that the workers who left wage employment status tended to receive lower wages than others

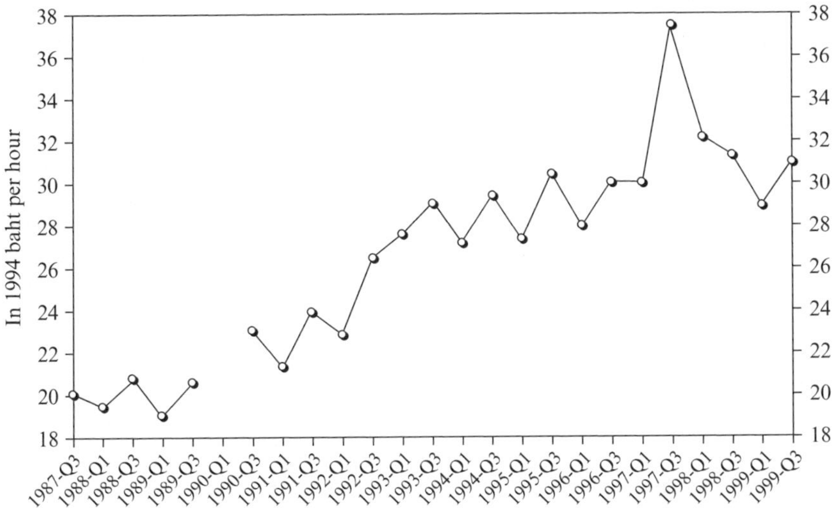

Note: No first round was conducted by the NSO in 1990 causing a gap in the plotted section.

Figure 7.1 Real hourly wage rate, 1987–99

before leaving wage employment because they were less productive regarding observed characteristics such as schooling or unobserved characteristics such as innate ability and motivation. If so, it is possible that mean wage rates for those in wage employment in the post-crisis period increased, even though the post-crisis wage rates for those who maintained wage employment through both periods hardly changed or even declined.

Table 7.2 summarizes relevant data for all workers and for subcategories defined by three characteristics of workers that are observed in the data and that are not likely to change (or at least not change much) due to labor market conditions: gender, age and schooling.[8] The first column gives the average wage rate for the indicated subgroup as a percentage of the national average wage rate for the pre-crisis period. These data permit the characterization of which types of workers received relatively high wage rates before the crisis. The next two columns include the percentage changes between the pre- and the post-crisis periods for wage employment and hours worked in wage employment.

Examination of this table suggests that wage employment shifted relatively from females to males, from younger to older workers, and from lower-schooled to higher-schooled individuals. Each of these three shifts was from lower to higher real wage rate categories.[9] This suggests that

Table 7.2 *Wages as percentages of national average wages in the pre-crisis period and percentage changes in wage employment and hours worked in wage employment before and after July 1997 for selected subgroups of workers*

Subgroups of Workers	Wage Rate as % of National Average Wage Rate in Pre-crisis Period	Percentage Change Between Pre- and Post-crisis in	
		Wage employment	Hours worked in wage employment
All workers	100.0	−5.5	−5.4
By gender			
Female	92.0	−13.5	−5.4
Male	105.3	−4.0	−5.4
By age			
15–19-year-olds	47.6	−29.1	−4.6
20–24-year-olds	66.8	−14.2	−4.9
25–49-year-olds	110.2	−0.6	−5.4
50+ year-olds	139.0	−0.4	−5.4
By schooling			
Less than primary	43.7	−22.5	−5.6
Primary	59.3	−17.4	−5.2
Secondary	99.5	14.8	−4.0
Vocational	149.4	1.3	−3.0
University	255.9	20.0	−1.8

compositional changes may have been important and, because they involved a shift from much lower wage rate categories to higher wage rate categories, the failure to account for them in the World Bank estimates mean that the estimated overall average real wage rate change is biased upwards.

Therefore, we obtain estimates that permit the control for changes in the composition of wage recipients with respect to age, gender and schooling. We estimate a *ln* real hourly wage rate equation, pooling individual data from all six quarters covering the pre- and post-crisis periods. By construction, this approach does not have any of the first three problems in the World Bank estimates that are discussed above. All coefficients of the wage equation are allowed to vary across the pre- and post-crisis periods. Using this equation, the actual change in real hourly *ln* wages (which would be the percentage change in real hourly wages between the pre- and post-crisis periods) can be decomposed into changes that might have occurred in the absence of any compositional changes in wage employment and changes

Table 7.3 Decomposition of crisis-induced change in ln *real hourly wage rates*

Change	Value	% Contribution
Changes due to varying coefficients (or wage returns)		
Intercept	−0.133	−701.2
Female	0.013	66.4
Primary schooling	0	0
Secondary schooling	0	0
Vocational training	0	0
University education	−0.011	−56.1
Ages 20–24	0	0
Ages 24–49	0.037	196.2
Ages 50 & over	0.016	83.9
Subtotal	−0.078	−410.8
Changes due to shifts in wage employment		
Female	−0.005	
Primary schooling	−0.027	−142.8
Secondary schooling	0.031	163.6
Vocational training	0.004	19.4
University education	0.082	431.5
Ages 20–24	−0.002	−11.7
Ages 24–49	0.012	64.4
Ages 50 & over	0.002	11.5
Subtotal	0.097	510.8
Total explained change in *ln* wages	0.019	100.0

Note: See Appendix 7A, Table 7A.1 for the estimates of the underlying *ln* wage equation.

that occurred because of compositional shifts. The estimates of the *ln* wage equation are presented in Appendix 7A, Table 7A.1, while the results of the decomposition analysis are given in Table 7.3.[10]

These estimates suggest that, controlling for the compositional shifts in wage employment, real hourly wage rates would have declined by 7.8 percent between the pre- and immediate post-crisis periods.[11] This estimate of a 'no-compositional shift' in the decline in real aggregate wage rates of 7.8 percent is strikingly different from the estimated increase in the aggregate real wage rate of the World Bank estimate adjusted for the first three biases discussed above. This comparison suggests that the World Bank estimate is biased upwards by 9.8 percentage points due to the failure to control for compositional shifts related to gender, age and schooling. This is a considerable bias. Of course, the actual unadjusted World Bank estimate was a decline of 4.6 percent because the biases due to the assumptions of no change in the share of employees who were wage workers and of no change in hours worked partially offset the biases due to the compositional shift and the weighting by hours worked instead of by wage recipients. But even with this serendipitous partial canceling of different biases, the estimate as presented in World Bank (2000) understates by about 40 percent the real wage rate decline that we obtain in our preferred estimate.

In summary, thus, our best estimate of how much real hourly wage rates would have declined had there been no change in the composition of wage recipients is 7.8 percent. Of course if the composition changed in terms of unobserved variables, such as ability and motivation, in the same way that it changed in terms of observable variables, such as schooling, as is suggested by some micro empirical estimates for other countries, the true decline for the same individuals controlling also for these unobserved factors would have been greater than 7.8 percent.

3.2 Who Fared Relatively Poorly in Terms of Real Wage Rate Changes?

Many have claimed that the poorer and more vulnerable workers – females, low-schooled, the young and the old – suffered most in the crisis (for example, Horton and Mazumdar, 1999; Kittiprapas, 1999; Kittiprapas and Intaravitak, 2000; Knowles et al., 1999; Pongsapich and Brimble, 1999; Sussangkarn et al., 1999). The compositional shifts in wage employment described near the end of section 3.1 are generally consistent with that claim. But that does not necessarily mean that the poorer and most vulnerable suffered the largest relative real wage rate declines.

Table 7.4 presents some evidence on this question with reference to gender, age and schooling. The first column gives the percentage change between the pre- and post-crisis periods in real wage rates. The second and third columns give regression estimates from the pooled data described for the decomposition in section 3.1 (and presented in Appendix 7A, Table 7A.1) for the interaction between the post-crisis dummy variable and gender, age and schooling (all relative, again, to males younger than 20 with less than complete primary schooling). Column 2 includes coefficient estimates for all of these characteristics; column 3 includes only those characteristics that have statistically significant coefficient estimates at least at the 10 percent level in column 2.

The percentage changes in real hourly wage compensation rates in the first column of Table 7.4 suggest that some of the groups that are often characterized as 'more vulnerable' did fare relatively badly in terms of wage rate changes. In particular, youth fared worse than prime-age adults. On the other hand, some of the groups usually characterized as more vulnerable fared relatively well: those with primary or less schooling (as well as those

Table 7.4 Percentage changes in real wage rates and coefficient estimates for interactions between crisis dummy variable and different groups in pooled real wage regression

Change	Percentage Change Between Pre- and Post-crisis Periods in Real Wage Rates		Change in Real Wages Relative to Reference Group (estimated coefficients for interactions with crisis dummy)
By gender			
Female	3.8	3.5*	0.030*
Male	1.2	–	–
By age			
15–19-year-olds	−4.6	B	B
20–24-year-olds	−3.7	−0.010	
25–49-year-olds	0.0	0.046*	
50+ year-olds	12.8	0.153*	0.161*
By schooling			
Less than Primary	−5.8	B	B
Primary	−4.7	0.027	
Secondary	−9.5	0.006	
Vocational	−4.6	0.025	
University	−11.5	−0.033*	−0.055*
Reference group (males < 20 years old, less than primary school)		−0.146*	−0.133*

Notes: * Calculations from the LFS data tapes. Changes are defined between the period before the crisis (first quarter of 1996, third quarter of 1996 and first quarter of 1997) to a comparable period after the initiation of the crises (first quarter of 1998, third quarter of 1998, first quarter of 1999). Real hourly wage rate includes cash wages plus monetary benefits, adjusted for the CPI, per hours worked. The second and third columns are from regressions 2 and 3 in Appendix 7A, Table 7A.1. * implies significantly non-zero at least at the 10 percent level. B means that included in reference group in bottom row.

with vocational schooling) had smaller declines than those with secondary or university schooling, females had larger increases than males, and older adults had much larger increases than any other age group. The first column gives the gross associations without controlling for other characteristics. The second and third columns give the changes for various groups with multivariate controls for other changes. These multivariate estimates again suggest that some of the more vulnerable groups fared relatively poorly. Based on column 3, males under 20 years of age with less than primary schooling had significant declines of 13.3 percent in wage rates.

But females had significantly greater increases than males by 3.0 percentage points and older adults had significantly and substantially greater increases than any other age group. The only other significant effect is that those with university schooling had *declines* that were 5.5 percentage points greater than the declines experienced by the reference group (those with less than completed primary school).

3 CONCLUSIONS

What happens to real wage rates at times of macro shocks is of considerable importance because of (1) the implications for purchasing power of workers and the design of appropriate anti-poverty and social safety net policies, (2) the impact on time allocations of workers, and (3) the implications for the extent to which labor market adjustments in response to the shock occur through price rather than quantity effects, which in turn is likely to affect how broadly the effects are spread and how quickly adjustment occurs. Conventional wisdom is that real wage rates fell, in some cases substantially, in Thailand and in the other Asian economies most hit by the financial crisis of the late 1990s, as well as in response to many other negative macro shocks experienced in developing countries.

The pre–post comparison of earnings per worker used by the World Bank (2000) and others to estimate the change in real wage rates due to the crisis in Thailand (and in other countries – see Table 7.1) has four problems that may result in substantial biases: (1) ignoring change in the share of wage employees in total employment, (2) ignoring changes in hours worked in wage employment, (3) weighting changes in real hourly wage rates by hours worked rather than treating individuals equally, and (4) ignoring compositional changes among wage recipients. We quantify the magnitude of these biases for the Thai experience and find that they are considerable – in absolute terms 2.5, 5.5, 1.3 and 9.8 percentage points, respectively. The usual methods, thus, are likely to give a misleading picture of what happened to average real wage rates. These methods do not provide good guides regarding the impact of real wage changes on purchasing power or time allocations of workers, nor of the extent of price adjustments in labor markets, nor do they inform policy choices well.

Our best estimate is that real wage rates declined by at least 7.8 percent due to the crisis, which is probably an underestimate of the true decline because of the probable composition changes with regard to unobserved characteristics such as ability and motivation that in many studies are found to be correlated with characteristics such as schooling. Though in the World Bank (2000) estimate the biases mentioned above are serendipitously partially offsetting, the severity of the impact of the crisis on declines in the real wage rate is underestimated by 3.2 percentage points or by over 40 percent even if the added problem of unobservables is ignored. In order to understand the impact of such crises and to inform policy-makers and other interested parties, it is important that the informational basis and the methodologies for estimating real wage rate changes are improved.

The best solution would be for longitudinal labor force data to be collected as a matter of routine so that comparisons could be made of the wage rates for the same individuals over time, thereby controlling for all individual unobserved as well as observed characteristics. Such data are collected in Labor Force Surveys for some developing countries (for example, Brazil has a rolling panel), but not many. Until such longitudinal surveys are available in other cases, a second-best solution is to follow the methods in this chapter, particularly with regard to controlling for compositional changes with respect to observed characteristics such as age, gender and schooling. An added by-product of such an approach is estimates of the extent to which different groups identified by such characteristics fared relatively poorly – which in the present case gives some, but limited, support to the widely-held understanding that the more vulnerable fared worse – and, in fact, females and older adults fared relatively well, while highly educated individuals fared relatively poorly.

NOTES

* This chapter builds upon work in Behrman et al. (2000) that was prepared for the World Bank by the Thailand Development Research Institute (TDRI). The authors alone – and not TDRI nor the World Bank – are responsible for all interpretations in this chapter. The authors thank Dr Worawan Chandoevwit and Mr Rangsiman Kingkaew for research and computational assistance on this project.

1. In 1997 speculation on currency devaluation intensified, official foreign reserves were rapidly depleted, the currency was subsequently allowed to float and devalued considerably, and over half of the finance companies were closed. The annual growth rate in real GDP per capita declined to –2.3 percent in 1997 and to –11.4 percent for 1998 from 4.8 percent for 1996 and from an average of 7.2 percent for 1990–95. Real GDP per capita relative to the underlying secular growth trend for the 1990s fell (from the peak in 1996) by 5.2 percent in 1997, 20.2 percent in 1998, and 20.5 percent in 1999 (based on the data for the 1990s as presented in Behrman and Tinakorn, 2000, Table 8; these estimates focus on how much real GDP per capita differs from the secular trend each year, and, because this secular trend is positive, incorporate the secular growth not realized in addition to any decline in measured real GDP per capita; see also Kakwani and Pothong, 1998).
2. To avoid long and perhaps awkward terminology, the 'post-crisis period' is used here and throughout this study to refer to what is really the 'post-initiation-of-the-crisis period' and *not* the period subsequent to the recovery from the crisis. That is, comparisons are made between average real wage rates for three labor force surveys prior to the initiation of the crisis in mid-1997 and for three labor force surveys subsequent to the initiation of the crisis in mid-1997 (see section 2.1 below).

3. Specifically, hourly wages were multiplied by 208 work hours per month, daily wages were multiplied by 26 days per month, and weekly wages were multiplied by 4.2 weeks per month.
4. The source is given as ILO (1999), 'Country Employment Policy Review for Thailand'. Given that inflation was positive (5.6 percent in 1997 and 8.1 percent in 1998 according to the CPI based on data from the Bank of Thailand, see Behrman et al. (2000, Table 2), it is not clear how the real drop in percentage terms can be less than, rather than greater than, the nominal drop in percentage terms.
5. As is standard in the literature, this procedure is using the average real wage per hour for each wage recipient rather than the marginal real wage rate per hour. The latter conceptually is preferable at least for some uses, but it is not clear how to calculate the marginal real wage rate per hour with information that is generally available in Labor Force Surveys.
6. The 1997 third-quarter real wage rate was strikingly high: 23.5 percent above the post-crisis average and 38.2 percent above the pre-crisis average. It should be emphasized, however, that if there is some anomaly for the 1997 third-quarter report, that does *not* affect our, nor the World Bank's (2000), pre–post comparisons because that period is not used for these comparisons.
7. The real wage rates declined between rounds within the post-crisis period: by 14.1 percent from 1997-Q3 to 1998-Q1, by 2.8 percent from 1998-Q1 to 1998-Q3, and by 7.7 percent from 1998-Q3 to 1999-Q1.
8. Schooling may be affected a little by labor market conditions for those near the margin of ending their schooling, but not much for older individuals in the prime working age ranges. We do not include in this table characteristics such as location, migration status, work status and occupation because these are likely to be affected by current and recent labor market conditions.
9. The third column indicates a further shift in average hours worked per worker in wage employment by schooling levels that reinforces this tendency, though no such shift in hours worked per wage worker by gender and a small partially offsetting shift in hours worked per wage worker by age groups. This shift in hours worked does *not* affect the estimate of the change in real wage rates if each wage recipient is weighted equally as we argue is preferable. But it affects the estimate if wage recipients are weighted by hours worked as in World Bank (2000).
10. This type of decomposition is different in some basic respects from the racial and gender decompositions of wage differentials along the lines pioneered by Oaxaca (1973) and Blinder (1973) and subsequently extended and refined by others such as Jones (1983), Cotton (1988) and Neumark (1988). In the Oaxaca–Blinder tradition, for example, the comparison is between two exclusive groups at the same point of time (not two overlapping groups in different time periods as in our case) and it makes a difference whether the estimates for one group or the other is used as the base for making the decomposition. Not only does the decomposition change depending on which estimates are used, but in the counterfactual in which 'discrimination' was changed, the relevant coefficients might change. In the present case we are merely describing the changes from the pre-crisis to the post-crisis periods, not attempting to indicate what would happen with movement in the opposite direction or with some counterfactual. Our procedure is equivalent, of course, to estimating separate *ln* real wage rate relations for the pre- and post-crisis period and comparing the coefficient estimates.
11. On the other hand, had real wage rates for every population subgroup remained unchanged during the crisis, the observed *average* wage rate would still have shown an increase of 9.7 percent. Most of this increase (8.2 out of 9.7, or 85 percent) would have occurred because of a shift in wage employment from lower-schooled to university-educated individuals (who typically earn substantially more). The difference between the increase of 9.7 percent (with only real wage rates unchanged) and the decline of 7.8 percent (with only the composition changed) is basically the same as the 2.0 percent increase with no concern about composition and with the other three adjustments in place.

REFERENCES

Behrman, Jere R. and Pranee Tinakorn (2000), 'The Surprisingly Limited Impact of the Thai Crisis on Labor, Including on Many Allegedly "More Vulnerable" Workers', *Indian Journal of Labour Economics*, **43** (3) (October), 513–44.

Behrman, Jere R., Anil B. Deolalikar and Pranee Tinakorn with Worawan Chandoevwit (2000), *The Effects of the Thai Economic Crisis and of Thai Labor Market Policies on Labor Market Outcomes*, Bangkok: Thailand Development Research Institute.

Betcherman, G. and R. Islam (2000), 'East Asian Labor Markets and the Crisis: Impacts, Responses, and Lessons', Synthesis paper prepared for the World Bank/ILO/Japanese Ministry of Labor/Japan Institute of Labor seminar on The Economic Crisis, Employment, and the Labor Market in East and South-East Asia, Tokyo, February.

Blinder, Alan (1973), 'Wage Discrimination: Reduced Form and Structural Estimates', *Journal of Human Resources*, **8** (Fall), 436–55.

Cotton, Jeremiah (1988), 'On the Decomposition of Wage Differentials', *The Review of Economics and Statistics*, **70** (2), 236–43.

Fallon, Peter R. and Robert E.B. Lucas (2000), 'The Impact of Financial Crises on Labor Markets, Household Incomes and Poverty: A Review of the Evidence', Discussion Paper Number 103, Boston: Boston University, Institute for Economic Development.

Horton, S. and D. Mazumdar (1999), 'Vulnerable Groups and the Labor Market: The Aftermath of the Asian Financial Crisis', Paper prepared for the World Bank/ILO/Japanese Ministry of Labor/Japan Institute of Labor Seminar on Economic Crisis, Employment, and the Labor Market in East and South-east Asia, Tokyo, November.

Jones, F.L. (1983), 'On Decomposing the Wage Gap: A Critical Comment on Blinder's Method', *Journal of Human Resources*, **18** (1), 126–30.

Kakwani, N. (1998), 'Impact of Economic Crisis on Employment, Unemployment and Real Income', Bangkok: National Economic and Social Development Board, mimeo.

Kakwani, N. and Jaroenjit Pothong (1998), 'Impact of Economic Crisis on the Standard of Living in Thailand', *Indicators of Well-Being and Policy Analysis*, **2** (4) (October), 1–20.

Kittiprapas, Sauwalak (1999), 'Social Impacts of Thai Economic Crisis', in Chalongphob Sussangkarn, Frank Flatters and Sauwalak Kittiprapas (eds), *Social Impacts of the Asian Economic Crisis in Thailand, Indonesia, Malaysia and the Philippines*, Bangkok: Thailand Development Research Institute.

Kittiprapas, Sauwalak and Chedtha Intaravitak (2000), 'Social Responses to Economic Crisis: Some Evidence during 1997–99 of Thai Crisis', Bangkok: Thailand Development Research Institute, mimeo.

Knowles, James C., Ernesto M. Pernia and Mary Racelis (1999), 'Social Consequences of the Financial Crisis in Asia: The Deeper Crisis', Manila: Asian Development Bank, mimeo.

Mahmoud, Moazam and Gosah Aryah (1999), 'An Appraisal of the Labor Market in the Context of the Macro Economy: Growth, Crisis and Competitiveness', Country paper prepared for the World Bank/ILO/Japanese Ministry of Labor/Japan Institute of Labor seminar on The Economic Crisis, Employment, and the Labor Market in East and South-East Asia, Tokyo, 13–15 October.

Neumark, David (1988), 'Employers' Discriminatory Behavior and the Estimation of Wage Discrimination', *Journal of Human Resources*, **23** (3), 279–95.
Oaxaca, Ronald (1973), 'Male–Female Wage Differentials in Urban Labor Markets', *International Economic Review*, **14** (3) (October), 693–710.
Pongsapich, Amara and Peter Brimble (1999), 'Assessing the Social Impacts of the Financial Crisis in Thailand', Bangkok: Chulalongkorn University and The Brooker Group, prepared for the Asian Development Bank, Regional Technical Assistance, mimeo.
Siamwalla, Ammar (2000), 'Anatomy of the Thai Economic Crisis', in Peter C. Warr, (ed.) *Thailand Beyond the Crisis*, London: Routledge.
Sussangkarn, Chalongphob, Frank Flatters and Sauwalak Kittiprapas (eds) (1999), *Social Impacts of the Asian Economic Crisis in Thailand, Indonesia, Malaysia and the Philippines*, Bangkok: Thailand Development Research Institute.
World Bank (2000), *Thai Workers and the Crisis*, Bangkok: Social Monitor 4.

APPENDIX 7A

Table 7A.1 Estimated real hourly ln *wage functions, using pooled data for six quarters (1Q96, 3Q96, 1Q97, 1Q98, 3Q98 and 1Q99)*

Independent Variable	Regression 1		Regression 2		Regression 3		Sample Means	
	Parameter	T-ratio	Parameter	T-ratio	Parameter	T-ratio	Pre-crisis	Post-crisis
Whether female	−0.193	−45.2	−0.208	−34.6	−0.208	−9.7	0.421	0.398
Whether primary schooled	0.348	36.6	0.334	24.5	0.346	31.5	0.585	0.507
Whether secondary schooled	0.822	78.8	0.820	54.9	0.821	87.6	0.172	0.210
Whether having vocational/ technical training	1.229	92.9	1.215	66.6	1.226	114.5	0.044	0.047
Whether having university education	1.740	168.2	1.758	118.4	1.768	156.3	0.148	0.194
Whether aged 20–24 years	0.133	15.9	0.139	12.4	0.135	5.5	0.178	0.162
Whether aged 24–49 years	0.374	50.3	0.354	36.2	0.350	12.6	0.642	0.677
Whether aged 50 years and over	0.571	47.7	0.498	30.1	0.495	15.3	0.095	0.099
Dummy for post-crisis period	−0.078	−18.6	−0.146	−6.2	−0.133	−5.9	0	1
Crisis × Female			0.030	3.5	0.030	1.9		
Crisis × Primary schooling			0.027	1.4				
Crisis × Secondary schooling			0.006	0.3				
Crisis × Vocational education			0.025	1.0				
Crisis × University education			−0.033	−1.7	−0.055	−8.5		
Crisis × 20–24 years			−0.010	−0.6				
Crisis × 24–49 years			0.046	3.1	0.055	9.6		
Crisis × 50 years and over			0.153	6.4	0.161	17.7		
Intercept	2.372	198.6	2.403	144.7	2.397	316.1		
Mean of dependent variable							3.269	3.289
R-square	0.505		0.506		0.506			
F-statistic	8179		4371		17570			
Number of observations	223484		223484		223484			

8. Exchange rate or wage changes in international adjustment? Japan and China versus the United States

Ronald I. McKinnon[1]

Seldom have the pages of the financial press in Europe and America been so full of grave editorializing on the need for a major depreciation of the dollar to correct the 'unsustainable' current account and trade deficits of the United States. Much of this international moralizing directs the high-growth East Asian countries to stop pegging their currencies to the dollar – or, in China's case, to allow a large appreciation of the renminbi before moving to unrestricted floating. The critics' message has two facets.

First, in order to reduce East Asia's large trade surpluses and thereby reduce America's even larger trade deficit, US and European critics suggest that Asian governments should let their currencies appreciate discretely against the dollar. For example, Fred Bergsten, Morris Goldstein, Nicholas Lardy and Michael Mussa from the Institute for International Economics (IIE) in Washington DC, all suggest that an immediate 20 to 25 percent appreciation of the renminbi is warranted (Bergsten et al., 2005). However, they provide no suitable conceptual model – let alone econometric evidence – that this would significantly reduce China's trade surplus with the United States.

Second, because of the very high ongoing productivity growth in some East Asian countries (notably China) relative to that in the United States and Europe, critics contend that subsequent continual appreciation of the renminbi (couched in terms of making its exchange rate more flexible) may also be required to balance fairly international competitiveness. And many outside critics see 'smooth' ongoing upward adjustments in the renminbi to be best obtained by China's government eventually allowing its currency to float freely – instead of intervening heavily to hold it down as is now the case.

In this chapter, I contend that these critics are wrong in both respects. Their 'conventional wisdom' is based on faulty, although unfortunately widely accepted, theorizing that fails to come to grips with how the international dollar standard works.

I will first discuss why a discrete appreciation by a dollar creditor country of the United States such as China or Japan would have no predictable effect on its trade surplus. I will then show how differential adjustment in the rate of growth of money wages will more accurately reflect international differences in productivity growth, that is, international competitiveness will be better balanced through time, when a peripheral country's dollar exchange rate is fixed. Finally, I will discuss the optimal degree of flexibility in the foreign exchanges for China at the present time.

1 THE EXCHANGE RATE AND THE TRADE BALANCE

Why is the common presumption that an exchange rate change by itself would have a predictable effect on a country's trade balance often incorrect? This presumption has been canonized in a model called the elasticities approach to the balance of trade that focuses on relative price effects. It is intuitively plausible because an appreciating country's exports obviously become more expensive in world markets and fall, whereas imports become cheaper and 'should' increase. The problem is that proponents of the elasticities approach focus on these relative price effects of an exchange rate change and either ignore the income (absorption) effects or believe them to be small and controllable.

But under the world dollar standard where foreign trade and asset flows are largely invoiced in dollars, a peripheral country will be exposed to major income and wealth effects should its dollar exchange rate change. In particular, an appreciation against the dollar would have (is having) unacceptable worldwide macroeconomic consequences *without* correcting the US trade and current account deficits.

Among financially open economies, sustained exchange rate changes must reflect relative monetary policies expected in the future: relatively tight money and deflation in the appreciating countries and relatively easy money with inflation in the country whose currency depreciates. After a sharp appreciation, multinational as well as national firms will see the country as a less good (more expensive) place in which to invest so that investment slumps. In creditor countries that have built up large dollar claims on foreigners, this deflationary impact of an exchange appreciation is further accentuated because these dollar assets lose value in terms of the domestic currency: a negative wealth effect that reduces consumption as well as investment. In summary, depressed domestic spending offsets the relative price effect of an appreciation so as to leave the effect on the net trade balance indeterminate.[2]

The high-saving countries in Asia and Europe (and including Canada), all creditors of the low-saving United States, face the specter of a growth slowdown or outright deflation should their currencies appreciate. For example, the repeated appreciations of the yen from 1985 to 1995 created the bubble in Japanese land and equity values from 1987 to 1990 and then, with the inevitable collapse of the bubble, threw Japan into a deflationary slump in the 1990s with a zero interest liquidity trap that made monetary policy helpless to revive the Japanese economy. In 2003 and 2004, the Japanese economy staged a partial recovery on the back of the China boom. But the current rise of the yen toward 100 to the dollar could well throw Japan, still in a liquidity trap, into a renewed deflationary slump in 2005. Similarly, with the 50 percent appreciation of the euro against the dollar in 2002–04, continental Europe is facing slower economic growth – although not yet as protracted as the earlier Japanese experience.

These exchange-rate-induced growth slowdowns or slumps in the appreciating economies sharply reduce their demand for imports. At the same time, their exports become more expensive in world markets. Because the fall in exports is coupled with a fall in imports, the net effect on their trade balances is unpredictable (McKinnon and Ohno, 1997, Chs 6 and 7). The ever-higher yen from 1971 to 1995 led to even bigger Japanese trade surpluses. All that is predictable is that the appreciating country will suffer deflationary pressure. However, if outside commentators and government officials persist in the mistaken belief that appreciation will reduce the trade surpluses of America's creditor countries, their 'talk' encourages hot money flows out of dollars into the currencies of creditor countries in Asia and Europe – a particularly acute problem for China currently. These countries then find it more difficult to avoid actual appreciation and unwanted deflation.

Conversely, if deflationary pressure in creditor countries is muted because of orchestrated joint appreciations of their currencies against the dollar, this would induce an outburst of unacceptably high inflation in the United States. For example, President Nixon's well-telegraphed depreciation of the dollar in August 1971 touched off a flight from dollar assets and also the high and volatile US inflation of the 1970s.

If exchange rate changes are not the answer to American trade deficits and Asian trade surpluses, what are the more fundamental causes? The major ongoing and long-run distortion in the world's financial system is America's saving deficiency, large fiscal deficits by the Federal Government and meager household saving, coupled with a virtually unlimited dollar line of credit on which to borrow from the rest of the world.[3] In addition, over the last two years, US monetary policy has also been too loose with short-term interest rates well below the rate of inflation leading to excess consumption – in part by inducing a bubble in housing prices.

The result is heavy US borrowing in international markets that is then transferred in terms of real resources by foreign countries running trade surpluses with the United States. The US current account deficit forces Canada and countries in Asia, Europe and now even in Latin America, into current account surpluses.

2 THE EXCHANGE RATE AND INTERNATIONAL COMPETITIVENESS

At least some of the critics of Asian countries' pegging to the dollar would agree that low saving in the United States, rather than misaligned exchange rates, is the root cause of the trade imbalance. However, suppose a country with very high productivity growth such as China trades with countries with much lower productivity growth. In the new millennium, Japan and Europe have overall trade surpluses, and the United States has an overall trade deficit. But all of these more mature industrial countries have much lower productivity growth than China's. Isn't exchange rate flexibility with ongoing appreciation of the renminbi more or less necessary to balance international competitiveness by offsetting the productivity differential between China and its slower growing trading partners? Indeed, because of foreign unease, China has promised that the yuan/dollar exchange rate will become more flexible in the future.

As long as the American price level remains stable, more flexibility in the *central* exchange rate of 8.28 yuan per dollar is neither necessary nor desirable for balancing international competitiveness with China's neighbors in the long run. International adjustment occurs by money wages naturally growing faster in the country with higher productivity growth. But this mechanism of differential wage adjustment, with more rapid wage growth in China than the United States, only works well when enterprises and workers in China are confident that the central rate will remain fixed indefinitely, and China's inflation remains more or less aligned with that in the United States. Then Chinese employers in the rapidly growing tradables sectors, largely manufacturing, will vigorously bid for workers subject to the constraint of having to remain internationally competitive at the fixed nominal exchange rate. Money wages, particularly for the increasingly skilled workers, then rise in line with the high-productivity growth. Similar wage growth than spreads out through the rest of the economy, including non-tradable services.

In the 1950s and 1960s under the Bretton Woods system of fixed dollar exchange rates, how differential wage growth became the principal mode of international adjustment was first articulated for high-growth Scandinavia when the Swedish, Norwegian and Danish currencies were all pegged to the dollar. But very high productivity growth in post-war Japan relative to the United States, when the yen/dollar rate was also convincingly fixed, provides an equally striking example of what is now known as the 'Scandinavian Model' of wage adjustment (Lindbeck, 1979).

2.1 Japan's Dollar Exchange Rate in Historical Perspective

When the yen was fixed at 360 to the dollar from 1950 to 1971, the importance of relative wage adjustment between Japan and the United States was pronounced. Table 8.1 gives the summary statistics for this remarkable era of very high Japanese growth in comparison to those of the wealthier, and consequently more slowly growing, United States. From 1950 to 1971, Japan's annual growth in real output was 9.45 percent while industrial production grew an even more astonishing 14.56 percent per year. Unsurprisingly, the annual growth in Japanese labor productivity of 8.92 percent was far in excess of the 2.55 percent in the United States. However, the balancing item was that average money wages grew at a robust rate of 10 percent per year in Japan and only 4.5 percent in the US. Figure 8.1 shows the dramatic rise of Japanese money wages relative to American wages under the Bretton Woods system of fixed dollar exchange rates.

Table 8.1 Key economic indicators for Japan and the United States, 1950–71 (average annual percentage change)

Wholesale Prices		Money Wages		Consumer Prices		Industrial Production	
US	Japan	US	Japan	US	Japan	US	Japan
1.63	0.69[a]	4.52	10.00	2.53	5.01	4.40	14.56
Real GDP		Nominal GDP		Narrow Money		Labor Productivity	
3.84	9.45[a]	6.79	14.52[a]	3.94	16.10[b]	2.55	8.92[c]

Notes:
[a]1952–71.
[b]1953–71.
[c]1951–71.

Sources: IMF, *International Financial Statistics*, CD-ROM, October 2003, unless otherwise noted. Japanese real income data, wholesale price data, and labor productivity data are from *Japan Economic Yearbook*, 1960–71, *Economic Survey of Japan*, 1954–59, and *OECD Economic Surveys: Japan*, 1964–71. Labor productivity data for the US are obtained from the index for the non-farm business sector as reported by the Bureau of Labor Statistics. Note that labor productivity refers to the industrial sector.

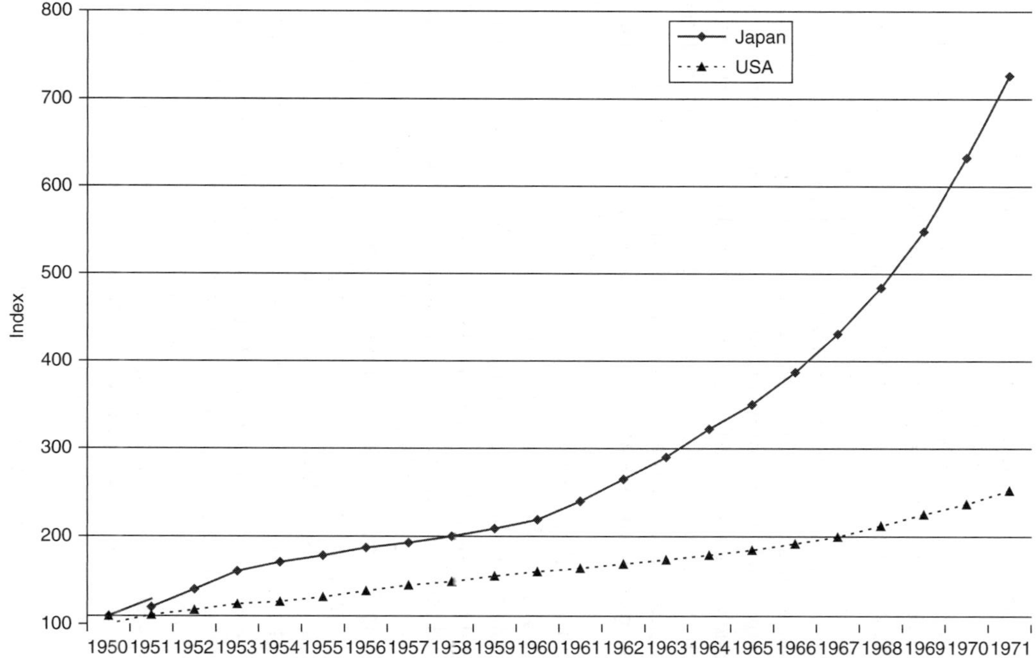

Source: IMF: IFS.

Figure 8.1 Nominal manufacturing wage growth for US and Japan: 1950–71 (base year 1950 = 100)

Keeping the yen at 360 per dollar effectively anchored Japan's price level for tradable goods. In the 1950s and 1960s, the Japanese wholesale price index (WPI) rose less than 1 percent per year whereas the American WPI rose a bit more than 1 percent (Table 8.1). Because the bulk of world trade was invoiced in dollars, fixing an exchange rate to the dollar was (is) a stronger anchor for the price level than the size of Japanese bilateral trade with the United States would suggest.

Employers in Japan's manufacturing export sector, with its extremely high growth in labor productivity, then bid vigorously for both skilled and unskilled workers subject to remaining internationally competitive at the fixed exchange rate. Wages rose rapidly in manufacturing so that workers received the main fruits from the productivity growth there. But then, as in the Scandinavian Model, these high wage settlements spread into the rest of the economy, such as in non-tradable services, where productivity growth was much lower. The result was that, within Japan, the price of services rose relative to goods prices. For 1950–71, Table 8.1 shows that Japan's CPI, which includes services as well as goods, began to increase much faster at 5 percent per year than its WPI, which contains only goods. But Japan's international competitiveness in its high-growth tradables sector remained balanced with the United States.

In Japan's bygone high-growth era, fashioning a purely domestic monetary anchor would have been more difficult. As in China today, restrictions on domestic interest rates proliferated; and the rate of growth in narrow money was high and unpredictable – more than 16 percent per year from 1950 to 1971 as Japanese households rebuilt their financial assets after the war. Thus having the Bank of Japan simply key on the dollar exchange rate was the most convenient instrument for stabilizing Japan's tradable goods price level while promoting high growth in money wages.

By the end of the 1960s, however, American monetary policy became too inflationary. The loss of America's foreign competitiveness was too great for the Bretton Woods system of fixed dollar exchange parities to survive. President Nixon had to choose between disinflating at home and thus maintaining the fixed rate system, or forcing a devaluation of the dollar against other major currencies while continuing to inflate. He chose to devalue in August 1971, and the United States suffered the great inflation of the 1970s.

2.1.1 The 'floating' yen: appreciation and deflation

For two decades after August 1971, productivity growth in Japan remained high relative to that in the United States. Japanese exports made major inroads into American markets for steel, autos, machine tools, semiconductors, and so on. In the midst of numerous trade disputes, the US government reacted by continually trying to 'talk' or force the yen up on the presumption that an appreciating yen would improve America's external competitiveness.[4] Indeed, the yen did appreciate all the way from 360 in 1971, to touch 80 to the dollar in April 1995, and threw Japan into its deflationary slump of the 1990s with a zero interest liquidity trap that lasts to the present day (McKinnon, 2005).

The deflation also reduced growth in Japanese money wages. It essentially destroyed the natural wage-adjustment mechanism for balancing international competitiveness that had held when the exchange rate was fixed. Once the yen began to appreciate, Figure 8.2 shows the breakdown in relative wage adjustment – albeit with a lag. Before 1975, money wage growth in Japan remained much higher than in the United States. Subsequently, as relative deflation in Japan set in (particularly from the sharp rise in the yen in 1977–78), Japan's money wage growth slowed sharply. From the 1980s into the new millennium, it became even lower than that in the United States. So, besides damaging the Japanese economy in a macroeconomic sense while failing to reduce its trade surplus, the erratically appreciating yen undermined the natural process of relative wage adjustment for balancing international competitiveness.

Although the yen has not appreciated on net balance since 1995, it has fluctuated widely against the dollar. Without the assurance of a fixed exchange rate anchor, re-establishing growth in Japanese money wages to reflect (potential) productivity growth accurately remains problematic. In 2004, annual money wage growth in Japan was close to zero; whereas in the US it was 2.4 percent.

2.2 Wage Adjustment in China under a Fixed Exchange Rate

Unlike Japan, China has kept its exchange rate stable since 1994 – and did not have the earlier misfortune of being pushed into a deflationary slump from an appreciating currency. Table 8.2 provides the key summary statistics comparing China to the United States. From 1994 through 2003, money wages in manufacturing increased by about 13 percent in China and by just 3 percent in the United States. This ten percentage-point wage-growth differential approximately reflected the differential growth of labor productivity: about 12.3 percent in China[5] versus 2.7 percent in the United States since 1994. Under the fixed yuan/dollar exchange rate, the appropriate wage-adjustment mechanism for balancing international competitiveness seems to be alive and well.

Figure 8.3 shows China's dramatically higher growth in money wages in manufacturing relative to the United States over the past decade. Within China, Figure 8.4 shows that wages in all sectors were rising fast – with wage growth in manufacturing about the median for the economy as a whole.

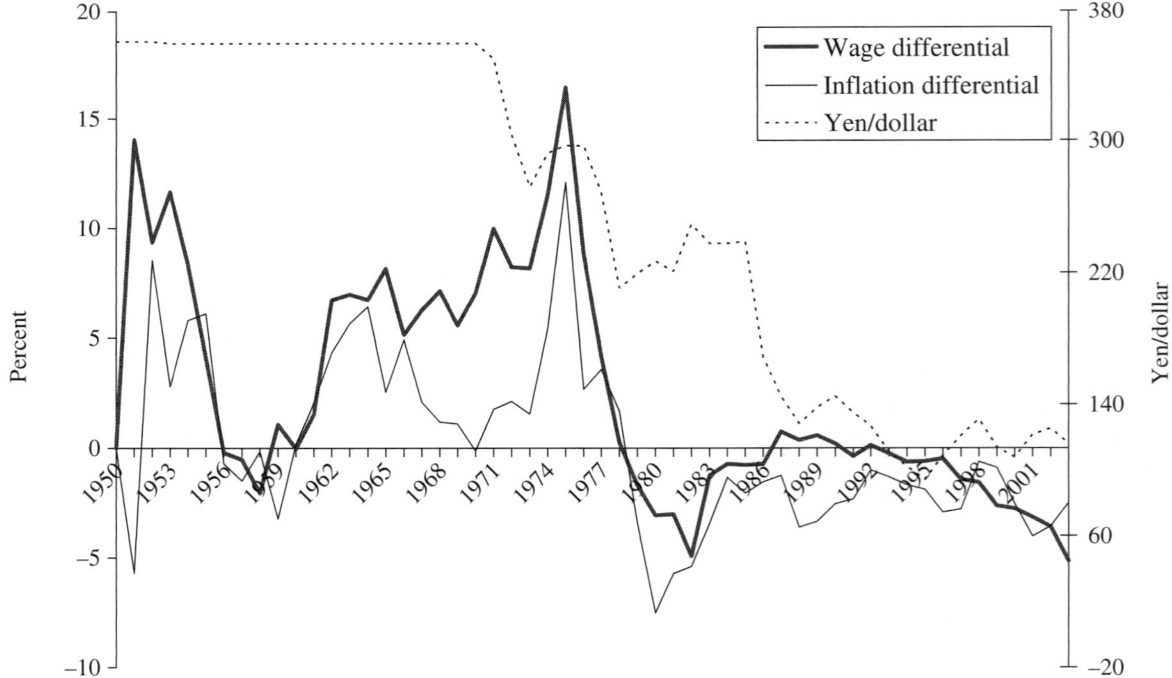

Note: Positive values indicate higher inflation and higher wage increases in Japan.

Source: IMF: IFS.

Figure 8.2 Inflation and wage differential between Japan and US, and yen/dollar rate, 1950 to 2004

Table 8.2 Key economic indicators for China and the United States, 1994–2003 (average annual percentage change)

Wholesale Prices		Money Wages (mfg)		Consumer Prices		Industrial Production	
US	China	US	China	US	China	US	China
1.53	1.26[a]	3.03	13.04[b]	2.43	2.84	3.00	12.17[c]
Real GDP		Nominal GDP		Narrow Money		Labor Productivity	
3.17	8.55	5.03	10.74	4.16	17.88	2.70	12.32[d] 9.48[e]

Notes:
[a] Ex-factory price index.
[b] 2003 data on manufacturing wages are projected from overall average wages from 1997–2003.
[c] 1994–2002.
[d] 1994–2001. Zhang and Tan (2004).
[e] 1994–2002. R. Fernholz (2004).

Source: IMF, *International Financial Statistics* CD-ROM, Nov. 2004, unless otherwise noted. Chinese CPI, manufacturing wage data, labor productivity data, real income data and wholesale price data are from *China Statistical Yearbook*, 2004. Labor productivity data for the US are obtained from the index for the non-farm business sector as reported by the Bureau of Labor Statistics. The China labor productivity data refer only to the industrial sector.

Much of this reflects the upgrading of skills and greater work experience of the labor force. True, at the margin, the wages of unskilled migrant workers may be lagging – and many of these seem to be absorbed into construction activities where average wages show the slowest rate of growth in Figure 8.4.

China's exchange rate stabilization in 1994 followed a major depreciation of the renminbi associated with the unification of the official exchange rate at the much higher 'free-market' swap rate. Figure 8.5 shows that the official rate jumped from 5.5 to 8.7 yuan per dollar. Because much of China's trade – particularly in manufacturing – had been transacted at the higher swap rate, this jump in the official rate overstates the effective devaluation. Nevertheless, because of a temporary burst of domestic inflation from 1993 to 1996 as shown in Figures 8.5 and 8.6, the 'real' devaluation was negligible. But the nominal devaluation certainly exacerbated the inflation. By 1996, the renminbi had appreciated slightly to 8.28 to the dollar where it remained until 2005. Chinese price inflation then settled down after 1996 and seems have converged close to the American level. In 2004, China's CPI

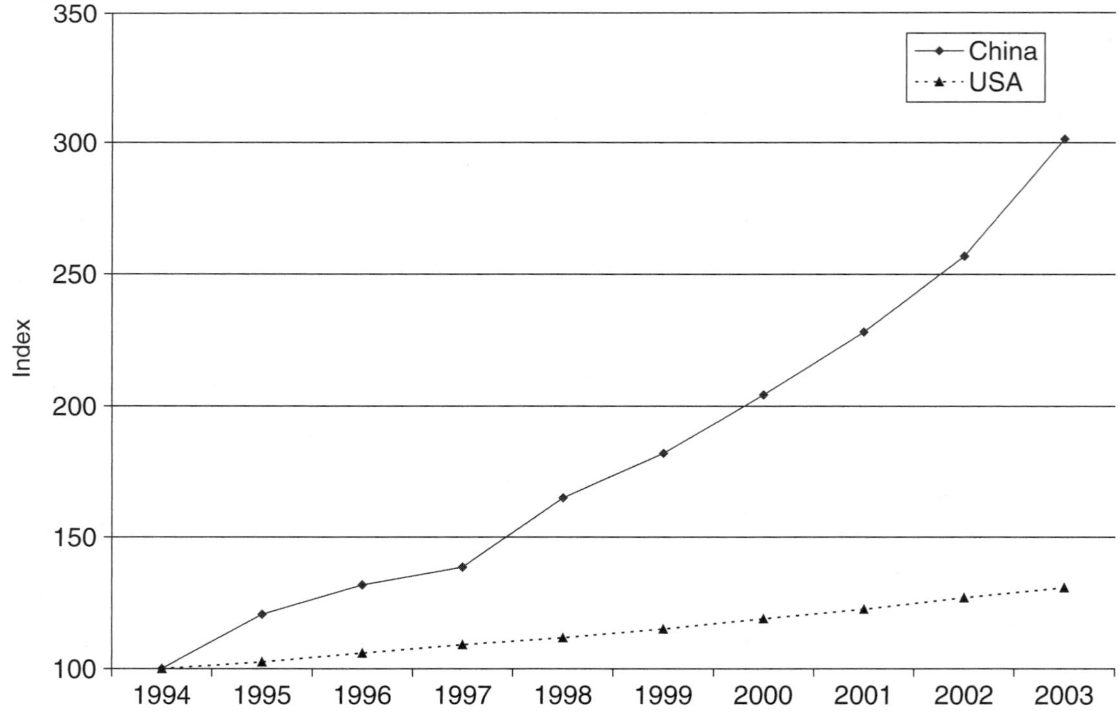

Source: IMF: IFS; Chinese manufacturing wage data are obtained from *China Statistical Yearbook*, 2004.

Figure 8.3 Nominal manufacturing wage growth for US and China, 1994–2003 (base year 1994 = 100)

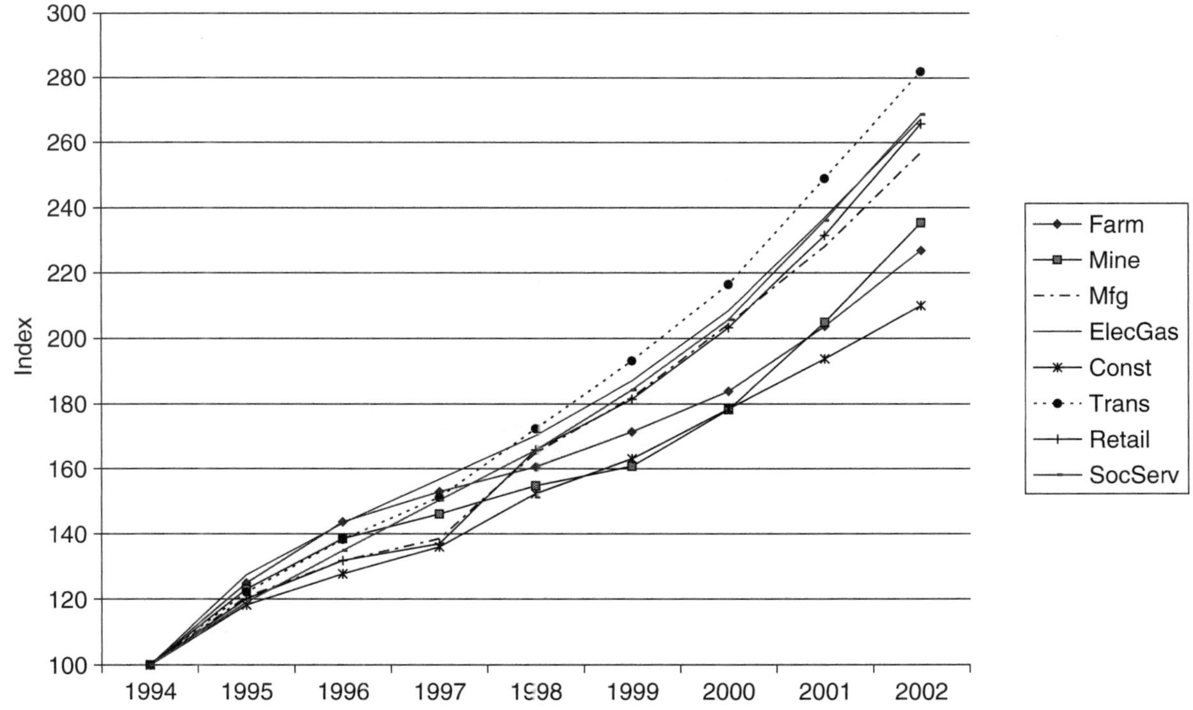

Source: *China Statistical Yearbook*, 2003.

Figure 8.4 *China: nominal wages across different sectors, 1994–2002 (base year 1994 = 100)*

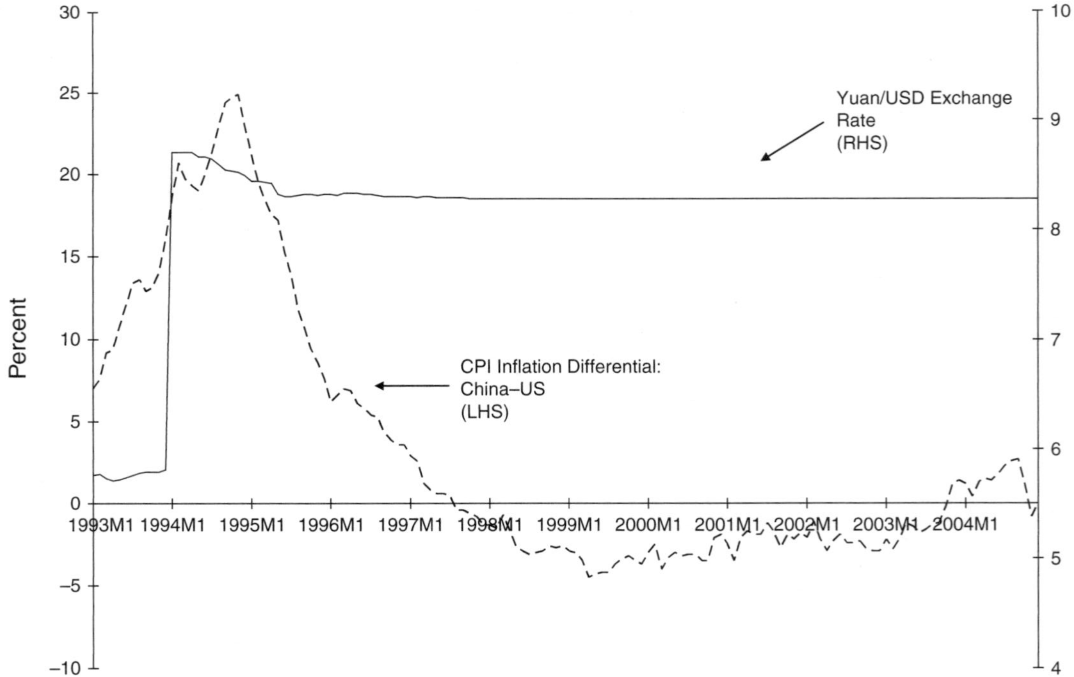

Note: M1 = January.

Source: EIU.

Figure 8.5 *China–US inflation differential and exchange rate, 1993–2005*

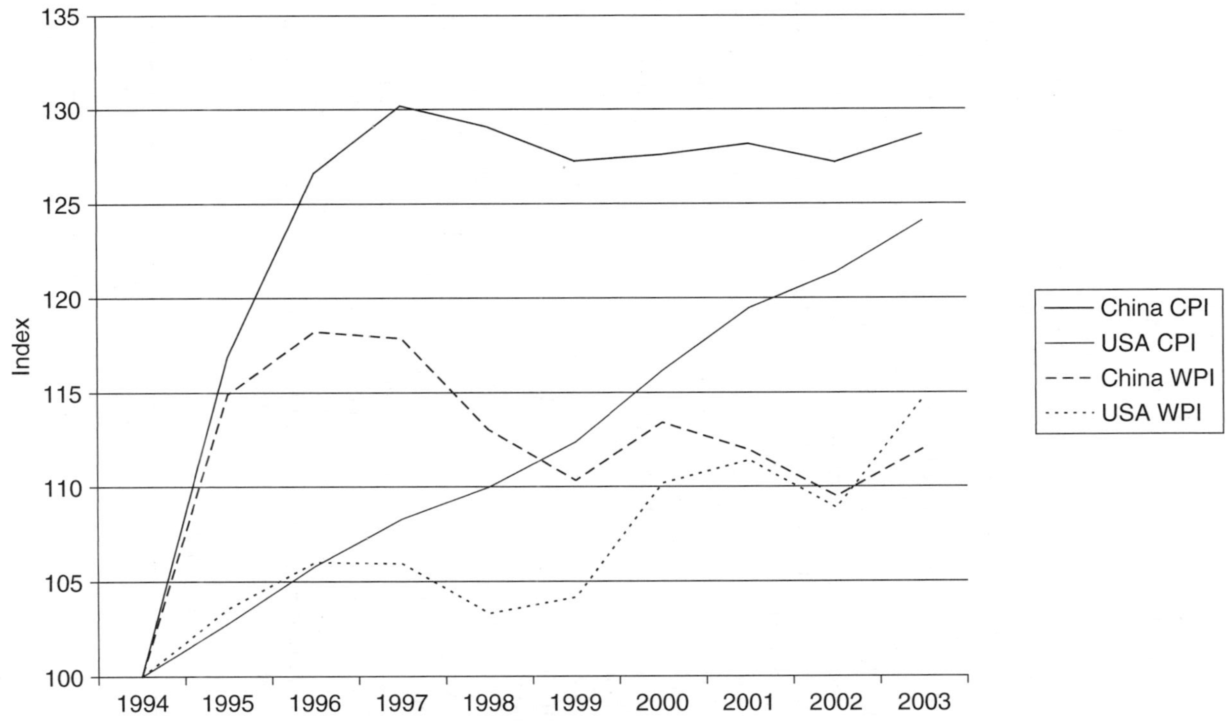

Source: IMF: IFS; Chinese ex-factory price data are obtained from *China Statistical Yearbook*, 2004.

Figure 8.6 CPI and WPI for US and China, 1994–2003

rose 3.8 percent while that in the United States rose 3.3 percent. The fixed rate regime served China as a nominal anchor for its price level much like the fixed yen/dollar rate served Japan in the 1950s and 1960s.

One might argue that, in 2004, inflation was too high in *both* China and the United States. But under the international dollar standard, only the center country can exercise monetary policy independently. Thus the onus is on the United States to disinflate. Fortunately, in 2005 and 2006, the Federal Reserve was committed to steadily increasing short-term interest rates back to more normal levels after its unprecedented monetary easing (low federal funds rates) in 2003 and 2004. Thus, inflation should calm down in both countries. China should have less trouble with inflows of 'hot' money, and even less trouble if outside commentators and government officials stop talking about the 'need' to appreciate the RMB.

More generally for the increasingly integrated East Asian economies, China's fix at 8.28 yuan per dollar became the key to intra East Asian exchange stability in the new millennium. All the others more or less peg to the dollar and thus to each other. If this fixed rate system continues, adjustment in relative wage growth in the other East Asian economies becomes the main vehicle for balancing international competitiveness.

In the context of the old Scandinavian model of wage adjustment, Table 8.3 below compares the 1950–71 Japanese and 1994–2005 Chinese experiences under fixed dollar exchange rates (the first row) with the post-1971 Japanese experience with a floating and erratically appreciating yen (the second row).

Under a fixed dollar exchange rate, the system converges to relative purchasing power parity (PPP): the rate of inflation in tradables in the peripheral country converges to that in the center country. Subject to the fixed exchange rate constraint, wage bargaining is determinate in the sense that employers bid up money wages to reflect fully the growth of labor productivity in the rapidly growing export sector. International competitiveness is balanced.

Under a floating rate that moves randomly or is hectored into appreciating as with the Japanese yen from 1971 to 1995, bargaining over money

Table 8.3 Wage bargaining

	Relative PPP	Wage Bargaining Process	Money Wage Growth
Fixed dollar exchange rate	Yes	Determinate	Reflects productivity growth in tradables
Floating exchange rate	No	Indeterminate	?

wage growth becomes indeterminate. Because risk-averse employers can no longer judge the future course of the (erratically appreciating) exchange rate, they hesitate to bid money wages up by the full amount of productivity growth in the tradables sector. This could be characterized as a negative risk premium in wage bargaining that parallels the negative risk premium in domestic interest rates arising out of fear of appreciation, which has driven short-term interest rates in Japan to zero (McKinnon, 2005, Chapter 4). When full-scale deflation sets in, money wage growth can also approach zero but, unlike interest rates, could even become negative.[6]

External pressure aside, the weakest link in the current East Asian monetary cum exchange rate system still seems to be Japan. The yen/dollar rate has not been credibly fixed within a narrow range despite massive interventions by the Bank of Japan to prevent the yen from appreciating. The fear of future yen appreciation and further deflation is still rife – and money wages are not adjusting properly. So the first order of business is for the Bank of Japan is to come up with a more credible dollar fix for the yen that would better stabilize intra East Asian exchange rates while ameliorating deflationary fears in Japan itself (McKinnon, 2005; McKinnon and Ohno, 1997).

However, China now faces more external pressure to appreciate, and the threat of trade sanctions if it does not – much like the 'Japan bashing' of the 1970s to the mid-1990s. The potential threat from being pushed into continual currency appreciation, as did Japan after 1971, is a consequent slowdown in China's economic growth and eventually outright deflation.

3 LIMITED FOREIGN EXCHANGE FLEXIBILITY FOR CHINA

Partly responding to foreign pressure but also because China could benefit from a more open foreign exchange market with decentralized transacting, it is important to pin down what the Chinese government should mean by greater foreign exchange 'flexibility'. This involves both the pace of liberalizing and rationalizing of capital controls (relaxing administrative constraints on foreign exchange transacting) and the optimal degree of flexibility in the exchange rate itself. Let us discuss each in turn.

In one respect China has been, and remains, very open to foreign capital flows. Inward foreign direct investment (FDI) at over US$40 billion per year since 2000 has been higher than China's multilateral trade surplus of about 3 percent of GDP. FDI has been an important vehicle for introducing the modern technology underlying China's rapid industrial transformation. It has also been a major contributor to the build up of China's liquid dollar assets, both held privately and increasingly as official exchange reserves – about US$660 billion as of March 2005. And outward FDI may be beginning in a significant way, as with Lenovo's purchase of IBM's PC division in 2005, and with large numbers of less publicized investments in African infrastructure projects.

However, there are two distortions in official Chinese policy that unduly amplify the financial magnitudes of inward FDI. First, the tax treatment of foreigners investing in China, particularly in special economic zones, is still more favorable than that accorded domestic investment – although much equalization has occurred. While entirely rational at the beginning of China's opening to international trade in the 1980s, such favoritism for foreign FDI is now counterproductive for encouraging domestic entrepreneurship. The second distortion is to limit foreign firms borrowing from domestic Chinese banks to help fund their operations in China. China wants and needs foreign technical expertise, but with its high domestic saving, it does not need foreign finance. Thus allowing foreign firms to borrow domestically would reduce unwanted financial inflows.

In foreign trade more generally, China has followed, and is following, the optimal order of (gradual) economic liberalization (McKinnon, 1993). In the mid-1990s, China consolidated its exchange rate system and achieved full current account convertibility for the renminbi in the sense of satisfying the IMF's Article VIII. In the new millennium, China is rapidly satisfying its WTO obligations by eliminating quota restrictions and drastically cutting tariffs. On capital account, it has liberalized relatively illiquid FDI flows *before* eliminating restrictions on shorter-term and more liquid financial flows. All this is according to what is now received textbook theory.

But this last stage, that of liberalizing liquid international financial flows, which can all too easily become 'hot' money, is best done very carefully in conjunction with an appropriate regulatory framework – or not at all. The most important principle is to contain (latent) moral hazard in financial institutions, implicitly or explicitly insured by the Chinese government, by limiting their ability to assume risk. In particular, undue foreign exchange exposure in banks and other financial institutions can imperil both themselves and the economy. *And foreign financial institutions should always be subject to the same stringent regulatory constraints as domestic ones.*

What is the best way to proceed with this delicate last stage in the liberalization process? One way is to assign foreign exchange trading exclusively to authorized banks that must keep their exposure in any foreign currency against renminbi within well defined limits. The State Administration for Foreign Exchange (SAFE) would then continuously monitor the net foreign exchange positions of these authorized banks relative to their capital positions. Only after this interbank foreign exchange market between renminbi and dollars is well established would further liberalization be considered. For example, free foreign exchange trading between major foreign currencies, such as yen against euros, would remain prohibited until a later stage.

Assuming that these prudential regulatory restraints are in place, what should be the range of variation of the yuan/dollar rate itself? In the 1960s during the old Bretton Woods system of fixed dollar parities for Western European countries and Japan, market rates varied within a 2 percent band around their central rates. Indeed, the foreign exchange margins (1 percent on either side of the official parity rate) were officially announced and corresponded to Article IV of the original IMF Articles of Agreement. On most trading days, their central banks did not have to intervene and all the clearing of international payments devolved to the authorized commercial banks. But the system was punctuated by occasional crises when official intervention became necessary.

In China today, allowing a similar 2 percent band around the central rate of 8.28 yuan per dollar, within which the market rate could fluctuate freely daily or weekly, would efficiently decentralize the foreign exchange market. Indeed, as capital controls are replaced by careful prudential regulation over the *net* foreign exchange exposures of authorized commercial banks, a widening of the band to, say, 1 percent on either side of the 'parity' rate of 8.28 yuan per dollar would make the foreign exchange market more flexible. The current margins are only about 0.3 percent on either side of 8.28, and unduly limit the private profitability of foreign exchange transacting.

If the 2 percent band is fully credible, in non-crisis periods, the People's Bank of China need seldom intervene to maintain it. Thus having the PBC officially announce what the band limits are reinforces regressive expectations: any deviation of the market rate away from 8.28 is expected to be followed by a move back toward 8.28. When the rate moved toward the top of the band, say, 8.4 yuan/dollar, then authorized banks would voluntarily intervene to drive it back down. When these banks know that the PBC is prepared to intervene decisively at either the upper or lower boundaries of the band, they will act as dealers (stabilizing speculators) to nudge the rate toward the middle of the band – without the PBC actually intervening. This ensures that the PBC need not itself intervene much in practice. Then, the clearing of most international payments would devolve from the People's Bank of China (PBC) to the commercial banks or other authorized financial institutions. Subject to constraints on their net foreign exchange position, they would be free to make hedging markets in foreign exchange futures and options for their non-bank customers.

However, if there is a crisis, as when foreigners put heavy political pressure on China to appreciate leading to hot money inflows, then the PBC has little choice but to intervene by however much is necessary to preserve the central rate.

Changes in the market exchange rate within such a narrow band would not significantly affect – or be intended to affect – a country's competitiveness in international markets for goods or services. It is simply a device for providing flexibility in decentralizing the foreign exchange market. As discussed in section 2 above, under a securely fixed central exchange rate, high growth in domestic money wages – reflecting China's very high growth in labor productivity – would remain the dominant mechanism for balancing international competitiveness.

NOTES

1. I would like to thank Hong Qiao and Ricardo Fernholz of Stanford University, and Gunther Schnabl of the University of Tubingen, for their great help in preparing this chapter.
2. In dollar debtor countries facing the threat of having their currencies depreciate against the dollar, the negative wealth effect tends to reinforce the relative price effect of an actual devaluation. Their trade balances could improve sharply from devaluation as domestic consumption (and imports) slumps even as their now cheaper exports expand into world markets. This was the case for Indonesia, Korea, Malaysia, Philippines and Thailand after the great Asian Crisis of 1997–98. Their current accounts went from being sharply negative before the crisis to positive immediately afterwards.
3. In a provocative paper, Ben Bernanke (2005) argues that the problem is more one of excess saving in other countries, particularly in Asia, than a saving deficiency in the United States. Either way, however, this international saving imbalance cannot be corrected by exchange rate changes.
4. As discussed in detail in Chapter 4 of McKinnon and Ohno (1997).
5. This estimate of productivity growth is not official, and was taken from Zhang and Tan (2004). In both countries, how best to measure labor productivity growth is controversial. Estimates for China can vary.
6. I am greatly indebted to Ms Hong Qiao for pointing out this interesting parallel between a negative foreign exchange risk premium in domestic interest rates and in bargaining over growth in domestic money wages.

REFERENCES

Bergsten, C. Fred, and the Institute for International Economics (2005), *The United States and the World Economy*, Institute for International Economics, Washington DC.

Bernanke, Ben (2005), 'The Global Saving Glut and the US Current Account Deficit', At the Sandridge Lecture, Virginia Association of Economics, Richmond, Virginia, 10 March.

Fernholz, Ricardo (2004), 'China, Japan, and Maintaining International Competitive Balance under a Fixed Exchange Rate', Senior Honors Thesis, Stanford University, 2004.

Lindbeck, Assar (1979), *Inflation and Unemployment in Open Economies*, Amsterdam, North Holland, 1979.

McKinnon, Ronald (1993), *The Order of Economic Liberalization: Financial Control in the Transition to a Market Economy*, Johns Hopkins University Press, 2nd Edition. (Translations: Chinese, Romanian and Arabic, 1995.)

McKinnon, Ronald (2005), *Exchange Rates under the East Asian Dollar Standard: Living with Conflicted Virtue*, MIT Press. (Translations: Chinese 2005, Japanese forthcoming 2007.)

McKinnon, Ronald and Kenichi Ohno (1997), *Dollar and Yen: Resolving Economic Conflict between the United States and Japan*, MIT Press. (Translations: Japanese 1998, Chinese 1999.)

Zhang, Xiaobo and Kong-Yam Tan (2004), 'Blunt to Sharpened Razor: Incremental Reform and Distortions in the Product and Capital Markets in China', International Food Policy Research Institute, DSGD Discussion Paper No. 13, August.

9. Adjustment to China's CPI-based inflation rate to account for the 'true' cost of living, 1993–2004

Lawrence R. Klein, Huiqing Gao and Liping Tao

INTRODUCTION

Much discussion has taken place during the past two or three years concerning China's growth rate, often dealing with the appraisal of statistical reliability and possible bias in the published figures. This discussion has taken place during a period when many people have seen for themselves the unfolding of a Chinese expansion that has been almost unbelievable in the speed, scope and depth of movement of the largest economy in the world, measured in terms of population. Most of the scholarly discussion and publication has dealt with the unbelievable numerical size and speed of the expansion, drawing the frequent conclusion that the magnitudes are overstated.[1] However, that is not the appraisal that comes from some of the authors of this chapter, who used quite different methods of measurement that seem to validate the impressions formed by the non- (economic) professional visitors who have actually experienced what has been taking place since 1978, especially on a year-after-year basis, so that the evolution of new developments are clearly exposed and China's stabilizing role in the crisis of 1997–98 is properly understood.

The main purpose of this chapter is to examine a crucial part of the issue at hand by concentrating on a neglected important part, namely, the rate of price level change, that is, the inflation rate that is needed to convert the nominal direct measures of GDP to *real* GDP. When it is claimed that China's GDP has roughly quadrupled between 1980 and 2000 or that the national growth rate since reform in 1978 has been about 9 percent, the statements implicitly mean GDP *adjusted for inflation*. There has been relatively little attention paid to the evaluation of the price deflator used to convert *nominal* into *real* values. In this chapter, we are going to argue that the magnitude of inflation has been overstated, because it does not take account of quality change or lifestyle change, in a broader sense.

It should be noted at the outset that the United States went through a period of significant change in the measurement of the economy's rate of inflation when some leading economic officials and scholars decided that the major price indexes for the US overstated the magnitudes. This was undertaken by the Boskin Committee, who examined such things as product quality, new products, place of purchase and other lifestyle features.[2] They concluded that the prevailing price indexes overstated US inflation by approximately as much as one full percentage point and that about half a point was due to quality improvement alone.

Without using the Boskin Committee's methods of analysis, which are not easily transferable to China because of unavailability of comparable data, we are going to estimate an adjustment to China's CPI by quite different methods and determine how to estimate the *real* growth rate of GDP.

The approach that we are using for China is through estimation of the 'true' economic cost of living index. During World War II, some British economists challenged the government's allowances for civilians, because the officials did not allow for enforced substitution of rationed for unrationed goods, thus lowering the *quality* of the available market basket. Following that debate, one of the authors of this chapter helped to produce a research paper in 1947 to show how one might specify an equation system that could be estimated from available data. This system is known as the linear expenditure system (LES).[3]

The relevance of the LES in the present context is that it provides a readily computable equation system that can be determined from Chinese data, and the formula for the 'true' cost of living for China for the period under dispute can be calculated to see how much the inflation rate might be lowered (and the growth rate correspondingly increased) for the economy as a whole. It should be borne in mind that the US *potential* growth rate, which used to be considered to be roughly 3 percent was raised to 4 percent or more by the work of the Boskin Committee. If the US can claim a higher rate of expansion by revising the price index, why not make a similar revision for China? It is quite evident that the Chinese economy has gone through a much faster and larger change in lifestyle since 1978 than has the US economy. The diet is better; clothing is immensely better; transportation is superior in many ways; retailing is better; services are better; tourism is far better; and so on and so on. Given these changes in living conditions, the economic goal for all progressive societies, surely one should try to take these changes into account when evaluating economic growth.

THE LINEAR EXPENDITURE SYSTEM

The LES equations are not unique, but just any comprehensive demand system is not suitable – it should have some economic-theoretical properties. Of course it need not be linear, but this property can be tested. The theoretical basis for the LES is that it satisfies the following properties from consumer theory:

1. Demand for each type of real expenditure should be homogeneous of degree zero in prices and incomes, that is to say, real demand should depend on relative prices and real income (that is, the ratio of income to price).
2. The equations should satisfy the Slutsky–Hicks symmetry conditions, that is, the partial derivative of the i-th demand with respect to the j-th price should equal the derivative of the j-th demand with respect to the i-th price, *both derivatives evaluated along a given indifference curve*.
3. The sum of individual expenditure amounts should equal total income, including future spending, that is, saving (adding up).

The LES can be written as

$$(p_{it}q_{it} - p_{it}\gamma_i) = \beta_i(r_t - \sum_{j=1}^{n} p_{jt}\gamma_j); \sum_{i=1}^{n} \beta_i = 1$$

⇕	⇕	⇕	⇕	
expenditure on the i-the category	minimum subsistence expenditure on the i-th category	total income	total minimum subsistence expenditure on all categories	β_i = marginal propensity to consume out of supernumerary income

This equation is expressed in current price values (nominal). It can also be transformed into real (constant price values). All statistical equations (except some definitions) should be expressed with explicit allowance for error. In this version, we have proceeded as though there is additive error for each equation as specified above in order to use properties of random variation for evaluation. It is written in such a way as to express intuitive behavior, that is, supernumerary expenditures are linear functions of supernumerary income.

The LES is easy to understand and provides some empirical information without making an elaborate effort, but there are drawbacks. In the first place the LES does not permit *inferior* goods/services. An *inferior* good or service is one whose consumption varies inversely with total income. In a typical family budget there are, indeed, many examples of inferior goods and, if the implicit equation system is to be integrated to the associated utility function, it becomes immediately obvious that *inferior* goods are not acceptable. Nevertheless, this defect can be dealt with by grouping. There are hundreds or thousands of goods and services in a typical family budget, but if they are grouped as we have used them in the present investigation, into only *eight* classes (Food; Clothing; Household Facilities, Articles and Services; Medicine and Medical Services; Transport, Post and Communication Services; Educational, Cultural and Recreation Services; Residence; Miscellaneous Commodities and Services), then we can treat each whole group as a non-inferior good. There can be much substitution between finely specified inferior and non-inferior goods in the process of given calculations.

The Engel curves that separately relate expenditure on each group of goods and services to total income should be linear in this model, given the implied utility function, and they are for 1993 or 1994, but are linear only up to the highest income class in 2002, where the curves turn up. The part of the Engel curves that we are using for parameter estimation is in a linear range. We would not be using Engel curves for 2002 in the present analysis, were it not for the matter of data availability. Our procedures treat urban and rural consumers separately, and the Engel curve database is not available for rural consumers at an earlier date.

This brings us to the technique for parameter estimation for determination of sample values for γ_i and β_i. The γ and β values range across the grouping of goods and services. There are eight values of each parameter, but since the β values are constrained to sum to unity, there are only seven free values of β_i.

There are two sources of variation in the sample. One source refers to cross-section variation from family budgets. One group of budgets refers to the urban population and another to the rural population, as their economic positions and choices are known to be quite different. The other source of variation is across time periods. For reasons of data availability and reliability, we have limited our samples to the period 1993–2002, although the effects of changes in lifestyle were also important in the earlier period 1978–93. Graphs and tables of Engel curve data from family budget data are given in Figures 9.1–9.8 and the corresponding Tables 9.1–9.8.

The parameters γ_i represent *necessary* levels of consumption in each grouping of goods and services. In order to measure supernumerary expenditures for each group of goods and services we need to have estimates of the minimal

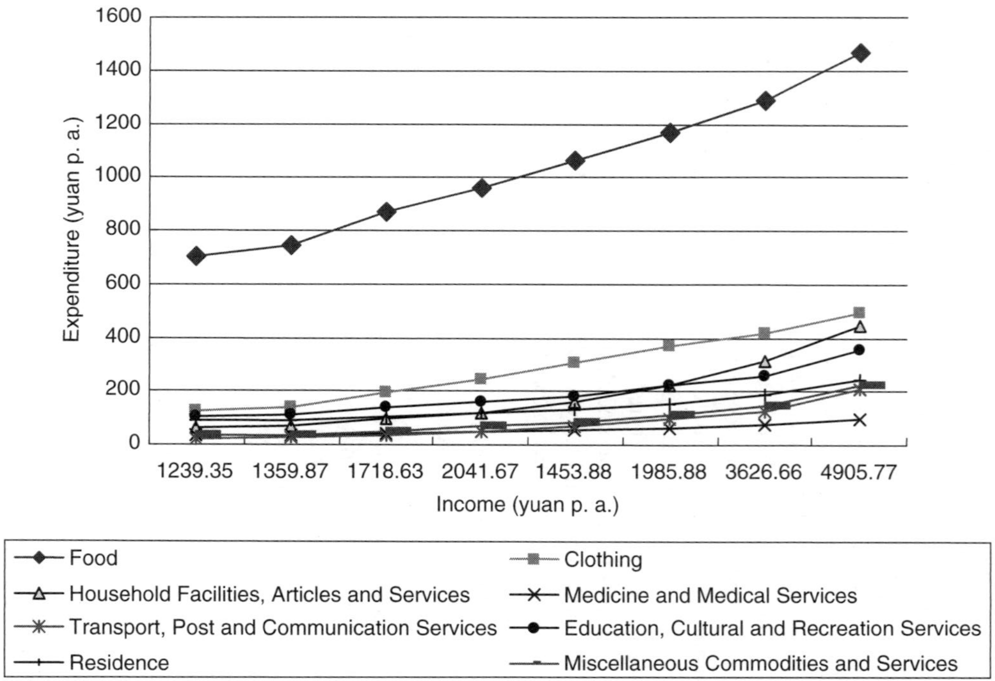

Figure 9.1 Engel curve for 1993 (per capita, urban)

Table 9.1 Engel curve for 1993 (per capita, urban)

	Poor	Lowest	Low	Lower Middle	Middle	Upper Middle	High	Highest
Income (yuan p. a)	1239.35	1359.87	1718.63	2041.67	1453.88	1985.88	3626.66	4905.77
Expenditure (yuan p. a)	1183.15	1261.36	1528.68	1770.17	2055.72	2404.13	2810.32	3533.49
Food	700.33	744.58	869.27	957.57	1064.65	1169.40	1284.57	1464.65
Clothing	127.01	142.50	195.79	246.43	303.32	367.20	418.16	492.62
Household Facilities, Articles and Services	60.00	66.51	94.42	120.06	163.10	220.27	314.16	446.75
Medicine and Medical Services	36.02	36.05	41.92	50.09	53.59	61.52	74.58	100.34
Transport, Post and Communication Services	24.18	28.34	35.69	51.04	68.72	99.60	127.27	212.16
Education, Cultural and Recreation Services	101.43	113.29	136.40	158.43	182.91	221.37	256.21	356.23
Residence	92.88	93.28	103.74	119.33	132.98	150.50	187.61	240.87
Miscellaneous Commodities and Services	34.69	36.81	51.45	67.21	86.45	114.26	147.76	219.88

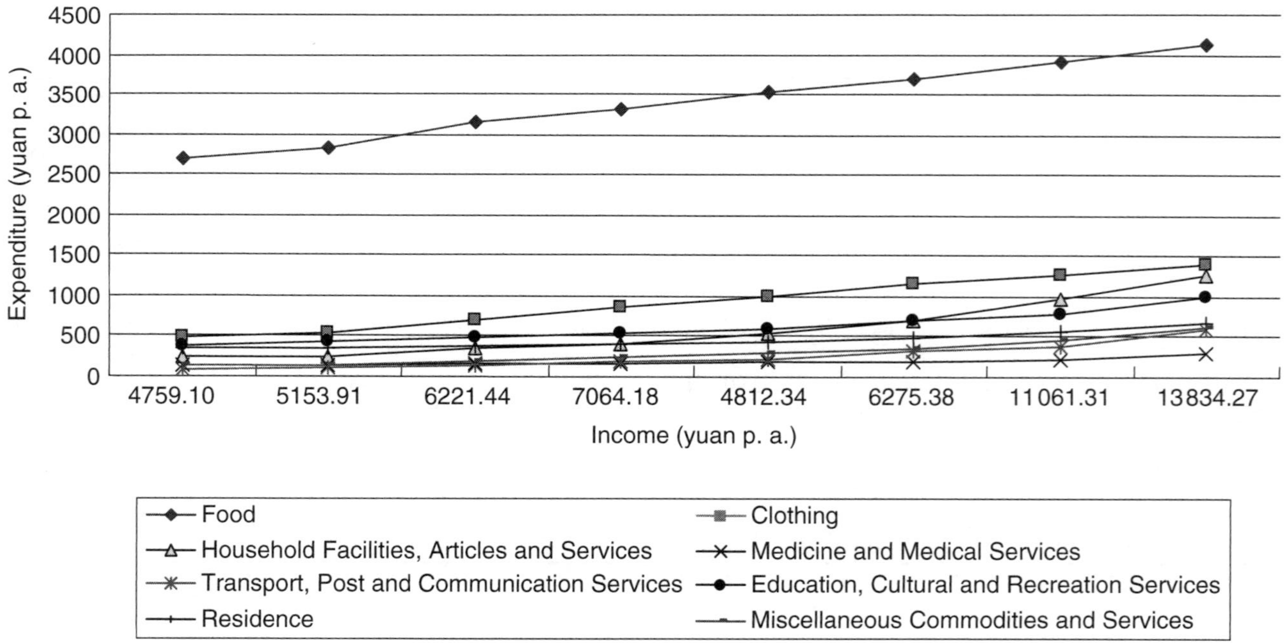

Figure 9.2 Engel curve for 1993 (family, urban)

Table 9.2 Engel curve for 1993 (family, urban)

	Poor	Lowest	Low	Lower Middle	Middle	Upper Middle	High	Highest
Size of family (persons)	3.84	3.79	3.62	3.46	3.31	3.16	3.05	2.82
Income (yuan p.a.)	4759.10	5153.91	6221.44	7064.18	4812.34	6275.38	11 061.31	13 834.27
Expenditure (yuan p.a.)	4543.30	4780.55	5533.82	6124.79	6804.43	7597.05	8571.48	9964.44
Food	2689.27	2821.96	3146.76	3313.19	3523.99	3695.30	3917.94	4130.31
Clothing	487.72	540.08	708.76	852.65	1003.99	1160.35	1275.39	1389.19
Household Facilities, Articles and Services	230.40	252.07	341.80	415.41	539.86	696.05	958.19	1259.84
Medicine and Medical Services	138.32	136.63	151.75	173.31	177.38	194.40	227.47	282.96
Transport, Post and Communication Services	92.85	107.41	129.20	176.60	227.46	314.74	388.17	598.29
Education, Cultural and Recreation Services	389.49	429.37	493.77	548.17	605.43	699.53	781.44	1004.57
Residence	356.66	353.53	375.54	412.88	440.16	475.58	572.21	679.25
Miscellaneous Commodities and Services	133.21	139.51	186.25	232.55	286.15	361.06	450.67	620.06

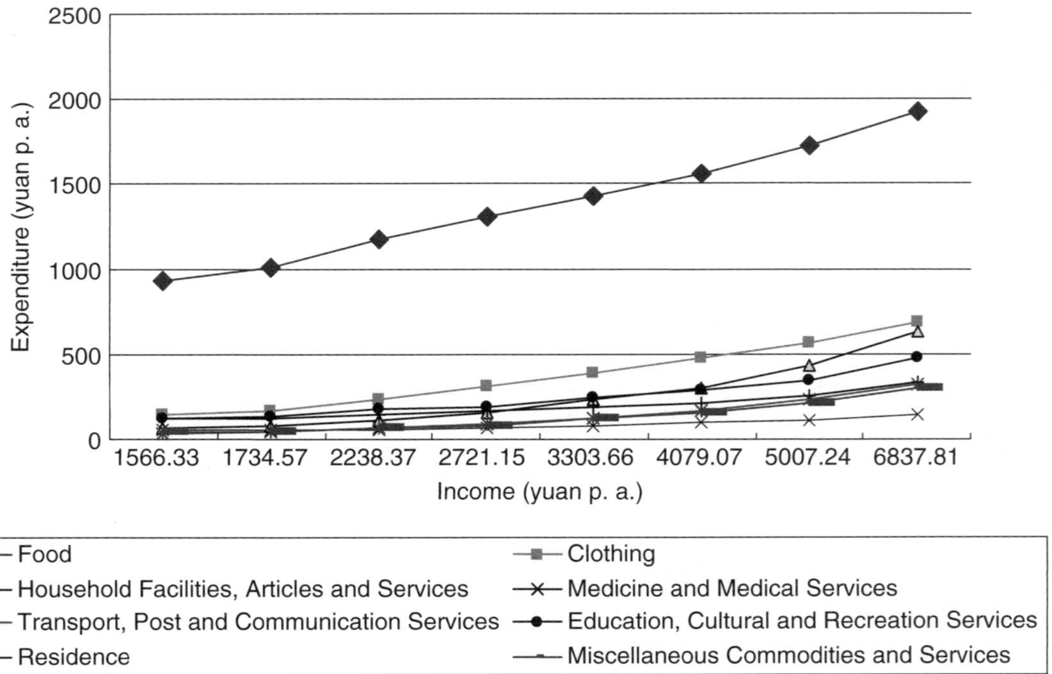

Figure 9.3 Engel curves for 1994 (per capita, urban)

Table 9.3 Engel curves for 1994 (per capita, urban)

	Poor	Lowest	Low	Lower Middle	Middle	Upper Middle	High	Highest
Income (yuan/p. a.)	1566.33	1734.57	2238.37	2721.15	3303.66	4079.07	5007.24	6837.81
Expenditure (yuan/p. a.)	1512.70	1644.56	2028.80	2351.56	2798.12	3252.70	3880.91	4799.83
Food	932.90	1005.76	1169.37	1305.41	1431.04	1563.81	1727.97	1921.61
Clothing	144.79	167.99	235.54	309.39	390.89	477.17	569.08	682.33
Household Facilities, Articles and Services	69.30	78.39	115.58	154.31	230.21	299.94	429.43	628.72
Medicine and Medical Services	52.68	53.82	60.30	67.39	78.89	96.97	109.40	138.48
Transport, Post and Communication Services	31.80	39.60	63.00	83.15	121.98	161.78	227.7	319.40
Education, Cultural and Recreation Services	120.07	130.80	174.16	187.47	244.29	288.61	346.62	479.11
Residence	116.18	121.54	143.23	161.58	183.24	211.41	259.70	335.98
Miscellaneous Commodities and Services	44.99	46.65	67.52	82.85	117.58	153.01	210.95	294.21

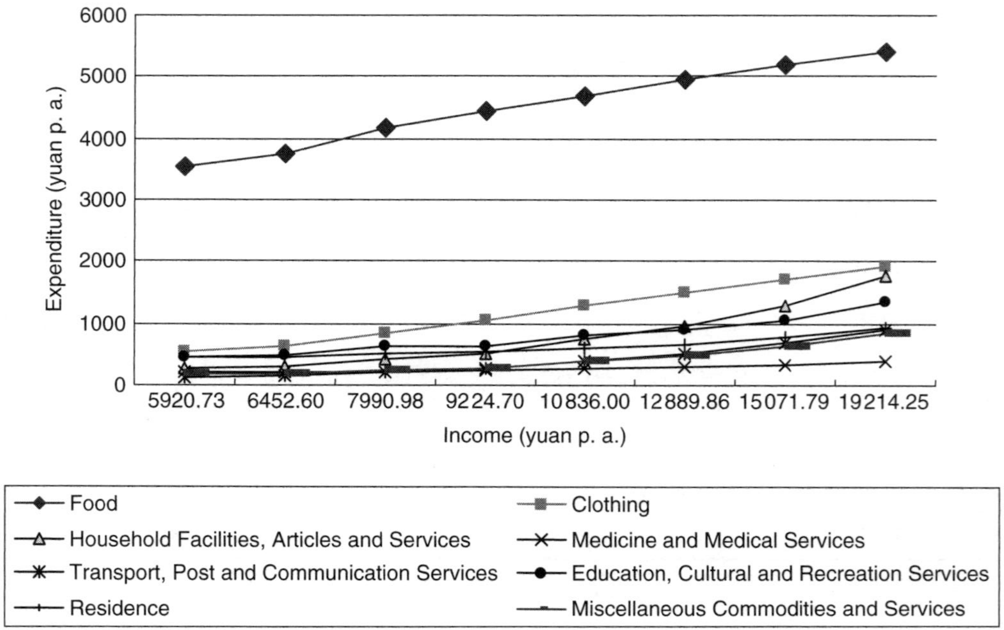

Figure 9.4 Engel curves for 1994 (family, urban)

Table 9.4 Engel curves for 1994 (family, urban)

	Poor	Lowest	Low	Lower Middle	Middle	Upper Middle	High	Highest
Size of family (persons)	3.78	3.72	3.57	3.39	3.28	3.16	3.01	2.81
Income (yuan p. a.)	5920.73	6452.60	7990.98	9224.70	10836.00	12889.86	15071.79	19214.25
Expenditure (yuan p. a.)	5718.01	6117.76	7242.82	7971.79	9177.83	10278.53	11681.54	13487.52
Food	3526.36	3741.43	4174.65	4425.34	4693.81	4941.64	5201.19	5399.72
Clothing	547.31	624.92	840.88	1048.83	1282.12	1507.86	1712.93	1917.35
Household Facilities, Articles and Services	261.95	291.61	412.62	523.11	755.09	947.81	1292.58	1766.70
Medicine and Medical Services	199.13	200.21	215.27	228.45	258.76	306.43	329.29	389.13
Transport, Post and Communication Services	120.20	147.31	224.91	281.88	400.09	511.22	685.50	897.51
Education, Cultural and Recreation Services	453.86	486.58	621.75	635.52	801.27	912.01	1043.33	1346.30
Residence	439.16	452.13	511.33	547.76	601.03	668.06	781.70	944.10
Miscellaneous Commodities and Services	170.06	173.54	241.40	280.86	385.66	483.51	634.96	826.73

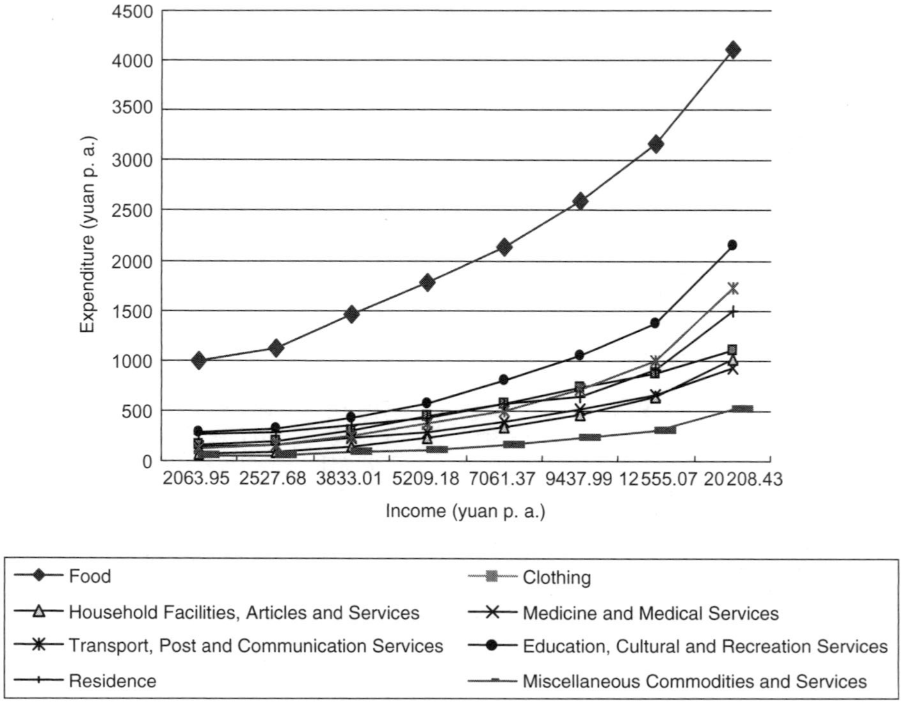

Figure 9.5 Engel curves for 2002 (per capita, urban)

Table 9.5 Engel curves for 2002 (per capita, urban)

	Poor	Lowest	Low	Lower Middle	Middle	Upper Middle	High	Highest
Income (yuan p. a.)	2063.95	2527.68	3833.01	5209.18	7061.37	9437.99	12 555.07	20 208.43
Expenditure (yuan p. a.)	2079.52	2387.91	3259.59	4205.97	5452.94	6939.95	8919.94	13 040.69
Food	988.19	1127.41	1457.87	1772.88	2140.34	2596.95	3171.36	4100.79
Clothing	152.38	193.09	309.49	438.38	571.19	737.20	866.38	1103.16
Household Facilities, Articles and Services	71.49	86.69	144.67	226.42	331.54	460.99	645.72	1014.63
Medicine and Medical Services	150.74	164.63	225.67	286.56	382.83	510.15	657.33	933.10
Transport, Post and Communication Services	126.34	157.64	257.63	367.72	505.78	718.92	991.17	1731.09
Education, Cultural and Recreation Services	280.53	317.57	425.33	576.71	797.52	1046.46	1373.85	2148.56
Residence	261.45	282.74	355.12	421.90	563.31	643.15	906.67	1485.72
Miscellaneous Commodities and Services	48.40	58.14	83.81	115.40	160.43	226.13	307.46	523.64

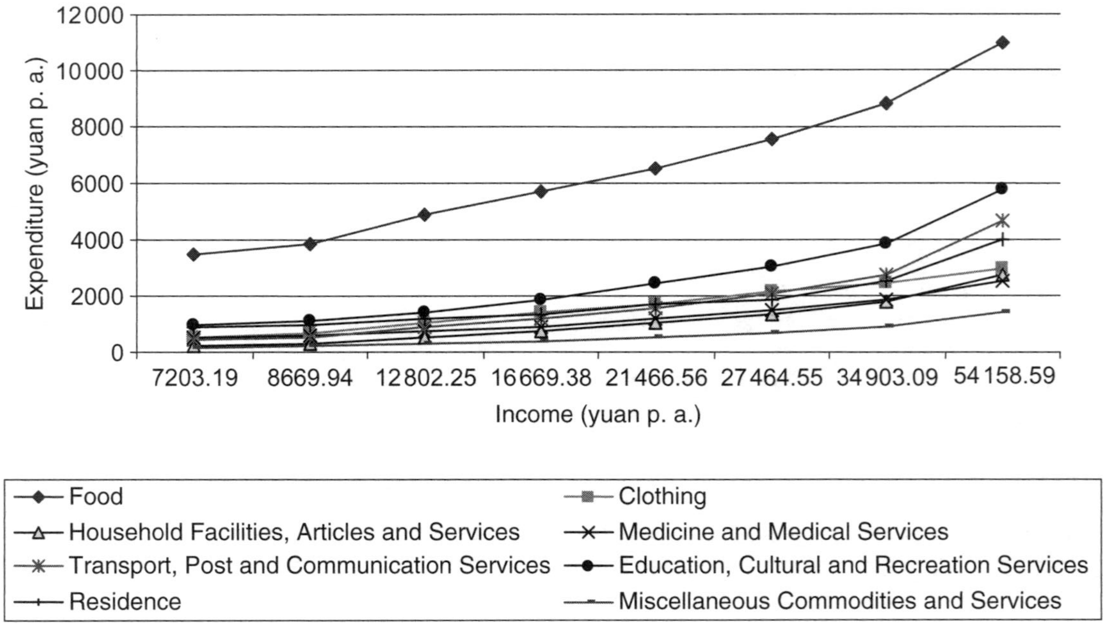

Figure 9.6 *Engel curves for 2002 (family, urban)*

Table 9.6 Engel curves for 2002 (family, urban)

	Poor	Lowest	Low	Lower Middle	Middle	Upper Middle	High	Highest
Size of family (persons)	3.49	3.43	3.34	3.2	3.04	2.91	2.78	2.68
Income (yuan p. a.)	7203.19	8669.94	12 802.25	16 669.38	21 466.56	27 464.55	34 903.09	54 158.59
Expenditure (yuan p. a.)	7257.52	8190.53	10 887.03	13 459.10	16 576.94	20 195.25	24 797.43	34 949.05
Food	3448.78	3867.02	4869.29	5673.22	6506.63	7557.12	8816.38	10 990.12
Clothing	531.81	662.30	1033.70	1402.82	1736.42	2145.25	2408.54	2956.47
Household Facilities, Articles and Services	249.50	297.35	483.20	724.54	1007.88	1341.48	1795.10	2719.21
Medicine and Medical Services	526.08	564.68	753.74	916.99	1163.80	1484.54	1827.38	2500.71
Transport, Post and Communication Services	440.93	540.71	860.48	1176.70	1537.57	2092.06	2755.45	4639.32
Education, Cultural and Recreation Services	979.05	1089.27	1420.60	1845.47	2424.46	3045.20	3819.30	5758.14
Residence	912.46	969.80	1186.10	1350.08	1712.46	1871.57	2520.54	3981.73
Miscellaneous Commodities and Services	168.92	199.42	279.93	369.28	487.71	658.04	854.74	1403.36

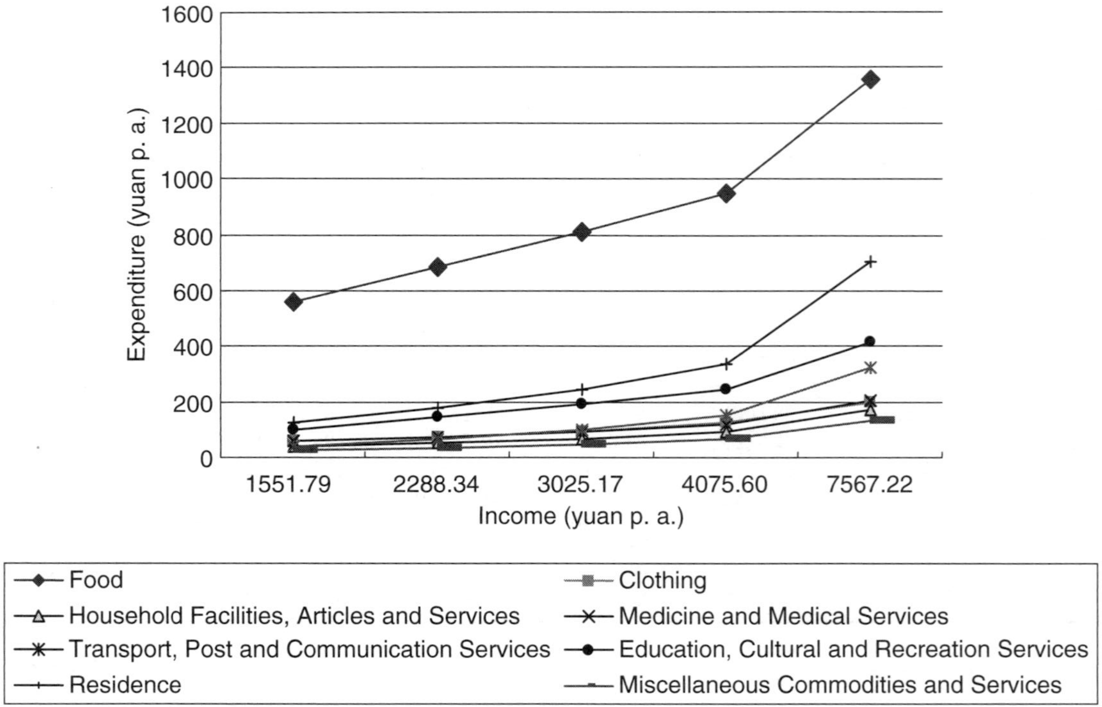

Figure 9.7 Engel curves for 2002 (per capita, rural)

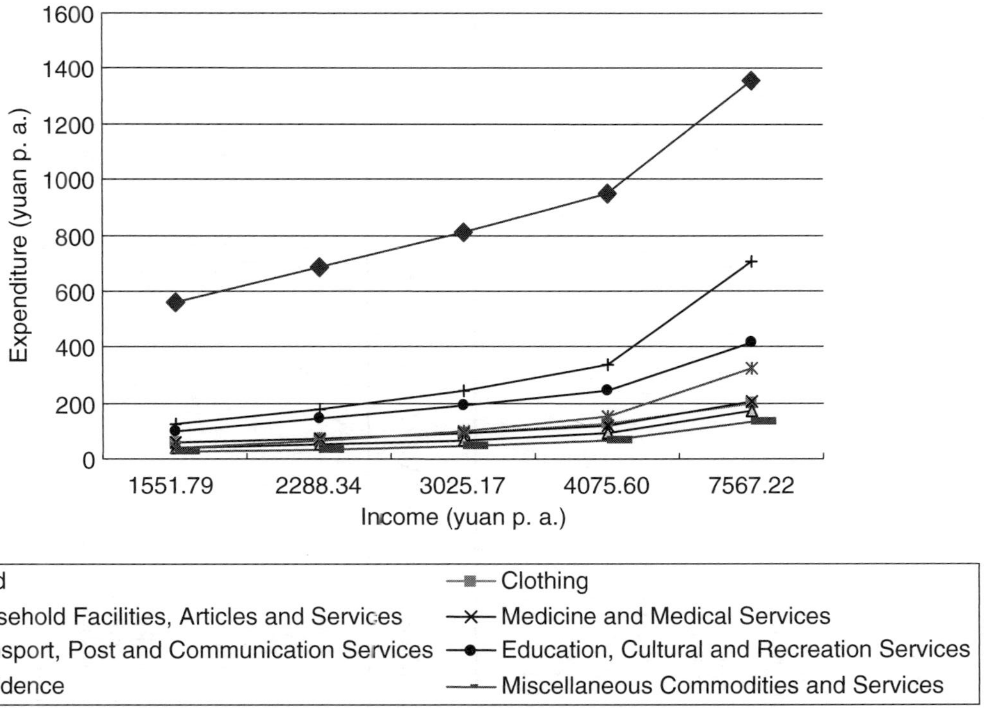

Figure 9.8 Engel curves for 2002 (family, rural)

Table 9.7 Engel curves for 2002 (per capita, rural)

	Low	Lower Middle	Middle	Upper Middle	High
Income (yuan p. a.)	1551.79	2288.34	3025.17	4075.60	7567.22
Expenditure (yuan p. a.)	1006.36	1310.34	1645.04	2086.72	3500.09
Food	562.37	686.76	808.99	949.52	1354.31
Clothing	56.75	74.23	93.98	122.86	198.89
Household Facilities, Articles and Services	38.95	52.83	67.77	93.32	168.51
Medicine and Medical Services	57.54	74.88	90.73	116.49	201.72
Transport, Post and Communication Services	41.76	67.65	100.50	153.64	321.40
Education, Cultural and Recreation Services	97.36	145.50	193.28	246.91	416.88
Residence	127.56	174.75	244.14	336.15	704.75
Miscellaneous Commodities and Services	24.07	33.74	45.65	67.83	133.63

Table 9.8 Engel curves for 2002 (family, rural)

	Low	Lower Middle	Middle	Upper Middle	High
Average size of family (persons)	4.66	4.36	4.15	3.92	3.56
Income (yuan/p. a.)	7231.34	9977.16	12 554.46	15 976.35	26 939.30
Expenditure (yuan/p. a.)	4689.64	5713.08	6826.92	8179.94	12 460.32
Food	2620.64	2994.27	3357.31	3722.12	4821.34
Clothing	264.46	323.64	390.02	481.61	708.05
Household Facilities, Articles and Services	181.51	230.34	281.25	365.81	599.90
Medicine and Medical Services	268.14	326.48	376.53	456.64	718.12
Transport, Post and Communication Services	194.60	294.95	417.08	602.27	1144.18
Education, Cultural and Recreation Services	453.70	634.38	802.11	967.89	1484.09
Residence	594.43	761.91	1013.18	1317.71	2508.91
Miscellaneous Commodities and Services	112.17	147.11	189.45	265.89	475.72

or necessary amounts. In order to estimate marginal propensities to consume, the β_i, we need estimates of supernumerary income, that is, income over and above that needed to buy the minimum in all groups, together.

The non-linearity in parameters could be handled by using some iterative technique for simultaneous estimation or in two-step procedures. In combinations of time series and cross-section samples it has been customary to estimate spending propensities from cross-section data (as Engel curve slopes, for example) and price coefficients from time series of market data. We have reversed the process by first estimating the γ_i (necessary or minimal amounts consumed) directly from the cross-section data and the marginal propensities from time series aggregates. This procedure is used, in order to make use of external information. Also, limited data are available for the rural group over the time period selected for analysis.

At best, it would be desirable to have expertise on the composition of *minimum subsistence* income, say, from specialists on social behavior and needs – many countries have such expert information. Instead we used information from Huiqing Gao and Liping Tao, who are confident that they know plausible values for the *minimal subsistence* levels of family budgets for base years, such as 1993, 1994 or 2002. The second income level from the bottom ('Lowest') was chosen as the minimum subsistence budget for urban consumers, while the bottom level ('Low') was chosen for rural consumers. In each case, the average amount spent in each of the selected income classes for each of the individual groupings (eight urban and eight rural) served as direct estimates of γ_i. If γ_i are estimated in this simple, straightforward way, then the remaining parameters can be computed from the linear relationship between supernumerary expenditures and supernumerary income. The constraint on the sum of β_i can readily be met if we use total expenditure rather than total income in the regressor variable. This is sensible, because total expenditure is to be preferred to total income, since total expenditure is generally felt to be a better indicator of long-run income, rather than direct measures of current period income, itself.

Having the γ_i and β_i estimated, we then evaluate the 'true' cost of living index from

$$\frac{r_i}{r_0} = \frac{C\prod_{i=1}^{n} p_{it}^{\beta_{ii}} - \sum_{i=1}^{n} \gamma_i p_{it}}{C\prod_{i=1}^{n} p_{i0}^{\beta_{ii}} - \sum_{i=1}^{n} \gamma_i p_{i0}}$$

The Engel curves provide estimates of γ_i (for a minimal subsistence value of total income) and regressions of supernumerary expenditure on supernumerary income provide estimates of β_i. The constants of integration are

Table 9.9 Percentage change, cost of living and official CPI

	Urban		Rural	
	Per capita	Household	Per capita	Household
Cost of living	4.55	4.56	3.96	3.42
CPI	5.47	5.47	5.13	5.13

determined by substitution in the above expression for all values of variables designated at $t=0$ (the base) and at the next adjacent year; that provides a formula for C. In other words, we find the value of C that makes the above expression hold for an adjacent year, $t=\pm 1$, given our estimates of γ_i and β_i. For example, in estimating values of the cost-of-living formula for base year 1993, we evaluate C such that the formula holds for

$$\frac{r_{94}}{r_{93}}=\frac{C\prod_{i=1}^{8} p_{i94}^{\hat{\beta}_i}-\sum_{i=1}^{8}\gamma_i p_{i94}}{C\prod_{i=1}^{8} p_{i93}^{\hat{\beta}_i}-\sum_{i=1}^{8}\gamma_i p_{i93}}$$

For rural as well as urban consumers in 2002, we compute estimates of γ_i for that year from the family budget table and then proceed to estimate supernumerary Engel curves for 1993–2002. The formula for r_i/r_{2002} is used to compute C (at 2001), for rural consumers only and then rebase the whole price series back to $t=1993$, as for the 'true' cost-of-living index base year.[4]

The results can be summarized, as follows in Table 9.9:

The lower inflation rate on the basis of 'true' cost of living translates into higher growth rates for real consumption. If the nominal consumption figures were to be adjusted for a lower CPI inflation rate we would estimate on a per capita basis higher real consumption growth (1993–2002) of 9.32 percent versus 7.65 percent. On a household basis the figures would be 9.57 percent versus 7.65 percent. These results combine both urban and rural consumption together; so slightly less than two percentage points could be added to the estimate of the country's growth rate of real consumption. This is not an estimate in a strict sense for real GDP growth but simply an example that shows the underestimate of a large GDP complement on the demand side.

As a crude check on these estimates, we make another estimate, urban areas alone, on a per capita and a family basis (see Tables 9.10 and 9.11), using the 2002 urban Engel curves, rebasing the time series of prices to 1993. For urban areas, we find the spread between the rate of growth of the

Table 9.10 Consumption expenditure (by per capita, 100 million yuan)

Year	Deflated by CPI			Deflated by 'True' Cost of Living		
	Total consumption	Urban consumption	Rural consumption	Total consumption	Urban consumption	Rural consumption
1993	15 682.40	7815.20	7867.20	15 682.40	7815.20	7867.20
1994	16 754.77	8401.20	8353.57	17 372.18	8748.44	8623.75
1995	18 518.03	9381.78	9136.25	19 849.04	10 157.92	9691.11
1996	20 399.18	9917.85	10 481.33	22 098.14	10 895.25	11 202.89
1997	21 508.85	10 635.38	10 873.48	23 599.33	11 887.34	11 711.99
1998	22 955.91	11 827.47	11 128.44	25 459.99	13 403.01	12 056.98
1999	24 791.37	13 186.25	11 605.11	27 875.81	15 198.75	12 677.07
2000	26 920.97	14 632.55	12 288.41	30 868.45	17 301.17	13 567.28
2001	28 587.02	15 690.91	12 896.10	32 826.60	18 566.56	14 260.04
2002	30 445.98	16 944.71	13 501.26	34 979.35	20 050.14	14 929.21
Average growth rate (%)	7.65	8.98	6.18	9.32	11.04	7.38

Table 9.11 Consumption expenditure (by family, 100 million yuan)

Year	Deflated by CPI			Deflated by 'True' Cost of Living		
	Total consumption	Urban consumption	Rural consumption	Total consumption	Urban consumption	Rural consumption
1993	15 682.40	7815.20	7867.20	15 682.40	7815.20	7867.20
1994	16 754.77	8401.20	8353.57	17 646.35	8753.97	8892.38
1995	18 518.03	9381.78	9136.25	20 528.49	10 167.29	10 361.20
1996	20 399.18	9917.85	10 481.33	22 941.82	10 904.00	12 037.83
1997	21 508.85	10 635.38	10 873.48	24 386.49	11 894.48	12 492.01
1998	22 955.91	11 827.47	11 128.44	26 195.16	13 408.07	12 787.09
1999	24 791.37	13 186.25	11 605.11	28 556.79	15 201.49	13 355.30
2000	26 920.97	14 632.55	12 288.41	31 521.56	17 299.18	14 222.38
2001	28 587.02	15 690.91	12 896.10	33 501.58	18 562.52	14 939.06
2002	30 445.98	16 944.71	13 501.26	35 685.86	20 045.78	15 640.08
Average growth rate (%)	7.65	8.98	6.18	9.57	11.03	7.93

CPI at 5.47 percent to be almost two percentage points higher than that of the 'true' cost of living at 3.51 percent per capita and 3.52 percent family, 1993–2002, using the Engel curve for 2002 but re-basing the associated cost of living index to 1993 (the initialization point for valuing the constant of integration). These results are shown in Figures 9.9–9.14 and Tables 9.12–9.18. The larger spread for this validation-checking calculation would imply a larger spread in the real growth rate of consumption.

Our procedures for estimating a bias in the consumer price index for China lack some data series that would be needed in order to make a definitive estimate of the increment to China's economic growth rate, but we can see that persistent overestimates of the price deflator for consumption is indicated by our various approximations. We come to the conclusion that one or two percentage points should be added to the growth rate.

Table 9.12 Cost of living and official CPI (urban, per capita, initialized at 1993, Engel curve at 2002)

	1993	1994	1995	1996	1997	1998	1999	2000	2001	2002	Average Growth Rate
CPI	1.00	1.25	1.46	1.59	1.64	1.63	1.61	1.62	1.63	1.61	5.47%
'True' cost of living	1.00	1.20	1.35	1.45	1.47	1.44	1.39	1.37	1.38	1.36	3.51%

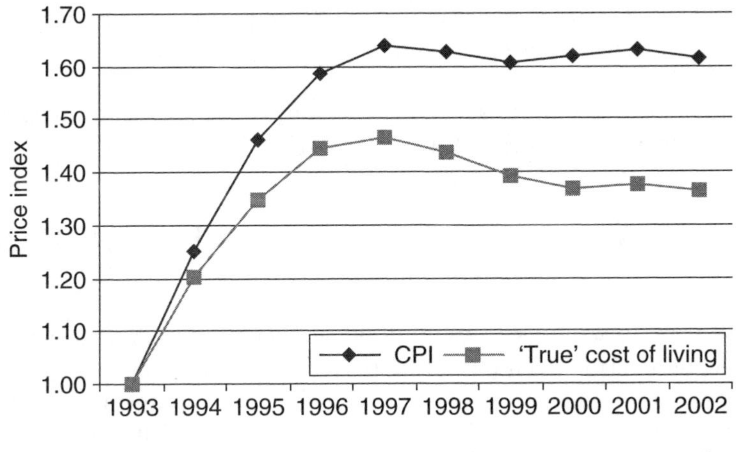

Figure 9.9 Cost of living and official CPI (urban, per capita, initialized at 1993, Engel curve at 2002)

Table 9.13 Cost of living and official CPI (urban, family, initialized at 1993, Engel curve at 2002)

	1993	1994	1995	1996	1997	1998	1999	2000	2001	2002	Average Growth Rate
CPI	1.00	1.25	1.46	1.59	1.64	1.63	1.61	1.62	1.63	1.61	5.47%
'True' cost of living	1.00	1.20	1.35	1.44	1.46	1.44	1.39	1.37	1.38	1.36	3.52%

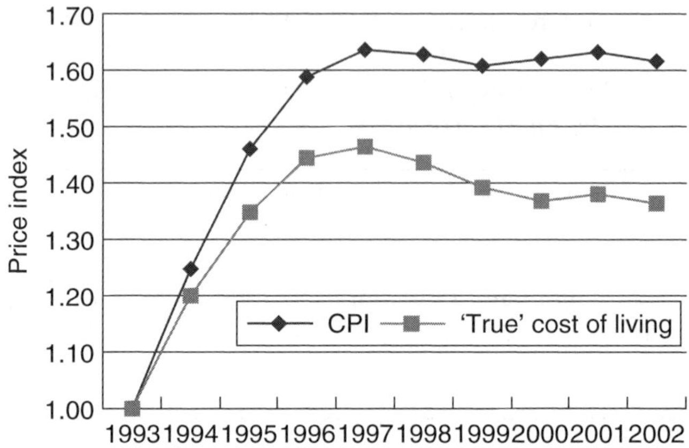

Figure 9.10 Cost of living and official CPI (urban, family, initialized at 1993, Engel curve at 2002)

Although we determine this for consumption, the same order of magnitude ought to be considered close for GDP as well.

SOME COMMENTS ON THE LINEAR EXPENDITURE SYSTEM

The linear expenditure system (LES) is, without doubt, a very special case and, as Samuelson pointed out in 1947, not a general case of *linearity*, such as in a first-order Taylor approximation. Yet the linear expenditure system is not linear in unknown parameters nor in individual prices, quantities, and income (total expenditures). Linearity depends on how the non-stochastic specification is transformed and how stochastic properties

Table 9.14 Cost of living and official CPI (rural, per capita, initialized at 1993, Engel curve at 2002)

	1993	1994	1995	1996	1997	1998	1999	2000	2001	2002	Average Growth Rate
CPI	1.00	1.23	1.45	1.56	1.60	1.59	1.56	1.56	1.57	1.57	5.13%
'True' cost of living	1.00	1.20	1.37	1.46	1.49	1.47	1.43	1.41	1.42	1.42	3.96%

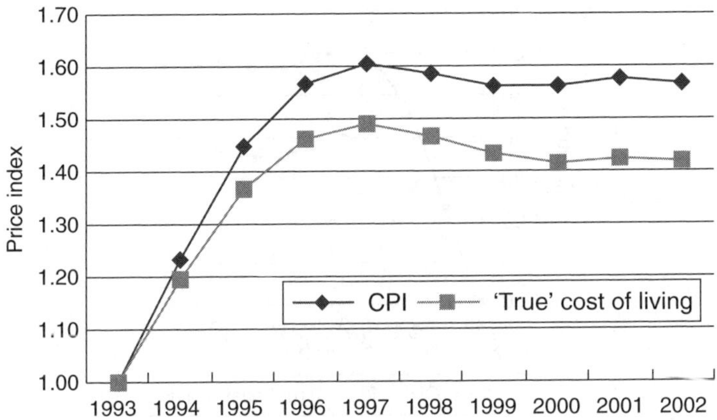

Figure 9.11 Cost of living and official CPI (rural, per capita, initialized at 1993, Engel curve at 2002)

are introduced. It is linear in nominal supernumerary expenditures and income.

It must be emphasized that our present interest in use of the LES is for determining growth, and, in the important Chinese case, growth means development since 1978; so the meaningful annual data samples are limited in scope, and as China is very much a *transition* economy it means that available data are not plentiful at a high degree of accuracy, although the situation is rapidly changing for the better.

In this system, the LES will be examined in a related, but somewhat different, setting, namely in the context of a cross-country sample built and maintained at the University of Pennsylvania by our colleagues Robert Summers, Alan Heston and (now deceased) Irving Kravis. In their 1985 volume on purchasing power parity (PPP) prices for evaluating GDP across countries in comparable world price values, they made an extremely

Table 9.15 Cost of living and official CPI (rural, family, initialized at 1993, Engel curve at 2002)

	1993	1994	1995	1996	1997	1998	1999	2000	2001	2002	Average Growth Rate
CPI	1.00	1.23	1.45	1.56	1.60	1.59	1.56	1.56	1.57	1.57	5.13%
'True' cost of living	1.00	1.16	1.28	1.36	1.40	1.38	1.36	1.35	1.36	1.35	3.42%

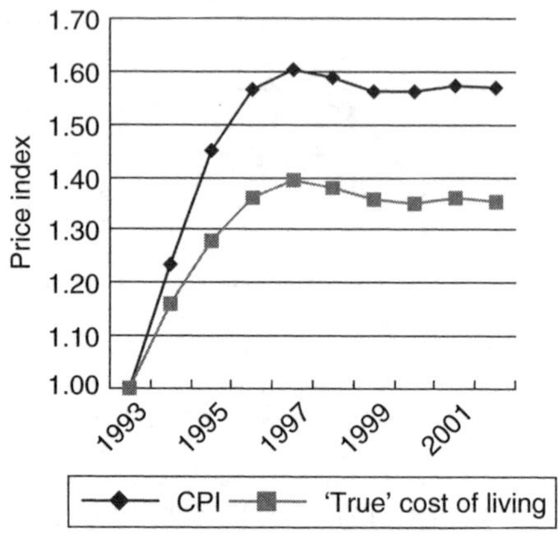

Figure 9.12 Cost of living and official CPI (rural, family, initialized at 1993, Engel curve at 2002)

interesting application of LES. They started this analysis with the provocative question, 'Are tastes the same the world round?' This question is akin, but not identical, to our preoccupation with measuring price changes in the context of a constant level of utility over time. Their within-sample variation comes from variability from country to country, while ours comes from variability from time period to time period within a given country – China. In the Summers–Heston–Kravis study, expenditures (or consumption volumes, in an aggregate sense) vary from country to country because incomes and prices vary, while tastes are assumed to be fixed. They show that LES can be written in three ways: (1) the dependent variable being expenditures, (2) the dependent variable being quantity consumed, (3) the dependent variable being budget share. They chose two forms (2) and (3), while we chose (1) for our analysis. They used four demand categories (Food, Clothing, Shelter, All others), while we chose eight demand categories.

Table 9.16 *Cost of living and official CPI (urban, per capita, initialized at 1993, Engel curve at 1993)*

	1993	1994	1995	1996	1997	1998	1999	2000	2001	2002	Average Growth Rate
CPI	1.00	1.25	1.46	1.59	1.64	1.63	1.61	1.62	1.63	1.61	5.47%
'True' cost of living	1.00	1.25	1.46	1.58	1.60	1.57	1.52	1.50	1.50	1.49	4.55%

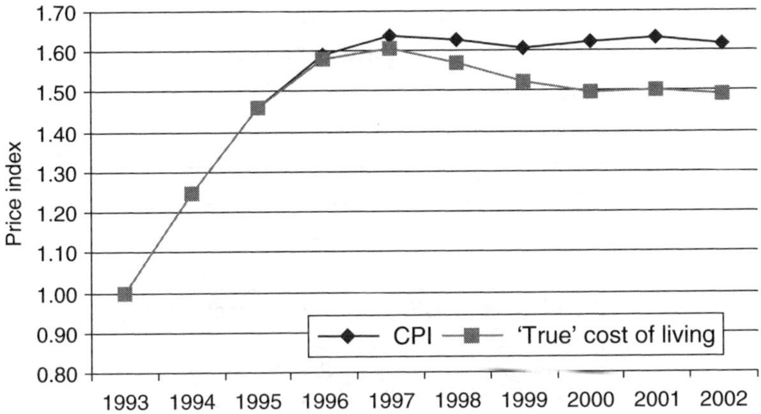

Figure 9.13 *Cost of living and official CPI (urban, per capita, initialized at 1993, Engel curve at 1993)*

For purposes of parameter estimation, either in a pure cross-section sample or a pure time series sample, it is straightforward to carry out the steps of statistical inference by non-linear means, often in iterated linear steps, until convergence is attained. That is the approach used by Summers, Heston and Kravis. By contrast, we have estimated LES by step-wise linear methods, without iteration. We achieve this by use of a priori information. In our case, the parameters obtained as estimates of essential minimal consumption expenditure in a given year are based on basic needs of a typical household. It is like the process used in many countries for establishing *subsistence* budgets, by expenditure category. Instead of using specialists' estimates of a minimal budget, we used the judgment of Gao and Tao (joint authors for this study) on the basis of their knowledge of norms that they estimate at the State Information Center. These are essentially *micro*economic estimates in association with

Table 9.17 Cost of living and official CPI (urban, family, initialized at 1993, Engel curve at 1993)

	1993	1994	1995	1996	1997	1998	1999	2000	2001	2002	Average Growth Rate
CPI	1.00	1.25	1.46	1.59	1.64	1.63	1.61	1.62	1.63	1.61	5.47%
'True' cost of living	1.00	1.25	1.46	1.58	1.60	1.57	1.52	1.51	1.50	1.49	4.56%

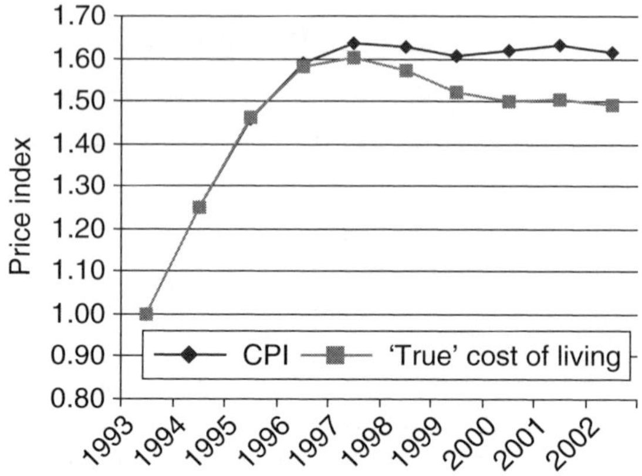

Figure 9.14 Cost of living and official CPI (urban, family, initialized at 1993, Engel curve at 1993)

family budget data samples. The other parameters are then estimated, given the minimum subsistence amounts, from the regression of supernumerary expenditure for each category on supernumerary income, which is taken to be total expenditure, serving as a proxy for long-run income. It seems reasonable to assume that the first set of parameter estimates does not depend on the second set, which uses time series of macro concepts – supernumerary expenditure, by categories of goods and services, in relation to total supernumerary income, from time series estimation. This is a linear estimator, given the estimates of minimum essential expenditure, on average, in the different groupings, over time periods in our sample of family budget data.

A remarkable property of the Summers–Heston–Kravis estimates is that the LES fits the data of the consumption estimate and their associated price indexes on a cross-country sample. An interesting application of the ana-

Table 9.18 Urban consumption expenditure (1993 price, 100 million yuan)

Year	Deflated by CPI	Deflated by 'True' Cost of Living (per capita)	Deflated by 'True' Cost of Living (family)
1993	7815.20	7815.20	7815.20
1994	8401.20	8401.20	8401.20
1995	9381.78	9362.54	9368.95
1996	9917.85	9958.47	9971.08
1997	10 635.38	10 858.98	10 872.53
1998	11 827.47	12 255.82	12 271.45
1999	13 186.25	13 929.52	13 947.86
2000	14 632.55	15 809.67	15 830.79
2001	15 690.91	17 003.79	17 026.41
2002	16 944.71	18 324.98	18 349.56
Average growth rate (%)	8.98	9.93	9.95

logue to the constant-utility property of the LES system in the context of a cross-country analysis is the use of the estimated LES consumption values to compute individual consumption values for each country. If the system is used to rank per capita consumption levels, country by country relative to the base country (the USA), the values listed in Table 9.19 below refer to how much the expenditures of the various countries would have to be increased in order to raise the level of satisfaction of the individual representative consumers to that of the representative US consumer. In place of maintenance of a given utility level over time variation, the results for the PPP consumption estimates maintain the taste levels across country variation.

The 34 countries in the sample used by Heston, Summers and Kravis show remarkable correspondence between their PPP rankings (Geary-Khamis) of per capita consumption and estimates of the same statistic computed from an empirical linear expenditure system from the cross-section sample of the same countries. The final results are all expressed in relation to per capita consumption in the US.

The sample used for the above table does not include all the countries chosen for the consumption tables (PPP) because some necessary data are lacking for a number of countries. The layout in Table 9.19 groups countries roughly by stage of development, and is, in a sense, an example of the usefulness of the LES system, which receives far less attention than does the PPP system of country comparisons of GDP and its components. In this case the component is consumption.

Table 9.19 Comparison of estimates of real per capita consumption expenditures using Geary–Khamis formulas and LES formulas (percentage of US per capita consumption 1975)

Geary-Khamis		LES
Malawi	4.76	4.49
Kenya	6.09	6.67
India	5.86	6.51
Pakistan	7.81	8.31
Sri Lanka	8.75	10.50
Zambia	7.25	7.46
Thailand	12.79	11.52
Philippines	12.14	14.09
Korea	18.69	17.95
Malaysia	17.14	18.33
Colombia	22.21	22.23
Jamaica	23.92	26.70
Syria	23.66	23.22
Brazil	22.21	22.82
Romania	26.00	27.89
Mexico	33.66	37.04
Yugoslavia	31.78	34.68
Iran	24.64	25.12
Uruguay	39.92	36.83
Ireland	43.70	44.38
Hungary	42.81	44.09
Poland	39.63	40.12
Italy	49.05	53.19
Spain	57.70	58.90
UK	61.03	62.70
Japan	55.34	55.96
Austria	72.01	74.95
Netherlands	66.11	68.35
Belgium	71.90	73.99
France	71.58	74.37
Luxembourg	71.69	77.71
Denmark	75.48	74.16
Germany	72.98	74.98
US	100.00	100.00

It is also interesting that R.C. Geary, who is a co-author of the Geary–Khamis method of making country comparisons for growth analysis, also made an independent derivation of the underlying utility function for the LES system. R.C. Geary derived the same utility function from Richard Stone's independent discovery of the LES system that P.A. Samuelson obtained from the Klein–Rubin version.

In conclusion, we state the final comments of Summers, Heston and Kravis as a piece of information supporting our use of the LES for evaluation of China's CPI; it too is a piece of understanding for the economic growth of China. 'The stochastic multilateral approach to international comparisons embodied in the LES differs from the Geary–Khamis multilateral approach, but still produces remarkably similar estimates'.[5]

ANOTHER APPROACH FOR ADJUSTMENT: VIA LIFESTYLE CHANGE

There are different ways of making adjustments to the official published price indexes. The changes made by the Boskin Committee in the United States to recognize product quality improvement is known as the method of *hedonic* price indexes. This has been introduced or investigated on a limited scale for specific goods and services such as optional equipment devices for motorcars, operational features of computers, or health care techniques. The specific technical detail for a large fraction of consumer spending was not available for our use in the present Chinese investigation, so we did not attempt to corroborate our studies with hedonic calculations, but we did attempt to measure aspects of lifestyle to see if we could estimate an index adjustment by referring to a variety of indicators of life quality or lifestyle in a wider sense. That is the objective of this section. In practice, hedonic index adjustments focus on quality improvements, but there are obvious cases of deterioration; that is a reason for not following that method.

In a sense we are looking for indicators of *human development*. The United Nations Development Programme (UNDP) provides an annual index made up of a real income measure, a literacy factor, longevity, and educational enrollment. In ordinary price indexes, unit prices are weighted by their associated quantities of goods and services. In a sense, these weighting factors, once they are put into appropriate units reflect the *volume* of economic activity, that is, their price valuations enable them to aggregate into real values of national income or national expenditure, or national production. They do not show the details of the composition of production and, in particular, quality improvement, over time, or lifestyle changes. As a single, uni-dimensional magnitude, life expectancy comes close to telling us about quality of life. We, however, did not want such a concentrated measure and looked for a variety of indicators, thus spreading the risk of poor judgment.

In a series of research papers, Nagar and Basu, have made cross-country estimates using the method of principal components to construct an index of human development.[6] Nagar and Basu recommend the construction of an index in which each principal component (which is a linear combination of indicators) is weighted by its eigenvalues.

Following the path laid out by Nagar and Basu, but using the time dimension in a time series sample for China rather than country designation in a cross-country sample Suleyman Özmucur and Lawrence Klein estimated five principal components from five variables:

- CO_2 emissions (metric tons per capita) inverted;
- secondary school enrollments (%);
- physicians (per 1000 people);
- infant survival rate (per 100 live births);
- life expectancy at birth (years).

These data were prepared (1980–2000), separately, for USA and China, interpolating values for specific years in which quantitative reports were not published and the results showed growth of the weighted aggregates to be 0.33 percent for USA and 0.53 percent for China.

For comparison without cost of living price deflators for China (and the USA for comparison) leads us to conclude that this source of variation shows that quality improvement grew about 60 percent (20 percentage points) faster in China than in the USA. This is about *growth* and not about *levels*.

There are some very important indicators for China that have not yet been investigated. For the USA, however, some of these indicators have been taken about as high as country performance could go. For example, illiteracy, in a practical sense, has been banished in the USA. Professor Teh-wei Hu of the University of California School of Public Health has suggested that we expand our list by adding data on access to tap water and public sanitation facilities for insight into improvement of China's quality of life.

In this chapter, we estimate the contributions of the following additional variables to China's principal component analysis: SO_2 Emissions; Urban Access to Tap Water; Urban Garbage Disposal; Urban Excrement and Urine Disposal (tons per capita), and Graduates of Higher Educational Institutions (per 1000 people). These variables are all measured for urban China. In the case of the USA, they are not necessarily relevant. They are year after year already at virtual saturation levels in the USA. So we have made an analysis of China alone, to be compared with the previous values for China, to see how much improvement, in an overall sense, has been taking place between the two countries.

We have, however, introduced a particular variable, namely SO_2 Emissions. The variable CO_2 Emissions, in an earlier study, measured possible environmental deterioration, but not directly a cause of individual human health problems; rather a cause of atmospheric conditions that could cause problems to existing cities or towns. CO_2 Emissions are generally associated with such problems as global warming, which could eventually cause human suffering. SO_2 Emissions are more likely to have direct effects on the health of exposed people so we have experimented with the use of this variable for China, either with or without simultaneous consideration of a CO_2 variable.

Below, we list ten indicators, including the original five variables used in the paper with Suleyman Özmucur (Klein and Özmucur, 2003):

1. Life Expectancy at Birth (years);
2. Infant Survival Rate (per 100 live births);
3. Physicians (per 1000 people);
4. Secondary School Enrollment (per 1000 people);
5. SO_2 Emissions (tons per capita);
6. Urban Access to Tap Water (%);
7. Urban Garbage Disposal (per 1000 people);
8. Urban Excrement and Urine Disposal (per 1000 people);
9. Graduates of Higher Education (per 1000 people);
10. CO_2 Emissions (tons per capita).

These are indicators of urban lifestyle change since data are not available for rural persons and areas.

The sample covers 1980–2002. In Table 9.20, we show the end results for annual growth, for an index computed as a ten-element weighted average, which grows from 100 in 1980 to 115.47 in 2002. The 22-year increase computed from

$$115.47 = 100.00\,(1 + r)^{22}$$

indicates that the estimated rate of growth is

$$r = 0.65596\%$$

This growth rate is nearly double that for the USA, 1980–2000. Thus the adjustment to China's growth rate could be as high as 1 percent or more, because the quality adjustment for the USA case has been estimated at 0.32 in a confidence interval of –0.1 to 0.8 percentage points.

Table 9.20 Index of lifestyle: China (ten indicators)

1980	100.00	1992	109.28
1981	100.53	1993	110.06
1982	102.11	1994	111.26
1983	102.12	1995	112.87
1984	103.06	1996	113.74
1985	103.55	1997	113.62
1986	104.50	1998	113.82
1987	105.35	1999	114.21
1988	106.51	2000	114.99
1989	107.14	2001	115.88
1990	108.11	2002	115.47
1991	108.58	0.65596% p. a. growth rate	

Table 9.21 Index of lifestyle, China (seven indicators)

1980	100.00	1992	106.67
1981	100.33	1993	107.00
1982	102.02	1994	107.92
1983	101.35	1995	109.04
1984	102.24	1996	109.78
1985	102.85	1997	110.15
1986	103.54	1998	110.67
1987	104.18	1999	111.66
1988	104.78	2000	112.71
1989	105.20	2001	113.87
1990	105.68	2002	114.41
1991	106.14	0.6138% p. a. growth rate	

While this calculation confirms our cost-of-living degree of superiority for China's growth rate, it is not entirely satisfactory. At least three of the variables considered (CO_2, SO_2 and urban excrement and urine disposal) have some problematic characteristics. In the first three components, the marginal values for CO_2 and SO_2 emissions show large positive coefficients, suggesting that higher values for CO_2 and SO_2 raise the index. It may require some years for the effects of these emissions to have their full negative effects on the environment and on personal health. All the indicator variables have complicated direct *and* indirect effects, but the large positive contributions leave us uneasy. Similarly, the disposal of urban excrement and urine have significant, but not overwhelming, negative effects.

If we delete these three indicators, and make a principal component analysis of the seven remaining indicators, we find sensible positive values for all the vector elements in the first principal component, with as much as 85 percent of the total variance of the seven remaining indicators explained by the first component. The index in this case seems to be more defensible. The results in Table 9.21 suggest a growth rate of 0.6138%, which is quite close to the growth rate of all ten indicators.

NOTES

1. See Klein and Özmucur (2002/03).
2. Advisory Committee to Study the CPI (2006).
3. Klein and Rubin (1947/48). Richard Stone (1954) independently discovered the same system at a later date. Both R. Geary (1950) and P.A. Samuelson (1947/48) pointed out the associated utility specifications.
4. It is to be hoped that in future research it will be possible to build up a whole time sequence of Engel curves for rural consumers.
5. Summers et al. (1982).
6. Nagar and Basu (1999).

REFERENCES

Advisory Committee to Study the CPI (1996), *Final Report of the Advisory Committee to Study the Consumer Price Index*, Chairman Michael J. Boskin, Washington, DC, Government Printing Office. http://www.ssa.gov/history/reports/boskinrpt.html.

Geary, R.C. (1950), 'A Note on a Constant-utility Index of the Cost of Living', *Review of Economic Studies*, **18**, 65–6.

Klein, L.R. and S. Özmucur (2002/03), 'The Estimation of China's Growth Rate', *Journal of Economic and Social Measurement*, **28**, 187–202.

Klein, L.R. and H. Rubin (1947/48), 'A Constant-utility Index of the Cost of Living', *Review of Economic Studies*, **15**, 84–7.

Klein, L.R. and S. Özmucur (2003), 'Estimates of Changes in Chinese Lifestyle', unpublished research paper, University of Pennsylvania.

Nagar, A.L. and Sudip Ranjan Basu (1999), 'Weighting Socio-economic Indicators of Human Development (A Latent Variable Approach)', National Institute of Public Finance and Policy, New Delhi.

Samuelson, P.A. (1947/48), 'Some Implications of "Linearity"', *Review of Economic Studies*, **15**, 88–90.

Stone, Richard (1954), 'Linear Expenditure Systems and Demand Analysis: An Application to the Pattern of British Demand', *Economic Journal*, **64**, 511–27, September.

Summers, Robert, Alan Heston and Irving Kravis (1982), 'Interspatial Demand Analysis', *World Product and Income*, Baltimore, MD: Johns Hopkins University Press, Ch. 9, p. 374.

10. Estimating China's core inflation rate*

Deming Wu

1 INTRODUCTION

The objective of this chapter is to measure the core inflation rate in China between 1997 and 2002. An accurate and timely measurement of inflation is a critical prerequisite for successful monetary policies. The conventional price indices, however, may not accurately capture the underlying inflation from a monetary policy point of view. Taking the consumer price index (CPI) as an example, it measures inflation as experienced by consumers in their day-to-day living expenses. However, the inflation from the consumers' perspectives may be different from the underlying inflation that concerns monetary policy-makers for reasons discussed below.

First, the prices of certain goods, such as agricultural products and oil, depend on factors such as weather and OPEC's oil production and pricing decisions, which are beyond the control of the central bank. Monetary policy as a response to inflation or deflation due to these kinds of price changes may be ineffective.

Second, some goods and services have very volatile prices whose movements typically reverse direction quickly. It is inappropriate for monetary policy to respond to these short-run fluctuations since it typically takes between 12 and 18 months, based on the US experience, for a monetary policy to begin to affect inflation significantly.

Third, some price changes are due to changes in the policy environment, such as those in the tax and tariff rates, or due to the increased competition in the distribution sector as a result of price reforms and trade liberalization. It is not necessary to respond to these one-time changes as if they are persistent.

Inflation as measured by the consumer price index is the sum of these different kinds of price changes. However, not all movements in the general price level are equally important from a monetary policy point of view. Instead, the central bank should focus on the underlying, or the core inflation, that is, the portion of inflation that can be affected through monetary policy.

Therefore, the focus of this research is to construct a measurement of the core inflation rate for monetary policy purposes. This measurement of the inflation rate should exclude the price changes due to factors beyond the central bank's control, temporary or one-time price changes, and cyclical price changes.

This research was also motivated by widespread concerns about the deflation threat among some economists and research organizations during the period of 1997–2002 (Bernanke, 2002; De Long, 1999; Erceg et al., 2002; Krugman, 1999a, 1999b, 2003; MF, 2003; Lau, 2003). In addition, China has been criticized as not being a full stabilization factor in Asia during the 1997–98 crisis. By measuring China's core inflation rate, however, I found that the expansionary monetary and fiscal policies in China did play a stabilization role during the crisis.

This chapter is organized as follows. In section 2, I briefly review the definitions of core inflation rate. Section 3 is a brief description of China's consumer price index by category. I also report the weights of individual categories in the CPI basket. In section 4, I estimate China's core inflation rate by excluding the price changes of agricultural products and energy. Section 5 estimates the impact of energy price changes. Section 6 reports an alternative estimation of the core inflation rate using a structural conditional error correction model with an unobserved variable. Section 7 concludes.

2 DEFINITION OF CORE INFLATION

In this chapter, the core inflation is defined as the portion of inflation that depends on monetary policy. This definition is based on the rationale that not all movements in the general price level are due to changes in monetary policy. Therefore, the central bank should focus on the part it can potentially control. Based on this rationale, the core inflation rate is measured by excluding agricultural products and energy, whose prices cannot be easily controlled by the central bank.

It should be noted that there are different interpretations of core inflation, which typically lead to different approaches to the measurement of the core inflation rate (Wynne, 1999). One interpretation, proposed by Okun (1970) and Flemming (1976), is that the observed inflation can be decomposed into two components: the general price change and the relative price change due to supply-side shocks. Core inflation can be thought of as the general price change that reflects the monetary policy. Therefore, the measurement of the core inflation rate is to remove the relative price changes from the observed inflation.

An alternative interpretation by Eckstein (1981) and Quah and Vahey (1995) defines core inflation as a persistent component of the headline inflation. According to this definition, the observed inflation includes a persistent component and a temporary or transitory component. Therefore, the measurement of the core inflation rate is to subtract the transitory component from the observed inflation. For example, Eckstein (1981) defines core inflation as a trend of production factor cost, which would reflect the long-run inflation expectation. Quah and Vahey (1995) define core inflation as the inflation that does not affect production in the long run. They propose a two-variable SVAR (structural vector auto-regression) model to estimate the core inflation rate. Their estimation method uses the identification condition that the core inflation shock does not have long-run effect on the growth rate. Bjornland (2000) uses a three-variable SVAR with oil price, GDP and CPI inflation to estimate the core inflation rate with the identification conditions that the oil price is influenced only by oil price shock, and the core inflation shock does not affect the growth rate in the long run.

The most commonly used estimation methods for core inflation are the methods of exclusion, which exclude some items from the basket of CPI. These methods attempt to exclude temporary non-monetary changes of prices from the observed inflation. On the other hand, there are different model approaches that attempt to extract the unobserved component of core inflation using different time-series-based estimation methods such as SVAR and Kalman filter. For example, Lee et al. (2003) propose a structural conditional error correction model for CPI and core CPI (VECM [vector error correction model]). In this model the core CPI indicator is an unobserved variable that is cointegrated with the headline CPI. They propose a state-space representation of this model, which is later estimated using a Kalman filter.

It is important to remember that the definitions of core inflation in different approaches are different. As a result, they do not measure the same thing. Therefore, it is difficult to compare the measurement of core inflation rate of one approach with another.

3 A DESCRIPTION OF CHINA'S CONSUMER PRICE INDEX BY CATEGORY

The composition of China's consumer price index underwent two major revisions in 1994 and 2001. The revision in 2001 introduced a new category called 'Tobacco, Liquor and Articles', and removed an existing category called 'Services'. As a result, the category definitions in the CPI market basket from 1994 to 2000 are different from those after January 2001. Table 10.1 and Table 10.2 list the categories in the CPI basket before and after 2001 respectively. The weights for calculating the consumer price index are determined according to the composition of the consumption expenditures of more than 90 000 urban and rural households. Table 10.3 and Table 10.4 report the composition of per capita consumption expenditures for urban and rural households respectively from 1997 to 2001.

As can be seen from these tables, in China, food-related costs comprise more than 40 percent of the per capita consumption expenditures. As a result, the weight for food-related costs in the CPI was above 40 percent before 2001. Because of this, the majority of the fluctuation in CPI was due to fluctuations of food prices. Changes in food prices in China depend on natural factors, such as the weather and the government restrictions on

Table 10.1 CPI categories before 2001

Category	2000 Weights
1. Food	0.4011
2. Clothing	0.1136
3. Household Facilities and Articles	0.0857
4. Medicine and Medical Articles	0.0769
5. Transportation and Communication	0.0652
6. Recreation, Education and Culture Articles	0.1196
7. Residence	0.097
8. Services	0.05

Source: National Bureau of Statistics of China.

Table 10.2 CPI categories after 2001

Category	2002 Weights
1. Food	0.3359
2. Tobacco, Liquor and Articles	0.0447
3. Clothing	0.0875
4. Household Facilities and Articles	0.065
5. Medicine and Medical Articles	0.0912
6. Transportation and Communication	0.0814
7. Recreation, Education and Culture Articles	0.1436
8. Residences	0.1507

Source: National Bureau of Statistics of China.

Table 10.3 Composition of per capita expenditures for urban households

Item	1997 (%)	1998 (%)	1999 (%)	2000 (%)	2001 (%)
Total living expenditures	100.00	100.00	100.00	100.00	100.00
1. Food	46.41	44.48	41.86	39.18	37.94
1.1 Grain	5.69	5.24	4.67	3.77	3.54
1.2 Meat, Poultry and Related Products	10.98	9.96	8.85	8.23	7.79
1.3 Eggs	1.76	1.55	1.42	1.13	1.07
1.4 Aquatic Products	3.37	3.29	3.12	2.87	2.86
1.5 Milk and Dairy Products	0.99	1.11	1.22	1.37	1.51
2. Clothing	12.45	11.10	10.45	10.01	10.05
2.1 Garments	7.84	7.18	6.94	6.75	6.86
3. Household Facilities, Articles and Services	7.57	8.24	8.57	8.79	8.27
3.1 Durable Consumer Goods	4.14	4.65	5.01	5.18	4.72
4. Medicine and Medical Services	4.29	4.74	5.32	6.36	6.47
5. Transportation, Post and Communication Services	5.56	5.94	6.73	7.90	8.61
5.1 Transportation	2.66	2.65	2.96	3.25	3.31
5.2 Communication	2.90	3.29	3.76	4.66	5.30
6. Recreation, Education and Cultural Services	10.71	11.53	12.28	12.56	13.00
6.1 Durable Consumer Goods for Recreational Use	2.69	2.91	2.93	2.94	2.62
6.2 Education	5.68	6.35	7.00	7.28	8.07
6.3 Recreation	2.35	2.27	2.35	2.34	2.30
7. Residence	8.57	9.43	9.84	10.01	10.32
7.1 Housing	3.55	3.99	4.24	4.03	4.09
7.2 Water, Electricity, Fuel and Others	5.02	5.43	5.59	5.98	6.23
8. Miscellaneous Commodities and Services	4.44	4.55	4.96	5.17	5.35
8.1 Personal Consumption	3.51	3.62	4.01	4.21	4.40
8.2 Other Commodities	0.43	0.41	0.43	0.41	0.41
8.3 Other Services	0.50	0.52	0.51	0.55	0.54

Source: China's *Statistical Yearbook*.

food imports. Because these factors are beyond the central bank's control, in order to construct a measurement of the core inflation rate that is more relevant from the central bank's perspective, we need to exclude food prices from CPI, as shown in Figure 10.1.

Table 10.4 Composition of per capita expenditure for rural households

Item	1997 (%)	1998 (%)	1999 (%)	2000 (%)	2001 (%)
Total living expenditure	100.00	100.00	100.00	100.00	100.00
Food	55.05	53.43	52.56	49.13	47.71
Clothing	6.77	6.17	5.83	5.75	5.67
Household Facilities, Articles and Services	5.28	5.15	5.22	4.52	4.42
Medicines and Medical Services	3.86	4.28	4.44	5.24	5.55
Transportation, Post and Telecommunication Services	3.33	3.82	4.36	5.58	6.32
Cultural, Educational and Recreational Articles and Services	9.16	10.02	10.67	11.18	11.06
Residence	14.42	15.07	14.75	15.47	16.03
Other Commodities and Services	2.12	2.07	2.18	3.14	3.24

Source: China's *Statistical Yearbook*.

4 ESTIMATING CHINA'S CORE INFLATION RATE

4.1 Estimation of Core CPI Inflation Rate

The core CPI inflation rate is defined as the CPI inflation rate excluding food and energy. In China's CPI basket, there is no explicit category for energy. There is a subcategory of 'Water, Electricity and Fuel' under the major category of 'Residences'. The weight for 'Residence' in the CPI is about 10 percent; the weight for 'Water, Electricity and Fuel' is about 5 percent of the total CPI calculation. Because of the lack of published data for the price index of the 'Water, Fuel and Electricity' subcategory in the CPI, I use the price index of the 'Fuel' subcategory under the RPI (retail price index) basket as a proxy.

I also have to estimate the weight by using the composition of per capita expenditure for urban and rural households. The expenditure shares of this category for urban households were 5.02 percent in 1997 and 6.23 percent in 2001; the expenditure share of this category for rural households was not available. It can be imputed by assuming the ratio of this category to its parent category is the same as that of the expenditure of urban households. In the research, I used the expenditure share for urban households as the approximation for this weight.

The inflation rate of core CPI is calculated using the following equations:

$$CPI = CPI_{food} * w_{food} + CPI_{energy} * w_{energy} + CPI_{core} * (1 - w_{food} - w_{energy}) \quad (10.1)$$

$$CPI_{core} = \frac{CPI - CPI_{food} * w_{food} - CPI_{energy} * w_{energy}}{1 - w_{food} - w_{energy}} \quad (10.2)$$

Table 10.5 and Figure 10.2 report the overall CPI inflation, the inflation of the food price index, the calculated CPI inflation excluding food, and the CPI inflation excluding food and energy from 1980 to 2003. As can be seen from the data, for 1998 and 1999, the overall CPI inflation rate was negative, but this was due to the large decline of food prices. If food prices were excluded from the basket, the core CPI inflation rate would have been positive in 1998 and 1999. For the year 2002, even after excluding food prices, the core CPI inflation rate was still negative. This indicates that the CPI decline in 2002 was likely to have been caused by factors other than food prices.

In Table 10.6 and Figure 10.3 I report the decomposition of the monthly CPI inflation rate between 1994 and 2004. I am taking advantage of the availability of monthly data because the annual data are somewhat misleading in that they are averages of the monthly data; so that the monthly positive and negative changes offset each other. As can be seen from Table 10.6 and Figure 10.3 the inflation rate of core CPI had been mostly positive until February 2002.

The decline of the consumer price index in 2002 was likely due to the effects of China's accession into the WTO and the reduction of the tariff rate in 2002. According to the WTO rules, and the commitments China made, China lowered the tariff rates of 5300 items in 2002, accounting for 73 percent of the total tariff items. The average overall tariff rate was cut down from 15.3 percent to 12 percent; the average tariff rate of industrial products was lowered to 11.6 percent; the average tariff rate of agricultural products, excluding aquatic products, was lowered to 15.8 percent; the average tariff rate of aquatic products was lowered to 14.3 percent. Lower tariff rates caused a large price reduction in imported goods, adding to the downward pressure on domestic price levels. The large increase of imported goods has also intensified the competition between imported and domestically produced goods. Domestic enterprises had to reduce their prices and costs in order to preserve their market shares.

The slowdown of economic growth in 2001 might also have contributed to the downward pressure on prices in 2002. Price changes

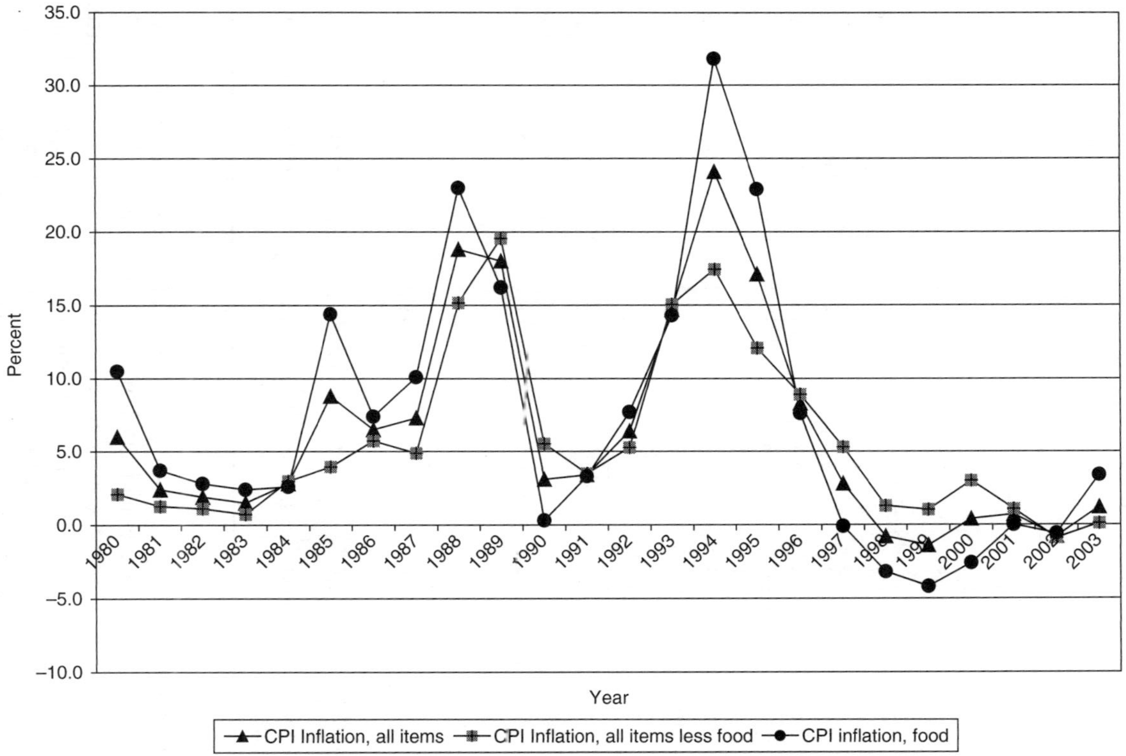

Figure 10.1 *Decomposition of annual CPI inflation in China, 1980–2003*

Table 10.5 Decomposition of annual CPI inflation 1980–2003

Year	CPI Inflation, All Items	CPI Inflation, All Items Less Food	CPI Inflation, All Items Less Food and Energy	CPI Inflation, Food	CPI Inflation, Energy
1980	6.0	2.1	2.2	10.5	0.7
1981	2.4	1.3	1.3	3.7	0.6
1982	1.9	1.1	1.2	2.8	0.8
1983	1.5	0.7	0.7	2.4	1.0
1984	2.8	3.0	3.1	2.6	2.2
1985	8.8	4.0	3.9	14.4	4.0
1986	6.5	5.7	5.9	7.4	3.6
1987	7.3	4.9	5.0	10.1	3.9
1988	18.8	15.2	15.1	23.0	16.1
1989	18.0	19.6	18.7	16.2	27.4
1990	3.1	5.5	5.2	0.3	8.2
1991	3.4	3.5	2.2	3.3	15.6
1992	6.4	5.3	4.3	7.7	14.6
1993	14.7	15.0	13.0	14.3	35.0
1994	24.1	17.4	17.7	31.8	15.1
1995	17.1	12.1	12.6	22.9	7.4
1996	8.3	8.9	9.3	7.6	5.0
1997	2.8	5.3	5.1	−0.1	7.3
1998	−0.8	1.3	1.8	−3.2	−3.9
1999	−1.4	1.0	1.1	−4.2	0.4
2000	0.4	3.0	1.5	−2.6	17.7
2001	0.7	1.1	0.9	0.0	2.4
2002	−0.8	−0.9	−1.2	−0.6	2.0
2003	1.2	0.1	−0.9	3.4	9.5
Weights (1997), 1980–2000	1.0000	0.5359	0.4857	0.4641	0.0502
Weights (2002), 2001–2003	1.0000	0.6641	0.6018	0.3359	0.0623

typically lag the GDP from half one year to one year. The GDP growth rates for the four quarters in 2001 were 8.1 percent, 7.8 percent, 7.0 percent, and 6.6 percent consecutively, declining quarter by quarter. This slowdown was reflected in price movement in 2002. In addition, there was a substantial decline of ex-factor prices and the purchase price of raw materials in 2001, which had a strong lagged influence on retail prices in 2002. Finally, the decline of stock prices in 2002 might have also contributed to the decline in the price of investment and consumer goods.

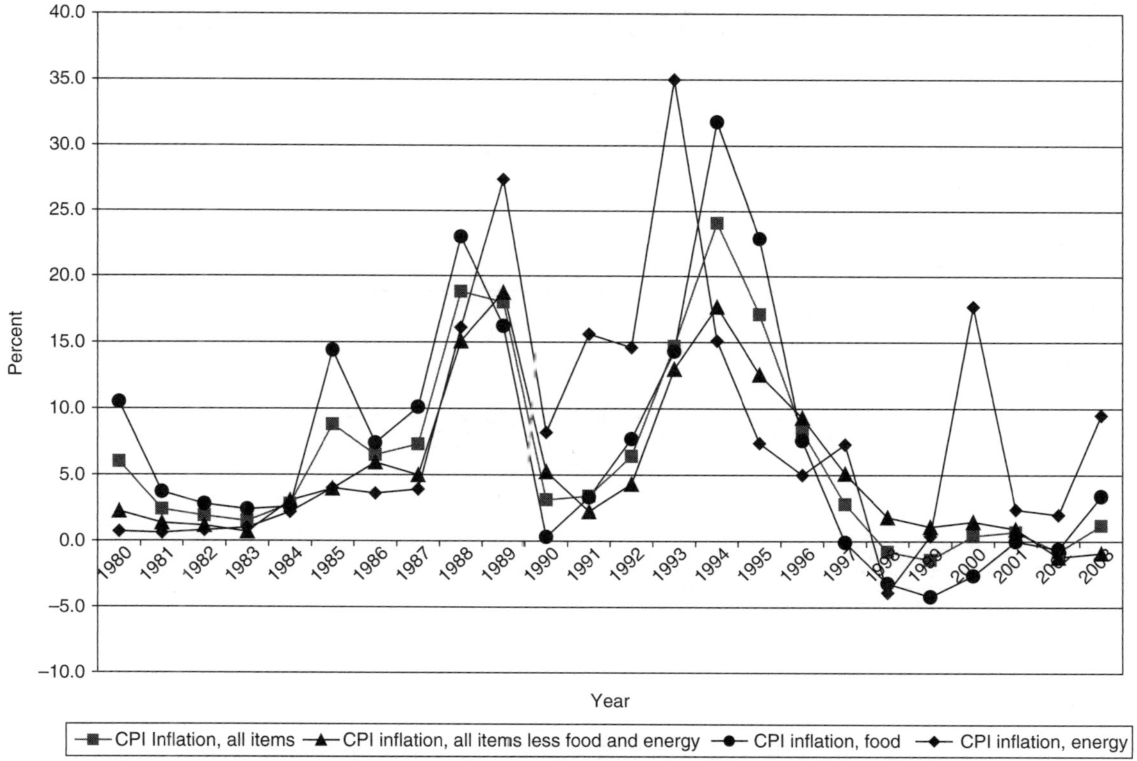

Figure 10.2 CPI Inflation, all items less food and energy, 1980–2003

Table 10.6 Decomposition of monthly CPI inflation, China, 01/1994–04/2004

Month	CPI Inflation, All Items	CPI Inflation, All Items Less Food and Energy	CPI Inflation, All Items Less Food	CPI Inflation, Food	CPI Inflation, Energy
Jan-94	23.2	22.1	22.0	24.6	20.9
Feb-94	25.9	21.1	20.9	31.7	19.1
Mar-94	24.5	20.9	20.6	29.0	17.4
Apr-94	23.2	20.6	20.3	26.6	16.5
May-94	21.8	19.3	18.9	25.1	15.2
Jun-94	22.7	19.1	18.3	27.8	10.1
Jul-94	24.2	18.1	17.5	31.9	12.1
Aug-94	27.1	18.3	17.8	37.8	13.4
Sep-94	27.5	18.5	18.0	38.5	13.0
Oct-94	27.0	18.3	17.8	37.6	13.0
Nov-94	26.4	18.1	17.7	36.5	13.4
Dec-94	24.1	17.5	17.0	32.3	12.4
Jan-95	22.5	14.5	14.0	32.3	9.1
Feb-95	20.4	13.5	13.1	28.8	9.4
Mar-95	19.4	12.6	12.2	27.7	8.5
Apr-95	19.7	12.8	12.4	28.1	8.4
May-95	19.7	13.0	12.5	28.0	7.7
Jun-95	18.1	13.0	12.5	24.6	7.3
Jul-95	16.7	13.0	12.5	21.6	7.1
Aug-95	14.1	12.4	11.8	16.8	5.7
Sep-95	12.9	10.6	10.1	16.1	5.9
Oct-95	11.9	10.4	10.0	14.1	5.8
Nov-95	12.1	10.9	10.4	14.1	5.1
Dec-95	11.1	11.1	10.5	11.8	4.7
Jan-96	9.0	10.2	9.7	8.2	4.6
Feb-96	9.3	9.8	9.3	9.3	4.3
Mar-96	9.8	10.2	9.6	10.0	4.3
Apr-96	9.7	9.9	9.4	10.0	4.9
May-96	8.9	9.7	9.2	8.5	4.4
Jun-96	8.6	9.7	9.2	7.9	4.4
Jul-96	8.3	9.2	8.7	7.8	4.1
Aug-96	8.1	9.0	8.5	7.6	3.9
Sep-96	7.4	9.2	8.7	5.9	4.3
Oct-96	7.0	8.5	8.1	5.7	4.9
Nov-96	6.9	8.4	8.2	5.4	6.3
Dec-96	7.0	8.7	8.7	5.0	9.4
Jan-97	5.9	7.5	7.8	3.7	10.6
Feb-97	5.6	7.1	7.4	3.5	10.6
Mar-97	4.0	6.1	6.4	1.2	9.6
Apr-97	3.2	5.6	5.9	0.1	8.4

Table 10.6 (continued)

Month	CPI Inflation, All Items	CPI Inflation, All Items Less Food and Energy	CPI Inflation, All Items Less Food	CPI Inflation, Food	CPI Inflation, Energy
May-97	2.8	5.2	5.5	−0.3	8.0
Jun-97	2.8	5.0	5.2	0.0	7.3
Jul-97	2.7	4.8	5.0	0.0	7.5
Aug-97	1.9	4.5	4.8	−1.4	7.4
Sep-97	1.8	4.2	4.4	−1.2	6.7
Oct-97	1.5	4.2	4.4	−1.8	6.2
Nov-97	1.1	3.9	4.0	−2.2	4.4
Dec-97	0.4	3.5	3.3	−2.9	0.8
Jan-98	0.3	3.0	2.6	−2.3	−1.5
Feb-98	−0.1	2.7	2.3	−2.9	−1.7
Mar-98	0.7	2.4	2.0	−0.8	−2.0
Apr-98	−0.3	2.3	1.9	−2.8	−2.8
May-98	−1.0	2.1	1.5	−3.9	−3.9
Jun-98	−1.3	1.8	1.2	−4.2	−4.3
Jul-98	−1.4	1.7	1.0	−4.2	−5.3
Aug 98	−1.4	1.6	0.9	−4.1	−5.7
Sep-98	−1.5	1.2	0.6	−3.9	−5.5
Oct-98	−1.1	1.3	0.7	−3.2	−5.2
Nov-98	−1.2	1.1	0.6	−3.3	−4.3
Dec-98	−1.0	1.1	0.6	−2.8	−4.2
Jan-99	−1.2	1.4	0.9	−3.6	−4.2
Feb-99	−1.3	1.3	0.8	−3.7	−4.5
Mar-99	−1.8	1.5	0.9	−4.9	−4.6
Apr-99	−2.2	1.1	0.7	−5.5	−3.9
May-99	−2.2	1.0	0.6	−5.4	−3.1
Jun-99	−2.1	0.8	0.5	−5.1	−2.4
Jul-99	−1.4	0.5	0.4	−3.5	−0.1
Aug-99	−1.3	0.2	0.5	−3.4	3.7
Sep-99	−0.8	1.3	1.7	−3.7	5.3
Oct-99	−0.6	1.4	1.7	−3.3	5.2
Nov-99	−0.9	1.3	1.7	−3.9	5.6
Dec-99	−1.0	1.3	1.9	−4.4	7.9
Jan-00	−0.2	1.5	2.3	−3.1	10.3
Feb-00	0.7	1.7	2.5	−1.4	10.9
Mar-00	−0.2	1.4	2.5	−3.3	12.5
Apr-00	−0.3	1.7	2.8	−3.9	13.9
May-00	0.1	1.3	2.9	−3.1	17.9
Jun-00	0.5	1.0	3.0	−2.4	22.3
Jul-00	0.5	0.9	3.0	−2.4	23.4
Aug-00	0.3	0.8	2.8	−2.6	22.0

Table 10.6 (continued)

Month	CPI Inflation, All Items	CPI Inflation, All Items Less Food and Energy	CPI Inflation, All Items Less Food	CPI Inflation, Food	CPI Inflation, Energy
Sep-00	0.0	1.2	3.2	−3.7	22.6
Oct-00	0.0	1.3	3.2	−3.7	21.3
Nov-00	1.3	1.6	3.3	−1.0	19.4
Dec-00	1.5	1.5	2.9	−0.1	16.2
Jan-01	1.2	0.8	2.0	−0.4	13.6
Feb-01	0.0	0.7	1.7	−3.3	10.9
Mar-01	0.8	0.7	1.7	−1.0	11.5
Apr-01	1.6	1.0	1.8	1.3	8.7
May-01	1.7	1.3	1.7	1.7	5.7
Jun-01	1.4	1.4	1.6	1.0	3.3
Jul-01	1.5	1.9	1.5	1.5	−2.1
Aug-01	1.0	2.1	1.4	0.2	−5.2
Sep-01	−0.1	0.2	−0.3	0.3	−5.5
Oct-01	0.2	0.3	−0.1	0.8	−3.7
Nov-01	−0.3	0.3	0.0	−0.8	−3.3
Dec-01	−0.3	0.5	0.0	−0.8	−5.0
Jan-02	−1.0	0.1	−0.5	−1.9	−6.8
Feb-02	0.0	0.3	−0.3	0.6	−6.2
Mar-02	−0.8	−0.4	−0.9	−0.6	−5.8
Apr-02	−1.3	−0.9	−0.9	−2.0	−1.6
May-02	−1.1	−1.0	−0.9	−1.5	0.3
Jun-02	−0.8	−1.4	−1.1	−0.2	1.4
Jul-02	−0.9	−1.3	−0.9	−0.9	3.3
Aug-02	−0.7	−1.5	−0.9	−0.4	5.6
Sep-02	−0.7	−1.8	−1.0	−0.2	6.8
Oct-02	−0.8	−1.8	−1.0	−0.5	7.6
Nov-02	−0.7	−2.0	−1.0	−0.1	8.4
Dec-02	−0.4	−2.1	−0.9	0.5	11.6
Jan-03	0.4	−2.6	−0.6	2.4	18.1
Feb-03	0.2	−2.7	−0.6	1.8	19.1
Mar-03	0.9	−2.3	−0.3	3.2	19.3
Apr-03	1.0	−1.6	−0.1	3.2	14.4
May-03	0.7	−0.7	0.1	1.9	8.1
Jun-03	0.3	−0.5	0.2	0.4	7.5
Jul-03	0.5	−0.5	0.2	1.0	7.0
Aug-03	0.9	−0.4	0.2	2.2	6.2
Sep-03	1.1	−0.4	0.0	3.2	4.6
Oct-03	1.8	0.0	0.1	5.1	1.6
Nov-03	3.0	0.2	0.4	8.1	2.5
Dec-03	3.2	−0.1	0.5	8.6	5.6
Jan-04	3.2	−0.6	0.8	8.0	5.6

Table 10.6 (continued)

Month	CPI Inflation, All Items	CPI Inflation, All Items Less Food and Energy	CPI Inflation, All Items Less Food	CPI Inflation, Food	CPI Inflation, Energy
Feb-04	2.1	0.3	0.3	5.6	3.0
Mar-04	3.0	0.2	0.5	7.9	3.2
Apr-04	3.8	0.1	0.6	10.2	4.9
Weights (1997), 1994–2000	1	0.4857	0.5359	0.4641	0.0502
Weights (2002), 2001–2004	1	0.6018	0.6641	0.3359	0.0623

4.2 Decomposition of RPI

Using the monthly retail price index (RPI) by category, I estimate the core rate of inflation as measured by the RPI by excluding the food and fuel categories. Because of the lack of published data for the weights of categories in the RPI baskets, I regress the overall RPI against the indices of subcategories to estimate the weights. To resolve the multicollinearity problem of highly intercorrelated indices of subcategories, I have to remove some categories from the right-hand side in order to get plausible estimated results. Table 10.7 reports the estimated weights of the major categories in the RPI basket for different periods. Using the estimated weights for the period between 04/1994 and 05/2003, Table 10.8 reports the decomposition of the inflation rate of the RPI by excluding food and energy.

As can be seen from Figures 10.3 and 10.4, one striking difference between the decomposition of RPI and that of CPI is that the inflation rate of RPI excluding food and energy has been consistently negative since October 1997. One possible explanation for the decline of the retail price index is the increased competition in the distribution sector, which has squeezed the gross margins of the wholesalers and retailers, and thus has put downward pressure on retail prices (Wu, 2004).

5 ESTIMATING THE IMPACT OF CHANGES IN PETROLEUM PRICES

In this section, I will assess the impact of changes in petroleum prices on China's domestic price levels. Although the weight of energy in the CPI

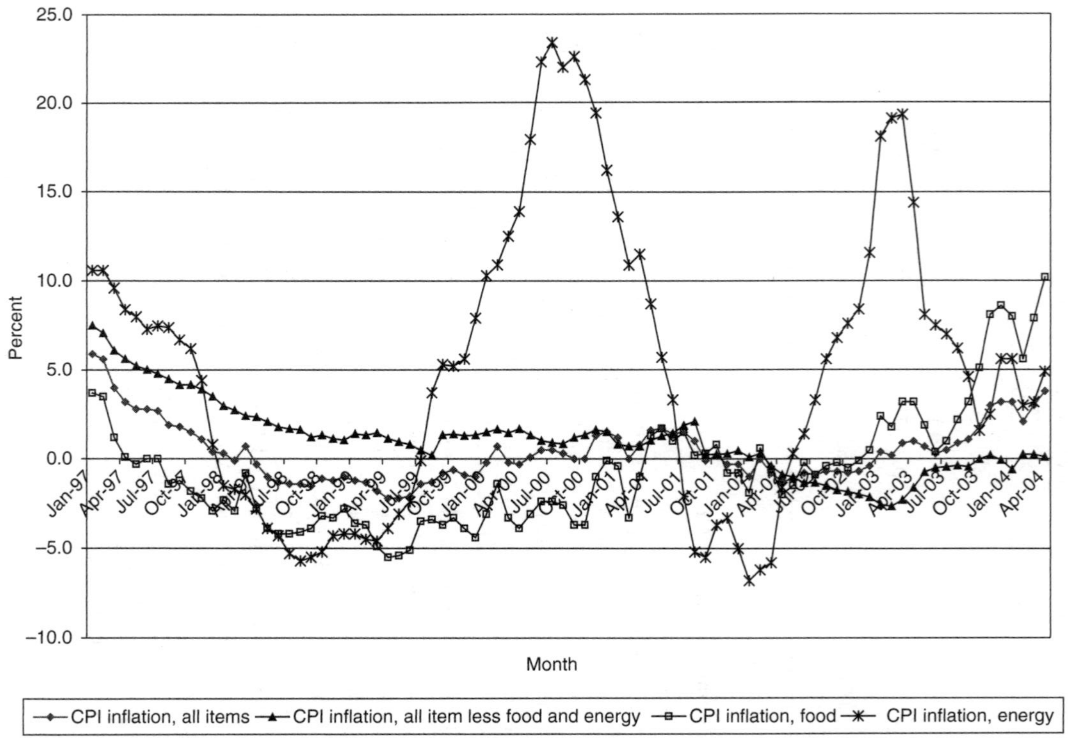

Figure 10.3 *Decomposition of monthly CPI inflation, 01/1997–04/2004, China*

Table 10.7 Estimated weights for categories in RPI basket

Category	01/94–12/00 (%)	01/94–05/03 (%)	01/97–05/03 (%)	01/99–05/03 (%)	01/00–05/03 (%)
1. Food	41.09	40.69	36.58	37.92	37.82
3. Clothes, Shoes and Hats	8.86	9.27	12.57	14.44	7.46
5. Medicines	0.19	2.31	4.38	4.38	5.91
7. Books and Magazines	1.91	1.91	3.25	2.37	2.34
8. Culture and Sports	7.23	7.77	1.70	1.70	6.21
9. Daily Used Articles	16.83	13.78	20.45	20.50	15.12
10. Household Electrical Products	10.54	5.19	3.64	3.33	1.60
12. Fuel	3.60	3.34	2.86	2.72	3.04
13. Construction and Decorative Materials	2.97	3.94	3.29	4.28	7.97
14. Mechanical and Electrical Products	4.30	5.93	6.67	5.87	4.50

basket is small, the indirect impact of oil price on domestic price levels could be large because energy cost accounts for a significant portion of the production cost in every industrial sector. Therefore, the simple index accounting approach used in the previous sections may underestimate the impact of petroleum price changes. In light of this limitation, I construct an input–output price model to estimate both the direct and indirect impact of changes in petroleum prices on the price levels.

5.1 An Input–Output Price Model for Petroleum Price Changes

In this section I derive a modified version of the Leontief input–output price model (Leontief, 1986). The derivation of this model is similar to that of Melvin's (1979). In the discussion below, upper-case variables denote the price level, and their corresponding lower-case variables denote price changes in percentages. Superscript T denotes the transpose of a matrix or vector. By default, vectors are represented as column-vectors, and row-vectors are represented using transpose.

Writing the condition that total cost equals total revenue, we have, for the j-th industry,

$$X_j P_j = X_{1j} P_1 + X_{2j} P_2 + \ldots + X_{nj} P_n + V_j \qquad (10.3)$$

Table 10.8 Decomposition of the monthly RPI inflation, 1996–2002, China

Month	RPI Inflation, Overall	RPI Inflation, Excluding Food and Fuel	RPI Inflation, Food	RPI Inflation, Fuel
Jan-96	7.6	6.9	8.8	4.6
Feb-96	7.7	6.4	9.8	4.3
Mar-96	7.7	5.8	10.6	4.3
Apr-96	7.4	5.4	10.4	4.9
May-96	6.5	5.2	8.4	4.4
Jun-96	5.9	4.8	7.6	4.4
Jul-96	5.8	4.5	7.7	4.1
Aug-96	5.8	4.5	7.8	3.9
Sep-96	5	4.4	5.9	4.3
Oct-96	4.7	4.0	5.6	4.9
Nov-96	4.6	4.1	5.2	6.3
Dec-96	4.4	3.8	4.8	9.4
Jan-97	3.3	2.7	3.5	10.6
Feb-97	2.9	2.2	3.2	10.6
Mar-97	1.7	2.0	0.7	9.6
Apr-97	1.1	1.7	−0.3	8.4
May-97	0.8	1.4	−0.6	8
Jun-97	0.8	1.1	−0.1	7.3
Jul-97	0.6	0.6	0	7.5
Aug-97	1.1	2.3	−1.1	7.4
Sep-97	0	0.3	−1	6.7
Oct-97	−0.4	0.2	−1.7	6.2
Nov-97	−0.8	−0.2	−2.1	4.4
Dec-97	−1.2	−0.2	−2.8	0.8
Jan-98	−1.5	−0.9	−2.3	−1.5
Feb-98	−1.9	−1.2	−2.9	−1.7
Mar-98	−1.2	−1.6	−0.6	−2
Apr-98	−2.1	−1.5	−2.8	−2.8
May-98	−2.7	−1.8	−3.8	−3.9
Jun-98	−3	−2.1	−4.1	−4.3
Jul-98	−3.2	−2.1	−4.5	−5.3
Aug-98	−3.3	−2.4	−4.4	−5.7
Sep-98	−3.3	−2.6	−4.1	−5.5
Oct-98	−2.9	−2.4	−3.4	−5.2
Nov-98	−2.8	−2.3	−3.3	−4.3
Dec-98	−2.7	−2.6	−2.7	−4.2
Jan-99	−2.8	−2.2	−3.5	−4.2
Feb-99	−2.8	−2.1	−3.6	−4.5
Mar-99	−3.2	−2.0	−4.8	−4.6

Table 10.8 (continued)

Month	RPI Inflation, Overall	RPI Inflation, Excluding Food and Fuel	RPI Inflation, Food	RPI Inflation, Fuel
Apr-99	−3.5	−2.1	−5.4	−3.9
May-99	−3.5	−2.1	−5.5	−3.1
Jun-99	−3.4	−2.2	−5.1	−2.4
Jul-99	−2.6	−2.4	−3.1	−0.1
Aug-99	−2.6	−2.7	−3	3.7
Sep-99	−2.8	−2.5	−3.9	5.3
Oct-99	−2.6	−2.6	−3.3	5.2
Nov-99	−2.8	−2.4	−4	5.6
Dec-99	−3	−2.4	−4.7	7.9
Jan-00	−2.1	−2.3	−2.9	10.3
Feb-00	−1.4	−2.5	−0.9	10.9
Mar-00	−2.1	−2.2	−3.1	12.5
Apr-00	−2.4	−2.2	−4	13.9
May-00	−1.9	−2.1	−3.3	17.9
Jun-00	−1.4	−2.1	−2.4	22.3
Jul-00	−1.2	−1.7	−2.5	23.4
Aug-00	−1.3	−1.8	−2.5	22
Sep-00	−1.5	−1.3	−3.7	22.6
Oct-00	−1.7	−1.3	−4.1	21.3
Nov-00	−0.6	−1.7	−0.7	19.4
Dec-00	−0.4	−1.8	0.2	16.2
Jan-01	−0.5	−1.6	−0.1	13.6
Feb-01	−1.7	−1.6	−2.9	10.9
Mar-01	−0.9	−1.9	−0.6	11.5
Apr-01	0.1	−2.0	2.3	8.7
May-01	0.1	−2.1	2.7	5.7
Jun-01	−0.1	−2.0	2.2	3.3
Jul-01	−0.2	−2.2	2.7	−2.1
Aug-01	−1.2	−2.3	0.6	−5.2
Sep-01	−1.3	−2.6	0.8	−5.5
Oct-01	−0.8	−2.4	1.6	−3.7
Nov-01	−1.7	−2.3	−0.8	−3.3
Dec-01	−1.8	−2.3	−0.8	−5
Jan-02	−2	−2.2	−1.3	−6.8
Feb-02	−1.1	−2.5	1.3	−6.2
Mar-02	−1.8	−2.4	−0.6	−5.8
Apr-02	−2.1	−2.1	−2.1	−1.6
May-02	−1.8	−2.2	−1.4	0.3
Jun-02	−0.8	−2.5	1.3	1.4

Table 10.8 (continued)

Month	RPI Inflation, Overall	RPI Inflation, Excluding Food and Fuel	RPI Inflation, Food	RPI Inflation, Fuel
Jul-02	−1.1	−2.4	0.3	3.3
Aug-02	−1.1	−2.2	−0.1	5.6
Sep-02	−1	−2.3	0.1	6.8
Oct-02	−1.2	−2.2	−0.6	7.6
Nov-02	−0.9	−2.4	0.4	8.4
Dec-02	−0.3	−2.2	1.3	11.6

Where P_j is the price of commodity j; and V_j is the value-added of commodity j. We can divide this equation by $X_j\, P_j$ to obtain

$$1 = a_{1,j} + a_{2,j} + \ldots + a_{n,j} + v_j \tag{10.4}$$

Here, $a_{1,j}, a_{2,j}, \ldots, a_{n,j}$ are the input–output coefficients, and v_j is the share of valued-added in commodity j.

Now assume sector n is the petroleum industry. Suppose the price of petroleum changes by p'_n, the direct impact of petroleum price changes on the price of commodity j is

$$1 + p'_j = a_{1,j} + a_{2,j} + \ldots + a_{n,j}(1 + p'_n) + v_j \tag{10.5}$$

That is,

$$p'_j = a_{n,j}p'_n \tag{10.6}$$

Here, we use the lower-case p'_j to represent the percentage of price changes. However, because prices of other inputs also change as a result of the change in petroleum prices, we need to consider both the direct and the indirect effects, therefore, we have

$$1 + p_j = a_{1,j}(1 + p_1) + a_{2,j}(1 + p_2) + \ldots + a_{n,j}(1 + p_n) + v_j \tag{10.7}$$

And the final price changes are

$$p_j = a_{1,j}p_1 + a_{2,j}p_2 + \ldots + a_{n,j}p_n \tag{10.8}$$

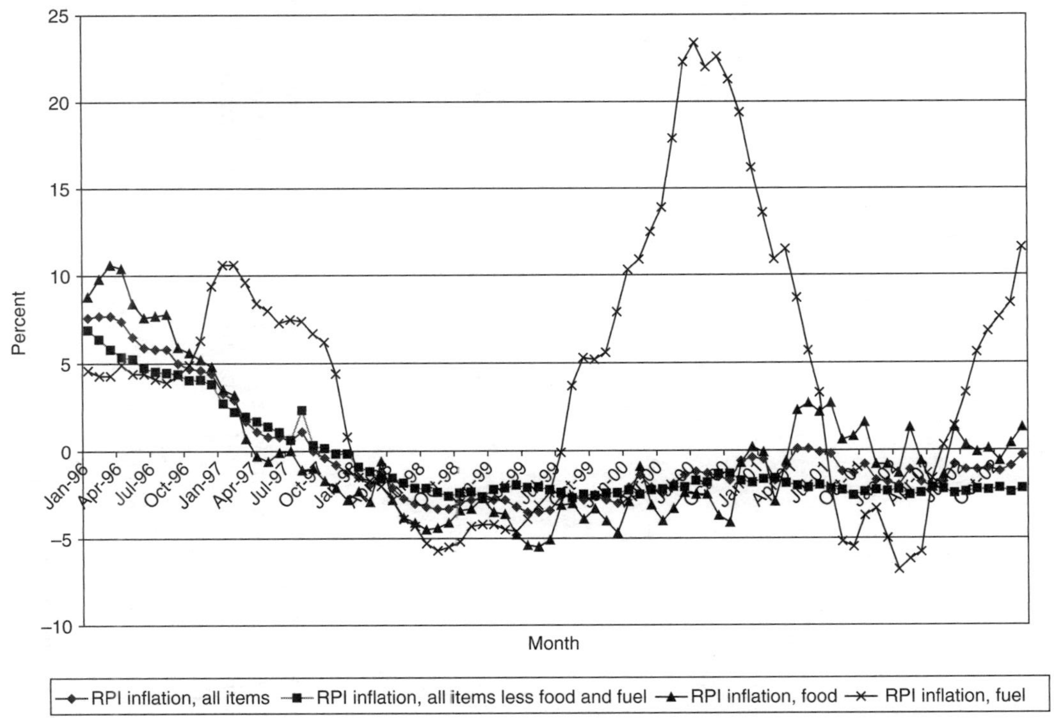

Figure 10.4 *Decomposition of monthly RPI inflation, 1996–2002, China*

Because there are similar equations for other sectors, we can write this total system in matrix notation to obtain

$$p = \mathbf{A}^{\mathbf{T}}_{\mathbf{n}-1}p + A^{n}p_{n} \tag{10.9}$$

Here we have

$$\mathbf{A}^{\mathbf{T}}_{\mathbf{n}-1} = \begin{pmatrix} a_{1,1} & \cdots & a_{n-1,1} \\ \vdots & \ddots & \vdots \\ a_{1,n-1} & \cdots & a_{n-1,n-1} \end{pmatrix} \tag{10.10}$$

and

$$\mathbf{A}^{\mathbf{n}} = \begin{pmatrix} a_{n,1} \\ a_{n,2} \\ \vdots \\ a_{n,n-1} \end{pmatrix} \tag{10.11}$$

and

$$p = \begin{pmatrix} p_1 \\ p_2 \\ \vdots \\ p_{n-1} \end{pmatrix} \tag{10.12}$$

Here, $\mathbf{A}_{\mathbf{n}-1}$ is the upper-left $(n-1) \times (n-1)$ sub-matrix of the input–output coefficient matrix of the intermediate input, A. And $\mathbf{A}^{\mathbf{n}}$ is a $(n-1) \times 1$ vector, derived from the first $n-1$ elements of n-th column vector of A^{T}. Solving this system gives

$$p = [I - \mathbf{A}^{\mathbf{T}}_{\mathbf{n}-1}]^{-1}\mathbf{A}^{\mathbf{n}}p_{n} \tag{10.13}$$

5.2 Estimation Results

Table 10.9 reports the estimated impact of a 1 percent change in petroleum prices using a 40-sector input–output table of China in 1997. As the table shows, a 1 percent decline in petroleum prices will cause the consumer price index to decline by 0.06 percent. In 2001, the world market oil price declined by 14 percent as shown in Table 10.10. Because there is time lag

Table 10.9 Estimated impact of a 1 percent change in petroleum price

Code	Name		2001–2002
	Change in petroleum prices, %	−1	−14.02
CPI	CPI	−0.06	−0.82
GDPI	GDP deflator	−0.08	−1.09
01	Agriculture	−0.02	−0.33
02	Coal mining and processing	−0.04	−0.53
03	Crude petroleum and natural gas products	−1.00	−14.02
04	Metal ore mining	−0.05	−0.73
05	Non-ferrous mineral mining	−0.07	−0.95
06	Manufacture of food products and tobacco processing	−0.02	−0.33
07	Textile goods	−0.03	−0.36
08	Wearing apparel, leather, furs, down and related products	−0.02	−0.33
09	Sawmills and furniture	−0.03	−0.47
10	Paper and products, printing and record media reproduction	−0.03	−0.45
11	Petroleum processing and coking	−0.07	−1.01
12	Chemicals	−1.00	−14.02
13	Non-metal mineral products	−0.06	−0.91
14	Metal smelting and pressing	−0.09	−1.24
15	Metal products	−0.06	−0.79
16	Machinery and equipment	−0.05	−0.67
17	Transportation equipment	−0.05	−0.65
18	Electric equipment and machinery	−0.06	−0.78
19	Electronic and telecommunication equipment	−0.04	−0.53
20	Instruments, meters, cultural and office machinery	−0.04	−0.56
21	Maintenance and repair of machine and equipment	−0.04	−0.58
22	Other manufacturing products	−0.04	−0.55
23	Scrap and waste	0.00	0.00
24	Electricity, steam and hot water production and supply	−0.21	−2.88
25	Gas production and supply	−0.02	−0.27
26	Water production and supply	−1.00	−14.02
27	Construction	−0.07	−0.97
28	Transportation and warehousing	−0.12	−1.72
29	Post and telecommunication	−0.03	−0.37
30	Wholesale and retail trade	−0.04	−0.49
31	Eating and drinking places	−0.02	−0.32
32	Passenger transportation	−0.14	−1.95
33	Finance and insurance	−0.02	−0.27
34	Real estate	−0.01	−0.20

Table 10.9 (continued)

Code	Name		2001–2002
35	Social services	−0.06	−0.79
36	Health services, sports and social welfare	−0.04	−0.60
37	Education, culture and arts, radio, film and television	−0.03	−0.38
38	Scientific research	−0.04	−0.50
39	General technical service	−0.03	−0.39
40	Public administration and other sectors	−0.04	−0.59

Table 10.10 The world market price of crude oil and China's average tariff rate

Year	TARIFF		OILP		OILPI	
	China's Average Tariff Rate	Change in %	Average Crude Price, US$/Barrel	Change in %	Average Crude Price Index, 1995=100	Change in %
1980	49.5		36.68		213.2	
1981	49.5	0.00	35.27	−3.84	205	−3.85
1982	49.5	0.00	32.45	−8.00	188.6	−8.00
1983	46.65	−2.85	29.64	−8.66	172.3	−8.64
1984	43.8	−2.85	28.55	−3.68	165.9	−3.71
1985	40.95	−2.85	27.37	−4.13	159.1	−4.10
1986	38.1	−2.85	14.17	−48.23	82.4	−48.21
1987	39.5	1.40	18.2	28.44	105.8	28.40
1988	39.7	0.20	14.77	−18.85	85.8	−18.90
1989	39.9	0.20	17.91	21.26	104.1	21.33
1990	40.3	0.40	22.99	28.36	133.6	28.34
1991	42.9	2.60	19.37	−15.75	112.6	−15.72
1992	41	−1.90	19.04	−1.70	110.6	−1.78
1993	39.9	−1.10	16.79	−11.82	97.6	−11.75
1994	36.3	−3.60	15.95	−5.00	92.7	−5.02
1995	35	−1.30	17.2	7.84	100	7.87
1996	23.6	−11.40	20.37	18.43	118.4	18.40
1997	17.6	−6.00	19.27	−5.40	112	−5.41
1998	16.8	−0.80	13.07	−32.17	76	−32.14
1999	16.55	−0.25	17.98	37.57	104.5	37.50
2000	16.3	−0.25	28.24	57.06	164.2	57.13
2001	15.3	−1.00	24.28	−14.02	141.1	−14.07
2002	12	−3.30	24.96	2.80	145.1	2.83

Source: The World Bank, IMF's *IFS*.

between the oil price changes and the price changes in the final market, this 14 percent decline in oil prices could have contributed to 0.82 percent decline of the consumer price index in 2002.

6 AN ALTERNATIVE MEASURE OF CORE INFLATION

In this section, I report an alternative measure of the core inflation rate based on a structural conditional error correction model. This model is similar to the ones suggested by Marques et al. (2002) and Lee et al. (2003). In this model, the core inflation is an unobserved I (1) variable, which is cointegrated with the observed headline inflation. This model can be represented as a state-space model and be estimated by a Kalman filter.

The state-space model (Kalman filter) can be represented as follows: Transition equation (or state equation)

$$\boldsymbol{\xi}_{t+1} = T\boldsymbol{\xi}_t + \upsilon_t \tag{10.14}$$

Observation equation (or signal equation)

$$\mathbf{y}_t = A'x_t + H'\boldsymbol{\xi}_t + \omega_t \tag{10.15}$$

Where $\boldsymbol{\xi}_t$ is the state variable vector, $\mathbf{y}_t$ is the observed variable vector, x_t is the exogenous variable, T is the transition matrix, and H is the observation matrix.

Below is the description of the model I estimated. I define the following variables:

$$\pi_t = \text{ CPI inflation}$$
$$g_t = \text{ Real GDP growth}$$
$$\pi_t^{core} = \text{ Core CPI inflation}$$

The observed variable vector is

$$\mathbf{y}_t = \begin{bmatrix} \pi_t \\ g_t \end{bmatrix}$$

The state variable vector is

$$\xi_t = \begin{bmatrix} \pi_t \\ g_t \\ \pi_t^{core} \\ \Delta\pi_t \\ \Delta g_t \\ \Delta\pi_t^{core} \end{bmatrix}$$

Where $\Delta x_t = x_t - x_{t-1}$.
The observation equation is defined as

$$\mathbf{y_t} = \begin{bmatrix} \pi_t \\ g_t \end{bmatrix} = \begin{bmatrix} 1 & 0 & 0 & 0 & 0 & 0 \\ 0 & 1 & 0 & 0 & 0 & 0 \end{bmatrix} \begin{bmatrix} \pi_t \\ g_t \\ \pi_t^{core} \\ \Delta\pi_t \\ \Delta g_t \\ \Delta\pi_t^{core} \end{bmatrix}$$

The transition equation is defined as follows

$$\pi_t = \pi_{t-1} + \Delta\pi_t$$

$$g_t = g_{t-1} + \Delta g_t$$

$$\pi_t^{core} = \pi_{t-1}^{core} + \Delta\pi_t^{core}$$

$$\Delta\pi_t = \alpha_1(\pi_{t-1} - \pi_{t-1}^{core}) + \beta_1\Delta\pi_{t-1} + \beta_2\Delta g_{t-1} + \beta_3\Delta\pi_{t-1}^{core} + \varepsilon_{1t}$$

$$\Delta g_t = \beta_4\Delta\pi_{t-1} + \beta_5\Delta g_{t-1} + \beta_6\Delta\pi_{t-1}^{core} + \varepsilon_{2t}$$

$$\Delta\pi_t^{core} = \beta_7\Delta\pi_{t-1}^{core} + \varepsilon_{3t}$$

Or

$$\xi_t = \begin{bmatrix} \pi_t \\ g_t \\ \pi_t^{core} \\ \Delta\pi_t \\ \Delta g_t \\ \Delta\pi_t^{core} \end{bmatrix} = \begin{bmatrix} 1 & 0 & 0 & 1 & 0 & 0 \\ 0 & 1 & 0 & 0 & 1 & 0 \\ 0 & 0 & 1 & 0 & 0 & 1 \\ \alpha_1 & 0 & -\alpha_1 & \beta_1 & \beta_2 & \beta_3 \\ 0 & 0 & 0 & \beta_4 & \beta_5 & \beta_6 \\ 0 & 0 & 0 & 0 & 0 & \beta_7 \end{bmatrix} \begin{bmatrix} \pi_{t-1} \\ g_{t-1} \\ \pi_{t-1}^{core} \\ \Delta\pi_{t-1} \\ \Delta g_{t-1} \\ \Delta\pi_{t-1}^{core} \end{bmatrix} \begin{bmatrix} 0 \\ 0 \\ 0 \\ \varepsilon_{1t} \\ \varepsilon_{2t} \\ \varepsilon_{2t} \end{bmatrix}$$

Where $\text{var}(\varepsilon_{1t}) = \sigma_1^2$, $\text{var}(\varepsilon_{2t}) = \sigma_2^2$, $\text{var}(\varepsilon_{3t}) = \sigma_3^2$.

Table 10.11 reports the estimation results; Table 10.12 reports the estimated core CPI inflation; Figure 10.5 plots the estimated core CPI inflation along with the overall CPI inflation. It can be seen from the chart that the core CPI inflation rates were all positive over the estimation interval.

It should be noted that the estimated core inflation rates based on this model are very sensitive to the initial conditions used in the estimation. For example, the estimated results for sample period 1980–2002 are significantly different from the estimated results for sample period 1978–2002. It is likely that there are multiple time series that are cointegrated with the headline inflation. As a result, the initial conditions will determine which time series get picked. As the core inflation is defined as

Table 10.11 Estimation results by Kalman filter

	Coefficient	Std. Error	z-statistic	Prob.
α_1	0.099733	0.030546	3.264962	0.001100
β_1	0.536499	0.091571	5.858822	0.000000
β_2	−0.008897	0.066462	−0.133870	0.893500
β_3	0.222716	0.152332	1.462038	0.143700
σ_1	1.859187	0.124553	14.926920	0.000000
β_4	−0.265674	0.298732	−0.889339	0.373800
β_5	−0.324210	1.039805	−0.311799	0.755200
β_6	3.333721	1.158122	2.878559	0.004000
σ_2	0.055450	79.019400	0.000702	0.999400
β_7	−0.269216	1.086708	−0.247736	0.804300
σ_3	1.958858	0.638306	3.068840	0.002100
	Final State	**Root MSE**	**z-statistic**	**Prob.**
π_t	0.139150	1.919737	0.072484	0.942200
g_t	8.128168	6.530537	1.244640	0.213300
π_t^{core}	5.461912	3.123347	1.748737	0.080300
$\Delta\pi_t$	0.999049	2.190233	0.456138	0.648300
Δg_t	−0.268281	7.669686	−0.034979	0.972100
$\Delta\pi_t^{core}$	0.000874	2.033565	0.000430	0.999700
Log likelihood	−528.1941	Akaike info criterion		11.72161
Parameters	11	Schwarz criterion		12.02313
Diffuse priors	6	Hannan-Quinn criterion		11.84331

Notes:
Method: Maximum likelihood (Marquardt).
Date: 04/25/04 Time: 11:04.
Sample: 1980:1 2002:4.
Included observations: 92.

Table 10.12 *CPI inflation and estimated core inflation using Kalman filter, 1980–2002*

OBS	CPI Inflation	Core CPI Inflation
1980:1	9.10	5.99
1980:2	7.60	5.87
1980:3	7.10	5.83
1980:4	6.60	4.85
1981:1	0.80	4.09
1981:2	0.80	4.09
1981:3	2.10	4.19
1981:4	3.60	5.53
1982:1	2.40	5.82
1982:2	1.90	5.78
1982:3	1.80	5.78
1982:4	1.70	3.01
1983:1	0.60	7.15
1983:2	1.00	5.54
1983:3	1.11	7.76
1983:4	2.10	6.92
1984:1	1.10	6.43
1984:2	1.70	7.09
1984:3	2.40	9.59
1984:4	1.77	10.06
1985:1	4.83	9.33
1985:2	9.37	8.36
1985:3	11.40	4.95
1985:4	11.73	4.77
1986:1	8.17	5.18
1986:2	4.43	5.51
1986:3	4.17	7.09
1986:4	5.93	7.17
1987:1	5.40	7.04
1987:2	7.40	7.19
1987:3	7.90	7.09
1987:4	8.20	6.67
1988:1	10.30	7.07
1988:2	14.20	7.67
1988:3	23.10	7.86
1988:4	27.30	8.07
1989:1	27.60	7.23
1989:2	24.70	5.69
1989:3	15.30	4.51
1989:4	7.50	2.98

Table 10.12 (continued)

OBS	CPI Inflation	Core CPI Inflation
1990:1	4.00	2.32
1990:2	2.30	3.43
1990:3	2.20	6.49
1990:4	3.70	6.46
1991:1	1.90	6.47
1991:2	3.10	6.00
1991:3	4.70	3.99
1991:4	4.60	5.56
1992:1	5.40	6.32
1992:2	5.50	6.45
1992:3	6.20	7.48
1992:4	8.30	11.66
1993:1	11.10	3.96
1993:2	13.90	4.36
1993:3	16.10	10.88
1993:4	17.20	10.60
1994:1	22.20	9.59
1994:2	21.90	9.37
1994:3	25.70	10.75
1994:4	26.90	4.29
1995:1	22.60	12.64
1995:2	20.00	12.08
1995:3	14.80	10.05
1995:4	11.10	11.85
1996:1	9.40	10.83
1996:2	9.10	7.74
1996:3	7.90	3.38
1996:4	7.00	5.75
1997:1	5.20	6.71
1997:2	2.90	6.90
1997:3	2.10	5.29
1997:4	1.00	5.93
1998:1	0.00	4.20
1998:2	−0.90	5.69
1998:3	−1.40	6.38
1998:4	−1.10	5.66
1999:1	−1.40	4.88
1999:2	−2.10	5.11
1999:3	−1.30	3.20
1999:4	−0.80	4.43

Table 10.12 (continued)

OBS	CPI Inflation	Core CPI Inflation
2000:1	0.10	5.54
2000:2	0.10	5.67
2000:3	0.30	5.19
2000:4	0.60	5.74
2001:1	0.10	5.55
2001:2	1.10	5.28
2001:3	0.80	4.60
2001:4	−0.10	4.80
2002:1	−0.60	5.11
2002:2	−1.10	5.50
2002:3	−0.80	5.45
2002:4	−0.60	5.47

an unobservable variable in this model, by nature it is very difficult to find out which series is the real core inflation. Because of this limitation, this measurement of core inflation will not be used for the rest of this chapter.

7 CONCLUSION

In this chapter, I have shown that although the overall CPI inflation rate was negative in the years 1998 and 1999, the core CPI inflation rate after excluding the price of food was positive in these two years. The core CPI inflation rate for 2002 was negative after excluding the food prices. This indicates that the CPI decline in 2002 might have been caused by factors other than food prices. It was highly likely that the decline of the consumer price index in 2002 was due to the effects of China's accession into the WTO and the reduction of the tariff rate in 2002. According to the WTO rules and the commitments China made, China lowered the tariff rates of 5300 items in 2002, accounting for 73 percent of the total tariff items. The overall tariff level was cut from 15.3 percent to 12 percent.

I have also decomposed the inflation rate of the RPI, and have found that a striking difference between the movement of the RPI and the CPI is that the inflation rate of the RPI, excluding food and energy, has been consistently negative since November 1997. A potential explanation (Wu, 2004) is that the increased competition in the distribution sector squeezed the gross margins of the distributors, hence adding to the downward pressure on retail prices.

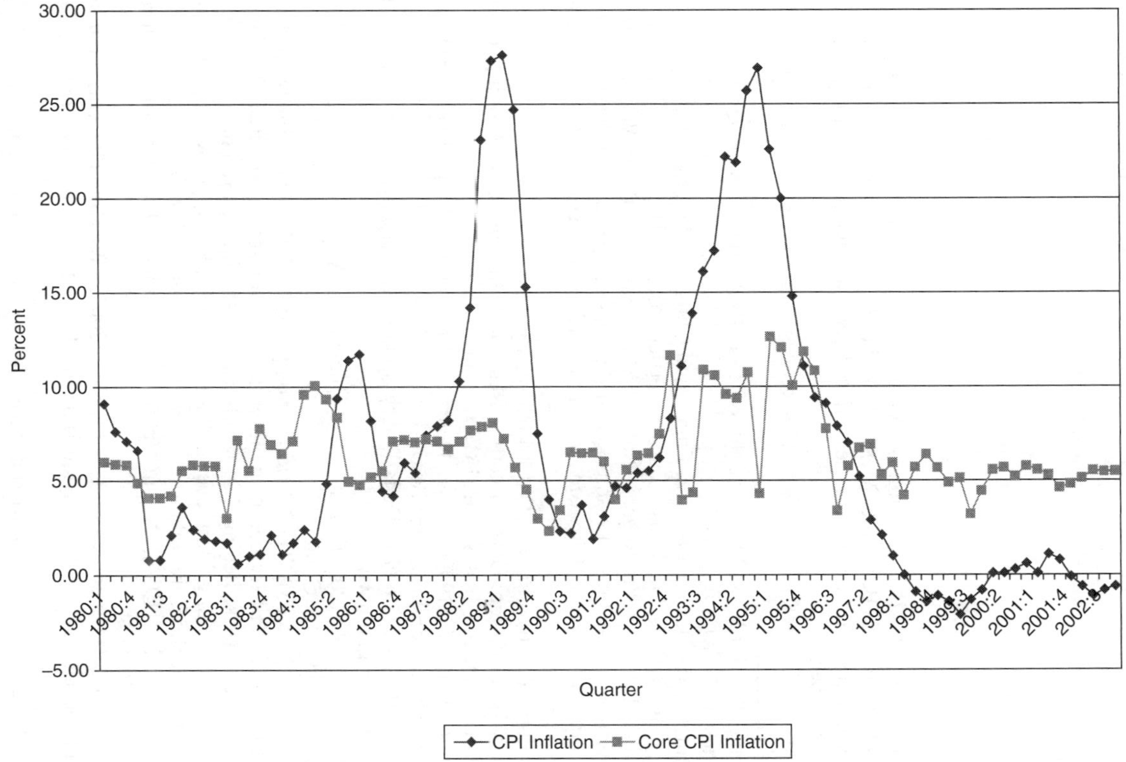

Figure 10.5 *CPI inflation and estimated core inflation by Kalman filter, 1980–2002*

NOTE

* The views expressed in this chapter are those of the author, and do not necessarily reflect those of the Office of the Comptroller of the Currency. This chapter is based on Chapter 2 of my doctoral dissertation at Stanford University. I am grateful to Professor Lawrence Lau, Professor Ronald McKinnon and Professor Takeshi Amemiya for their invaluable guidance.

REFERENCES

Bernanke, Ben (2002), 'Deflation – Making Sure "It" Doesn't Happen Here', Speech by Ben S. Bernanke, Member of the Board of Governors of the US Federal Reserve System, before the National Economists Club, Washington, DC, 21 November.

Bjornland, H.C. (2000), 'Identifying Domestic and Imported Core Inflation', *IMF Working Paper.*

De Long, Bradford J. (1999), 'Should We Fear Deflation?', *Brookings Papers on Economic Activity*, **1**, 225–41.

Eckstein, O. (1981), *Core Inflation*, Engelwood Cliffs, N.J: Prentice-Hall.

Erceg, Christopher, Jon Faust, Luca Guerrieri, Carter Hemphill, Linda Kole, Jennifer Roush, John Rogers, Nathan Sheets and Jonathan Wright (2002), 'Preventing Deflation: Lessons from Japan's Experience in the 1990s', *International Finance Discussion Paper*, Board of Governors of the Federal Reserve System.

Flemming, J. (1976), *Inflation*, Oxford University Press.

IMF (2003), 'Deflation: Determinants, Risks, and Policy Options – Findings of an Interdepartmental Task Force', IMF working paper.

Krugman, Paul R. (1999a), 'Can Deflation Be Prevented?', Krugman website, http://web.mit.edu/krugman/www/.

Krugman, Paul R. (1999b), 'Deflationary Spirals', Krugman website, http://web.mit.edu/krugman/www/.

Krugman, Paul R. (2003), 'Fear of a Quagmire', *New York Times*, 24 May, Section A, Page 15, Column 5.

Lau, Lawrence J. (2003), 'The World Economy and Deflation', working paper presented at the Fifth Meeting of the International Advisory Council of the China Development Bank, Beijing, 7 November 2003, Stanford University.

Lee, Jong Wong, Sang Don Lee and Ki-Ho Kim (2003), 'New Approach to Estimation of the Core Inflation', *Journal of the Korean Economy*, **4** (2), 315–43.

Leontief, Wassily (1986), 'Input–output Economics', 2nd Edition, Oxford University Press.

Marques, C.R., P.D. Nerves and A.G. Da Silva (2002), 'Why Should Central Banks Avoid the Use of the Underlying Inflation Indicator', *Economics Letters*, **75**, 17–23.

Melvin, James R. (1979), 'Short-run Price Effects of the Corporation Income Tax and Implications for International Trade', *The American Economic Review*, **69** (5), 765–74.

National Bureau of Statistics of China (1999), 'Input–output Table of China', China Statistics Press, China, Beijing.

Okun, Arthur M. (1970), *The Political Economy of Prosperity*, Brookings Institution, Washington DC.
Quah, Danny and Shaun P. Vahey (1995), 'Measuring Core Inflation', *The Economic Journal*, **105** (432), 1130–44.
Wu, Deming (2004), 'Was there Deflation in China between 1997 and 2002? An Empirical Study of Price Movement in China', PhD dissertation, Stanford University.
Wynne, Mark A. (1999), 'Core Inflation: A Review of Some Conceptual Issues', working paper, European Central Bank.

Index

Abiad, A.G. 27, 28, 74–5
accountability, IMF 125–6, 128
accounting standards 163, 181, 184, 187
Adams, F. Gerard 13–15, 197–218
adverse selection problem 155
age and wage rates 229–34
Akamatsu, K. 198
Alba, Pedro 184
Allen, Franklin 148
Alper, C.E. 27, 31, 134, 136
Alvarez-Plata, Patricia 31
APEC (Asia-Pacific Economic Cooperation) 149
Argentina
  bankruptcy infrastructure 183
  crisis (2002) 31
  IMF rescue package 125, 128
  poverty 57
Arrow, Kenneth 155
artificial serial correlations 27–8
Aryah, Gosah 222, 225
ASEAN (Association of Southeast Asian Nations) 44
Asia
  in 21st century 53–5
  bond markets 148–9
  new developments 6–8
Asia before and after financial crisis (1997–98)
  currency crisis theories 24–32
  new Asian miracle 53–5
  overview 8, 23–4
  predictability of crisis 44–53
  societal impacts 55–65
  vulnerabilities of affected countries 32–44
Asia-Pacific Economic Cooperation (APEC), *see* APEC
Asian Bond Fund 126, 189
Asian Development Bank 181, 201
Asian Financial Crisis (1997–98)
  currency crisis theories 24–32
  impact on growth and productivity 13–15, 213–15
  new Asian miracle 53–5
  overview 8, 23–4
  predictability of crisis 44–53
  questions raised by 2–8
  secular aftermath 5–6
  societal impacts 55–65
  Thai wage rates during 15–17
  and third-generation crisis models 72–3
  vulnerabilities of affected countries 32–44
  see also economic development; economic growth; Thailand, wage rates
Asian Policy Forum 187–9
Association of Southeast Asian Nations (ASEAN), *see* ASEAN
Australia
  borrowings 177
  corporate borrowing 173
  economic information quality 167
  financial infrastructure 164
  judicial system 166
Austria, domestic consumption 290

balance of payments, Malaysia 144
Baldacci, Emanuele 56
bank deposits/loans 158–9
Bank for International Settlements 3
bank lending, reliance on 185–6
Bank Negara 137
Bank of Japan 246, 255
Bank of Thailand (BOT) 9, 69, 80, 81, 149, 185–6
bankruptcy infrastructure 183
banks
  and debt financing 172–3
  implications of absence of bond markets 13, 174–5

Barro, Robert 160
Basel Capital Accord 121
Basu, Sudip Ranjan 292
Behrman, Jere R. 15–17, 221–35
Belgium, domestic consumption 290
benchmark yield curve 177–8, 180, 186
Bergsten, Fred 240
Bernanke, Ben 297
Betcherman, G. 222
Bjornland, H.C. 298
Black, Bernard 172–3
Black, Fischer 169, 170
bond markets
  absence of 169–76
  development of 126
  failure of 167–8
  financial sector overview/flow of funds analysis 150–62
  new flotations 122
  overview 12–13, 148–50
  role of financial infrastructure/efficient financial markets 162–76
  role of government as issuer 176–80
  Thailand 5, 180–90
borrowers
  monitoring of 174
  preferences 158
Boskin Committee 261, 291
Bosworth, Barry P. 198, 209
Brady Plan 121
Brazil
  domestic consumption 290
  exchange rates 123
Bretton Woods Institutions 11, 121, 127–8, 243–6, 257
Brimble, Peter 225, 232
Brunetti, C. 31
business cycle 199, 209

Calvo, G. 72, 134
Camdessus, Michel 121
Canada, bond market 149, 189
capital account indicators 85, 86
capital account variables 83
capital controls
  main characteristics of macroeconometric model 137–8
  overview 11–12, 134–5
  review of studies 135–7
  simulations with model 138–45
capital flight, Thailand 32
capital growth 205
capital inputs 208–11
Capital Management Crisis (1998) 124
capital market
  China 7
  reforms 4–5, 8
capital mix 4
capital mobility 123
Caprio, Gerard, Jr 172
carry trade 73
cartel pricing 174
Central and Eastern Europe, current account deficits 130–31
Chatusripitak, Nathporn 5, 12–13, 148–90
Chile, foreign borrowing 127
China
  in 21st century 53–5
  capital growth 205
  domestic saving 206
  economic growth 121–2
  exchange rates 126, 247–58
  export growth 207–8
  GDP growth 200–201
  inputs 210–11
  investment 203–4
  labor productivity 202–3
  new developments 6–7
  petroleum price increases 10
  total factor productivity 212–13, 217–18
  wage adjustment under a fixed exchange rate 247–55
China, core inflation rate
  alternative measure of core inflation 319–24
  definition of core inflation 297–8
  description of consumer price index by category 298–301
  estimation of core inflation rate 301–9
  impact of changes in petroleum prices 309–19
  overview 19–20, 296–7
China, cost of living
  comments on linear expenditure system 284–91

lifestyle change 291–5
linear expenditure system (LES) 262–84
overview 17–19, 260–61
Chuppe, Terry 148
Claessens, Stijn 156, 184
classification errors 28
clothing expenditure, China 263–78
CLSA Asia-Pacific Markets 187
collective action clauses (CACs), debt securities 125
Collins, Susan M. 198, 209
Colombia, domestic consumption 290
commodities expenditure, China 263–78
consumer price index (CPI), China
by category 298–301
comments on linear expenditure system 284–91
core inflation rate estimation 301–9
lifestyle change 291–5
linear expenditure system (LES) 262–84
overview 17–19, 260–61
US 253
consumer price index (CPI), Japan 246
consumer prices
China/US 249
Japan/US 244
consumption expenditure, China 262–91
contagion 25–6, 32, 57, 72, 105, 136
Copeland, Morris 150
core inflation rate, China
alternative measure of core inflation 319–24
definition of core inflation 297–8
description of consumer price index by category 298–301
estimation of core inflation rate 301–9
impact of changes in petroleum prices 309–19
overview 19–20, 296–7
corporate borrowing 172–4
corporate governance reforms 5, 127–30
corporate performance, Thailand 184
Corsetti, G. 197
cost of living, China
comments on linear expenditure system 284–91
lifestyle change 291–5
linear expenditure system (LES) 262–84
overview 17–19, 260–61
Crafts, Nicholas 198, 209
credit culture, creation of 126
credit risk, pricing 170–71
creditor countries 241–2
creditor rights 162–3, 181
creditworthiness information 157, 163
crises
aftermath 5–6
cures 3–5
impending 10–11
lessons learned 3
nature and dynamics 2
crony capitalism 13
cross-border financial transactions 122, 161–2
cultural services expenditure, China 263–78
currency crisis theories
early warning systems 26–8
Markov-switching approach 28–32
overview 24–6
currency crises, vulnerability indicators/analysis
definition of currency crises/methodologies for identifying 80–84
empirical results 85–108
overview 9–10, 69–71
review of selected studies 71–80
summary 108–12
currency devaluation 53
current account (CA)
Indonesia 39, 40
Korea 37, 38
Malaysia 42
Philippines 45, 46
relative 48
Thailand 33, 34, 83, 85–9, 91, 98–100, 104, 106, 107, 110, 111
current account deficits 121–2
current account imbalances 4

Da Silva, A.G. 319
Dalla, Ismail 148
De Long, Bradford J. 297
de Mello, Luiz 56
dealer markets 179
debt claims 167–8
debt financing, dominance of banks 172–3, 174–5
decomposition analysis 209
default 163, 168
definitions
  core inflation 297–8
  currency crisis 81–2
deflation 242
  China 297
  Japan 246–7
delivery versus payment (DVP) system, Thailand 186
Demirgüç-Kunt, Aslï 26, 172
Denison, Edward F. 208
Denmark, domestic consumption 290
Deolalikar, Anil B. 15–17, 221–35
deposit rates, Thailand 85–9, 96, 98–100
Detragiache, E. 26
Diamond, Douglas 172
differential wage adjustment 243–4, 247
direct financial claims 156–7, 159–60, 162
  with no secondary market 153–6
disclosure standards 181, 187
Djankov, Simeon 156, 184
Dodd, R. 73
Doing Business in 2004 (World Bank) 181
dollar standard 240–58
domestic credit, Thailand 85–9, 95, 98–100, 110, 111
domestic saving 205, 206

early warning systems
  currency crises 9, 26–8
  Thailand 69–70
East Asia
  economic growth 13–15
  income inequality 57–62
  new developments 6–7
Eckstein, O. 298
econometric predictive models 8, 24, 28–32
economic development 197–9
economic fundamentals, long-term deterioration 32, 33–44
economic growth
  China 7, 18, 53–5
  East Asia 13–15
  India 7–8, 53–5
economic growth during Asian Financial Crisis
  overview 197–9
  growth record 199–208
  input/total factor productivity approach 208–18
economic indicators
  China/US 249
  Japan/US 244
Edison, H.J. 134, 135, 136, 142
education and wage rates, Thailand 229–34
education expenditure, China 263–78
education indicators 62–4
Eichengreen, Barry 2, 3, 5, 10–11, 26, 72, 121–31, 135
elasticities approach, balance of trade 241
emerging crises 121–31
empirical results, currency crisis indicators
  assessment of future vulnerability 105–8
  composite indicator and probability of crisis from signals approach 100–101
  crisis indicators from signals approach 85–100
  Markov-switching models 31–2
  profit estimates 101–5
empirical studies, currency crisis indicators 73–80
employment
  Malaysia 137–8
  Thailand 15–16, 222, 227
energy prices, China 301–2, 304–19
Engel curves 18, 263–91
Engwatana, Pipat 74, 77, 81
equity markets 167–8, 171
Erceg, Christopher 297
Esquivel, Gerardo 73, 75–6
ethnic tensions 56
Europe, bond markets 189

European Monetary System (EMS) 72
European Union
  bond markets 149, 180, 189
  reform agenda 129–30
exchange rate differentials, China/US 252
exchange rate dynamics 29–32
exchange rate mechanism (ERM) crisis (1992–93) 25
exchange rate policy, appropriate choice of 3–4
exchange rates
  China 7, 247–58
  and international competitiveness 243–55
  Japan 244–7
  Malaysia 145
  Thailand 74, 78–80, 81–2
  and trade balance 241–3
  see also flexible exchange rates; floating exchange rates, pegged exchange rates; real effective exchange rate
exchange rates in international adjustment
  exchange rates and international competitiveness 243–55
  exchange rates and trade balance 241–3
  flexibility, China 255–8
  overview 17, 240–41
exclusion windows 27–8
Executives' Meeting of East Asia-Pacific Central Banks (EMEAP) 149, 189
export growth rates
  Asia 205, 207–8
  Indonesia 39, 40
  Korea 37, 38
  Malaysia 42, 43
  Philippines 45, 46
  relative 50
  Thailand 33, 34, 85–9, 91, 98–100, 104, 107, 111
export-led growth
  China 8
  East Asia 197–8
exports during Asian Financial Crisis 13–15, 215–18
external debt, Thailand 85–9, 94, 98–100, 110, 111
external sector variables 111

Fallon, Peter R. 222
family-controlled industrial conglomerates 155–6, 184
Fan, Joseph P.H. 184
Faust, Jon 297
Federal Reserve (FED), US 10, 121, 130, 254
Fernholz, Ricardo 249
financial claims 153–6
financial crises
  impact on income inequality 57–62
  impact on living standards 62–4
  impact on poverty 56–7
  impending 10–11
  overview 55–6
  policy implications 64
  review of studies 135–7
financial development, importance of bond market
  financial sector overview/flow of funds analysis 150–62
  overview 12–13, 148–50
  role of financial infrastructure/efficient financial markets 162–76
  role of government as issuer 176–80
  Thailand as example 180–90
financial infrastructure, role of 162–76
financial intermediaries 156–9
financial markets
  efficiency in 162–76
  saving/investment with lack of 150–53
  Thailand 180–90
financial sector
  flows with direct financial claims but no secondary market 153–6
  government and international sector 159–62
  Malaysia 138
  savings and investment without financial markets/institutions 150–53
  with financial intermediaries 156–9
financial variables 83, 85, 86, 111

first generation currency crisis models 24–5, 71, 72
fiscal balance
  Indonesia 39, 40
  Korea 37, 38
  Malaysia 42, 43
  Philippines 45, 46
  relative 49
  Thailand 33, 34, 85–9, 92, 98–100, 104, 106, 107, 111
fiscal discipline 123–4
fiscal policy, post-crisis 56
Fischer, Stanley 125
fixed exchange rate, China 247–55
Flatters, Frank 232
Flemming, J. 297
flexible exchange rates 123, 126–7, 255–8
floating exchange rates 254–5
  Japan 246–7
flow of funds analysis
  flows with direct financial claims but no secondary market 153–6
  government and international sector 159–62
  savings and investment without financial markets/institutions 150–53
  with financial intermediaries 156–9
'flying geese pattern' 198
food expenditure, China 263–78
food prices, China 299–300, 302, 304–9, 310–16
foreign borrowing 127
foreign capital flows, China 255–6
foreign debt, Thailand 74, 184–5
foreign direct investment (FDI) 14–15, 135, 216, 217–18, 255–6
foreign reserves, accumulation of 123
forward markets/contracts 169–70
France, domestic consumption 290
Fund of Bond Funds, Asia 189
futures markets/contracts 169–70

Gale, Douglas 148
Gao, Huiqing 17–19, 260–95
GARCH(1,1) model 136
Gaussian cumulative distribution function 29
GDP (gross domestic product)
  China 249, 260–61
  Japan/US 244
  Malaysia 140, 141
  Thailand 83–4, 85–9, 91, 92, 95, 98–100, 104, 106, 107, 110, 111
  US 249
GDP growth rates, Asia 200–201
Geary–Khamis method 289–91
Geithner, Timothy 130
gender and wage rates, Thailand 229–34
general price changes 297
Gerlach, S. 72
Germany
  borrowing 177
  domestic consumption 290
Gilson, Ronald 172–3
Gini coefficient 57–62
global economic growth 121–2
Global Financial Stability Report, IMF 124
Goldfajn, Ilan 73, 75–6
Goldsmith, Raymond 148, 150, 156
Goldstein, Morris 134, 240
goods consumption, China 263–78
governance problems, IMF 127–8
government as issuer of bonds 176–80
government budget balance, Malaysia 143
government consumption, Malaysia 141
government debt, Malaysia 143
government fixed investment, Malaysia 141
government policies, unsustainability of 24–5
government sector, impacts on flow of funds 159–62
government securities, Thailand 180–81
Greenspan, Alan 130
gross domestic product (GDP), *see* GDP
growth accounting framework 198–9
Guerrieri, Luca 297
Gultekin, B.N. 27, 31, 74–5, 134, 136
Guttentag, Jack M. 179

Hakansson, Nils H. 171
Hamilton, James B. 30

Hart, Oliver 172
Hausman, Jerry A. 160
Headcount Index, East Asia 58–62
headline inflation 298
health indicators 62–4
hedging 124, 170, 175
hedonic price indexes 291
Hemphill, Carter 297
herding behavior 26
Herrick, Bruce 197
Herring, Richard J. 5, 12–13, 148–90
Herstatt Crisis (1974) 121
heterogeneity across countries 28
Hong Kong
  bond market 148–9, 180, 189
  borrowings 177
  capital growth 205
  corporate borrowing 173
  economic information quality 167
  export growth 207
  financial infrastructure 164
  GDP growth 201
  inputs 211
  investment 203
  judicial system 166
  labor productivity 203
  total factor productivity 213, 217
Horton, S. 222, 232
household facilities/services expenditure, China 263–78
household savings, increases in 160–61
household sector, sources and uses of funds 151–9
Hu, Teh-wei 292
human development indicators 291–5
Hungary
  current account deficit 131
  domestic consumption 290

IBM 256
import growth rate
  Indonesia 39
  Korea 37
  Malaysia 42
  Philippines 45
  relative 51
  Thailand 33, 85–9, 98–100
Inada, Yoshihisa 53
Inchauste, G. 56
income inequality, impacts of financial crises 57–62
India
  in 21st century 53–5
  domestic consumption 290
  new developments 7–8
indicators, currency crisis
  empirical results 85–108
  empirical studies 73–80
  identifying 80–84
  overview 82–4
indirect financial claims 156–9
Indonesia
  bankruptcy infrastructure 183, 189
  bond market 149
  borrowings 177
  capital controls 136–7
  capital growth 205
  corporate borrowing 173
  domestic saving 206
  economic information quality 167
  export growth 207–8
  financial infrastructure 164
  GDP growth 200–201
  income inequality 59–62
  inputs 209–11
  investment 203–4
  judicial system 166
  labor productivity 202–3
  living standards 63
  macroeconomic indicators 36, 39–41
  poverty 57
  real wage rates 222
  societal impact of crises 23–4
  total factor productivity 212–13, 217
  vulnerability 53
industrial production
  during Asian Financial Crisis 215–18
  China/US 249
  Japan/US 244
inferior goods/services 263
inflation differentials
  China/US 252, 254
  Japan/US 248
inflation rate
  Indonesia 39, 40
  Korea 37, 38
  Malaysia 42, 43
  Philippines 45, 46

relative 52
Thailand 33, 34, 85–9, 95, 98–100, 110, 111
see also core inflation rate, China
information flows 163, 171
input–output price model, petroleum price changes 311–16
inputs 198–9, 208–11, 215–16
Institute for International Economics (IIE), US 240
Institute of Directors, Thailand 187
Institute of International Finance 122
Intaravitak, Chedtha 225, 232
Inter-American Development Bank 127
interest rates
government bonds 178
Malaysia 142, 145
term structure of 169–71
international adjustments
exchange rates and international competitiveness 243–55
exchange rates and trade balance 241–3
foreign exchange flexibility, China 255–8
overview 240–41
international competitiveness, effect of exchange rate 243–55
international dollar standard 240–58
international financial markets, structure of 127
international financial system
agenda for reforms 126–30
reforms 122–6
international issuance of bonds 173–4
International Monetary Fund (IMF)
Articles of Agreement 256, 257
Capital Markets Division 124
Financial Sector Assessment Program 124
Independent Evaluation Office 129
International Monetary and Financial Committee (IMFC) 129
Korean package 136
reform agenda 122–30
Reviews of the Observance of Standards and Codes (ROSCs) 124
Special Data Dissemination Standard (SDDS) 112, 124–5
Special Drawing Rights 129
surveillance role 3, 124–6
Thai package 9–10, 69–70, 78–80, 136
international reserves, Thailand 9–10, 69, 78–80, 81–2, 85–9, 94, 98–100, 110, 111
international sector, impacts on flow of funds 159–62
investment
bias in decisions 172
during Asian Financial Crisis 13–15, 203–4, 215–18
without financial markets/institutions 150–53
investors
implications of absence of bond markets 172–4
portfolio allocation preferences 178–9
Iran, domestic consumption 290
Ireland, domestic consumption 290
Islam, R. 222
Italy, domestic consumption 290
Ittisupornrat, Anotai 74, 77, 81

Jamaica, domestic consumption 290
Japan
bond market 149, 173, 189
borrowings 177
corporate borrowing 173
dollar exchange rate in historical perspective 244–7
domestic consumption 290
economic information quality 167
financial infrastructure 164
international adjustment 17
judicial system 166
new developments 7
Jeanneau, S. 73
judicial systems 163, 166, 168
Jun, Lwang 148

Kahler, M. 134
Kakwani, N. 225
Kalman filter 298, 319–24, 325
Kaminsky, G.L. 9, 26, 27, 70–71, 73–4,

75–6, 81, 82–3, 84, 99, 101, 104, 105, 134
Kane, Edward J. 163, 166, 167
Kaplan, E. 136
Kenya, domestic consumption 290
Khatdhate, Deena 148
Kim, Ki-Ho 298, 319
Kindleberger, Charles P. 197
Kittiprapas, Sauwalak 225, 232, 233
Klein, Lawrence R. 1–20, 23–65, 134–46, 260–95
Klein, M. 146
Knowles, James C. 232
Kojima, K. 198
Kole, Linda 297
Kondury, Kali 148
Kravis, Irving 285–6, 287, 288–9, 291
Kruger, M. 73, 75–6
Krugman, Paul 25, 53, 72, 73, 134, 198, 297
Kumar, M. 26

La Porta, Rafael 162, 163, 166
Labor Force Surveys (LFSs) 224–5
labor inputs 208–11
labor market conditions 55
labor market, Thailand 221
labor productivity
  Asia 201, 202, 203
  China/US 249
  Japan/US 244
Lang, Larry H.P. 156, 184
Lardy, Nicholas 240
Larrain, Felipe 73, 75–6
Latin America
  current accounts 122
  exchange rates 123, 127
  fiscal discipline 123–4
  income inequality/poverty 57
  living standards 62–3, 64
Lau, Lawrence J. 53, 199, 297
leading-indicator approach 26–8
  Thailand 69–70, 80–84, 108–9, 111
Leblang, D. 135
Lee, Jong Wong 298, 319
Lee, Sang Don 298, 319
legal frameworks, bond markets 162–3
legal infrastructure, Thailand 181
lending rate, Thailand 85–9, 96, 98–100
Lenovo 256
Leontief, Wassily 311
letter stocks 179
leverage 124, 172, 175, 184
Levine, Ross 148
liberalization
  capital account 11, 135–7
  capital markets 4–5
  China 256–7
Liberty Bonds, US 176–7
lifestyle change 19, 261, 263, 291–5
Lindbeck, Assar 244
linear expenditure system (LES) 262–84
  comments on 284–91
  overview 18–19, 260–61
liquid secondary markets 178–80
liquidity shocks 175
literature, real wage declines 224–5
living standards, impacts of financial crises 62–4
Lizondo, S. 9, 71, 73–6, 81, 82–3, 84
loan contracts 159
logit model 26–8, 73, 75–6, 80–81, 84
London Interbank Offered Rate (LIBOR) 85–9, 96, 98–100
Lopez-de-Silanes, Florencio 162, 163, 166
Lucas, Robert E.B. 222
Luxembourg, domestic consumption 290

M1 85–9, 97, 98–100
M2 9, 29, 73, 85–9, 94, 97, 98–100, 104, 106, 107, 110, 111, 136–7
macroeconometric model, Malaysia
  main characteristics 137–8
  overview 11–12, 134–5
  simulations 138–45
macroeconomic indicators 24
  Indonesia 36, 39–41
  Korea 36, 37–8, 44
  Malaysia 41–4
  overview 12
  Philippines 44, 45–6
  Thailand 33–6
macroeconomic performance 135–7
Mahmood, Moazam 222, 225
Makino, J. 53
Malawi, domestic consumption 290

Malaysia
bankruptcy infrastructure 183
bond market 148, 149, 189
borrowings 177
capital growth 205
capital market reforms 5
corporate borrowing 173
domestic consumption 290
domestic saving 206
economic information quality 167
export growth 207–8
financial infrastructure 164
GDP growth 200–201
income inequality 57–8, 60–62
inputs 209–11
investment 203–4
judicial system 166
labor productivity 202–3
macroeconomic indicators 41–4
total factor productivity 212–13, 217
Malaysia, capital controls
main characteristics of macroeconometric model 137–8
overview 11–12, 134–5
real wages 222
review of studies on capital controls 135–7
simulations with model 138–45
societal impact of crises 23–4
management accountability, IMF 128
manufacturing wage growth
China 247, 249
China/US 250
Japan/US 245–6
Marcos regime, Philippines 44
Mariano, Roberto S. 4–5, 11–12, 27, 28, 31, 74–5, 134–46
market sentiment 26
Markov-switching models 28–31, 65, 136
empirical results 31–2
Marques, C.R. 319
Martinez-Peria, M.S. 28
Masson, P. 26
Mazumdar, D. 222, 232
McKinnon, Ronald 4, 17, 148, 240–58
mean absolute error (MAE) 138
mean absolute percentage error (MAPE) 138
mean consumption, East Asia 58–62
medicine/medical services expenditure, China 263–78
Melvin, James R. 311
Merton, Robert 162
Mexican Crises (1982/1994–95) 53, 73, 121
Mexico
bankruptcy infrastructure 183
domestic consumption 290
living standards 62–3
loans 127
poverty 56, 57
Micu, M. 73
minimum lending rate (MLR) 85–9, 96, 98–100
monetary policy, post-crisis 56
money markets, net flows 122
money wages
China/US 249
Japan/US 244
monitoring of borrowers 174
Moore, John 172
Moorthy, U. 26
moral hazard 155, 256
mortality rates 62–3
Mussa, Michael 240

Nagar, A.L. 292
narrow money
China/US 249
Japan/US 244
National Economic and Social Development Board, Thailand 112
negative shocks 91–5, 98–100
Nerves, P.D. 319
Netherlands, domestic consumption 290
new developments
China 6–8
East Asia 6
India 7–8
Japan 7
new issues, government bonds 178
New York Stock Exchange (NYSE) 179
Nixon, Richard 242, 246
nominal GDP
China/US 249
Japan/US 244

non-inferior goods/services 263
non-parametric approach, analysis of leading indicators 84
non-performing loans (NPLs) 3, 71, 137, 175

Obstfeld, M. 25, 72
OECD (Organization for Economic Co-operation and Development)
  Code of Good Corporate Governance 187
  use of leading indicators 70
Ohno, Kenichi 242, 255
Okun, Arthur M. 297
OPEC (Organization of the Petroleum Exporting Countries) 296
option contracts 170
Organization for Economic Co-operation and Development (OECD), *see* OECD
Organization of the Petroleum Exporting Countries (OPEC), *see* OPEC
Osakwe, P.N. 73, 75–6
overinvestment, Thailand 184
Özmucur, Süleyman 4–5, 11–12, 27, 28, 31, 134–46, 292, 293

Page, J. 73, 75–6
Pakistan, domestic consumption 290
Pan-Asia Bond Index Fund 189
parametric approach, analysis of leading indicators 84
pegged exchange rates 6, 25, 53; *see also* dollar standard
People's Bank of China (PBC) 257–8
per capita expenditures, China 300–301
Pérez, J. 26
Pernia, Ernesto M. 232
Perraudin, W. 26
Pesenti, P. 197
petroleum price changes, impact in China
  estimation results 316–19
  input–output price model 311–16
  overview 10, 298, 309–11
Philippines
  bond market 149, 189
  borrowings 177
  capital controls 136, 137
  capital growth 205
  corporate borrowing 173
  domestic consumption 290
  domestic saving 206
  economic information quality 167
  export growth 207–8
  financial infrastructure 164
  GDP growth 200–201
  income inequality 59–62
  inputs 210–11
  investment 203–4
  judicial system 166
  labor productivity 202–3
  macroeconomic indicators 44, 45–6
  societal impact of crises 23–4
  total factor productivity 212–13, 217
Poland, domestic consumption 290
policy implications, financial crises 64
Pongsapich, Amara 225, 232
Poonpatpibul, Chaipat 74, 77, 81
positive shocks 89, 95–7
post-crisis patterns of economic fundamentals 33–44
Poterba, James M. 160
poverty, impact of financial crises 56–7
Pratt, Shannon P. 179
pre-crisis patterns of economic fundamentals 33–44
predictability, Asian Financial Crisis 8, 9, 44–53
predictive models, currency crises 28–32
primary market, Thailand 185–6
principal–agent problem 155
private capital flows, Malaysia 142
private consumption, Malaysia 141
private fixed investment, Malaysia 141
probit model 26–8, 73, 74, 75–7, 80–81, 84, 101–8, 109, 111
production function approach 199
production sector, Malaysia 137–8
productivity
  China 240, 243
  during Asian Financial Crisis 13–15
  see also total factor productivity (TFP)
public sector, Malaysia 138
purchasing power parity (PPP) 254, 285–6, 289

pure loans 158–9
pure security 159

Quah, Danny 298
quasi-financial systems 155–6

Racelis, Mary 232
Radelet, Steven 197
Rajan, Raghuram 176–7
Rao, D.C. 148
real assets 150–56
real effective exchange rate (REER) 29, 31, 136–7
  Indonesia 39
  Korea 37
  Malaysia 42
  Philippines 45
  Thailand 33
real exchange rate, Thailand 85–9, 93, 98–100, 104, 106, 107, 110, 111
real exports, Malaysia 139, 140
real GDP growth
  China/US 249
  Indonesia 39, 40
  Japan/US 244
  Korea 37, 38
  Malaysia 42, 43, 139, 140
  Philippines 45, 46
  relative 47
  Thailand 33, 34, 85–9, 92, 98–100, 104, 106, 111
real government consumption expenditures, Malaysia 139
real imports, Malaysia 140
real indicators, Malaysia 141
real private consumption expenditures, Malaysia 139
real sector variables 83, 85, 86, 111
real wage rates, Thailand
  overview 5–6, 15–17, 221–3
  re-examination of real wage rate changes 226–34
  summary of previous literature 224–5
recreation services expenditure, China 263–78
reforms
  capital markets 4–5
  China/India 54–5
  corporate governance 5
  exchange rate policy 3–4
  international financial system 3, 11, 122–6
Reinhart, C.M. 9, 26, 27, 70–72, 73–4, 75–6, 81, 82–3, 84, 99, 105, 134, 136, 142
relative price change 55, 297
representativeness, IMG 128–9
Republic of Korea, *see* South Korea
residence expenditure, China 263–78
retail price index (RPI), China 309–16
review of studies
  capital controls 135–7
  currency crises 71–80
Ricci, L. 134, 135
risk
  management of 3, 174–5
  settlement obligations 179–80
Rodrik, D. 134, 136
Rogers, John 297
Romania
  current account deficit 131
  domestic consumption 290
root mean square error (RMSE) 138
Rose, A. 26, 72
Roubini, N. 197
Roush, Jennifer 297
rural household expenditure, China 263, 276–8, 279, 280–83, 285, 286, 301
Russia, poverty 57

Sachs, Jeffrey D. 197
Salvatore, D. 134
Samuelson, P.A. 284, 291
savers
  implications of absence of bond markets 171–2
  preferences 158
savings without financial markets/institutions 150–53
Scandinavian model of wage adjustment 243–4, 246, 254
Scholes, Myron 170
Schrooten, Mechthild 31
Scotti, C. 31
second generation currency crisis models 25, 71, 72

secondary markets
direct financial claims with lack of 153–6
nurturing 162, 178–80
Thailand 181, 185–6
secular aftermath, Asian Financial Crisis 5–6
sensitivity analysis 209
services expenditure, China 263–78
Shabbir, Tayyeb 1–20, 23–65, 74–5, 134, 136, 197–218
Shaw, Edward 148
Sheets, Nathan 297
Sheng, Andrew 149
Shleifer, Andrei 162, 163, 166
Siamwalla, Ammar 225
signals approach
composite indicator and probability of crisis 100–101, 111
crisis indicators from 85–100, 105–8
overview 9, 26–8, 73–4, 75–7, 80–81, 84
significance testing 28
simultaneous equation macroeconomic model 11–12
Singapore
bond market 149, 189
borrowings 177
capital growth 205
corporate borrowing 173
domestic saving 206
economic information quality 167
export growth 207
financial infrastructure 164
GDP growth 201
inputs 211
investment 203
judicial system 166
labor productivity 203
total factor productivity 213, 217, 218
Singh, A. 135
Slok, T. 134, 135
slumps, exchange-rate induced 242
Slutsky–Hicks symmetry conditions 262
Smets, F. 72
Smith, Clifford, Jr 169–70
Smithson, Charles 169–70
societal impact of crises 2, 5–6, 23–4, 55–65
Solow, Robert M. 208
Sonakul, M.R. 149
South Asia, new developments 7–8
South Korea
bankruptcy infrastructure 183
bond market 149, 189
borrowings 177
capital controls 136, 137
capital growth 205
corporate borrowing 173
domestic consumption 290
domestic saving 206
economic information quality 167
export growth 207–8
financial infrastructure 164
GDP growth 200–201
income inequality 58, 60, 61
inputs 210–11
investment 203–4
judicial system 166
labor productivity 202–3
macroeconomic indicators 36, 37–8, 44
real wage rates 222
societal impact of crises 23
total factor productivity 212–13, 217
Spain, domestic consumption 290
speculative attacks
early warning systems 26–8
impact of 81
Markov-switching approach 28–32
vulnerability to 73
spillover effects 26, 32
Sri Lanka, domestic consumption 290
stabilization role, China 260, 297
staff surveillance, IMF 129–30
stakeholder representation, IMF 128
State Administration for Foreign Exchange (SAFE), China 256–7
State Information Center, China 287
statistical analysis, determinants of TFP 211–18
step-wise linear methods 287–8
Stiglitz, J.E. 135, 168
Stock Exchange of Thailand (SET) 85–9, 90, 98–100, 104, 106, 107, 110, 111, 184, 187
Stone, Richard 291
structural conditional error correction model 319

structural problems, Thailand 181–4
structural vector auto-regression (SVAR) model 298
Stulz, René 148
subsistence income 279–80, 287
Summers, L. 135
Summers, Robert 285–6, 287, 288–9, 291
surveillance of financial systems 124–6
Sussangkarn, Chalongphob 232
swap contracts 169–70
swap operations 81
swap rates 249
Syria, domestic consumption 290
Szirmai, A. 199

Taipei
  capital growth 205
  export growth 207
  GDP growth 201
  inputs 210–11
  investment 203
  labor productivity 203
  total factor productivity 212–13, 217, 218
Taiwan
  borrowings 177
  corporate borrowing 173
  economic information quality 167
  exchange rates 127
  export growth 208
  financial infrastructure 164
  judicial system 166
Tan, A.H.H. 28, 31, 74–5
Tan, Kong-Yam 249
Tao, Liping 17–19, 260–95
tariffs, China 302
tax revenues, Malaysia 142, 143
taxation, China 256
technology change 211, 213, 216
technology-intensive production 198
Tequila Crisis (1994–95) 105
Thai Bond Dealing Center (BDC) 181, 186
Thai Central Bank 189
Thai Rating and Information Services Company (TRIS) 184
Thai Securities and Exchange Commission 186
Thailand
  bankruptcy infrastructure 183
  bond market 5, 13, 149, 180–90
  borrowings 177
  capital controls 136, 137, 146
  capital growth 205
  capital flight 32
  corporate borrowing 173
  domestic consumption 290
  domestic saving 206
  economic information quality 167
  export growth 207–8
  financial infrastructure 164
  GDP growth 200–201
  income inequality 57–8, 60–62
  inputs 209–11
  international reserves 7
  investment 203–4
  judicial system 166
  labor productivity 202–3
  macroeconomic indicators 33–6
  poverty 57
  total factor productivity 212–13, 217
  vulnerability 53
Thailand Securities Depository Corporation (TSD) 186
Thailand, vulnerability to currency crisis
  definition of currency crisis/ methodologies for identifying 80–84
  empirical results 85–108
  overview 9–10, 69–71
  selected studies on currency crises 71–80
  societal impact of crises 23–4
  summary 108–12
Thailand, wage rates
  overview 5–6, 15–17, 221–3
  re-examination of real wage rate changes 226–34
  real wage decline literature 224–5
theoretical explanation of currency crisis, Thailand 71–3
third generation currency crisis models 25–6, 72–3
time-series-based estimation methods 298
Timmer, M.R. 199
Tinakorn, Pranee 2, 9–10, 15–17, 69–112, 221–35

Tobin Tax 134
total factor productivity (TFP) 208–11
  overview 13–15, 198–9
  statistical analysis of determinants 211–18
trade balance, effect of exchange rate 241–3
trade balance/growth, Thailand 85–9, 90, 98–100, 110, 111
trade surplus 4
trading volume, Thai bond markets 188
transactions costs 157
transparency 3
  IMF 11, 125
transport expenditure, China 263–78
Turkey
  bankruptcy infrastructure 183
  current account deficit 131
  fiscal discipline 124

UK
  borrowings 177
  corporate borrowing 173
  cost of living 261
  domestic consumption 290
  economic information quality 167
  financial infrastructure 164
  judicial system 166
unemployment 56
United Nations Development Programme (UNDP) 291
University of California School of Public Health 292
University of Pennsylvania 285
urban household expenditure, China 263, 264–75, 279, 280–83, 284, 286, 287, 288, 289, 300, 301
Uruguay, domestic consumption 290
US
  bond market 149, 176–7, 180, 189
  borrowings 177
  corporate borrowing 173
  current account deficit 121–2, 130–31
  dollar exchange rate 244–7
  domestic consumption 290
  economic information quality 167
  financial infrastructure 164
  inflation rate 261
  interest rates 10
  international adjustment 17
  judicial system 166
  price indicators 291–3
  treasury bonds 123
US and international adjustment
  exchange flexibility, China 255–8
  exchange rates and international competitiveness 243–55
  exchange rates and trade balance 241–3
  overview 240–41
US Treasury 128

Vahey, Shaun P. 298
Valdés, Rodrigo O. 73, 75–6
vector error correction model (VECM) 298
venture capital sector 173
Vishny, Robert 162, 163, 166
volatile prices 296
vulnerabilities
  competing hypotheses as explanations of crisis 32–3
  early warning systems 26–32
  macroeconomic indicators 24
  pre-crisis/post-crisis patterns of fundamentals 33–44
vulnerability, Thailand
  definition of currency crisis/methodologies for identifying 80–84
  empirical results 85–108
  overview 9–10, 69–71
  selected studies on currency crises 71–80
  societal impact of crises 23–4
  summary 108–12

wage adjustment, China 247–55
wage bargaining, China 254–5
wage changes in international adjustment 17
wage differentials, Japan/US 248
wage rates in international adjustment
  exchange flexibility, China 255–8
  exchange rates and international competitiveness 243–55
  exchange rates and trade balance 241–3
  overview 17, 240–41

wage rates, China 251
wage rates, Thailand
overview 5–6, 15–17, 221–3
re-examination of real wage rate changes 226–34
summary of previous literature 224–5
wage recipients, Thailand 227–32
Wakeman, Lee 169–70
Weinstein, D.E. 173
Weiss, Andrew 168
wholesale price index (WPI), Japan/US 246
wholesale prices
China/US 249
Japan/US 244
working hours, Thailand 227–8
World Bank
lending 127
studies of Thai real wage rate declines (2000) 15–16, 221–3, 224, 225, 226–32
study of Asian bond markets 148–9
World Development Report (2000–01), World Bank 57, 64
Wright, Jonathan 297
WTO (World Trade Organization) 256, 324
Wu, Deming 19–20, 296–325
Wynne, Mark A. 297
Wyplosz, C. 72

Yafeh, Y. 173
Yam, Joseph 149
Young, A. 198
Yugoslavia, domestic consumption 290

Zambia, domestic consumption 290
Zhang, Xiaobo 249
Zingales, Luigi 176–7